Praise for *The Wealthy Spirit*:

"Read a page a day to multiply your money, decrease your stress and vastly improve your life and lifestyle!"—Mark Victor Hansen, co-author of *Chicken Soup for the Soul*

"Chellie Campbell will show you how to love money...giving it, getting it and most importantly, receiving it. The stories are hysterical and the tools practical. A winning combination."—Rhonda Britten, author of *Fearless Living and Fearless Loving*, Star of NBC Television Series, *Starting Over*

"Regardless of what's happening out in the world, with *The Wealthy Spirit*, your inner relationship to self-worth, money and prosperity will shift. There has never been a more important time for you to read this fabulous book and use it to make your dreams a reality."—Marcia Wieder, CEO & Founder, Dream University®

"Through Chellie and this book, making, saving, investing, and spending money is a joyous adventure. I never tire of her wise stories, and my bottom line always benefits!" —Linda Sivertsen, co-author of *New York Times* bestseller, *Harmonic Wealth*

"*The Wealthy Spirit* is a must-have guide for maintaining a positive outlook about money and receiving abundance...no matter what's going on in the world around you. Read it every day and reap the rewards!"—Christine Kloser, author of *The Freedom Formula*

"*The Wealthy Spirit* is a fun, upbeat, page-a-day inspirational guide filled with heartwarming personal stories that show you how you can conquer your financial fears, make more money, and love your life. An extremely valuable book and a great read!"—Marci Shimoff, *New York Times* bestselling author, *Happy for No Reason* and featured teacher in *The Secret*

"*The Wealthy Spirit* is an easy yet powerful book that is broken down into doable bite-size steps. With each daily lesson, you'll be transforming your attitude about money and your pocketbook!"—Cynthia Kersey, author of *Unstoppable* and *Unstoppable Women*

"*The Wealthy Spirit* is just the daily reminder we need to keep money in its proper perspective as a valuable tool, not the goal, for a joyful and harmonious life."—Sarah & Paul Edwards, authors of *Working from Home* and *The Practical Dreamer's Handbook*

"A page a day will keep the recession fears away. *The Wealthy Spirit* offers bite-sized doses of energizing inspiration and practical strategies for taking charge of your monetary well-being. Chellie makes her points with wisdom and humor, both of which will reduce your financial stress."—Elizabeth Cogswell Baskin, author of *Hell Yes: Two Little Words for a Simpler, Happier Life*

"*The Wealthy Spirit* is such a beautiful book. It's truly amazing that one person can tell so many incredible, poignant stories. This book is so soulful and inspiring while being very practical, giving easy-to-follow steps that really work to boost your money and your fulfillment. I want to give this book to everyone I know!"—Carol Allen, Vedic Astrologer, author of *Love is in the Stars*

"It now seems obvious, but how you think about money determines whether you will have it or not. This book teaches you how to think about money in a new way—a way that is practical and constructive. Thanks to Chellie Campbell, I'm no longer afraid to want it, to expect it, and to have it. *The Wealthy Spirit* is an essential primer on money and on life."—Jan B. King, author of *Business Plans to Game Plans: A Practical System for Turning Strategies into Action*

"Chellie is an inspiration. Not only does she have wisdom that will transform your relationship with money, but she reveals that wisdom in heart-warming, poetic personal stories. She's a woman who walks her talk each and every day. If you're serious about increasing your peace and your prosperity, read *The Wealthy Spirit* today."—Victoria Loveland-Coen, author of *Manifesting Your Desires* and *The Baby Bonding Book*

"Chellie is probably going to be the next Suze Orman—she's that good! Her book contains not JUST affirmations, but small daily ACTIONS that move you toward personal and financial success."—Lin Painchaud-Steinman, Park Edge Books

"Let's see, I have purchased at least a dozen copies of your book to share with friends! I say your Top 50 affirmations every morning and every night, and 'people really do love to give me money.' I actually am astounded at how much money has come to me in the last 3 months... thanks to you! Even my two daughters are open to affirmations and participate with me sometimes. Actually, one morning I had gotten aggravated... my little Sophia (age 9) said, 'Mom, I think it's time for an affirmation!' And, by the way, you said something that I cannot forget and that changed my life. You said to me, 'I love my life.' That one saying has stayed with me. I think of it everyday. I love my life!"—Karen Caplan, President, Frieda's, Inc.

"Have just started reading your absolutely wonderful book. Am not through with it yet despite grabbing every minute I have left from work and chores but am determined to finish reading it soon and start all over again. Your book is very inspiring and I have already sent out ships. Shall keep in touch with you. THANKS A MILLION.—Warm regards, Archana Kulkarni, Mumbai, India

"I just finished Chellie Campbell's book *The Wealthy Spirit*. To you and all those at Sourcebooks whose hands helped bring this book to market, thank-you. The book generated so many aha moments, I read it cover-to-cover, turning each page with anticipation. Now, I plan to work her book, one day at a time. I've been inspired. Thanks again!"—Sincerely, Gretchen McKeon, Letter to the publisher

"I love your book! In fact, I have used it so much, and carry it with me nearly all the time so that it is page-marked, highlighted, post-it-ed, and dog-eared and looks well, used...During one of my first BIG talks I gave, I used the book to show the audience how sometimes I just open the book, knowing I will get just the message I need. I nearly started crying when the page read: 'No More Fear of Public Speaking.' We all laughed...Thank you. A lot of us were waiting for you to write your book!"—Fawn Chang, Feng Shui

"I ran a 4-week teleclass for therapists recently to help them with their money issues resetting, negotiating, and collecting fees from their clients. As a bonus for joining the group, I sent each one a copy of *The Wealthy Spirit*. They have been going crazy over it!! They love, love, love it.In fact, one of my clients in San Luis Obispo bought a copy for her friend in Denver and that friend loved it so much she is buying copies for her friends. Just wanted you to know how much you are adored! Blessings to you!"—Casey Truffo, www.BeAWealthyTherapist.com

"I am currently reading your book *The Wealthy Spirit*. I found your book exceptionally inspirational and confidence building, and I thank you for all the work and good will you have put into this book. I live in Sri Lanka. Unfortunately this area was badly affected by the tsunami on the 26th of December 2004. I am doing my daily affirmations as mentioned in your book and I know things will improve... I just want to thank you for giving me that extra push to enable me to get on with my life. Thank you."—Nilani, email

"I read your book almost every day. Since I started working with the book diligently this summer, my income has tripled!!! I'm delighted and continue to send out ships as I joyfully receive the riches the other ships are bringing in. Thank you for your amazing work. As a coach I always recommend your book as a text book for my clients who want to reduce their financial stress. Blessings to you."—Beth Davis, Life Coach

"I am an Indonesian working in Singapore. Several months ago, I saw one of my life mentors reading your book. I bought your book and started to read it every day. I find your writing to be serious, funny, down-to-earth, light to read yet very dense in content. In short, I like your book very much. I keep finding a lot of AHAs from your book… I sincerely thank you for giving me and other people your gift of love, peace, freedom, and inspirations in your writings. I wish you keep soaring with your beautiful work."—Warmest regards, Solihin Jinata, Singapore

"Took out this magical book three times at the library. Ordered one at the local book store. Before it arrived, my wife had already picked up one for our ten-year anniversary. I'm self-employed. I think she's thinking with the extra income I'll be making from all my ships coming in and affirmations, she'll get a much bigger gift next year. Thanks, this book seems like it was written just for me. Great job! I hope your life is as magical, fun, and blessed as mine." —Mark, email

"This book changed my entire outlook on money. Making money becomes effortless. I didn't realize until I began reading *The Wealthy Spirit* that the reason I wasn't making the kind of money I wanted was because my thoughts didn't support me making the kind of money. That has all changed thanks to Chellie!"—Amy Applebaum, Bootcamp for Your Mind Life Coach

"I really think your book is brilliant. It was given to me as a gift and I have given it to a number of people myself. What I love about your book is reading short stories EVERY SINGLE DAY. Most books do not reinforce the principles of positive thinking like yours does. I am sure once I hit page 365, I will start all over again. Cheers!"—Robert S. Grossman, Founder, President & CEO, Focus Creative Group

"Thank you so much for all the help your book (*The Wealthy Spirit*) has given me. I use to get caught up in all the negative things in life and I never realized that some of the things I use to say and think were actually negative affirmations…I have been reading your book for some time and I am almost done. I can't wait to start reading it again. I am now a full time realtor living on Cape Cod enjoying my life and making tons of money. I am referred to as The Realtor with Turn Key Results now and I owe you a lot of thanks for that. Your book isn't just about money it's about love and living. I can't believe the turn my life has taken. Thanks for everything."—Ken Oliver, Realtor

"I wanted to share a quick story. While I was away my dad stayed at our house to house sit and watch his grand cats. I had told him about your book and left it for him to read. When I returned he had earmarked so many pages that I know exactly what to give him for Christmas. And, he can't stop talking about how beneficial all of this is. My dad is 78 years old. Go Chellie!"—Gwendolyn Young, Young Communications Group

The Wealthy Spirit

Daily Affirmations for Financial Stress Reduction

Chellie Campbell

Sourcebooks, Inc.®
Naperville, Illinois

Published by Sourcebooks, Inc.
P.O. Box 4410, Naperville, Illinois 60567-4410
(630) 961-3900
FAX: (630) 961-2168
www.sourcebooks.com

Library of Congress Cataloging-in-Publication Data

Campbell, Chellie.

The wealthy spirit: daily affirmations for financial stress reduction/by Chellie Campbell.

p. cm.

Includes bibliographical references and index.

1. Self-Help/Affirmations I. Title.

HG179 .C3165 2002
332.024—dc21

2001 1032270

Printed and bound in the United States of America
AMZ

Dedication

"A father is a banker provided by Nature."—French proverb

To my parents:
Mark Ervin Campbell—in this world
Chellie LeNell Campbell—in the next
Without whose regular loving deposits into my emotional and financial bank accounts none of these pages would have been written.

Acknowledgments

This book is the result of many minds and many hands. On this page, I thank all those wonderful dolphins in my life, past and present, without whom I would still be a baby tuna swimming in circles, afraid of the open sea: Thank you, Theresa Stephens and Jim Jermanok, who led me to Lisa Hagan, who not only became my agent, but my guiding light, the buoy that kept me afloat when the seas were rough. And most of all, my friend, Lisa, thanks for your constant support and whispered prayers. I couldn't have done this without you.

Lisa found me my wise and brilliant editor, Deb Werksman, who believed in my project immediately. Deb, I treasure all your notes in the margins of my manuscript, from "This is so good!" to "I don't think you want to go there." You were always so right.

To all of the wonderful team at Sourcebooks: Thank you for turning this dream into a reality. I am especially grateful to copy editor Jon Malysiak for fine-tuning the completed manuscript; to Jennifer Fusco, Amy Baxter, and their team for brainstorming the perfect title; and to the fabulous sales and publicity teams: No book gets anywhere without you.

My sincere love and appreciation to my writers group, the Wild Women Writers, who laughed at my jokes, cried over my sad stories, praised me when I needed it, and sympathized when I needed that: Rhonda Britten, Linda Sivertsen, Victoria Loveland-Coen, and Carole Allen. Your loving friendship and honest appraisals of my work helped me grow and enjoy the growing. And to all the wait-staff at Marmadalade's, thank you for putting up with our exuberance and demands for slightly warmed chocolate cake with extra whipped cream at lunch meetings.

Heartfelt thanks to my parents, for without the strong family bond and values they instilled in me, I would not be the person who could write this book. I also thank my sisters, Jane Markota and Carole Wiltfong, and their families: the Markotas—Dick, Robert, Marissa, and Lindsey; and the Wiltfongs—Lloyd, Katie and Nicholas. You are the dolphins of my heart, who swim by my side every day.

Thank you, Shelley Lavender, for your generosity and help in hosting my workshops when the storms raged and it looked like the ships might sink. Your friendship is greatly appreciated.

To all of the members of my wonderful networks: The Women's Referral Service founded by Nancy Sardella, the National Association of Women Business Owners, the Executive Le Tip of West Los Angeles, the Ventura County Professional Women's Network, Women in Management, and all the groups that invited me to speak, thank you for teaching me that the best way to get referrals is to give them.

Finally, my thanks to all the dolphin graduates of the Financial Stress Reduction Workshops. This book could not have been written without your courage, your strength, and your faith. Your stories shaped my teachings and made me a better person. May you continue to swim far and wide and joyfully, knowing that we all depend on each other in this blue ocean.

Introduction

"I have all the money I'll ever need—as long as I die by four o'clock this afternoon."

—Henny Youngman

Over one million people filed bankruptcy in 1998, the *Los Angeles Times* reported. The credit card industry is a $556 billion a year business and nearly 50 percent of all borrowers do not pay their balances off in full each month. Forty percent of Americans spend more than they make, and Consumer Credit Counselors declared that it is not unusual for their clients to have forty to sixty credit cards. Relationships are in trouble: 50 percent of all marriages end in divorce; in 80 percent of the divorces, finances are a significant issue. People are working more hours than ever before, yet the life savings of the average fifty-year-old is only $2,300. A 1997 study by the Oppenheimer Fund found that one in seven women had nothing saved for retirement; of those that do, one in three owe more on their credit cards than they have saved. According to a Social Security Administration report, nine out of ten people are either dead or dead broke at age 65. And this when the economy had been booming for a record nine years. Something is wrong.

As the owner of a business management firm for twelve years, I worked with hundreds of clients to help them manage their finances. All of them—no matter what their level of income—had financial stress. In fact, it often seemed the more money they made, the more stress they had. I consulted with people who couldn't make ends meet on $15,000 per month. If their unconscious habit pattern was to spend more than they made, it didn't matter how much they made. They were just broke at a higher level. What was needed was something that would stop the *habit* of money woes they were experiencing in their lives—at every income level. What was needed was *Financial Stress Reduction*®.

Simple one-on-one consultations with my own clients, explaining money management principles, techniques for success, and how to be happier at the same time, became in 1990 an eight-week course. I designed it to help people achieve wealth in their work, serenity in their spirits, and a balance between the two. It struck a nerve with people from all walks of life: doctors, attorneys, CPAs, business owners, construction workers, government employees, photographers, housewives, plumbers, and the unemployed. The techniques and principles apply to all, no matter what their income level.

The results amazed me. Whatever their circumstances, participants in the workshop found they could lift themselves to the next level of success. One woman made $35,000 the first week of the class and went on to develop a nationwide executive search firm. A roofing contractor increased his sales 300 percent in just four weeks; an unemployed man found a new job and a six-figure income within three months. Stuck at a plateau of $100,000 per year annual sales, a woman in advertising specialties booked over $2,000,000 the next year.

But the class was about more than money. It was about living a rich life in every area. Plato said, "The unexamined life isn't worth living," but the unlived life isn't worth examining. One woman brought her husband to class because, although they made plenty of money, they had no time in which to enjoy it. The owner of his own public relations firm, he had become a workaholic through fear of losing business if he wasn't available—even for *a day*. By the end of class, they were able to schedule a trip to France with friends for an entire month. Another young couple realized that, although they made plenty of money, they never spent any of it on personal enjoyment. Loosening up and realizing that some part of their money could be spent on pleasure, they remodeled their kitchen and bought a vacation home.

It was a joy and a thrill to help people prosper and I loved doing it. I had developed a comfortable, small niche in Los Angeles, teaching workshops in my home, making a lot of money, not working very hard, and having lots of time off to play. When people suggested to me that I write a book, produce audio and video tapes, and travel the world on a speaking tour, I said, "Why? It sounds like too much work! I'm happy where I am."

Then one of my clients, Ruth Mahoney, was so struck by the changes she had produced in her life that she sent me thirteen friends who signed up for the course. When I called to thank her, she said, "Well, that's fine, Chellie. But what am I going to do about my friend in New York? Or my friend in Arizona? And the ones in Seattle? They can't come to Los Angeles for an eight-week course. But they need it. How can you help them?"

She shocked me out of my complacency in that moment. I remembered Marianne Williamson's statement, quoted by Nelson Mandela in his Inaugural address: "Our deepest fear is not that we are inadequate. Our deepest fear is that we are powerful beyond measure. It is our light, not our darkness, that most frightens us. We ask ourselves, who am I to be brilliant, gorgeous, talented, and fabulous? Actually, who are you *not* to be? You are a child of God. Your playing small doesn't serve the world." Oh. It wasn't about *me*. Here was the reason to put my business and my life on a bigger scale: To help other people. So, I started to write.

Then, of course, it was about me. What you teach best is what you need to learn most....

How to structure the book was the first problem. Throughout my life, I have taken many workshops. I have seen how people can receive incredible amounts of useful information, and go home energized and excited from the experience they had—they are on "workshop high." It lasts about three days. Then they wake up one morning struggling to apply what they learned, without knowing how to systematically put all the new information into practice in their daily lives. The same thing often happens when people read self-help books. They start out with great intentions and maybe they are able to implement one or two positive changes from hundreds of new suggestions. Then a problem comes up, their old habits intrude, the old negative voice plays its rusty recording once more, and the good feeling evaporates. Grudgingly, helplessly, they fall back into the same patterns of behavior they were trying to avoid.

To cope with this problem, I designed my workshop to take place over eight weeks, so participants could assimilate the information and put it into practice over time. The goal was to help people create new habits of thinking and behavior, which would produce actual results during the class. Learning should be fun, so I teach by story, participation, and example. I wanted to translate this workshop process into the book, without having it degenerate into a "to do" list of instructions, chapter by chapter.

That is why I wrote this book in a page-a-day format. It was designed to help you succeed through changing your attitudes and beliefs about money and motivating you to take actions that produce abundance through a *daily practice*. You don't have to try to take in all the information at once; you don't have to twist yourself into a complete transformation today. Just take one step every day: one thought, one goal, one action every day of the year and you can change your financial condition, increase your income, live debt-free, and have work you love. Half of financial stress reduction is "minding your money":

1. Think positive
2. Send out ships
3. Count your money

The other half is just as important—"without losing your mind":

1. Swim with dolphins
2. Survive the storms
3. Seek balance and enlightenment

Do this and you will find you have more joy, better relationships, and a sense that you are fulfilling your life's purpose. Take each lesson one day at a time—it's a daily practice and a daily meditation. Be determined, be diligent, be consistent and you will find you have retrained your mind and your body with new habits of success, happiness, and fulfillment. And the treasures available in life will be yours.

Please know that this book comes not from an author who's always done everything right, or on whom Providence has always smiled. I learned it the hard way, through rock-bottom personal experience. I've been a "starving actor," a battered wife, an alcoholic; I've been robbed at gunpoint, had my house foreclosed, and filed bankruptcy. I've been "Pity Party Patty"—the one who always had a sob story to tell. It took me years to figure out that the victim stories were what kept me a victim. There were nights I cried myself to sleep, looking at the moon deep in the night sky outside my window. "One day," I vowed, "it will be six months from now and I won't hurt this bad."

And one day, it was and I didn't.

However financially stressed-out you are, I have been there. However unhappy you are, I have been there. And I know that you have the power to change it because I have done it. If you follow the principles outlined in this book, it can get better. In fact, it can get great. I now have a business I love, work that doesn't feel hard, and clients who praise me and pay me. I'm not Donald Trump, I'm not Bill Gates; I can't teach you how to make billions. There are other books for that. I'm just a middle-class, middle-aged girl, who once was miserable and broke, and now is living rich, inside and out. I make a six-figure income, am debt-free, have savings and investments, a retirement plan, and travel the world on exciting vacations every year. My recreational beverage of choice is Diet Coke. I have wonderful relationships with family and friends and a spiritual foundation to my life and my work that deepens every day. I'm making more money and having more fun than ever before in my life.

Consciously or unconsciously, we create our lives. We create them out of our thoughts, attitudes, beliefs, and feelings and the choices we make from them. Our life story is the sum total of our decisions. We have such power and yet so many people feel powerless. We give up our power to the things we have chosen and then think we are helpless to change it. But we are responsible for it all. We choose where we live, who our friends are, what our work is. We choose whether or not we exercise, smoke, take drugs, donate to charity, get a degree, have pets, have spouses, have children. We pick what we read, what we think, and what we believe. Our lives are testimonials to our choices. Each moment is the point of power. Each moment, we can continue to choose what we have already chosen or we can choose to choose again.

Not what you see, but what you *think* is what you get. Focus on fear, and your fear will make manifest the object of your fear. Focus on love, and love will surround you. Worry about the lack and limitation of your finances, and you will produce scarcity. Faithfully concentrate on the solutions to financial problems, visualizing the success beyond, and you will produce abundance. Mind your money and mind your life. A life filled with abundance—inside and out—is yours for the taking.

There is a road from poverty to prosperity. I know, because I have walked it myself. You know it, too, but perhaps you have forgotten. Let me remind you. The road beckons. Come. I will walk it with you.

Operating Instructions

These are the six principles of *The Wealthy Spirit*.

1. **Think Positive:** Like mind over matter, mind over money begins with believing you deserve it and can get it.

2. **Send Out Ships:** You can wait for your ship to come in but if you don't send any out, it's going to be a long wait.

3. **Count Your Money:** Money is a game and you have to know the score. The money score will tell you how well you're doing at steps one and two.

4. **Swim With Dolphins:** Being "in the swim" will depend largely on who you're swimming with. Look for dolphins and avoid sharks and tuna.

5. **Survive the Storms:** It takes the sun to create a shadow—accept that the dark and the light live side by side in all of us. You must weather the interior storms as well as the exterior ones. Persistence is key.

6. **Seek Balance and Enlightenment:** Promote Peace and Prosperity for All. I suggest you start with yourself.

Each of the 365 entries in this book relates to one of these six keys, and will either illustrate it, encourage you to put it into practice, or take you to a new level with that key principle. To achieve financial stress reduction, you must practice each of the six keys. You can't leave any of them out, or you will not get the desired result.

Many stories have multiple meanings. Think.

Notice when you resist reading certain pages. That's when you have hit your issue.

This book is designed to be habit-forming. If you read one page every day for twenty-one days in a row, you will have established the daily habit of reading it. If you miss a day, the count starts over.

Each day, repeat a daily affirmation to yourself throughout the day. To accelerate your progress, select several affirmations to repeat.

Periodically, I recommend that you take a review day. Did you practice affirmations every day? How many ships did you send out? How many came in? Did your income and spending match your budget? How much debt did you pay off? How much money did you save or invest? You may want to create a system for yourself to review these questions weekly, monthly, or whatever works for you.

Form a Money Mastery Network of like-minded friends with whom you can read and practice the principles in this book. If possible, hold a meeting with group members each month and support each other to think positive, send out ships, count your money, swim with dolphins, survive the storms, and seek balance and enlightenment.

1

Celebrate a New Beginning

"There are some people who live in a dream world, and there are some who face reality, and then there are those who turn one into the other."

—Douglas Everett

This is a day of celebration: awake and sing the song of a bold new beginning. The point of power is in the moment, and this moment you can start your new path towards success, wealth, and happiness. Whatever came before is buried in the snows of last year. You can and you will—whatever you desire.

We are all graduates of MSU—Make Stuff Up. Whatever you have done in your life so far, you made it all up. You chose where you live, what you wear, what friends you have, what profession you're in, how much money you make. And you choose again each day to maintain and build upon those things or to let go of them and pick up new things, new roads, new directions. On this day of your new beginning, all paths are open, all doors unlocked, all possibilities unlimited. What will you choose to be, do, and have now and going forward?

At the beginning of each *Financial Stress Reduction® Workshop*, I ask participants to write down their "Intended Results." It is a list of goals they want to accomplish in the course. I ask you to do this as well. What is your intention in reading this book? What do you want to have achieved by the end of it? Make a list of your goals for the next one-year period—financial, emotional, and spiritual. Goals have been called "dreams with deadlines." Writing them down brings them from the metaphysical realm into the physical. No longer just a fantasy, the idea now exists in concrete form as a written document. If you have written goals down in the past, look at them, and acknowledge yourself for the ones you have accomplished. Whatever remains undone may be transferred to your new list.

Make wealth—internal and external—your goal this year. Believe you will make more money with less stress and have more time off for fun with your family and friends. Be willing to risk change and survive the storms to find your highest good. Counting your money will make your money count—and remember to count your friends and your blessings as well.

Then celebrate—you have taken the first step along the path to great achievement!

Today's Affirmation: "Something wonderful is happening to me today—I can feel it!"

2
Rules for Affirmations

"Getting ahead in a difficult profession requires avid faith in yourself. You must be able to sustain yourself against staggering blows. That is why some people with mediocre talent, but with great inner drive, go much farther than people with vastly superior talent."

—Sophia Loren

Great inner drive is sustained by daily positive thoughts about yourself and your expectations for your future. Affirmations are designed to help you with this process, but they only work if you say them. Knowing about them isn't the same as doing them.

When you make the commitment to practicing positive thinking on a daily basis, what affirmations should you use? You can use the affirmations in this book, collect them from other books, or write your own. Whichever you choose, make sure that they follow the three rules for creating affirmations:

1. **State affirmations in the present tense.** Affirmations must be stated in the present tense, such as "I am prosperous" or "I am rich and wonderful", because if you put them in the future tense, "I'm going to be rich", you will be creating a picture in your mind that someday you'll be prosperous, but not now. It's like a sign posted at a bar: "Free Beer Tomorrow." When does the customer get free beer?

2. **State affirmations in the positive.** When you speak your affirmations, you are giving instructions to your subconscious mind. Neuro-linguistic programming has determined that the subconscious has no picture for "not," "don't", and other negative qualifiers. For example, if I tell you, "Don't think about pink elephants," I'm sure you are picturing pink elephants in your mind. You can't help it. So, when you create an affirmation, say "I always have plenty of money in my bank account" rather than "I'm not going to be overdrawn on my bank account again." Picture what you want instead of what you don't want.

3. **Be specific.** A photographer friend of mine told me how much she wanted to go to Greece. She thought a great way to get there would be if she was paid to go, by getting a photography assignment there. Excited by the concept, she started doing affirmations for this trip daily: "I have a photography assignment in Athens! I have a photography assignment in Athens!" Four months later, she received the call—she had her assignment for a photo shoot in Athens. Athens, Georgia. Oops. Make sure you state *exactly* what it is you want.

Today's Affirmation: "I always have plenty of money!"

3
The Waitress and the Short-Order Cook

*"Two men look out through the same bars:
One sees the mud, and one the stars."*

—Frederick Langbridge

The waitress has worked here since time began. Ageless and calm, her eyes see through to the end of the world. She smacks her gum, gives the customer a lop-sided grin, and smoothly asks in her professional voice, "May I take your order now?" She stands there expectantly, pencil poised to write on her order pad.

"I don't know exactly what I'm hungry for. I can't make a mistake. I'm really sorry this is taking so long—I'm so stupid!" In discomfort and confusion, the customer gropes for the right words and the right order.

"One don't, one can't, and a side order of shame!" the waitress hollers to the cook. He stands behind the counter, ready to serve up another batch of cold reality. He's heard this order before. In a second, the plate is prepared.

"I really want to help people. I don't care about the money," the customer explains.

"Hold the money!" the waitress hollers.

The cook silently removes the money from the plate.

A new customer bursts into the diner: "I'll have the talent, drive and determination to be a top caliber professional writer, I write a book that helps many people and easily makes me rich and famous!"

The waitress laughs and gives the order to the cook: "One successful bestseller smothered in money and a side order of fame!"

"It's already been delivered," smiles the cook.

This is Earth's Universal Diner, where you always get exactly what you ask for. Would you like to change your order?

Today's Affirmation: "I always get exactly what I want!"

4

Declare Your Abundance

"The greatest discovery of my generation is that human beings can alter their lives by altering their attitudes of mind."

—William James

"I don't care who else wants it, I am winning that basket!" Heather Moreno declared at the networking dinner. A blond, brown-eyed dynamo of a fitness instructor, Heather avowed her intention in no uncertain terms. The gift basket that would be given to a lucky winner that evening was filled with gifts, coupons, and cash worth over six hundred dollars in goods and services.

Sitting next to Heather, I looked over at the basket and said, "Well, I want to win it, too!" She looked at me calmly and declared again, "That's nice, Chellie, but that basket is *mine*!" I chuckled and recognized that my intention and commitment to having that prize was not as strong as Heather's. She was clear as a bell about having that basket and she told everyone at our table that it was hers. In fact, she told everyone at the meeting.

The moment arrived, and Linda Soto, who designed the basket, drew a business card from the bowl. Her eyebrows raised in surprise, she announced, "The winner is—Heather Moreno!" Heather gleefully ran to the podium to collect her prize.

In recent months, I have given a cash prize at the end of my speaking engagements. The last two were won by people who declared out loud to the room that they were going to win. Once I asked a man to draw the winning ticket, and as he walked up to the front of the room he said, "You know I'm going to pick my own name and win the money!" And he did.

Have you had this experience? Have you known people who declared the door prize was theirs before the drawing and then actually won it? Watch these people! Look how they do it. See the determination, the confidence, the winning attitude that succeeds. They just *know* they are going to win.

Winning a door prize is just practice. Like anything else, you learn to create winning experiences in your life by starting small. As the German philosopher Friedrich Nietzsche said, "He who would learn to fly one day must first learn to stand and walk and run and climb and dance; one cannot fly into flying." Don't start with trying to win the lottery, start with winning the next door prize. Declare your abundance and success before they draw the ticket. Visualize getting the job before you go on the next interview, instead of focusing on the fear of being rejected. Confidence sells—fear repels.

Today's Affirmation: "I am a winner! I win often and I win big!"

5
People Love to Give Me Money

"Money swore an oath that nobody who did not love it should ever have it."

—Irish proverb

When I work with groups, I always ask if anyone ever took a class on making and managing money in grade school or high school. Very few hands go up. Without official training in this subject, people are left to formulate their own ideas based on what they heard, read, or saw others do. So what did you hear about money when you were growing up? What did your parents say to you when you asked for money? What did you read about money? What were the old clichés you heard? These thoughts became your "money mantras" and they resound in your mind whether or not you are conscious of them. And they create your financial reality. Try completing the following sentences:

"Money doesn't grow ____________." "The love of money is the root ____________." "The rich get richer and ______________." "Save for a ____________." "It takes money to __________." "It's just as easy to marry _______________." "Money can't buy _____________."

My workshop participants call out the answers immediately. As each one is mentioned, I write it on the white board for everyone to see. As I add more and more negative statements, the room gets quieter and quieter. I ask them to feel the energy in the room and they all notice it's more depressed. Then I ask, "How many people believe in the power of positive thinking?" Many people raise their hands, but then I run to the board and point out all the negative statements and ask, "Then what's this?!"

This generally gets a good laugh as people realize that they may believe in thinking positive, but they haven't really taken the time to evaluate their thoughts. The very first affirmation I teach them is, "People love to give me money!" People start laughing—it's fun, and it feels so different to say a positive, fun, money affirmation. I say, "See, you can't say it without smiling!"

Many people make this statement a part of their daily affirmation program. And the results have been amazing. One attorney thought it was silly, but was game to try it, and so repeated this statement all the way home from the class. As he walked up to his front door, his roommate ran out and handed him a check for money he had owed him for *nine months*. Effie, a young photographer, was saying this affirmation in her car. When she stopped at a traffic light, a homeless man knocked on her window. When she rolled it down, *he* handed *her* five dollars!

Change your mind about money today and change your experience with money tomorrow. Try it and see.

Today's Affirmation: "People love to give me money!"

6
Prosperity Thinking

"One plus one is two. Two plus two is four. But five will get you ten if you know how to work it."

—Mae West

We create our lives each day by choosing what we focus on. What you focus on expands—focus on fear and you will become more afraid. Focus on love and acceptance and you will get more of that. As you focus on and believe in your ability to create financial abundance in your life, you will begin to receive it: believing is seeing, not vice versa. Saying prosperity affirmations daily will help you to do this.

Yes, yes, I know you've heard of this before. Prosperity affirmations aren't new. But I ask you: *are you doing them*? Consistently? Every day? Because you are thinking about money every day, and I know from experience, what most people are thinking about money is not prosperous or affirmative. Do you clench your teeth when bills arrive in the mail? Do you shudder when you hear the word "taxes"? If so, you need to start reprogramming your consciousness to develop a healthier attitude toward money so that you can attract it into your life.

Now, if you try doing prosperity affirmations for three days and then give up in disgust, it's not going to work. Neuro-linguistic programming states that it takes twenty-one days to establish a new habit. In order to reframe our attitudes and beliefs about money, we need daily practice for twenty-one days in a row. That means that if you practice saying positive affirmations for ten days and then forget a day, you have to start all over again.

Claude Bristol, in his book *The Magic of Believing*, suggests a technique called "mirroring." Stand in front of a mirror and say your affirmations out loud with power, meaning, and energy. There is something utterly transforming about talking yourself up this way.

Obviously, if we say positive affirmations for five minutes each day but then go back to our old negative groove for the other twenty-three hours, fifty-five minutes of the day, it will take a long time to notice any progress. It is important that you monitor your thoughts and words throughout the day and catch yourself in any negativisms. When you notice one, repeat two positive affirmations—one to counteract the negativism and the other to move yourself forward.

Find additional times and places to practice your affirmations. Standing in line at the post office or the grocery store, waiting for a bus or a friend at a restaurant, or while taking a shower are great times to run through your list. Another great affirmation time is while driving. It only takes 5 percent of your brain power to drive, so use the rest of your brain positively!

Today's Affirmation: "My affirmations work for me, whether I believe they do or not!"

7

Write "Thank You!" on All Your Checks

"If a fellow isn't thankful for what he's got, he isn't likely to be thankful for what he's going to get."

—Frank A. Clark

It is important for your personal prosperity to take joy in the process of sending people money. As you write the check or pay the cash for your purchase, know that you are creating financial benefits for many unseen individuals who make their living from these transactions. Smile and write "Thank you!" on the bottom of every check in the memo portion. "Thank you!" that I can buy this wonderful product or service that I want. "Thank you!" for providing it for me. "Thank you!" that I have the money to buy it—and that the check is good.

Andrea James, a bright young financial planner, took this idea to heart and decided to try it. Her boyfriend was applying for an exclusive apartment through a rental agency. He knew that there would be many applications for this apartment, and prepared his with care. Andrea insisted that he write "Thank you!" with a big exclamation point on the deposit check he submitted with his application. A skeptic, he scoffed, rolled his eyes and snorted with derision, but finally acquiesced, and wrote it on the check.

He got a call two days later. Although there were some seventy-five applicants for the apartment, he was the one who got it! He asked why he was the one who was chosen. The apartment manager said she picked him because he had written "Thank you!" on his check! It had brightened her day, and she said that a person who would do that was the kind of person she wanted living in her building.

He writes "Thank you!" on all his checks now.

Give of your abundance happily to other people and they will likely do the same—happiness is catching. Send the money back out and around, and eventually it will circle back to you. Then you will send it out again. We are all linked together in the circle of abundance.

Today's Affirmation: "Thank you, God, for the abundant gifts you provide for me every day."

8
Send Out Ships

"The vision must be followed by the venture. It is not enough to stare up the steps—we must step up the stairs."

—Vance Havner

Thinking positive is your first step to living rich, inside and out. But it is not enough. You have to take action to achieve your goals. I call this "Sending Out Ships."

In the nineteenth century, the merchants in London built grand, tall-masted sailing ships. It would take many months, sometimes years, to build them. Then they would hire a crew, outfit the ship, and store provisions for the long sea voyage. One fine day, the ship would weigh anchor, hoist her sails, and sail out of London harbor, on her way to visit foreign ports, and trade for gold, jewels, silks, and spices. The trip would take many months —often years—and there were no communication lines open then: no ship-to-shore radio, no telegraph, no cellular telephones. Once the ship had sailed, the merchant could do nothing more; only wait for that future day when the ship would return, sailing into London harbor laden with treasure. On that day, the merchant's fortune was made. And that's where the expression "I'm waiting for my ship to come in," comes from.

Some people are going down to the dock, waiting for their ship to come in—but they haven't sent any out! If you want the fortune, your responsibility each day is to send out some ships. And you had better send out more than one, because stuff happens to ships: One runs aground just outside of the harbor, another sinks in a hurricane. A few get commandeered by pirates, the whirlpool gets one, and on the next one there's a mutiny and they sail off to Pitcairn Island and aren't heard from for another twenty years. Then, of course, there's the one that hits the iceberg! Once you send the ship out, it's out of your control. You are only in charge of sending it out, not when it comes in.

When you get into the habit of sending ships out on a daily basis, even if you know some ships aren't going to make it back home, you are still confident and optimistic because you know you have a whole fleet sailing out there. It creates a positive expectation that ships are going to be sailing in, docking at your pier, and unloading riches for you any minute. Positive energy shines from you. You feel good about yourself because you've been doing what it takes to succeed. This is what Tony Robbins, in his book, *Awaken the Giant Within*, calls "massive, positive, constructive action on a daily basis." (Although that sounds a little too much like hard work to me.) I prefer the image of breaking the champagne bottle and waving goodbye to a proud clipper ship on a beautiful spring day as it sets forth on my behalf. And then celebrating the ship's safe arrival with all my wealth.

Send those ships out every day. Then prepare to unload your treasures.

Today's Affirmation: "Today is a big money day!"

9
Flying Without a Net

"One day John and George showed up...and told me we had a gig. I said, 'No. I've got a steady job here....I can't expect more.' And I was quite serious....But then I thought, 'Sod it.' I bunked over the wall and was never seen again by Massey and Coggins. Pretty shrewd move really, as things turned out.'"

—Sir Paul McCartney

The successful corporate executive had just been fired after twenty years. He told me he had always wanted to be an entrepreneur, but had been afraid to "fly without a net." I have seen many people like him give up their dreams for the illusion of security, trading their hopes and aspirations for what they think is a safety net. The tragedy is, there is no net. There never was—and never will be. We are all, always, flying without a net. There is no job from which you can't be fired, no house that can't be destroyed, no life that can't be lost, no gold that can't be stolen, no stock that can't lose its value, no security that can't disappear.

So you might as well do what you want!

When I decided to sell my business management company and teach the *Financial Stress Reduction® Workshop* full-time, it was really scary. I didn't know if I would be able to sell enough workshops, on an ongoing basis, to make a living. With the bookkeeping service, my clients paid me a fee every month. This created a regular income stream. With the workshop business, however, a customer paid once for the workshop and then was gone. I had to generate new customers every eight weeks. I didn't know if I could do that. I was terrified.

But I loved teaching this workshop. All of my performing skills and financial skills were married in this creative outlet. My students were giving me great reviews and producing extraordinary results in their income. I had to go for it. I talked to people endlessly about the class and one by one, people enrolled. I would relax a bit at the beginning of each new course—I was safe for another eight weeks! But then, I'd look at the next course—no one was enrolled in it yet—and fear would strike again.

It took about three years before I started to trust that, if I followed my own program assiduously, there would always be people in the workshop. As long as I take action—think positive, send out ships and count my money—I make a wonderful income from work I love. And as long as I stay centered—swim with dolphins, survive the storms, and seek balance and enlightenment—I am happier than I have ever been in my life.

Make no decisions based on security. There is none. The safety net is an illusion. The only net you will ever have is the internal one you make for yourself. It is woven of goals, grit, determination, will, planning, resilience, creativity, and optimism. And the belief that if you fall, you have what it takes to get back up.

Today's Affirmation: "I soar to tremendous heights of success!"

10

The Money Is in the Phone

"Everything you want is out there waiting for you to ask. Everything you want also wants you. But you have to take action to get it."

—Jack Canfield

As a single person working alone in my own seminar and public speaking business, I send out ships on a daily basis. Some are medium-sized cargo ships like speaking at a networking meeting where I can meet many potential clients. Appearing on television or speaking at a national conference are large cruise ships. Writing this book was an aircraft carrier! But my bread and butter canoes are follow-up telephone calls to people I've met who are interested in my work. I close all of my sales on the telephone so I know that "The money is in the phone." To remind myself of this, I spray-painted my telephone gold. I paint my fingernails gold, too. It's a mnemonic device, reminding me that the riches I desire are often just a phone call away. It's not "Cold Calling," it's "Gold Calling"!

Follow-up phone calling is a discipline. I work alone at home, and often people will ask me how I stay focused on work with all the distractions that are possible. You know, the laundry, personal chores, housekeeping, food, *Oprah*. (Oops, well I do watch *Oprah*—she's terrific—and I plan my afternoon break for that. And I hate laundry, so that's no distraction.) But for the most part, it's easy to stay focused on my job. All I have to do is pay some bills. When there's no more money, I remember, "The money is in the phone." I get busy and call potential clients.

Where is your money? If you're a business owner or in sales, your money is in the phone. If you're employed, you sold your boss on hiring you. Ask your boss where she thinks the money is in your business. Pay most attention to your tasks at work that produce income. Businesses must make money to survive and pay you—how can you help them make more money more efficiently?

Focus on sending out the ships that bring in the treasure.

Today's Affirmation: "My phone is ringing off the hook with people calling to give me money!"

11

Playing the Piano

"If people only knew how hard I work to gain my mastery, it wouldn't seem so wonderful at all."

—Michelangelo

You can learn how to play the piano. You can study music composition and theory, learn to read music and build dexterity in your fingers. You can buy the finest piano money can buy, rent an auditorium, sell tickets, and gather an audience.

But if you don't actually put your fingers on the keyboard and play—nothing will happen. You can sit in front of the piano and think "Ohmmm, I'm playing beautiful music, ohmmm..." but unless you've rigged a player piano, no music is going to come out of it.

I meet a lot of people who repeat their positive money affirmations every day, but never send out ships. They are not affirming—they are wishing. Affirmations aren't magic words. They don't conjure money out of the air. You use them to build your positive energy to the point where you start feeling and believing in your success—and with enough repetition, it becomes real to you, physically and emotionally in your body. From there you start feeling yourself motivated to take action. Action, backed up by the positive beliefs, creates the music.

A client of mine told me she was practicing her affirmations every day, but wasn't sending out any ships. When I told her affirmations weren't enough, that she had to reach out to people to sell her services, she rebelled. "Well," she said sulkily, "I have a friend who's in business and she doesn't have to do that—she gets a lot of business through word-of-mouth referrals and never has to market her services."

"Great!" I said. "I suggest you call her up and find out how she does it. If there is a magic way to get business to come to you without having to do any marketing, I'd love to know what it is. Let me know what you find out."

She hasn't returned my calls lately. My guess is, wishing isn't working.

Are you practicing? Sending out ships? Or wishing?

Today's Affirmation: "My affirmations inspire me to send out ships with abundant enthusiasm!"

12
Goal-Getting

"If you look up, there are no limits."

—Japanese Proverb

Goal-setting is very important to achieving our desires. But goal-*getting* is the next step—taking action to get the goal you set.

When I enrolled in Roger Lane's *The Finance Course*, he called me to find out what I had on the list. I told him I wanted a brand-new Mercedes Benz. He said, "Great!" and asked me, "What model?" I said, "I don't know." Then he asked, "What color?" I said, "I don't know." "How much does it cost?" "I don't know." Roger got impatient with me at this point. He said, "Well, you'd better find out exactly what you want because that's what we're going to do in the class—get you the things you want." I said, "Oh! I'd better go shopping!"

Now, you need to understand that at this particular moment in my life, my business was going very well and I was making good money, but I thought that there was no way I could really afford to buy a Mercedes Benz. My belief was that those cars were driven by rich people and movie stars. Well, I wasn't that rich and I certainly wasn't a movie star, so I "just knew" I couldn't have one. I had already looked at, and was ready to buy, another medium-priced car.

As luck would have it, two days after this conversation with Roger, I went to a networking group and a woman who sold Mercedes Benz automobiles stood up and said that there was currently a special savings on car leases. I made an appointment to see her the next day. When I walked into the Mercedes showroom, there in the middle of the room, sparkling in the sunlight, was a beautiful metallic teal-green sedan with gold pin-striping. I was in love. Barbara came over to me and I told her, "I want this one." She, good salesperson that she was, said, "You can have that one!" "Yeah, sure," I said, disbelieving. "Show me the money."

We proceeded to calculate the costs of this purchase. She gave me a great deal, and it turned out not to be anywhere near as expensive as I thought. In fact, the monthly payments were only thirty-two dollars per month more than the other car I was going to buy. I thought about how many times I might have stopped myself from having things I wanted merely because of a mistaken belief. Goal-getting is knowing what you want, investigating what it will take to have it, and then taking the action steps to have it.

I bought the car. I drove it home that day. And then I drove it to Roger Lane's workshop that weekend! I told him I knew what color of car I wanted. He said, "Good. What color?"

I said, "Green. Want to see it?" And I took him to the parking lot and showed him.

Today's Affirmation: "I am a money-making machine and I'm making a lot of it today!"

13

The Black Limo Fantasy

"Things may come to those who wait, but only the things left by those who hustle."

—Abraham Lincoln

Annie shared her dream of being an artist. Well, she was an artist of course, but she wanted to be paid to be an artist. This is a distinction I run into with many people. They bubble with creativity, pour their souls out onto canvas and marble and paper, then sit in the middle of their wonderful work and cry, "But how do I get recognized? Why isn't the world beating a path to my door? Why doesn't this work sell?"

They remind me of the Black Limo Fantasy: when I was eight, the nation was in love with *The Mickey Mouse Club*—and no one more than I. I wanted to play with them, dance with them, be one of them. I hadn't a clue how that could happen. My fantasy was that talent scouts were driving up and down the streets in a Black Limo, looking for talented children to whisk away to stardom. I kept my eyes peeled for the Black Limo with the talent scout in it. Alas, it never came to my neighborhood.

So I look at my beautiful artist friends and don't want them to wait one more day for the Black Limo. It's not coming for them, and it's not coming for you. It is parked at a corner somewhere in your future, its motor running, waiting for you to arrive. And you don't find it in one seven-league boot stride. You find it by every day making one baby step towards your dream. Find out where the Black Limo is parked by asking everyone you know, then even calling people you don't know. Talk to gallery owners, corporate art buyers, interior decorators, architects. Enter contests, display at the local art fair, form a support group of other artists, and share connections. This is called "Sales and Marketing" by business people. I call it "Sending Out Ships." They are the delivery system for your creations, whatever they may be. You have to get them out where people can buy them; otherwise they're just hobby-crafts that you give away at Christmas.

Annie never thought she could make a sale. Not only was she afraid to make a phone call, she was reluctant to make a sale when someone called her and *asked* to buy one of her paintings. There were people in her life who wanted to invest money, time, and connections in her dream, and she wasn't letting them help her. She was afraid. The fear stopped her cold. I told her that I wasn't a therapist and I couldn't find the source of her fear. I could only tell her to get over it, or on her deathbed she'd be regretting instead of reminiscing.

The next week, she started selling paintings. She found her Black Limo. Where is yours?

Today's Affirmation: "I am now earning a great big income doing what makes me happy!"

14

See It, Want It, Get It

"You have to have a dream so you can get up in the morning."

—Billy Wilder

My first career goal was to become a professional actress. I fantasized about the applause of adoring crowds, fame, stardom, and tears of joy streaming down my face as I collected my Academy Award for Best Actress. I dreamed of moving audiences to joy and laughter, rage and sorrow, and the wonderful acclaim I would receive. Great fantasy. I saw it, and I wanted it.

The trick was to get it—to bring my fantasy into reality. Maria Nemeth, in her book *The Energy of Money*, describes the difficulty of crossing the border from metaphysical reality to physical reality as "trouble at the border." I had to make some effort to put my dream into being. I had to take risks; I had to step out into the unknown. I had to put myself on the line, without knowing whether or not I would measure up. I had to send out ships.

So these are some of the "become an actress" ships:

I auditioned to be in a play at my high school. I asked a friend what I had to do. When she told me I had to sing, I backed off—I was much too frightened to do that. But then she said, "Well, you've been taking dance lessons for years, so go to the dance audition and try out for a dancing part." That felt like something I could do, so I joined the crowd at the dance audition, did the steps they showed me, and was cast in the show. Success! I loved it. I loved the rehearsals, the people, the creativity, the teamwork solving problems—it was all terrific, just like in my fantasy.

So I went to my school counselor, told her I wanted to be an actress, and signed up for all the drama curricular and extra-curricular activities. I took dance lessons, acting and singing lessons, read and studied plays, auditioned and performed in plays. Subsequently, I got a degree in Dramatic Art from the University of California at Santa Barbara, and made the trek to Hollywood as countless thousands before me. I had my professional pictures taken, got an agent, and auditioned everywhere I could. I got my Actors' Equity card performing in *Hello, Dolly!* with Martha Rae, my Screen Actors Guild card in *The Time of Your Life* with James Whitmore, and did odds and ends of dinner theaters, commercials, and Disneyland.

Then the dream shifted, and I followed a new path: bookkeeper(!?). It seemed strange at the time, but now I see how the two seemingly different career paths were necessary training grounds for my current profession, financial stress reducer.

You never lose anything, no time is wasted, all experience is meaningful. But you have to put ships in the water to get anywhere or you'll never hear the lookout shout, "Land ho!"

Today's Affirmation: "All paths lead to my highest good."

15
Consistency Is Everything

"We are what we repeatedly do.
Excellence, then, is not an act, but a habit."

—Aristotle

Money is a metaphor in life. It allows you to test your ability to manifest reality from your thoughts. It is tangible, concrete: You can count it; you can calculate your results exactly.

Demonstrate it for yourself. Practice affirmations daily. Just as importantly, stop all the negative thoughts about money.

Then translate your new positive thoughts about money into positive actions with money—making it, saving it, spending it. Send out your ships with the fresh new air of your joyful beliefs billowing in the sails. Notice how much easier your work becomes, enjoy the increasing richness of your surroundings. At the end of the month, count your money. Do you have more than you did before?

Now the trick is to keep doing it. Consistency is everything. Amazingly, many people stop after having great results for two or three months, and revert to their old, ingrained habits. They stop doing the affirmations, and behold! Their ships sink and they don't know what happened. Or they keep doing the affirmations (thinking they're some sort of magic charm) and stop sending out ships. No ships, no money. Very tangible. Very concrete.

When this process has become internalized and your new habit, you have consciously learned the art of manifesting your reality. I believe that's one of life's greatest lessons that we're on this planet to learn. Money is just a concrete, easy, and convenient way to learn it. It's school.

You are supposed to graduate, however. If you get stuck in the school of manifesting money, you can be a very unhappy person. That's why you see many people who have achieved great wealth give away a lot of it. They've learned how to manifest money and now they're on to the next lesson. Now they're looking for the ships that arrive with intangible treasures: love, community, integrity, honor, authenticity, peace.

Conversely, some people are trying to avoid the money school. They want the intangibles, but want to somehow skip the grades that involve feeding and clothing the body. They often suffer from the fear of financial insecurity, resent the jobs they take that don't pay well, and have spiteful opinions of people who've mastered money school. Well, they don't seem to have the intangibles down either, do they? You can't help the poor if you are the poor.

There is internal wealth and external wealth. They are not mutually exclusive.

Today's Affirmation: "My ships are piled high with treasure and I'm unloading them today!"

16

Baby-U-Deserve-Getting-Every-Thing (Budget)

"It's amazing how fast you can go through $7,000 with beer, pizza, and The Gap."

—Ben Affleck

What is your reaction to the word "budget"? A sinking, depressed, deprived feeling? You are not alone. Many people audibly groan at the mention of the word. For the vast majority, it connotes scarcity, lack, and limitation—none of which are very pleasurable concepts. "Budgeting" in common usage usually means cutting the fun, frivolity, entertainment, and spontaneity out of your life, and creating a bare-bones, austere, nothing-but-the-basics spending plan—something you do when you're stressed about not having enough money.

That is not my idea of budgeting. I have reframed it above: it means designing a spending plan to achieve your number one priorities, and getting all those things you *really* want. This can and should be a very enjoyable process, and not the bitter, restrictive pill you fear.

It is important to know that a budget is not written in stone. It is a flexible, adjustable plan that reflects how you give valuable products or services to others (income) and how you choose to support others by buying their products or services (expenses). All of these are decisions you make, therefore you have the power to change them. We often feel so trapped by our previous decisions that we think that we're stuck, but a closer examination will reveal that we can change everything if we are willing.

The power of budgeting is that we decide before each month how we will spend our income, then as the month goes on, we write down our actual income and expenses. When we tally up the score at the end of the month, we can see whether or not we want to change our decisions for next month. Design a plan that works for you, and then work your plan!

Today's Affirmation: "I happily spend the money I make in all the wisest ways!"

17

Mom's Envelopes

"A budget is telling your money where to go instead of wondering where it went."

—C.E. Hoover

I grew up in the typical '50s middle class household: Dad worked at the office, brought home the paycheck, Mom stayed home and raised the three kids. My childhood was mirrored on televisionland shows like *Father Knows Best*, *Leave It To Beaver*, and *The Donna Reed Show*. Those were the days when, since I both lived in and watched it on TV, I thought everyone's life was like that. All the girls in the neighborhood were Donna Reed-ettes looking for their Carl Betz.

My mom deposited dad's paycheck at the bank, paid the regular recurring bills by check, and got cash for the discretionary spending. She had a system of envelopes for the cash: one envelope for clothing, one for school activities, one for entertainment, etc. When we came home from school asking for money for something special like a school sweater, Mom would take us to the envelopes. She kept them in her chest of drawers in her bedroom, and would put them on the bed while we sat and looked at what money remained in each one. If there was no money in the corresponding envelope, she would see what money was available in the other envelopes.

Then she would give us choices: we could have the school sweater by taking money out of one of the other envelopes. But that meant trading one thing for another, and whatever envelope we took from would be empty. We could have the sweater, but it meant no new dress or no going out to dinner. We had to choose what we wanted most.

I learned a lot from Mom's envelopes:

1. Dad worked to put the money in the envelopes.
2. The money in the envelopes was all the money there was.
3. If there was no money in the envelopes, we didn't get to buy anything.
4. Having one thing meant not having another.
5. I got to choose what I wanted most.

Create some envelopes for your discretionary spending, and put cash in them. You will quickly learn what your spending priorities are.

Today's Affirmation: "I am a smart money manager and always make smart financial decisions."

18

Count Your Money

"A man who both spends and saves money is the happiest man, because he has both enjoyments."

—Samuel Johnson

To achieve success, you must think positive and send out ships. But if you want to achieve *financial* success, you have to add the third step: count your money. Keeping track of how much you're making, how much you're spending, and how much you're saving will tell you how effectively you're doing the first two steps. In other words, budget.

I suggest that everyone should have not just one, but *three* budgets, all with complicated names: Low, Medium, and High. You start with Medium Budget, which is the average income and expenses that you have right now. Then you create Low Budget—this is your bare-bones plan to reduce expenses if you have an unexpected financial problem such as a bill or a reduction in income. Then create a High Budget—this is your goal budget, how you're going to spend the money you plan to make in the future. If you don't have a plan for how you are going to spend it and save it, you won't have a reason to make it, or if you do, you might fritter it away on low priority items. These flex-budgets will give you a written plan to follow, no matter what happens with your money. And each budget is only for one month.

People hate budgeting because they're afraid of Low Budget. They think that's the only budget there is and that they'll be stuck with it forever. Who'd want that? No wonder people don't do budgets. But Low Budget is never forever, it's just for now. Anyone can go on Low Budget for a month! And when you're on it, stay light-hearted about it and double up on your prosperity affirmations. Make it a game! See how much money you can avoid spending each day. Look for opportunities to trade or barter services. Clean out your home and have a garage sale. What work can you do part-time that would also bring in extra cash? What can you fix instead of buying new? Create new outfits to wear by mixing and matching separates in new ways. And each day you succeed in conserving your cash with creative ideas, congratulate yourself on your wisdom and money mastery.

The real fun is creating High Budget. This is your Prosperity Plan. Spend some time each day looking at it and feeling rich. What do you want to have and do when you're on High Budget? Go shopping and price-compare for the best values. (Just because you have a lot of money doesn't mean you have to spend it foolishly.) Get pictures and brochures of the things you really want and put them on your wall. Start a special savings plan for major purchases. Be specific: if you want a new car, what make, model, and color is it? What features and options does it have? Smile and feel the pleasure now as if you already owned it. Affirm your ability to create this abundance in your life. It won't be long before it shows up!

Today's Affirmation: "I spend money wisely and happily, blessing myself and others."

19

The Sparkly New Dress

"All right, so I like spending money! But name one other extravagance!"

—Max Kauffmann

Elizabeth was "between jobs." A beautiful girl with a great smile, she spoke of her dissatisfaction with her current job on the first day of the workshop. She longed for a better position with better pay. The next week, she came to class and laughingly told us how she had been fired. "I know I created that happening!" she exclaimed. "I was doing affirmations for a better job, but wasn't sending any ships out to look for one. So I guess my higher self took charge and got me fired so I would have to get up off my duff and find what I really want." We laughed and applauded, and helped her with suggestions about a new career.

After class, in which we had focused on creating Low, Medium, and High Budgets, Elizabeth approached me with a question. "I'm going to a friend's wedding on Saturday, and I went shopping for a dress. I found this beautiful sparkly lavender dress that looked wonderful on me and I really want to have it. But I'm on Low Budget now, having just lost my job. And the dress costs $143. So you don't think it would be a good idea for me to buy it, do you?"

I loved the way she asked me this question. Clearly, she understood that the reasonable answer was "No!" She really shouldn't buy a dress—sparkly or otherwise—when she's on Low Budget with no job and no income. I congratulated her on coming to me with the question, because we both knew she was looking for support to maintain her financial control. It might be fun for one day to wear a new dress and get lots of compliments, but it would all be over the next day. Then she'd be really depressed knowing that a bill for $143 would arrive any day—and she couldn't pay it.

I suggested she go shopping in her closet: look in the back of the closet for something great that she hadn't worn in a while. Perhaps she could dress it up with a scarf or different jewelry or shoes. She could create a new outfit or two from existing items combined in new ways. Or perhaps she could trade dresses with a friend who wore the same size, and they'd both feel like they got something new. Her eyes gleamed with the challenge, and a brilliant smile radiated across her face.

"Elizabeth," I said, "You don't need a sparkly dress—you have sparkly eyes!" She told me she liked that compliment even better than the one she might have gotten on a new dress.

Today's Affirmation: "Money and love are attracted to me. They flow to me from all directions in larger and larger amounts."

(Contributed by Mark Roevekamp)

20
Shopping for Love

"An object in possession seldom retains the same charm that it had in pursuit."

—Pliny the Younger

"Can't buy me love," sang The Beatles. But we can buy its cousin: praise, which we use as a poor substitute for love. People crave love and acknowledgment beyond all other things. In a survey conducted by Ken Blanchard, author of *The One Minute Manager*, employees ranked "Feeling 'in' on things" and "Appreciation of work" as the number one and number two benefits they wanted most from their jobs. Higher wages ranked a distant fifth. We want to feel included, we want to be special, we want compliments, we want attention.

When we don't get it, we go shopping. We buy things to make us noticed, to get praised. Women buy clothing, jewelry, shoes, handbags, scarves, and makeup to be beautiful, to be admired. Men buy cars, electronic equipment, tools, hardware, businesses to be powerful, to be admired. The problem is that after everyone has "oohed" and "aahed" over our fabulous purchase and we've had our fix of the praise drug—the rush is over. It isn't long before we need another fix, another dress, another car. The praise is over—but the payments aren't. We're stuck with endless monthly bills for items that don't get us any more praise, but still we need more praise. So we charge the next fix on our credit cards, even though we're ashamed of ourselves for spending more than we should. It is a habit as destructive as drugs, alcohol, or cigarettes.

Now we have a cycle of buying praise and feeling shame for doing it. The worse we feel about ourselves, the more praise we need to buy. So credit cards in hand, we shop again. "Love me!" the silent scream floats beneath the surface of our ocean of debt.

The solution? Look for love in better places. It isn't in the new shoes, it isn't in the new computer whiz bang. Love is in the eyes of a friend who's happy to see you, regardless of what you wear. Praise comes from a customer or boss you've served above and beyond the call of the ordinary. Acknowledgment is what you give yourself as you master your spending and pay off your debts.

Send out a ship into someone else's harbor today. Reach out with love to compliment someone on their thoughtfulness, their kindness, their ability to love, or the light in their eyes instead of their new dress. Do your job better than you've ever done it—every menial task. Be extraordinary by putting just a little extra in the ordinary. Send out love, and love will come sailing back to you. You can't buy it. You just have to practice it.

Today's Affirmation: "I am peaceful and content with all the riches in my life."

21
Ballet Lessons

"I write only when I'm inspired. Fortunately, I'm inspired at 9 o'clock every morning."

—William Faulkner

"I'm sorry I haven't paid you yet," my former student wailed, "but the job I told you about fell through. I don't know why it's so hard to find the right position!"

I calmed her down and let her tell me her sad story of lost opportunities. "Just one more thing," I said as we were about to hang up the phone, "Are you still doing your affirmations?"

"Well, no," she said. "I've just been too depressed."

I can't tell you how many times I've had similar conversations with past participants of my workshops. Things are going along great, they're practicing their affirmations, sending out ships and counting the money as it rolls in. Then somewhere, somehow, they get busy and skip a day's affirmations. Then two. Then two weeks. By that time they're out of the habit and the old negative voice pipes up once more. A ship sinks in the harbor and the bad news broadcasts loudly in their minds. Fear and anxiety gather like boa constrictors around their throats. Everything starts going wrong. The car breaks down; the babysitter quits; the company downsizes their paycheck or their job.

It reminds me of the dancer's life. No matter how famous, successful, brilliant, and accomplished, great dancers take class and practice every day. Baryshnikov, Nureyev, Fonteyn—all the great stars, stood at the barre with beginners and performed their dancer's ritual. Their rule was that if you missed class one day, you could tell. If you missed two days, the other dancers could tell. But if you missed three days, the audience could tell.

In the same way, daily practice of your prosperity affirmations is required for abundance maintenance. It must be developed as a habit as necessary as brushing your teeth. If you miss a day, you will be able to tell. If you miss two days, your bank account can tell. And if you miss three days, your ships can tell and they sail into someone else's harbor. Let your affirmations shine the way home to guide your ships to your shore.

Today's Affirmation: "My net worth and my self worth are rising every day!"

22

Irregular Expenses

"Just about the time you think you can make both ends meet, somebody moves the ends."

—Pansy Penner

Irregular expenses are often budget-busters. This is because they aren't a part of our regular, monthly expenses, and we tend to forget them. Then suddenly, like a harbinger of doom, there they are looming over your checkbook, cackling with glee that they've given you this nasty surprise. Your car breaks down and the repair bill is five hundred dollars. The water heater goes out, or the computer suddenly develops amnesia. It's time for your yearly vacation, but you didn't put money aside to take that cruise you want.

The solution is to make a list of all your irregular expenses by month. Insurance premiums, taxes, vacation expenses, and club membership dues are not regular monthly expenses and should go on this list. Make a list for each month of the year, then total the amount of money for the entire year. Divide this number by twelve and you will have the average amount of money you spend on irregular expenses. Put this figure as a line item on your budget.

Now open an interest-bearing savings or money market account and deposit this amount into it every month. Then when bills come due that are on your irregular expense list, you pay it from your savings account. No more anxiety over forgotten expenses—the money is there! You now have knowledge and control over all your spending.

A woman I consulted with had a tutoring business with a healthy income during the months that school was in session. But during the summer months when school was out, her income plummeted. I suggested she use an irregular expense account, which she started immediately. She divided her yearly income by twelve and made a budget to live within that income. The additional income she earned during her regular working season, she deposited into her irregular expense savings account. By the time summer came around, she had plenty of money saved to live on for the summer.

Now the side benefit kicked in. She like having savings and didn't want to spend it. So she got into her creative mode and started inventing new ways to make money during the summer months. She developed a summer school curriculum and then started enrolling students. She made enough additional money that she didn't need to take money out of her savings—and went on vacation for a month as well!

Today's Affirmation: "I have positive cash flow right here, right now, and always!"

23

Magic Money Wish List

"The two most beautiful words in the English language are: 'Check enclosed.'"

—Dorothy Parker

Every so often, as I worked with my chosen monthly budget, I would think of something I wanted to have that wasn't on my budget. It could be something I had forgotten to plan for by putting it on my "Irregular Expenses" list like new stationery, additional advertising specialty items like coffee mugs or pens, or a new piece of computer equipment. Or it could be something fun or extravagant that I wanted to create more money for, like new clothes, new office furniture, or a piece of jewelry.

Whenever I thought of something, I wrote it down on a piece of paper at the back of my time management calendar on my desk. I labeled it my "Magic Money Wish List," because I knew I had to create extra, magic money, above and beyond my budget, in order to have the things on this list.

Without paying much attention to it, I started regularly receiving extra money. In fact, the amounts I received almost always totaled the amount of money I needed to buy the things on this list. I remember one day in particular, when I had gotten a surprise bill for $800 that I had not planned for. I wrote this amount on my list and started doing "magic money" affirmations, because I didn't want to take $800 out of my savings. Three weeks later, I got a check in the mail from a real estate transaction that had closed three years before. Some accountant in the lender's office had done an audit and discovered a discrepancy—I had not been paid the full amount I was due, so they were sending me a check to take care of the balance due me.

The check enclosed was for $806.32. True story.

When that happened, I suddenly became conscious of what I was doing. I was naming a goal, writing it down, and telling my subconscious and the Universe to create it for me. Whenever I bought one of the items, I crossed it off of the list by highlighting it in green. After several years, I had several pages of nice things highlighted in green—this was working! Right then, I added the "Magic Money Wish List" instructions to my *Financial Stress Reduction® Workshop*.

What would you like to have "magic money" for? Write out your wish list today!

Today's Affirmation: "I create 'Magic Money' for all the wonderful things I desire!"

24

"Magic Money" and the "PDQ" Plan

"Bills travel through the mail at twice the speed of checks."

—Unknown

Personal bankruptcies soared in the late '90s and credit card debt was at an all-time high. Consumer Credit Counselors declared that it was not unusual for their clients to have 40-60 credit cards. They also reported that the average per family debt, in credit cards and cards, was $52,000. Although these statistics might change somewhat from year to year, they don't change enough.

Too much easy credit coupled with too small minimum monthly payments keeps too many people slaves to their debt. Make a decision now to become debt-free! It may take some time, but a commitment today to the "PDQ" (Pay Debts Quick) Plan will have your debt unloaded sooner than you think. There is a freedom and self-satisfaction that comes with acting on your plan that makes you walk, talk, look, act, think, and be richer!

Look at your current budget and see what amount of money you can dedicate each month to paying off debt. For example, let's assume that you have ten credit cards and can afford $250 per month towards paying them off. So you pay $25 to each credit card every month. Eventually, one of the cards will get paid off and most people will continue to send $25 to the other nine cards. But that's reducing your debt repayment commitment to only $225 instead of $250. What happens to the other $25? It disappears. (Eating up unallocated money is the actual purpose of the "black holes" in the universe. There is one in every checkbook, wallet, and credit card.)

Instead, take that $25 and add it to the $25 payment you're making on the credit card with the highest interest rate. Now that card is being paid off at $50 per month instead of $25 per month—twice as fast. As soon as that card gets paid off, take the $50 and add it to the next card on your list. Now that one is getting paid off at $75 per month—three times as fast!

A magical thing happens next. Out of the integrity of your commitment and follow through, unexpected money starts appearing in your life. I call it "Magic Money." You feel more prosperous, more confident, and like a good money manager because you have taken control of your finances. Money flows to people who think like this. And always use part of your "Magic Money" to pay down your debt even further—and faster!

Today's Affirmation: "I am a creative money generator!"

25
Luck

"If you bet on a horse, that's gambling. If you bet you can make three spades, that's entertainment. If you bet cotton will go up three points, that's business. See the difference?"

—Blackie Sherrod

People always smile and look askance when I tell them I play poker. "You teach finance and you *gamble*?" they ask incredulously. Ah, but any poker player will tell you: poker isn't gambling. It is a game where, as in life, luck always plays a part, but over the long-term it is a certainty: good players win and bad players lose. If you play well, it is possible to win consistently at poker. (Contrary to what the media commonly reports: Barbara Enright, one of the top women poker players, spent days filming a segment for *48 Hours*. It was "too positive," however. Instead, they profiled a gambling addict who lost all her money.)

Poker is fun, challenging, and takes a combination of skill and luck. It is a game of strategy, assessing risks vs. rewards, and taking your best shot when the odds are with you. The great players have strong minds, strong wills, patience and knowledge of people honed by many hours of observation. They also understand that luck runs in cycles and have a feel for when they are "running good." And they have a positive winning attitude—they believe in their skill as well as luck.

John Kluge, whose net worth was estimated by *Forbes* magazine to be $5.6 billion dollars, had this to say about poker: "If you want your kid to succeed in business, maybe you shouldn't send him or her to business school. Teach him to play cards instead. Card-playing teaches you that luck is important, but how you play your luck is even more important."

Some people go broke playing poker. Some people make their living playing poker. Just like life. For me, poker is fun. It challenges my skills, gives me adrenaline rushes when I'm running good, and I'm working on taking my "bad beats" with grace. I don't have to dress up, I don't have to be "on," I can talk and be sociable if I want to, or sit quietly if I don't. This is a relaxing balance of energy for someone often in the public eye. I have a budget category under "Entertainment" labeled "Poker." If I have fun and don't exceed my budget, I consider it money well-spent. When I win and have extra money, I'm happy.

Poker is fun and can be a rewarding hobby. But before you step inside the casino with your hard-earned cash, I suggest you study the game—the winning players do. Otherwise, you may lose your shirt.

Whatever your hobby is, have a budget for it, stay within it, then have as much fun as you can.

Whatever your life is, have a budget for it, stay within it, then have as much fun as you can.

Today's Affirmation: "I am a lucky person. A powerful winning force surrounds me!"
(Mike Caro, *Fundamentals of Poker*)

26

Why Swim with Sharks When You Can Swim with Dolphins?

"Why do some people always see beautiful skies and grass and lovely flowers and incredible human beings, while others are hard-pressed to find anything or any place that is beautiful?"

—Leo Buscaglia

There are three kinds of fish in the sea: Dolphins, Sharks, and Tuna.

Dolphins are wonderful creatures: intelligent, happy, and playful. They communicate; they swim in schools. They've been known to ward off a shark attack and protect the other fish. They are fun-loving and beautiful, arcing in graceful leaps over the waves.

Sharks are eating machines. It's not their fault; they were born that way. But their job is to eat you. If you find yourself in the water with a shark, put your shark fin on or get out of the water. It's very difficult for a dolphin to act like a shark, and you'll never be as good at it as a real shark, so I recommend getting out of the water.

Tuna fish are food. They don't know that the blood in the water is their own. They think everything that happens to them is somebody else's fault. They take no responsibility for their choices. It's like there are three kinds of people: the people that make things happen, the people that watch things happen, and the people who say, "What happened?" (Those are the tuna.)

Sharks will steal your money and tuna will leech money from you. Real money is made when you have dolphins on your team.

Who are the fish in your sea?

Today's Affirmation: "I now attract people who reflect my highest good!"

27
Your People

"About all you can do in life is be who you are. Some people will love you for you. Most will love you for what you can do for them, and some won't like you at all."

—Rita Mae Brown

As I've gone through life, I've been greatly influenced by wonderful self-help books by marvelous teachers, giving me life lessons in moments of illumination. One such moment came from a passage in Wayne Dyer's book *Your Erroneous Zones*, where he reminds us that half of the people in the world aren't going to like you, and there's nothing you can do about it.

I was shocked. It was definitely an "Aha!" moment. I had been raised to be a good girl, a people-pleaser, always trying to make sure everyone around me was happy and that I didn't offend anyone with any statement or act. What an impossible task! I was doomed to failure, and I became nervous and unhappy when I couldn't please everyone. I was one of those people who would go to a party, find ninety-nine people out of one hundred liked me, but follow around the one who didn't, trying to change his mind.

How much money is lost in life by people chasing people who don't like them, trying to make them happy? It can be a boss, a client, or a family member. This person clearly isn't one of Your People. Let them go! You will never please them, satisfy them, or measure up to their vision of how you ought to be. You'll make yourself crazy spending any time or effort on them.

Look for Your People—pick dolphins to be on your team. When someone asks me how you can tell who they are, I tell them it's easy: you know Your People because you like them—immediately. And they like you back. Just listen to your gut instinct, your feelings. You can tell from the chemistry that flows between you, the quickening interest in their eyes, the body language that tells you they're awake and listening. They have praise for you, your products or services, your ideas. If they are a client or a boss, they pay you well.

The Other People have "out of body" experiences around you. You know how this happens: you're talking to them and their eyes glaze over and you know that mentally, they just left the room. Or some anger surfaces in the conversation, they take offense to something you said, or disagree strongly with your core values. They never think you're good enough, they put you down, they "should" on you. If they're a boss or a client, they will never be happy with your performance, they will niggle you to death over the smallest of details, and they won't pay you what you're worth—if they pay you at all! Instead of buy-buy, say bye-bye!

Today's Affirmation: "All My People praise me and pay me!"

28
Other People

"If you don't make a total commitment to whatever you're doing, then you start looking to bail out the first time the boat starts leaking. It's tough enough getting that boat to shore with everybody rowing, let alone when a guy stands up and starts putting his life jacket on."

—Lou Holtz

A friend sent Lillian to me. We met for lunch and had a good discussion of her goals and desires. She thought my course would help her, and enrolled. As we stood up to leave the restaurant, I offered her some affirmations to get her started, beginning with "People love to give me money."

Her face fell. "I don't believe in affirmations!" she exclaimed.

Uh-oh, I thought. "Would you be willing to put aside your disbelief for the eight weeks of the class and give it a try anyway?" I asked.

"Well, I guess so…" she replied reluctantly.

Lillian called to argue with me after the first class and I coached her to put aside her "Yeah, buts." Second class, same story. After the third class, she called again. "I'm not coming back," she said. "I've thought about it and this class just doesn't work for me."

I said, "Okay."

She laughed at that. "Okay?" she asked. "You mean you're not going to argue with me?"

I said, "Nope."

"But I have all my arguments prepared!" she exclaimed.

"I'm sure you do," I answered. "But we don't need to go there. If after three classes, you don't think this workshop is what you need, then it isn't."

She offered to pay for the classes she attended, but I refused. Pay for what? She didn't get it and wasn't using it. She thanked me and we wished each other well on our separate journeys.

You are only looking for Your People. They have Your Money. They will love you and pay you. Other People won't understand you and usually won't pay you either. Why fight to try to get them, keep them, teach them what they resist learning? They don't want what you have. Move on.

Today's Affirmation: "There is plenty of money in this world and I'm receiving mine today!"

29
Jaws

"Keep away from people who try to belittle your ambitions. Small people always do that, but the really great make you feel that you, too, can become great."

—Mark Twain

A bright, talented attorney in my workshop was having a terrible time. John had been hired by a client who was giving him many headaches. Nothing was ever good enough, fast enough, or cheap enough. He told the story in great detail one class session, looking for ideas and creative help from the group on how he could turn around this situation.

As he started describing the details of the interaction with this terrible client, I drew a red flag on the white board. He continued his impassioned, anxious narrative. I drew some waves under the red flag. He described the next problem. I drew a shark fin amongst the waves. He went on. I drew "Doo-doo-doo-doo" under the waves. He kept going. Then the whole class, as one voice, started singing the theme music from *Jaws*. He burst out laughing. He said, "Okay, I get it. He's a shark, he's not a dolphin, and there isn't anything I can do with him but send him on his way."

The class cheered.

Do you want to work and not get paid? Or *not* work and not get paid? You don't have to work for the crazy client or the rage-aholic boss. Who told you that you had to make the best of a bad situation? Get out! Go swimming in a different ocean with better fish. You don't have to put up with bad behavior from anyone. You don't have to pay any more dues.

Today's Affirmation: "All my dues are paid in full."

30
The City Girl and the Farmer's Wife

"The hardest arithmetic to master is that which enables us to count our blessings."

—Eric Hoffer

I'm a city girl. Born and bred in suburbia, visits to the country were visits to another planet. Then I met Stan, who was raised on a farm in Montana. As our relationship progressed, he suggested a visit to the farm to visit his parents. I had never been on a farm.

"Big Sky Country" they call it. Montana's sky is vast, blue, and sometimes thundercloud-filled, where eagles sweep through craggy mountain passes and geese honk in V-formation flight squadrons. My heart drank in Nature. I loved it.

I loved fishing in the lake for perch and sunfish, after digging for fish-hook night crawlers just before dawn. I gloated over my catch and reeled in fish after fish, blissfully unaware of the "you catch 'em, you clean 'em" rule. I loved collecting the eggs from underneath the hens, milking the cow, and then eating the fruit of our labors at meal-time. Stan worked with his father and brothers in the fields. His mother, Mae, his sisters, and I took our turns driving the tractor and cooking. I left my fancy clothes in my unpacked suitcase and wore denim every day. Worry was only for whether or not you'd get the hay baled before the rain fell.

One morning after breakfast, when Mae and I had finished the dishes and the men had gone out to the hay fields, Mae said she was going birding. "Could I come along?" I asked. Surprised, Mae said hesitantly, "You want to come?" I nodded and she said okay. That's when I developed a life-long fascination with sneaking up on our feathered friends and watching them, collecting the names of different species I had seen for my "life list." We saw bald eagles, evening grosbeaks, hairy and downy woodpeckers, marsh hawks, Canadian geese, and dozens of ducks. When the time came to head for home, I lamented that there were no birds in the suburbs of Los Angeles except sparrows and pigeons (oops, I mean "rock doves"; no respecting birder calls them pigeons). "Take another look," Mae said with a twinkle in her eye. "There are more birds there than you think." Of course she was right.

Mae and I started writing to each other with tales of our different lives. As Stan and I fell out of love, Mae and I fell in. When Stan and I broke up, she called me with tears in her voice and said, "I'm not just Stan's mother. I'm your friend." And so, although Stan and I lost touch with each other, Mae and I never did. I sometimes think I just met Stan in order to meet Mae.

Life presents us with many gifts—they're just not always the ones we think we're looking at. Remember to be grateful for your surprise packages. You might find a dolphin in a lake.

Today's Affirmation: "I gratefully receive and enjoy life's surprise packages!"

31
The Day of My Enlightenment

"I walked for miles at night along the beach, composing bad blank verse and searching endlessly for someone wonderful who would step out of the darkness and change my life. It never crossed my mind that that person could be me."

—Anna Quindlen

The world and reality shifted for me on an excruciatingly awful day, a culmination of many awful days. I was a young actress in the fifth year of marriage to a brilliant young actor. We had little money and the stresses of two creative artists trying to succeed in a difficult business made our relationship a cauldron of roiling emotions. With each failed audition, his rages and my fear intensified. I had no tools for dealing with anger; in my family, if you got angry, you were sent to your room to cool off until you could be nice again. I had never seen anyone put a fist through a door, or throw a chair across a room. In shocked silence, I waited for the anger to subside. We were both frozen in our positions, and neither of us knew how to reach the other.

On this particular day, I sat in a rocking chair in our home, miserably reviewing my messed-up life. My husband was out of town, performing in a play. I noticed that a lot of my unhappiness went with him, and the distance between us gave me the courage I needed to fight back when the telephone rages started. Finally in touch with my own anger, I rocked in my chair, raging and blaming him for my life. Rock, rock, blame, blame. I was the martyr, the good one, the oppressed. Rock, rock. He was the bad guy, the perpetrator, the oppressor. Blame, rock.

I sat and rocked, rocked and blamed, blamed and cried all afternoon.

All of a sudden, a voice from out of nowhere spoke in my ear three words that changed my life: "You picked him."

Thunderbolt! Electrified, my breath caught in my throat, my next blame dying in my mind, I froze in my chair. "I did!" I answered the voice, "I picked him! No one chained me to him at birth, no one told me I had to live this way, I chose it!" I was horrified at what I had done—not at what *he* had done, but what I had done! "And I continue to choose this every day that I stay here," my thoughts progressed. "How did I choose this? And how can I get out of it and choose something else?"

When I went in search of answers to that question, I took back control over my life and my destiny. A different woman got up out of that rocking chair. You can't blame a shark for eating a tuna—it's your responsibility not to be a tuna! My husband and I divorced, but I bless him and bless every difficult experience because it was what I needed to bring me to this point of realization and enlightenment.

What have you chosen in your life that it's time to change?

Today's Affirmation: "I create a wonderful, fulfilling life for myself and help others do the same!"

32
Winter

"Sunshine is delicious, rain is refreshing, wind braces us up, snow is exhilarating; there is no such thing as bad weather, only different kinds of good weather."

—John Ruskin

Perhaps it is winter now for you. Winter, when the trees have shed the last of their clothes and a chill is in the air whether or not snow is on the ground. If the frost has reached in and touched your heart—and your pocketbook—and left you frozen with grief and helplessness, there is comfort to be found in the continuum of the seasons. Spring will come again. The snows will melt from around your heart, your frozen assets will thaw, the seedlings of the money tree will sprout new leaves of green cash.

Winter is a time of quiet hibernation, a drawing within, harboring your inner resources. Take time to breathe and relax. Meditate. Pray. But stay away from desperate, needy entreaties! Remember that they're *affirmations*, not *desperations*. Make your prayers ones of gratitude for whatever warmth remains in your life. Thank God for the gifts of fortitude, endurance, patience, persistence, and faith. Remember with assurance that spring will arrive—and on time—again. Focus on the abundance that is coming, rather than on the cold hearth of the present. Beneath the surface of the barren ground, vibrant life is waiting for its rebirth in spring. Brilliant diamonds lie hidden in the heart of coal, and golden threads of a new dawning are just around the corner from the stars and moonbeams of the night. The sun will warm the earth again, the grass will grow, your heart will lighten. Love and money will renew their acquaintance with you, tipping their hats and nodding good day.

Today's Affirmation: "The joys of springtime are bursting into bloom in my life!"

33
Waiting

"The sea does not reward those who are too anxious, too greedy, or too impatient. To dig for treasures shows not only impatience and greed, but lack of faith. Patience, patience, patience, is what the sea teaches. Patience and faith. One should lie empty, open, choiceless as a beach—waiting for a gift from the sea."

—Anne Morrow Lindbergh

My ship is becalmed in still waters. No wind in the sails (or sales). A publisher has said, "Everyone loves your book! I'll call you tomorrow."

Now a week has gone by with no call. A friend tells me, "When a woman says she'll call you later, she means when she gets home. When a man says he'll call you later, he means before he dies."

I've done all I can do. I built the ship, provisioned it, hired the best crew I could find. Launched it with the crash of a Sparkling Cider bottle against the hull (no alcohol for me) with great fanfare. Crowds along the shore shouted and waved goodbye with great hopes in their hearts.

Now nothing. I can still see the ship, but it isn't moving.

I appreciate King Agamemnon's rage and frustration as all his ships sat in the harbor, with no wind to carry them to Troy to recapture Helen. Finally, he sacrificed his daughter, Iphigenia, to the gods, and then the wind came.

Okay, so who do I have to kill?

I pause to think about that. I have no daughter of my body to sacrifice. What is the daughter of my soul that needs to be laid on the altar and given to God? The answer whispers in my mind: my will, my impatience, my pride.

I surrender. I decide to enjoy the moment of unknowing, where all dreams and wishes still remain possible. The wind can pick up at any moment, the "Yes!" can still arrive on the next wave. If "No" comes and this ship sinks, I will build another ship tomorrow.

We are only in charge of sending out ships. God is in charge of which ones come in. And on what timetable.

Today's Affirmation: "The divine plan of my life now takes shape, leading me to perfect joy!"

34

What Looks Like Bad News Isn't Always Bad News

"Today I know that I cannot control the ocean tides. I can only go with the flow."

—Marie Stilkind

When we are in the midst of our hurly-burly lives, we cannot always see where the threads of our days have taken us, or where we stand in the warp and woof of time. It is hard to see the overall design because our focus is so narrow—we're looking at today, tomorrow, next week, last week. We don't spend much time in review to see how all the threads intertwined to create the present moment.

I started out with the burning desire to act, and trod many stages in sixteen years of performances. Then I became a bookkeeper!? It seemed an odd choice, a complete departure from all I had ever known or wanted. For twelve years, bookkeeping and business management held my attention and passion.

The catalyst that brought the two halves of my life together looked, at first, like a disaster. My biggest account, worth $300,000 per year, fired me. But what looks like bad news isn't always bad news. The struggle that I underwent to solve my financial stress made me strong and taught me things I would never have known any other way. And so when, a year later, the big recession of the late 1980s hit California, I was prepared with tools to help others weather financial storms.

My clients knew I had had problems—I talked about them to anyone who'd listen—and that I'd solved them. Suddenly, everyone was taking me to lunch and asking how I handled creditors, how I renegotiated leases, how I made deals and closed sales. When three people in the same week told me I should teach a class, the *Financial Stress Reduction® Workshop* was born.

Suddenly, my whole life made sense. Sixteen years of performing skills coupled with twelve years of financial management skills gave me all the tools I needed to teach a financial class that was practical yet entertaining. I couldn't see the design of the tapestry before that defining moment. But then I knew that my whole life, I had been training for this purpose. Even when I thought I was off the path, I was on the path. All my mistakes, upsets, and disasters were material to share with my clients: were they broke, stressed out, in debt, scared? I had been there. Abused? Alcoholic? I had been there, too.

Yes, I make money—I teach making money. But the real payday for me is when one of my clients turns her money and life around, when she closes a deal she didn't think she could get, when she finds the job that makes her soul sing—and pays her well, too! With tears in her eyes, she thanks me for it. And with tears in mine, I thank God.

What glories have the disasters of your life brought you?

Today's Affirmation: "Every day, I follow my life's design to my heart's desire."

35
Inner Voices

"We all walk in the dark and each of us must learn to turn on his or her own light."

—Earl Nightingale

I saw a television commercial in which a woman was shopping for groceries in the supermarket. As she walked up and down the aisles, looking at all the food, she had an angel perched on one shoulder and a devil perched on the other. The angel whispered sweetly, "Oh, yes, yes, buy the vegetables, they're good for you," while the devil coaxed, "Buy the chocolate cake! And ice cream!" This is a perfect illustration of the two voices we have in our heads that promote or demolish us, our goals, and our self-esteem. Sometimes there are more than two—there's a whole committee.

I was very fortunate. My mother always said to me, "You can do anything you put your mind to," and when I wailed and said, "I can't!" to anything, she would answer back, "Can't never did." I have a strong interior voice that keeps saying, "I can do anything." This is the voice of Saint Chellie-in-my-mind. But I also have a powerful negative voice that speaks up on occasion. I don't know where this one originated, but it's the one that tells me I'm not good enough, beautiful enough, strong enough, or worthy enough to get what I want. I haven't been able to get it to take its mask off, but ultimately, it doesn't matter. I just want it out of my head. I call this one Demon Chellie-in-my-mind.

Do you have such a voice? Or several voices? A committee? A mob? The whispers of our thoughts, good ones and bad ones, are with us always. I think the practice of meditation is just to shut *everybody* up. To be still, quiet, peaceful, content, at one with our bodies, God, and the Universe. Our paths in life take us through light and shadow; we constantly face choices between good and evil, truth and lies, kindness and coldness. Our interior voices face each other over the battlefield of our minds. Our souls are the prize.

You may not completely escape them or shut them up entirely, but you can definitely turn down the volume on the demon voices and change the radio station and play the saints instead. It will require diligence, however. Repetition of positive statements can help to replace the old messages we don't want with new ones we do. Once in a while won't do the trick; it must be a constant, consistent, constructive application of the preferred thought, attitude, belief, or feeling. Daily, daily, daily. You will observe your interior voice change, and along with the change of voice will come a change in your results. When you take charge of your interior voice, you can tell it what to tell you. And you can make it good.

Today's Affirmation: "I think loving and empowering thoughts about myself every day."

36
Change

"It is not the strongest of the species that survive, nor the most intelligent, but the one most responsive to change."

—Charles Darwin

How big a risk is it that you're afraid to take?

To take a risk is to embrace change. It's been said that the only thing that likes change is a wet baby—and they cry about it. We long for the new, hoping it will be better than the old, but we are terrified it won't be as good. So we spin a web of habits and endlessly repeat them, forgetting that the web was of our own making. Sometimes it takes what seems, at the time, a tragedy to knock us down so that we are freed to weave a new and finer web of life. We weep and wail and hate the change and curse our fate—and then, so often, find we are better off because of it. A lost job paves the way to a new and better career. A failed business shows us our mistakes so we do better next time. A friendship's end opens our lives to new relationships. Our victories in survival create in us depths of understanding, compassion, and empathy.

Life, excitement, drama, experience, learning, and love are on the other side of change. The seed must turn into the flower and the caterpillar into the butterfly. Change leads to growth and the growth to new fulfillment. We must keep growing through the changes, even though we don't know what's on the other side. Every experience is valuable. What doesn't kill us makes us stronger. What a pity if the seedling were to refuse to flower because it had never done it before. If the caterpillar stayed locked in the cocoon, we would never have butterflies' shimmering colors gliding on the breeze.

Change. Grow. Flower. Fly. Love.

Today's Affirmation: "I am endlessly creative. Money flows naturally from my creative endeavors."

37

Buy the Artichoke

*"When I'm about to take a risk, I consider the down side.
If it's not death, I do it."*

—Nancy Sardella

Amy Frelinger, one of my class participants, came in one afternoon exasperated about an experience she had at the grocery store. She had seen an older woman in the produce section looking over the artichokes. The woman picked up one, then another, of the vegetables, turning them around and around in her hands, frowning. Noticing Amy watching her, she smiled and said, "I don't know how to cook these, do you?" Amy said that she did, and gave her some simple directions on how to steam the artichoke and then eat it with melted butter.

Another woman overheard the conversation and chimed in with the suggestion that she dip it in herb salad dressing. Soon there were several people making suggestions on different ways to cook artichokes, encouraging the woman to try it. The woman listened and seemed to enjoy the conversation, but eventually put the artichoke back, saying, "I'm just not sure about this."

Amy was aghast. She was incredulous that the woman couldn't take the risk to cook an artichoke. "It only cost $1.49!" she exclaimed. "How big a risk could it be?"

Step outside your comfort zone today. Take a risk. You don't have to quit your job, get divorced or move to another country yet. Practice with little risks. Shop at a different grocery store. Drive a different route to work. Try out a new restaurant. Watch a foreign film with subtitles. Cut your hair. Go to a concert. Sleep on the other side of the bed.

Cook an artichoke.

Today's Affirmation: "I relish new experiences that enrich my life!"

38

"Yeah, Buts"

"You can have what it is you want, or you can have your reasons for not having it."

—Werner Erhard

It is an interesting phenomenon that when told of a problem, most people will try to be helpful and offer advice to try to help solve it. It seems to be just naturally what people do. The response to the helper's advice often sounds like this: "Yeah, but that won't work for me because...," or, "Yeah, but I tried that once and it didn't work...," or, "Yeah, but my case is different...." This is the voice of someone who is defending their position, not looking for solutions. They are great at finding evidence for why problems can't be solved rather than actively looking for help to change their situation.

"Yeah, buts" have a very negative psychological effect on the person trying to help. They've just been rejected, essentially told that their advice is no good, inappropriate or doesn't work. It's very difficult to keep trying to make positive suggestions to Yeahbutters. "Yeah, buts" build a big dam in the river of creative ideas.

I had buttons made for my workshops that have the words "Yeah, but" on them surrounded by a red circle with a red line through it—"No yeah, buts." I explain that that phrase is not allowed in my classroom. So during each class, when someone is offered advice and forgets and says, "Yeah, but..." I throw them a button. Sometimes, with incorrigible Yeahbutters, other people in the class get up, grab a button and throw it at them. People have been known to leave class wearing eight or ten buttons!

You will find yourself getting richer and happier when you eliminate the words "yeah, but" from your vocabulary. Instead of "Yeah, but" say, "Thank you for the suggestion! Help me see how I can apply that to my situation." Now you have two people working on the problem side by side, instead of two people, with the problem between them, arguing about it.

Think you can make it through today without one "yeah, but"?

Today's Affirmation: "I am grateful for all suggestions because they help me improve my life."

39

How Badly Do You Want It?

"Only put off until tomorrow what you are willing to die having left undone."

—Pablo Picasso

Alice Kahn wrote an article in the *Los Angeles Times* in which she told of walking on a beach on a cold winter's day. A chill was in the air, fog and mist dampened her clothes as she trudged through the wet sand. There were no lifeguards on duty, and the lifeguard stations stood as empty sentinels surveying their deserted kingdom.

As she passed one lifeguard station, she noticed there was a sign posted on the side of it. Curious, she detoured over to it so she could read what was written there:

Air Temperature: 58 degrees

Water Temperature: 55 degrees

Swimming Conditions: It's there if you want it—but you gotta want it bad!

Why does success elude so many talented people? Because they don't "want it bad" enough. There are risks to take, challenges to overcome. There are discomforts to be endured. Without a clear vision of a goal and very strong desire and will to achieve it, they will falter along the way.

One of my acting teachers years ago told me that the key to analyzing any character in a play was to ask two questions: "What do they want?" and "What are they willing to do to get it?"

This test has served me well throughout my business career as well. There are people who are consistent and persistent in achieving their goals, and others who give up when it gets difficult. Some people are even willing to commit crimes in order to get what they want. (Shark warning… Aaoougha!…Get out of the water.)

What do you want? How badly do you want it?

Today's Affirmation: "I am strong and confident and I always get my goals."

40

Challenges

"Success seems to be largely a matter of hanging on after others have let go."

—William Feather

I was always a good student in high school English class, but I had heard terrible things about the low grades typically given to freshman English students. So when my teacher, Mr. Hathaway, asked if anyone had questions, I raised my hand and said, "I've heard a nasty rumor that only C's, D's, and F's are given in this class. Is that true?" And he smiled and answered, "Yes." Surprised that he would admit to it, I asked him "Why?" He replied that freshmen students usually didn't write well enough to get a better grade than that.

The challenge was issued. I resolved then and there that I was going to get an A in this class.

I turned in my first paper and waited anxiously for my grade. 'C+' slashed the mark at the top of the paper. Used to receiving 'A's, I stared at this low mark. I made an appointment to see Mr. Hathaway after class.

He smiled as I walked into his office for the meeting. "How can I help you?" he asked. I said, "I'm unhappy with my grade, and I want to know what's wrong with my paper." "It's a very good paper," he replied, "You got the highest grade in the class." "That's good," I said quietly, "but not good enough. What makes this paper a 'C' instead of an 'A'?" He looked somewhat surprised, but then got to work explaining in detail where my paper lacked power.

On the next paper, I got a 'B.' "Good," I thought, "I'm making progress." At the end of the lecture, I walked over to Mr. Hathaway and said, "I'd like to make an appointment to see you after class." "Why?" he said. "You got the highest grade in the class!" "That's wonderful," I replied, "But I want to write 'A' level papers, and it's your job to teach me how to do that." We made another appointment and he taught me more about writing.

I received an 'A' on the next paper, and the next, and on nearly every paper from then on. I still have the postcard he sent me to notify me of my final grade in the class: "This is the only 'A' I have given in a group of forty-six students. You earned it: You performed well and you seemed to care about what you learned. I especially hope that I am right when I say you care about what you learn—I hope you believe there is meaning in all that you do. You can do very well in school; don't ever work for an 'A,' however, when to do so would mean spending time doing something that won't get you anywhere worthwhile." I appreciated his final lesson: He wanted me to win the war, not just the battle.

Determination is everything. I got this "A" because I was determined to have it, and I was going to do whatever it took to have it. Be determined about something today. Anything you want.

Today's Affirmation: "I relish the challenges that lift me higher and make me better!"

41

Ski School

"I will not participate in a sport where there is an ambulance parked at the bottom of the hill."

—Erma Bombeck

I had always wanted to learn to ski, and when one of my clients offered me the use of his condo at Mammoth Mountain, I jumped at the chance. When I got there, I signed up for ski school. All went fine for the first couple of days. I learned the basic "plow" stance and could remain on my feet on the bunny slopes. But I was excited as the third day dawned bright and crisp, for this was the day the ski class was going up the mountain. There were about twenty-five students in the class and we all watched intently as the instructor showed us how to do turns. I was at the end of the line as we practiced our turns skiing down the slope concentrating very hard, eyes on my skis. Finally, I made it to the bottom of the slope, and I looked up proudly.

No one was there. The entire class had disappeared. I was at an intersection of eight trails and I had no idea which way they had gone. I had no map. Shocked and scared, I took my skis off, sat down in the snow and burst into tears, crying and feeling sorry for myself for about ten minutes. Then I thought, "Well, this isn't going to get me down the mountain." So I picked a trail and skied down it, only to find that at the bottom, there was nothing but another chair lift. Panic set in—the last thing I wanted to do was go back up the mountain! I needed help. I looked at all the people in line, picked out a sympathetic young man, told him my sad story, and begged for assistance. He was terrific and coached me up the chair lift and skiing down the hill to the main ski lodge.

As I waved goodbye to my hero, back safe and sound at the lodge, all of my fear turned into rage. I marched into the ski school and complained bitterly about having been lost on the mountain by their instructor. The nice young man at the desk didn't miss a beat and offered me a free class the next day. (Well, what else was I going to do for a week at a ski resort?)

I arrived at ski school the next day as usual—with one difference. Now I wore a big, bright pink hat. I introduced myself to the instructor and told him that the last instructor had lost me on the mountain. I said, "Do you see this pink hat? Whatever happens today, I want you to make sure that this pink hat is with you every step of the way." And he did, and I learned to ski.

There are several morals to this story: 1. The price of success is failure. 2. Crying about failures won't get you where you want to go. 3. When you fail, ask for help. 4. If someone else fails, ask for reimbursement. 5. If all else fails, wear a pink hat.

Today's Affirmation: "Every day I will persevere in order to bring my best goals near."

42
The Glad Game

"The sun is always shining. Even though clouds may come along and obscure the sun for a while, the sun is always shining. The sun never stops shining. And even though the earth turns, and the sun appears to go down, it really never stops shining."

—Louise Hay

When I was young, my sisters and I would sometimes run home to mother, crying over some tragedy that had just befallen us. We would be heartbroken because the boy we liked didn't ask us to the prom, or we lost the election, or didn't get the part we wanted in the school play. Whatever the problem was, Mom would always hold us and murmur sympathetically, letting us know she was sorry for our hurt—for about five minutes. Tops.

Then she would say, "Well, let's play the glad game!" (I think she got this from the movie, *Pollyanna.*) She would brighten up, smile, and get us to think about all of the things we had that were positive, that we were grateful for, or glad about. It wouldn't be long before we were happy again, having learned to move on from the bad things, and to reconnect with all that was good in our lives.

This became a life-long habit for me. Whenever something bad happens, I cry about it for a while, have my little pity party, and then focus on what's still good in my life. It lifts my spirits immediately. For example, one Sunday afternoon, after visiting an art affair with friends, I walked back to my car and tried to start the engine. Nothing happened—it was dead as a doornail. "Rats!" I fumed (or words to that effect). "Why did this have to happen?" I spent a few minutes being angry about it, then called the Auto Club to come get me. That started my grateful list: "I'm glad I belong to the Auto Club...I'm glad I have a car phone to call the Auto Club...I'm glad it's daylight and I'm in Beverly Hills and not some bad neighborhood in the middle of the night...." You see how it works? I got my attitude back to gratitude: There are a lot of good things in life, and I have a lot of them. The cup *is* half full, thank you.

A car that won't start is a small thing. But playing the glad game works with big events, too. I used the glad game to get me back to positive thinking after my divorce, after losing a $300,000 per year account, after losing a friend to cancer. It takes more time, but the process is the same. I mourn my losses, and then I refocus on my abundance. It is a coping strategy that keeps me in a state of happiness and well-being most of the time.

Thanks, Mom!

Today's Affirmation: "My attitude of gratitude creates more and more blessings in my life."

43
Saint Chellie in My Mind

"Finish each day and be done with it. You have done what you could. Some blunders and absurdities no doubt crept in; forget them as soon as you can. Tomorrow is a new day; begin it well and serenely and with too high a spirit to be cumbered with your old nonsense."

—Ralph Waldo Emerson

Saint Chellie lives in my mind. She is perfect. She never makes mistakes, never says the wrong thing, never makes anyone angry. Never gets angry herself!

Saint Chellie loves everyone and everyone loves her back. She is never anxious or afraid. People admire her, but she modestly deflects adulation and reflects it back to its originators. She knows the glory is to the message, not to the messenger. She is ideal.

If I focus too much on her, Saint Chellie makes me feel bad about myself. I can never measure up to her perfection. No matter how good I am, I am never good enough because I can always imagine her being better, doing better, living better.

Saint Chellie makes me crazy.

I am not a saint. I am a person. I am a good person, and I love and care for those around me. I do the best I can to spread joy and cheer in the world, take care of my responsibilities, and be honest, faithful and true to myself and others. If I fail today, I will try to do better tomorrow. No mistake is worthless if I learn something from it. But I hold myself harmless from perfection. I accept myself unconditionally just the way I am.

Saint Chellie is not real. I am real.

And in spite of all my foibles, fancies, and failures, I am good enough.

Today's Affirmation: "I am enough. I am more than enough. And I accept myself unconditionally just the way I am."

44

Suze Orman Is Living My Life

"There is no greater glory than love, nor any greater punishment than jealousy."

—Lope de Vega

Stayed up late last night, reading and writing...it was 12:30 A.M. but I was just charged up and couldn't sleep. Finally, I got into bed and turned on the television so I could drowse off. And there she was, best-selling author of *The 9 Steps to Financial Freedom*, bright, cute, and smiling all over Oprah. It wasn't enough that she had her own PBS special running forever like the Tae Bo of financial fitness. The whole *Oprah* show was a paean to her. Money sparkled in her eyes, success dripped off her nose, and her stature proclaimed "Millions of Books Sold, Millions of Books Sold!"

Meanwhile, I didn't have a publisher yet.

Saint Chellie chirps, "Isn't that wonderful? She deserves her success and is helping many people. There's room for everyone!" Demon Chellie howls at the moon. I want a stiff drink and twelve cigarettes, but I swore off those things and won't go there. So screw the diet—I eat pie for breakfast. Marie Callender apple pie. Turns out it's fat free. Rats. Saint Chellie's been messing with my grocery list.

I reread Anne Lamott's chapter on jealousy in *Bird by Bird*, her wonderfully irreverent instruction book on writing. She writes you're going to have to deal with jealousy, "because some wonderful, dazzling successes are going to happen for some of the most awful, angry, undeserving writers you know—people who are, in other words, not you." I read her story of how she processed her envy through talking with friends, reading books, and finally, writing her way back to equilibrium. I realize I'm doing that, too. She makes me laugh, quoting a Clive James poem that begins "The Book of My Enemy Has Been Remaindered. And I am pleased." The sun peeks out from behind my mood and the day lightens.

I check my e-mail: My cousin has a group that wants to pay me to come speak in Atlanta. I know this is a sign: the world's big enough for the two of us, Suze and me. She'll reach some people with her work and I'll reach some with mine. We're different people with different voices singing in the same choir. She's a soprano and I'm an alto. She's a blond and I'm a redhead. She's famous and I'm...getting there!

Today's Affirmation: "I applaud other people's successes because they point the way to my own."

45

Chellie Campbell Is Living My Life

"Too many people miss the silver lining because they're expecting gold."

—Maurice Setter

It was Tuesday afternoon, and I was at the Westside lunch meeting of Women's Referral Service. I showed my friend, Lynn Kerew, my page on "Suze Orman is Living My Life." She laughed, but then looked me straight in the eye. "Don't you know there are people here who are looking at you, saying 'Chellie Campbell is living my life'?" she said. "You're a Life Member, a Member of the Year Award winner, you know everybody, and half the people in the room have taken your workshop. In this circle of people, you're the Suze Orman!"

Oh, thank you, Lynn, for the reminder. I was focusing on what I didn't have instead of what I do have. I was looking at how successful I wasn't instead of how successful I was. Lynn got me back to reality—by playing the "Glad Game" with me. It was great.

She went on to say that she was moaning to herself the week before that she only had one hundred fifty patients a week in her chiropractic practice and her goal was to have three hundred. But then she remembered that a year ago she only had fifty! So she had a choice: she could moan about what she didn't have, or she could celebrate what she did have. And she decided she would live in celebration. Then she told me where she learned it.

From me.

Today's Affirmation: "I am the most successful me I know!"

46

Valentine's Day

*"Today I forgive all those who have ever offended me.
I give my love to all thirsty hearts, both to those who
love me and to those who do not love me."*

—Paramahansa Yogananda

One Valentine's Day fell on a Friday, when I had a regularly scheduled business networking meeting. Joe Reber, an estate planning attorney, had brought a valentine for each member of the group—one of the small valentines that we used to give each other in grade school. I could see everyone's face light up with pleasure as they received their card, remembering with nostalgia their grade school Valentine's Days. Joe told me he gave one to an older woman he saw at the grocery store and she started to cry. She said she hadn't gotten a valentine in forty years.

Is it good business for him to do this? Yes.

Is that *why* he does it? No.

It is clearly a gift from the heart, meant only to give people a moment's happiness. That's why it's good for business.

I want to refer business to a man like that.

Today's Affirmation: "I give gifts from the heart and they flow back to me in return."

47

Love of Flying

"Aerodynamically, the bumblebee shouldn't be able to fly. But the bumblebee doesn't know that, so it goes on flying anyway."

—Mary Kay Ash

Carol Allen is a high-energy, darling astrologer who loves to travel. While taking my workshop, she created a new affirmation for herself: "Money is flying at me from all directions." Here is her report.

"I started saying this for ten minutes a day and within a week, money started to come to me through flying. First, my long-distance boyfriend sent me a round-trip ticket to visit him in New Mexico. Then, while using the ticket at the airport, Southwest airlines gave me a voucher for twenty dollars off my next flight. In all my years of flying, I'd never heard of such a thing. At the gate of my connecting flight, they gave me another voucher for another twenty dollars. I had a *fabulous* trip!

"Two weeks later, still saying my affirmation, my father sent me a surprise round-trip ticket to visit him in San Francisco for Father's Day weekend. At the airport, I handed the ticket agent my 'frequent flyer card.' I needed two more round-trip travels to earn a free round-trip ticket. She said, 'Right now, we're having a special. You have enough round-trip travel for a free ticket.'

'No, I don't,' I foolishly argued. 'I need two more round-trip travels after this one.' 'No, you don't. Just for today, you qualify!' She handed me the necessary documents for a free trip anywhere in the U.S. I had a wonderful visit with my father.

"I returned and my beau called to inform me that he was sending me another free round-trip ticket to meet him in New York City (my *third* free trip in six weeks!) I'd known him eight years and he'd never flown me anywhere before, so this was a pleasant surprise. Another great trip.

"A month later, I used my free round-trip pass from Southwest Airlines that I'd been given on the way to meet my father to visit my then fiancé again in New Mexico. (I was still saying the affirmation ten minutes daily, of course!) I was feeling guilty for taking more time off to go on another wonderful vacation—my fourth in less than three months. At the airport, I quickly checked my messages at a pay phone. I heard a message that made my day: I was offered a media opportunity which lead to more business in one month than I usually had in four.

"The whole time I said the affirmation, money kept coming to me through flying!"

Want to fly, anyone?

Today's Affirmation (of course!): "Money is flying at me from all directions!"

48

Practice with Parking

"The man who removes a mountain begins by carrying away small stones."

—Chinese proverb

The process of actualizing your desires is simple:

1. Pick a goal.
2. Visualize yourself having it.
3. Positively affirm having it.
4. Send out ships to get it.
5. Celebrate getting it!

Visualizing having the goal is a step that is most important to master. Pick something small and easy to practice on at first. You could visualize getting a cab quickly and easily, or getting good news in the mail. Since I live in Los Angeles, where it sometimes seems there are a *billion* cars, I tell people to practice by manifesting a parking space at a busy shopping mall, theater, etc. The trick to getting parking spaces is to visualize the empty space instead of the crowd of cars.

My mother called me one day and she was very excited. She told me that she had always had trouble parking at the country club on the days she played golf—it was always very crowded. But this particular day, she remembered my stories of manifesting parking spaces and decided to try it. "I drove right up to the front entrance of the club, visualizing an empty space, and just as I arrived, a car pulled out of a space right in front of me! Chellie, this stuff really works!"

She reminded me of a date I had to go to the movies. As we drove to the shopping mall where the theater was located, Bill said to me, "The only problem with going to this theater is that the parking is always so terrible. It's much too crowded there."

"Oh, I can fix that," I assured him, "I'll just visualize a space for us."

He looked at me very strangely and I could see him thinking about what kind of weirdo had he gotten mixed up with. Soon after, we pulled into the mall parking lot and he slammed on the brakes and stared. The parking lot was practically empty! Bill slowly turned and looked at me with his eyes wide and his mouth open.

I said, "Oops. Sorry. I guess I overdid it." It was a very funny moment.

Practice visualizing what you want instead of what you don't want. See if you can clear a parking lot.

Today's Affirmation: "I visualize and create marvels in my life!"

49
Confidence

"Do not attempt to do a thing unless you are sure of yourself, but do not relinquish it simply because someone else is not sure of you."

—Stewart E. White

When I was in high school, just beginning to be interested in a career in the theater, I tried out for the school musical. The year before, I had been in my first musical in a small dancing role. This time I wanted a speaking part, but to get one, you had to sing a song at the audition. It took place in front of the teacher and all the other students—my entire peer group!—who were trying out for parts. Although I had been singing in the church choir for years, I had never sung a solo in front of anyone before. I decided to sing "Tonight" from *West Side Story*, which sounded pretty good when I rehearsed it at home in the shower. But in front of all my friends that day, I was so nervous, my poor voice just wavered tremulously, and I barely squeaked out the last high note. Finally relieved to be finished, I smiled at the applause as I returned to my chair. Then the teacher said, "That's all right, Chellie, you just keep dancing until you learn how to sing!" and the entire room erupted in laughter. I was devastated.

I never sang again in high school. I felt the humiliation of that day too intensely to brave its like again. But I kept practicing and improving. When I went to college, I tried again, and won some small parts, but always the fear of ridicule was with me. It all changed when I got into a summer theater program at the University of Oregon at Eugene. I flew there scared but excited. I had determined that I was going for broke with the audition the next day. After all, I reasoned, I wouldn't ever see any of these people again, so if I made a fool of myself, so what? I had to sing full and strong and joyously, without the crippling fear that strangled the notes in my throat.

It worked! I sang "I Can't Say No" from *Oklahoma*, a funny character piece that suited me perfectly. I had fun with it and the audience had fun with me. When I finished, one of the directors ran up on stage, took my hand, handed me a script—and cast me as the lead in their first show, *Celebration*. I was elated, triumphant, vindicated! I could sing.

Confidence ebbed and flowed over the years as I wrestled with my fear demons whenever I took on new challenges. But I never forgot this one shining moment of triumph and how I achieved it: I sang for myself because I thought it was good and did not dwell on how it would be received. And that is the lesson of confidence: work and improve until *you* think you're good. Your People will think you're good, too! The others don't matter.

Today's Affirmation: "I have confidence in me!"

50
Flower Power

"Remember the turtle progresses only when he sticks his neck out."

—Anonymous

Summer vacation! Wonderful. But summers at the beach were only a fond high school memory. For I was eighteen now, and had just finished my first year at college. Home for the summer this year meant getting a job. After answering some want ads in the paper, I finally had gotten an interview with the Auto Club. Alas, my typing skills were apparently abysmal, and I didn't qualify for an office job with them.

Depressed, I turned my car towards home and thought about what kind of job I might find. The previous year, I had gotten my very first job—as a telephone solicitor. It was horrible. I was dreadful. That was out! After that, I got a job at Zody's, a now-defunct, low-end department store, working the return desk. The line of people returning things they had purchased was always long, and the people were always angry. I wasn't going to go back there.

Now it looked like office jobs were out, at least until my typing improved. As I thought about what I might be qualified for, suddenly I started thinking about what I might *like* to do. Until that moment, I hadn't really thought about liking a job. I rather had the idea that I was doomed to drudgery. But I perked up at the idea I might like something. It suddenly occurred to me that I might like working in at a flower shop. I loved flowers, gardening, and hiking. Maybe that would be fun!

At that moment, I saw a sign that read "Whittier Florists." Without giving myself too much time to think about it, I impulsively turned into the parking lot, got out of my car, and marched into the flower shop. The woman behind the desk asked if she could help me. I told her I was looking for a job. "Are you a designer?" she asked, sizing me up. "Yes!" I blurted out. (Where had *that* come from? Oh well, I've done it now.) She nodded and said, "All right, come back here and design something." (Gulp!)

She walked me back to the workroom, handed me a vase and a bunch of flowers, and went off to the front of the shop. Well, I thought, what's the worst that could happen? I don't get the job? I don't have the job now. The worst that can happen is that I break even and leave here the same as I started. But I will have tried. I quickly looked around at the vases of flowers to see how they were put together, and dove in. Who knows? Maybe I'll just get this job!

I did. The woman came back, looked at the floral arrangement I had made, and said, "Fine. Come back tomorrow to meet the owner. I'll tell him about you." I showed up bright and early the next morning, and they put me to work immediately. I worked there every holiday and vacation for the next three years.

Instead of thinking about what you *can* do, think about what you'd *like* to do. Then go for it!

Today's Affirmation: "I can do anything I put my mind to!"

51
Crime and Punishment

"When I want your opinion, I'll beat it out of you."

—Chuck Norris

Have you ever done something you're ashamed of? Made a bad decision, a blunder which you later regretted?

There was a time when I was very unhappy with myself. I had done something dumb and the committee inside my head was giving me a very hard time. "You're so stupid!" the voice said. "How could you have done that?" chimed in another. "You'll never get ahead if you keep doing things like that," said the third. On and on the committee raged.

Disgusted with myself, I went to the grocery store, but the litany of inadequacies continued while I shopped. The negative voices had really taken over my consciousness and were punishing me.

Finished at the store, I drove home and into my parking lot. I got out of the car, opened the back door, and leaned over to grab my brown paper grocery bag. Somehow it had gotten wedged in tight between the floor and the seat and was stuck. Angrily, I tugged and pulled at the bag. All of a sudden the paper bag tore, and the force of my tugging sent my arm flying up, my hand in a fist—and I punched myself in the nose!

I fell down flat on my back in the parking lot. My eyes welled with tears—it really hurt! But at the same time I burst out laughing. What a sight I must have been as I lay there giggling in the dust. But in that moment it had become so clear to me what had happened. I had been mentally beating myself up and the power of my negative thoughts was so strong I had actualized it.

What we think is what we create. I have never had such a clear and powerful demonstration of it as that day in the parking lot. I vowed never to waste my creative energy beating myself up again.

Do you worry and fret about money? Does your committee tell you that you're financially inadequate? Do you spend your creative energy focused on what's not working with your finances? Stop that! Go back to all your positive affirmations. Say them out loud to yourself in the mirror until you believe it. Every time you think a negative money thought, you have to do two positive affirmations—one to cancel out the negative thought, and the other to move you to a more positive frame of mind. The committee is trainable—you give it direction and power. Teach it to tell you good things about you and your financial condition.

Or you might be punching yourself in the nose in a parking lot.

Today's Affirmation: "My mind is full of powerful, loving thoughts about myself."

52
Work Hours

"I believe that people who work twelve hours a day should go home with bigger loaves of bread than people who work eight."

—Michael Levine

No, no, I disagree! I enjoyed a lot of Michael Levine's *Lessons at the Halfway Point,* but this one I take exception to. Success cannot be a matter of how many hours of the day you work. At some point—namely twenty-four—we run out of hours. What then?

Late one evening in the fall of 1985, I was hard at work with running the business management firm I co-owned with two attorneys. We shared office space, and Merv, one of the partners, was working late that night, too. He came by my desk to say good night and I looked up at him in frustration. "There's so much to do!" I exclaimed. "I could work every hour in the day and never get it all done!"

"That's right, Chellie," he said, "Work will expand to fill the time you're willing to devote to it. At some point, you just have to say, 'That's enough' and go home."

I thought about that many times in the next few years as I tried to find how many work hours were "enough" for me. When I was president of the National Association of Women Business Owners Los Angeles Chapter, the first motion I put on the table at the first Board of Directors meeting was this: "I move that there will now be thirty-six hours in every day." It was seconded in a heartbeat, and passed unanimously, amid riotous laughter.

Would that we could solve our time management problems so easily! But even if we could make thirty-six-hour days a reality, we would have the same problems managing our time as we do today. We spin like tops trying to do too much. There is so much to do in the world! We want to do all of it and we want to do it today. I see people on the overwork treadmill every day, and it isn't pretty. People have the equation wrong—they think more work will equal more money. They look at some successful people who are working twelve-fourteen hour days and mistakenly draw the conclusion if they want to be successful, they will have to work twelve to fourteen hours per day, too. But what they fail to notice is that the successful person isn't working that many hours because they *have* to. They're doing it because they *want* to—this is their fun! Don't put more hours in your work—put more fun in your work hours. It's the passion and drive that's fun, and that's what creates success.

Even if you enjoy work and work a lot, at some point you're going to run out of hours. Everyone has only twenty-four hours in a day, but we are all making different amounts of money. Bill Gates, Donald Trump, and Stephen Spielberg aren't making more money because they're spending more time at work than you. They're making more money because they're leveraging their time differently. What can you do today to work lighter instead of longer?

Today's Affirmation: "I have all the time I need to have all the fun I want!"

53

How Do You Spend Your Time?

"Procrastination is the art of keeping up with yesterday."

—Don Marquis

There are 168 hours in every week. What are you spending your time on? How many hours are you spending on your number one priorities? Sending out ships? Eating? Sleeping? Having fun? How many hours are you spending on income producing activities? List a typical week below:

TYPE OF ACTIVITY:	# OF HOURS PER WEEK:	INCOME EARNED:
Sleep	________	________
Eat	________	________
Read	________	________
Watch TV	________	________
Entertainment	________	________
Cultural Activities	________	________
Charitable Activities	________	________
Educational Activities	________	________
Paperwork	________	________
Phone Calls-Business	________	________
Phone Calls- Personal	________	________
Computer Time-Business	________	________
Computer Time-Personal	________	________
Networking	________	________
Sales	________	________
Other work tasks	________	________
Hobbies, Arts, Crafts	________	________
Exercise/Sports	________	________
Relationship Time	________	________
Time with Children	________	________
Household Chores	________	________
Driving	________	________
Doing Nothing	________	________
TOTAL:	________	________

If you want to double your income, double the time you spend on income producing activities!

Today's Affirmation: "I have all the time in the world to make all the money I desire."

54
Ships Logs

"In any business, there are jobs that are productive and sometimes confrontational, for they test you. And then there is all the other work, none of which earns any money."

—Stuart Wilde

Wilde is talking about sales. Where there are no sales, there is no money. If you are in business for yourself, it won't matter how good you are if you don't have any customers. Getting and retaining customers must be high on your list of daily activities. Otherwise, you aren't going to be in business for long.

In my seminar business, if I don't "send out ships" to get people to attend the workshops, there won't be anyone in them, and I won't make any money. End of business. But since this was the most "confrontational" aspect of my work, I found I'd do just about anything else during the day. That's what paperwork is for—it's an excuse not to market your business. I'd reach the end of the day and feel like I'd worked hard, but stayed unconscious as to how many sales calls I'd made.

Then one day, I was complaining to a friend about working too hard and not making enough money. He asked how many sales calls I made each day. I looked at him blankly. "I don't know, exactly," I said. He only had to raise his eyebrows and I got the picture.

That's when I invented the "Ships Log." It is my daily record of my sales calls: how many times I dial the phone, how many people I actually talk with, how many appointments I make, how many meetings I go to, and how many clients result from all that activity. Before starting work in the morning, I decide my target numbers in each of these categories. Then throughout the day, I make hatch marks on my log to record my actual numbers.

Keeping track in this way does several things for me. First of all, it keeps me on purpose about my activities. It's very easy to shuffle papers and talk on the phone (too long) and yet not make any sales. When I record the number of calls, I can see the effectiveness of my efforts as I go. By the end of the day, I know exactly how many sales I made, what income I produced, and what it took for me to produce it. By consistently keeping track, I have statistics on the average number of phone calls it takes to make a sale. If I want more income, I can just make more calls. If I learn new skills, or improve the ones I have, the number of calls it takes to make a sale will go down. But I won't know what's working and what isn't if I don't measure the results.

When you're diligent about counting your ships, eventually you're counting your money.

Today's Affirmation: "All my beautiful ships are bringing me fabulous money!"

55
Julie and the One Hundred Calls

"God gives every bird its food, but He does not throw it into the nest."

—Josiah Gilbert Holland

Julie, a sensational public speaker, hated making her sales calls. She loved speaking and was really good at it. She had valuable lessons to share and wonderful experiences to recount; people loved listening to her and learning from her. But "sending out ships" was hard: pick up the phone, call strangers who may or may not want to talk to her, get rejected, rebuffed, put off, disconnected...oh, this was not fun at all.

She knew this was a necessity in her business, however. And it's a necessity in every business! Until you become known, with so many repeat and referral clients, you have to be out there talking to people. The more you talk to people, the more you become known. You can't wait for people to discover you and call you—it could be a long wait, and how will you eat and pay your bills in the meantime? Not making phone calls is like standing in the shadows at a party—you know you're there, but no one else does. You have to pick up the golden phone and smile and dial.

She made one hundred phone calls over the next two days. And the hundredth call resulted in a speaking engagement for four thousand dollars! That's her motivation for the next one hundred calls.

Am I hearing "Yeah, buts" from you now? Are you wondering how this story applies to you if you aren't in your own business or in sales? Well, how about making one hundred calls to help your boss or your company improve their profitability and see what happens? Or one hundred calls to get a better job? Or one hundred calls to raise funds for your favorite charity?

What could happen for you in one hundred calls?

Today's Affirmation: "I receive tremendous rewards every time I dial the phone!"

56

Commitment

"Do or do not. There is no try."

—Yoda in *Star Wars* by George Lucas

Punkin, Corinne's cat, had just had kittens. Five of the cutest little calico kitties you could imagine. I hadn't had a pet in years, and had always had dogs. Now I thought it might be fun to have a cat. So, on this bright June afternoon, I visited Corinne, Punkin, and the kittens in order to choose one for my own.

The littlest, scaredy-cat, runt of the litter with the big ears and wide golden eyes was mine the minute I saw her. "She looks like Yoda from *Star Wars*," I declared, and that promptly became my kitten's name. I told Corrine I wanted her, but was going on vacation in a couple of weeks and didn't want to leave the kitten alone, so could I please leave her there and pick her up after I got home? Corinne thought about this and said okay, but pressed me to make sure I was committed to owning this cat. She wanted to make sure I wasn't going to change my mind and bail out of the deal at the last minute. I gave her my assurances, but could tell Corinne wasn't totally convinced.

I left Corinne's house and immediately went to the pet store to go shopping for my new kitty! I bought her food bowl, her water dish, some play toys, lots of cat food, a litter box, and a big, carpeted cat tree. After I unloaded all my cat loot at home, I called Corinne.

"I just spent $150 on my cat," I told her. "I'm committed!" And now she knew I was.

When there's money on it, there's commitment. I remember this when I'm enrolling people in my workshops. If they pay for the workshop or send a deposit before the class, I know they're going to show up for the class. No matter how committed they say they are, if they don't put money on it, they are likely to cancel at the last minute or just be a "no show." The expression "Put your money where your mouth is" is apt.

What have you been putting off committing to? The fence is a most uncomfortable place to sit. Any grass is greener than the fence post. Make a decision. Jump off the fence. Land on your feet. Just like a cat. Put money on it. Buy a cat.

Today's Affirmation: "I relish the commitments I make and keep."

57

"Ship Shape" Dollars

"Money won't make you happy...but everybody wants to find out for themselves."

—Zig Ziglar

My friend, Korey, and I went on a cruise. We worried about gaining weight, since there was so much scrumptious, abundant food supply on board that we couldn't believe it. There were about twelve meals per day: pre-breakfast snack, breakfast, after breakfast snack, mid-morning snack, pre-lunch snack, lunch, after lunch snack, afternoon tea, cocktail hors d'oeuvres, dinner, mid-evening snack...by the time the midnight buffet arrived, I couldn't get so much as another cracker in my mouth! We decided that we would counter all the food by exercising: always using the stairs instead of the elevator, making sure to do a lot of walking, dancing in the disco, and going to aerobics class every morning.

We showed up for aerobics class the first morning bright and early. There was a good crowd at the class and the instructor, Debbie, was energetic and upbeat, so a good time was had by all. Debbie was dressed in a cute yellow Royal Caribbean T-shirt and matching visor. At the end of the hour, she gave each one of us a yellow "Ship Shape" dollar and told us that we would get one at the end of each exercise program on the ship. If we collected ten "Ship Shape" dollars, we could redeem them for a yellow T-shirt and visor just like hers. Everyone's eyes lit up. A free prize? Cool!

You might guess that, as the week wore on, and we partied and danced 'til the wee hours of the morning, it became increasingly difficult to get up at 7:00 A.M. to go to aerobics class. The wake-up call would ring in our rooms, shattering our slothful sleep, and we would groan in chorus. I would say, "I don't want to get up and go to aerobics this morning, do you?" Korey would say, "No...but I only have five 'Ship Shape' dollars. How many have you got?" "I've only got four—how did you get five?" "Oh, they gave me one for shuffleboard yesterday." "That's cheating!" "No, it isn't, it was exercise!" "Well," I said, "I've got to get up and go to class so I can catch up." And we'd both get up and drag our tired bodies to aerobics class.

There were a lot of tired bodies there! But I noticed everyone telling versions of our story: "Well, I was really tired and didn't want to come today, but I only have six dollars and I need four more to get my T-shirt," or "I wanted to sleep in, but I need three more dollars!" It was amazing how people were plugged into this competition for a T-shirt while on this cruise that cost $800 (they could definitely afford to buy themselves a T-shirt if they wanted one.)

The lessons of the "Ship Shape" dollars are: 1) Rewards and prizes are fun. 2) People will work hard to get their prizes, no matter what they are. 3) The actual value of the prize doesn't matter. 4) Therefore, pick prizes to reward yourself when you accomplish your goals!

Today's Affirmation: "I accept rich rewards—and I deserve them!"

58
Campbell Cash

"Just as a sunbeam can't separate itself from the sun and a wave can't separate itself from the ocean, we can't separate ourselves from one another. We are all part of a vast sea of love; one indivisible divine mind."

—Marianne Williamson

I invented "Campbell Cash" for my workshops, in order to play a game like the cruise line's "Ship Shape" dollars. I had pretty green coffee mugs made to use as a prize, with dollar signs, hearts, and prosperity affirmations on them.

I was excited about putting this game into practice at my next workshop. At the first session of the eight-week class, I explained that participants could buy them only with "Campbell Cash" dollars on the last day of the class. They would receive a "Campbell Cash" dollar every time they came to class, and each time they did their homework. I would also give out additional dollars from time to time when people had special "wins" or accomplishments in managing or making more money. They needed fifteen of them in order to buy the mug.

Just as on the cruise ship, people jumped into the game of getting as many "Campbell Cash" dollars as they could. They looked for "wins" in their week that they could share in class, they came to class, and they did their homework. People learned to ask for money—they got very creative and kept asking me, "Do I get a dollar for that?" It built an energy and excitement that carried over throughout the workshop.

A few people still had some difficulties with the homework, or with asking for a special dollar. What was I going to do if some people didn't get their fifteen dollars needed to buy the mug on the last day of class? God forbid anyone should leave class without a mug. I was still unsure of the best thing to do when the day of the last class arrived. Looking around the room, I asked everyone to count their dollars. As they added up their total, I saw some people looking proud and happy, and others looking a little sad.

I asked Linda in the front row how many dollars she had. "Seventeen," she said proudly. "Congratulations!" I said, "You get a mug!" I turned to Lana sitting next to her and asked how many she had. "Only fourteen," she said sadly. Without the briefest hesitation, Linda turned to her and gave her a dollar. A ripple of love and wonder thrilled through the room as everyone sighed with happiness and understanding. They knew what to do. The next person had sixteen dollars, got her congratulations, then promptly handed her extra dollar to the man following her who only had fourteen. It continued this way until everyone in the room had enough to win their mug. There was a loving smile on every face, and a tear in every eye. Especially mine. And it has happened like that in every class since.

Is there someone in your life who needs your dollar in order to get their prize?

Today's Affirmation: "I have great abundance in my life and plenty to share with others."

59

Having Fun on Low Budget

"There were times my pants were so thin I could sit on a dime and tell if it were heads or tails."

—Spencer Tracy

If this is a month you have chosen to be on "Low Budget," remember that it is just for now, not forever. Make it a game! Your goal each day is to spend as little as possible. How can you have a great time without spending money? You can get the whole family involved—have a prize for the best idea. Here are some suggestions to get you started:

1. Go shopping in your closet. Create new outfits from all the assorted shirts, skirts, pants, scarves, shoes, belts, and jewelry. Discard anything you haven't worn in a while and donate it to charity. You'll be doing good for others and at the same time creating space for more abundance when you get to "High Budget."

2. Write a poem, a play, a story, or a song. Draw a picture. Play the musical instrument you haven't picked up in a while.

3. Organize a family or neighborhood talent show and encourage everyone to contribute their talent. Create "First Place" Awards for everyone: Each person will be the best in their own unique category (for example, "Best Song by a Blond Girl Scout").

4. Spend an afternoon at the library. Check out books in categories you don't usually read.

5. Learn a new language or practice one that's rusty. Call a friend to help!

6. Go for a walk in nature, to a park, the mountains, the lake or the seashore. Get a field guide to birds or plants in your area and really look at the myriad life forms all around you.

7. Get involved in a charity event. Volunteers are always welcome and you'll feel good helping others less fortunate than you.

8. Play "The Glad Game." Look around you at all you have to be grateful for, and thank God for your abundance.

Today's Affirmation: "My life is rich in fun and adventure!

60

High Budget Is Lifting Me Higher

"With money in your pocket, you are wise, and you are handsome, and you sing well, too."

—Jewish proverb

The class had just completed their Low, Medium, and High Budgets, their homework assignment for the week. Diane raised her hand, exclaiming, "Low Budget was easy for me—I'm used to trying to reduce spending and save money. But I just didn't understand how to do High Budget, or what its purpose is."

"You have to have a *reason* to make the money, otherwise you won't make the money," I told her. "If you don't have a goal or a plan for spending additional money, you won't bother to do what it takes to make it. You'll keep making what you're already making and just getting by."

When you create your High Budget, dream your dream: pick an amount of money that is what I call "high reasonable." If you've only been making $15,000 per year, I suggest you don't write out a budget for $50 million—it's too wide a discrepancy and when you look at it you're likely to think, "Shoot, I'll never make that much money unless I win the lottery." Winning the lottery is a 14 million to one shot, and I like people to pick something with better odds. Pick a High Budget number that you believe is possible for you to achieve in the next year or two. You can find this number by investigating what other people make who do what you do—who is at the top of your field, and how much are they paid?

Write this figure on your High Budget under "Income." Now decide how you want to spend this income. Do you want a new car? What make, model, year, color is it? A new house? In what neighborhood, style, how many bedrooms, bathrooms—describe it, collect pictures to drool over. How much money will you spend on travel, contributions to charities, education, a beautiful wardrobe, toys? Remember to allocate money for stocks, bonds, income property, and other appreciating assets that build your net worth. This world is filled with fabulous treasures, exciting things to do, exotic locales to visit—and they can be yours if you want them. What do you want the money *for*?

When you get passionate about what you want, then you get passionate about doing what it takes to have it. Bruce worked for years in "enough to get by" Low Budget mode, until his wife got pregnant. Then he set a goal to have $10,000 saved by the time the baby was born. This goal lit a fire under him, and nine months later he told me, with eyes shining, that he had accumulated $12,000 in savings. "And before that," he said, "I never saved a dollar."

Have fun creating your High Budget today!

Today's Affirmation: "I am high on High Budget and its fabulous treasures are mine!"

61

Spree Money

"If you gave up your morning coffee for a year, you could make an extra mortgage payment. But man, you'd be grumpy."

—Citibank advertisement

Every so often, I read about someone who lived a penurious life, saving every nickel, never allowing themselves the slightest luxury. The cleaning woman who worked every day of her life, never took a vacation or bought a fancy dress, died and left a fortune of $10 million to a college that she hadn't even attended. The "millionaire next door" who lived in a modest house, wore modest clothes, and left a $35 million fortune to her heirs. The relatives of these people were always shocked at the size of their fortunes, never having guessed at the riches they hoarded yet refused to enjoy. Newspapers wrote their stories, bemused over their life choices.

These are painfully sad stories, the other side of the spectrum from the lotto winners who splurge their millions on spending sprees until they're broke again. The purpose of money is neither the relentless hoarding to hold on to every penny nor the frantic spending to get rid of it.

It is the equal balance of prudent saving for the future and fun spending in the present.

"Give up the daily cappuccino!" some financial advisors cry. "If you save that three dollars every day, with compound interest in fifteen years you'll have $36,000 in the bank!" But maybe that cappuccino really starts your day off happily on a positive note. Maybe it makes you feel good to treat yourself to your special coffee at the neighborhood café so that you're reminded that you are special and deserve some special goodies from all your labor. The manicure that makes you feel pampered, the massage that relaxes your body, the lunches with friends and co-workers—these are the little things that can make your life rich with pleasure.

You need to have "Spree Money" on your budgets. It's part of keeping balance in your life. It's a reminder that money can buy fun, and you deserve to have some. Have "Spree Money" allocated even on low budget, for if there is none, you will feel trapped, broke, envious of others, and focused on lack and limitation. A little "Spree Money" will keep you reminded of the pleasures available in life, and the smarter you get about making money, the more pleasures will be available to you.

If you just hoard all your money and never enjoy it, someone else will. After you're gone.

Today's Affirmation: "I enjoy planning my spending and spending what I plan!"

62
Risk: Gambling

"Experience is a good teacher, but she sends in terrific bills."

—Minna Antrim

"Do you ever gamble, Fred?" the player in seat two asked the dealer, a handsome black man with a bright smile.

"Oh, noooo!" he exclaimed, shaking his head with a grin as he shuffled the cards. "I go to Gambler's Anonymous three times a week. I lost $85,000 in one year, the house, and the wife. I don't gamble any more."

Whenever I read an article or watch a television program about gambling, it is usually filled with stories like the one above. There are many of them. So why is gambling a $500 billion industry? Why are new extravagant hotels being built every year in Las Vegas? How can people continue to take these kinds of risks?

Gambling has been a part of human experience since the dawn of time. Archaeologists have discovered gaming dice among the ruins of many ancient civilizations. (Cheating has existed just as long; a recent discovery at an ancient city site was a die with two fives on it.) With all of the negative press, the horror stories of terrible losses, and the railings of anti-gambling forces in every era, gambling persists. Why?

Because some people win. And win big! For every story of loss and heartbreak, there is a story of the person who put two dollars in the slot machine and bells clang, whistles blow, lights flash, and they're an instant millionaire. Because we are all at the bottom of our souls eternal optimists who love the idea that one day we may hit the big time, that Lady Luck will smile on us, and maybe it's our turn today! Our hearts pound, the adrenaline rushes, we hold our breath in fear of the outcome, yes, *yes*, oh, no, we lost, curses, depression, tears...but maybe next time, we'll win and scream and yell and life will be great! I bet! It's an adventure, and, bottom line, it's *fun*.

Fun. That means that this is on the entertainment portion of your budget. It is not a job-related expense, it isn't your retirement plan, it isn't a charitable contribution, rent, school, or a tax deduction of any kind. It's part of your spree money, movie money, extra splurge entertainment money. Keep track of your expenditures in this area and notice if this really is your priority for spending your money. If the amount of money you're spending on entertainment is okay with you, then there's no problem. But if the amount gets too large, and you find you've gambled away the rent money, you may want to join Fred at Gambler's Anonymous.

Today's Affirmation: "I have a wonderful budget for fun and entertainment!"

63
Jury Duty

"Reflect upon your present blessings, of which every man has many...not on your past misfortunes, of which all men have some."

—Charles Dickens

In Los Angeles, they recently changed the requirements for jury duty so that if called, you only had to serve for one day or one trial. As a single, self-employed person, I had always been excused from jury duty because it would cause a financial hardship. But this new system made it possible for me to participate. Rather than regarding it as an onerous duty, I rather looked forward to the new adventure. It made me think about our system of government and how lucky we are to have a judicial system in which judgments are rendered by a jury of our peers. Beats tyranny and oppression every time.

So my peers and I showed up at the Van Nuys courtroom, checked in and waited to be called.

There were about three hundred of us in a large, comfortable waiting room. Fifty at a time, they called our names, upon which we proceeded to a courtroom, where we were to be interviewed as prospective jurors.

In the courtroom, the panel involved a murder case, expected to last for eight days. The defendant was accused of murdering his estranged wife. One by one, the bailiff called the jurors to the jury box, where they were asked a set of questions. Many jurors were excused, based on their answers. They completed the jury before I was interviewed, and my jury service of one day was over. But the answers I had to the questions they asked struck me:

Have you ever been a victim of a crime? "Yes, my home has been burglarized three times; my car has been broken into three times, stolen once; I have been robbed at gun point once and physically attacked in my home in the middle of the night once."

Have you or anyone you know ever been a victim of domestic violence? "Yes, I have."

Have you ever abused alcohol? "Yes, I am a sober member of Alcoholics Anonymous."

I had never added up all this information about my past in quite this way. And I saw how much of a victim I had been. I believe it's because, at that time, I had a victim mentality; I thought negative, fearful thoughts and attracted those experiences to me. I noticed, too, that since I had actively practiced positive thinking, my experiences had also changed, and I was a victim no more.

Please note I am not blaming all victims here, just noting that if you are a victim *over and over again*, maybe it has something to do with you. Like the old Marvin Gaye/Kim Weston song says, "It takes two, babee-ee-ee." So I determined to stop thinking like a victim, stop telling victim stories, and decided to focus on winning. Now I tell success stories. How about you?

Today's Affirmation: "I am victorious over my past and creating abundance today!"

64
Getting Past the Past

"The hardest years in life are those between ten and seventy."

—Helen Hayes

Chuck was having a hard time. He was trying to do his positive affirmations, but the negative voices kept coming up. He was very conflicted about his past, the negative upbringing, the angst in his family. You could tell from the look on his face and the energy with which he talked about his past that he relished the struggle. I've seen this problem many times, watching people take class after class, ostensibly to learn to overcome their problems and become successful, but, in actuality, to wallow in their difficulties and celebrate their inadequacies. They are victims and it's never their fault.

I sensed that Chuck was on the verge of changing this behavior. He approached me after class one evening, told me of his struggle and asked if he could take me to lunch the next day. "I just know you have the answer and I will be able to get past my past!" he said. "Maybe I do," I answered, "Let's go to lunch and see."

We met at noon and sat under the trees at the little sidewalk café. For forty-five minutes, he regaled me with stories of his childhood, the struggles with money, the poverty consciousness of his family, and the continuing problems throughout his working career that stemmed from his past. He had been in therapy, had taken classes and read books, and seemed to have a thorough understanding of how the negative programming of his childhood had created negative habit patterns in the present. I could see that he was ready to be done with the past and create a new present.

"I just know you have the answer," he said towards the end of our lunch hour.

"I do," I said.

"Great!" he exclaimed. "I knew you would! Tell me the answer! What do I have to do?"

I paused, looked him straight in the eye and said, "Get over it."

His eyes widened in shock. He looked at me for a long moment, then started to smile and then to laugh. He said, "That's it exactly. I knew it; I just needed somebody else to confirm it. Thank you."

We laughed together, sitting in the sun. After that day, his tension eased, he relaxed, he appeared more self-assured, he started thinking more positively, sending out ships, and his business prospered.

You may not be ready to "get over it" today. Maybe you need more psychotherapy. Maybe you need more time to wallow. But if you want treasure, one day you must stop mourning over the sunken ships and build new ones.

Today's Affirmation: "With a glad heart, I welcome the treasures of today!"

65
Michael Douglas' Jacket

"Did you ever feel like the world was a tuxedo and you were a pair of brown shoes?"

—George Gobel

After high school, I went to the University of California at Santa Barbara to major in Dramatic Art, joining other ambitious students eager to create their dreams out of the raw material of talent. One of those students was Michael Douglas. He was a couple of years ahead of me, beautiful and talented. Oh, yes, and rich, too. Unlike the others of us, unknown and unknowing of future fortune, he represented the assurance of dreams fulfilled. We knew he was going to be a star. I couldn't help being enamored of him.

My sophomore year, we were cast in a play together: Pirandello's *Henry IV*. Michael played Henry, and I had one of the two women's roles, Frieda. It was quite a coup to have been chosen from the hundreds of students who auditioned for roles in the play, and I was delirious with joy. I was now a part of the in-group, the A-team, my abilities and potential acknowledged. I was going to get to work with Michael. A little star dust glittered in my eye.

One evening, the director was rehearsing a scene that neither Michael nor I were in. Michael lounged in one of the theater seats, wearing a beautiful leather jacket. Now was my chance to talk to him. Hesitantly, I walked over to him and commented, "Great jacket, Michael. Where'd you get it?" He smiled up at me and said, "Switzerland."

He might as well have said, "The Moon." The gap between us yawned before me with that one word. I had never been to Switzerland. I hadn't even been out of the country. The only vacations my family had ever taken were car trips—alternating visits to Mom's relatives in Mississippi and Dad's in Oregon and Washington. His dad was a movie star. I didn't know what to say. I didn't feel adequate. Not because he thought he was better than I was. But because I thought he was. This was tuna thinking at its worst. "Oh," I mumbled and walked away. I vowed that someday, I was going to be somebody and travel the world, too.

Poor Chellie! I didn't know I already was somebody. The poverty consciousness and the inadequacies I felt were products of my own mind. They had to be rooted out before I could get the things I wanted. Years later I started reading philosophy and self-help books. Then I got some therapy. I developed quality friendships with wonderful people, who loved me and supported me in my goals. And slowly, I learned to love myself. I still haven't been to Switzerland. But I got a suede jacket in Hong Kong. And a gold bracelet in Santorini, a necklace in Athens, a painting in Paris...and self-esteem right here at home.

You, too, can travel, prosper, collect treasures, enjoy experiences. It all starts with loving yourself. You deserve it. You are good enough. Think like a dolphin. And if someone tells you his jacket came from Switzerland, just say, "Great! I haven't been there yet. Tell me about it!"

Today's Affirmation: "Great riches are heaped upon me just because I'm me!"

66
Self-Esteem

"Low self-esteem is like driving through life with your hand-break on."

—Maxwell Maltz

Self-esteem begins here: anyone who doesn't like you is an idiot.

Really—aren't they?

I used to bend myself into all kinds of pretzel shapes, trying to get people to like me. It was usually futile, because there wasn't much there to like—or dislike for that matter. I didn't know who I was. I just knew I wanted to be accepted, and thought of as smart, talented, and beautiful. I was afraid that I wasn't any of those things. I looked up to other people that I judged to be better than me, and gave them the power to judge me. If they liked me, I was relieved. If they didn't, I was crushed. But I was never safe, never secure. How could I be? If people like the mask I show them, they don't really like me, they like the mask. I have no chance of being loved for who I am if I never show who I am.

Eventually, I figured this out. If I find out who I really am, then show it, I figure my chances of having someone like what they see in me is approximately fifty-fifty. A 50 percent chance is a big improvement over a zero percent chance.

I am a self-confessed acknowledgment junkie. I love applause and compliments. But I used to want them from everyone. Now I just want them from "My People." My People are fabulous, smart, terrifically talented, discerning, intelligent, successful, spiritual, and loving. Like you.

Everyone else is an idiot.

Today, act as if this were true for you, too.

Because it is.

Today's Affirmation: "I am a fabulous person and all fabulous people think so, too!"

67

Boulders in the Road

"He who postpones the hour of living is like the rustic who waits for the river to run out before he crosses."

—Horace

You know what you want. You probably even know how to go about getting it. But then you don't go get it. Why not? What is it that stops you?

Sometimes it's other people who put boulders in your road. They block your path with "Yeah, buts." Years ago, when I was looking for a job, I answered an ad in the newspaper. The gentleman doing the interviewing asked me where I lived, and I answered that I lived in the San Fernando Valley. "Oh, that's too far away," he said. "This job is in Pacific Palisades."

"That doesn't matter to me," I replied brightly. "I can drive."

"But you might get tired of making a long drive and then want to quit," he protested.

"Look," I insisted, "for the right job, I won't mind driving. Not only that, for the right job, I can *move*!"

I think he liked my reasoning, because he went ahead and set up an interview for me. Hired me, too. Four years later, I bought the company from him.

When people put boulders in your path, show them your steam shovel.

Today's Affirmation: "Everybody loves a winner and knows that I am one!"

68

Stopping Points

"We can throw stones, complain about them, stumble on them, climb over them, or build with them."

—William Arthur Ward

Sometimes you're the one putting the boulders in your path. Then the "Yeah, buts" you hear are in your own mind. Recognize any of these?:

1. Yeah, but I don't have the time.
2. Yeah, but I don't have the money.
3. Yeah, but I don't have the education.
4. Yeah, but I don't have the talent.
5. Yeah, but I'm not pretty (handsome, smart, strong, or ____) enough.
6. Yeah, but I have too many other things on my plate.
7. Yeah, but I already tried that once and it didn't work.
8. Yeah, but that works for other people, not for me.
9. Yeah, but my husband (wife, partner) won't let me.
10. Yeah, but I'm too sick.
11. Yeah, but my husband (wife, partner) is too sick.
12. Yeah, but I wasn't born rich.
13. Yeah, but I have to make a living.
14. Yeah, but my case is different.
15. And the biggest stopper of all: Yeah, but that's just the way I am.

Think you can go all day today without saying any "Yeah, buts"? Try it. If you think it but don't say it out loud, that's a victory. You might want to write down all the "Yeah, buts" that come up during the day, so you can see what the dark side of your mind is telling you, and where your biggest problem lies. Then at the end of the day, rewrite the list as positive affirmations and start practicing them daily. Your inner talk will start to shift, and as it does, your outer behavior will shift, too. With new positive thoughts, followed by positive action, you will receive positive results.

Today's Affirmation: "I love myself the way I am!"

69

Angels in Disguise

"The person who says it cannot be done should not interrupt the person doing it."

—Chinese proverb

It was a beautiful Saturday morning at the L.A. *Times*' Festival of Books, held on campus at U.C.L.A. It was fun to roam among the books and booksellers and hear some authors speak of their experiences writing and publishing. At one panel, Chris Bohjalian, author of *Midwives*, a national bestseller, was asked if he had ever taken any writing courses. He laughed, and said no, but it wasn't through lack of trying. He had once applied for acceptance into a writing program and had sent in samples of his work. Nervous, nineteen and hopeful, he had entered the monolithic building for his interview with the well-known writing instructor. She sat behind a huge, overpowering desk, looked at him coldly and said, "Be a banker."

Whenever you step out of the norm, you will encounter sharks. Out of moments of their own despair, possibly even thinking they're helping, they will throw challenges at your dream in the shape of criticism. Remember that they do not know you and they do not hear your music. Perhaps they are really angels in disguise, whose mission is to make you angry, to goad you, to create the cement that will glue you to your dream with grit, determination, and power. As a friend of mine once said, "I didn't know I *had* a dream until this man told me I couldn't have it."

So, who told you "no"—you can't have that, be that, do that? Everyone who ever wanted to do something powerful, rich, or different was told "no" a thousand times: "It isn't done." "You haven't got what it takes." "You're too intelligent, stupid, short, tall, fat, thin, plain, pretty, to do that." They will have all manner of reasons and evidence that what they say is true.

They lie. They only see what exists now, not the possibility of what may be. That exists in your mind and soul, and you can create its reality. Honor your vision. Go for your goal. What you end up with may be different from what you set out to achieve, but you will live a rich life in pursuit of your quest. The dream may change along the way, as we are changed as we move through life. But dreams given up too early become the restless dissatisfaction of "what if" and "if only."

When you challenge the norm and take the risk, step outside your comfort zone, you find the happiness that only the brave know. Risk and you may fail. But not to risk is to surely fail. Somewhere there is an author who never put a pen to the page. A champion tennis player who never picked up a racquet. A world-class composer who never picked up a musical instrument. A lover who never asked for a date. Until you take a risk, you don't know who you are.

Laugh at the naysayers, the sharks who don't want you to succeed, the tuna who are afraid you will succeed. And when they tell you that you can't do something, just say, "Oh yeah? *Watch this*!"

Today's Affirmation: "I am successful and follow my dreams all the way to reality!"

70
The Nay Sayers

"A ship is safe in the harbor, but that is not its purpose."

—Anonymous

No matter who you are, how brightly you shine, how loving, smart, talented, rich, successful, kind, caring, or wonderful you are, there will be someone who doesn't think so. Some of the most difficult challenges to overcome are the boulders that other people put in our path. They are the "Nay Sayers."

Years ago, on the same day, Burt Reynolds and Clint Eastwood were both released from their contracts with a major motion picture studio's talent development program. They were told they would never make it in show business. Reynolds was told that he couldn't act and Eastwood that his Adam's apple was too large.

As they walked off the studio lot, they passed some workmen who were already painting out their names on their parking spaces. I imagine that they were depressed, hurt, and scared. Their dreams of stardom and success must have dimmed on that day. But Reynolds turned to Eastwood and said, "Well, I think I have a better chance than you of becoming a star anyway."

Eastwood looked at him suspiciously and asked, "Oh, yeah? Why is that?"

With a twinkle in his eye and his inimical comic style, Reynolds replied, "Well, I can always learn how to act. But what are you going to do about that Adam's apple?"

Both talented men rose to great heights of motion picture stardom. Their faces and films are familiar to me. I know Burt Reynolds's name. I know Clint Eastwood's name.

I don't know the name of their Nay Sayer. Do you?

Today's Affirmation: "All my good is on its way to me now!"

71

Making Movies

"Behind every successful woman...is a substantial amount of coffee."

—Stephanie Piro

My first movie role was in *The Lucifer Complex*, a low-budget sci-fi movie starring Robert Vaughn, Aldo Ray, and Keenan Wynn. It was about a group of women who are kidnapped by a bunch of neo-Nazis who want to impregnate them with little Hitlers. Very excited, the first day on the set I arrived before my call at 7:00 A.M., adrenaline pumping through my system, eager to participate and learn and enjoy every minute of the experience. I got into costume, makeup, and coffee with some of the other girls on the set.

Then we got to experience the real truth of being on the working set of a movie: waiting. We waited while they set up the camera, then we waited while they changed the scenery. Next we waited while they reset the camera, tested the sound, changed the scenery again, set the props, reset the camera...get the picture? At 3:00 P.M., they were finally ready for us to shoot a scene. By then, I was exhausted. My excitement had been at fever pitch all morning—now my nerves were shot. But I cranked up my energy to act, determined to do a great job.

The director blocked the scene for us, showing us where to stand and what to do. Then we did a run through. Then we did another run through. And another. Finally, we were ready to film. We did the scene. Oops, a fly buzzed around the microphone—do it again. Someone flubbed a line—do it again. A plane flew overhead—do it again. And again. By the time we were done, I could barely drag myself home. But I was happy! I was living my dream.

I didn't have a call again for two days and thought I would just sleep. But during the night I had a horrible pain in my chest and couldn't sleep a wink. In the morning I saw the doctor, who informed me that I had pneumonia. "Walking pneumonia?" I asked. "Well," he said, "you might be walking but you shouldn't be. You have *pneumonia*." He gave me a prescription and told me to stay in bed for the next couple of weeks. Right. I'm making my first movie and I'm going to call in sick. No way.

Of course I showed up on the set the next day. I explained to the director that I was a trifle under the weather and needed to lie down someplace between takes, so they found a spot for me—Robert Vaughn's trailer. Robert ran into his trailer one afternoon when I was lying there and asked, "What's wrong with you anyway?"

"I have pneumonia," I replied.

Horrified, he said, "You should be home in bed!"

"I can't do that!" I exclaimed. "I'm making a movie!"

"Oh, of course," he smiled. He understood: When you're living your dream, you don't let minor irritations like pneumonia get in your way.

Today's Affirmation: "I am happy, healthy, and living my dream!"

72
Daughter of Jaws

"Do not try to fight a lion if you are not one yourself."

—African proverb

The money is in the phone—but not in every phone call. Let me tell you about Bridget.

A corporate client of mine invited me to his company trade show. When I arrived, he introduced me to the woman he was sitting with, and very nicely praised my skills as a motivational speaker. The woman, Bridget, said, "Oh, you should come and give a talk where I work at XYZ (a major television station)—they have speakers in all the time." I thanked her for the suggestion and asked for her card. When I saw that her title was essentially "Big Honcho of Talent and Casting," I felt as though I had won the lottery!

I immediately sent Bridget a nice thank you note and my usual speaker's package of information and testimonials. After a week, I made a follow-up phone call to her office. The secretary asked my name, then put me on hold. The next thing I heard was shouted at me: "Don't call me! I only met you for five minutes! Don't call me!"

I was shocked speechless for a moment, unprepared for this reaction! I said, "Excuse me. When we met, you gave me your card and suggested I send you some information, which I did. This is the first call I have made to follow up."

"Don't call me! I can't do anything for you. I got your stuff, I forwarded it on—there's nothing more I can do for you. I only met you for five minutes! Don't call me!"

Well, I just couldn't think of anything brilliant to say in that moment so I said, "Okay," and hung up. I felt awful! Then the phone rang. I picked it up and meekly said, "Hello?" "For heaven's sake, what's wrong with you?" my friend Judy St. James asked. I told her the story and she said, "Well, who pissed in her coffee?" "Oh," I said, "what a great comeback that is. I wished I had said that!" Judy was the perfect person to talk to in that moment. A business coach and seminar leader, she had my self-esteem back in shape in no time. We laughed and giggled together. I gave myself an hour break, then went back to my sales calls.

This story is a perfect example of the worst that can happen to you when you send out a ship in the shape of a phone call. And this is why many people never succeed—they let this fear stop them. Yes, this was an unpleasant experience. But if I let the fear of this experience stop me from pursuing my success, Bridget wins. And she's just not worth being broke for.

Was someone mean to you? Did you give something up because of them? Take it back!

Today's Affirmation: "The money is in the phone and I get richer and richer with every call!"

73
Daughter of Dolphin

"None of us has gotten where we are solely by pulling ourselves up from our own bootstraps. We got here because somebody bent down and helped us."

—Thurgood Marshall

It was December of 1988 and I had just lost the major client of my business management firm. I was struggling with debt, with bills I couldn't pay, trying to get more business and keep the doors open. My friend, Sharlee Bishin, called me up and asked me if I had seen the article in the paper about the new pilot program the Small Business Administration was starting up called the "Women's Network of Entrepreneurial Training" or WNET. They had enlisted twelve successful women business owners in California to act as mentors to other women, and they were taking applications from potential mentees.

I had seen the article and had even cut it out and put it on my desk, but hadn't done anything about it. When I told her that, Sharlee just about leapt through the phone. She said, "This is perfect for you and with what you're going through, you have to apply for this program. You could get matched up with somebody like Patty DeDominic, who runs a multi-million dollar employment agency here in Los Angeles and was mentioned in the article!" I had had the instinct myself that this would be a good program for me, but I just hadn't taken action. Sharlee gave me just the push I needed to take the time to fill out the application and send it in.

Three weeks passed, and I forgot about it until one afternoon when I got a call from an SBA representative. She told me, "We've got a mentor for you." I was delighted. "Who?" I asked. And she said, "Patty DeDominic!" The synchronicity floored me—I knew this was meant to be and was going to be great.

Patty was incredible. We hit it off immediately the first time we met. When I told her of my recent problems, she told me about the time she had a cash flow crunch early in her career and wasn't going to be able to make the payroll for all her temporary employees. When the bank turned her down for a loan, she ended up borrowing the money from her accountant. But she weathered the storm, and here she was, one of the most successful women entrepreneurs in the country. She had overcome obstacles and she believed I could, too.

We worked together over the next year, meeting once every three or four weeks, and talking on the phone regularly. She opened her business, her home, and her heart to me, and her faith and sound advice were a lifeline I clung to during some of my darkest hours. Much of what I know about successful business practices, I learned from her. Patty Dolphin DeDominic.

Have a mentor? Write them a thank you letter today. Don't have one? Get one. Then be one.

Today's Affirmation: "I surround myself with supportive, loving friends and mentors."

74
Ocean

"It will never rain roses. When we want to have more roses, we must plant more trees."

—George Eliot

When I speak of sharks, dolphins, and tuna, I want to stress that I am not advocating segregation of fish, or saying that some fish are bad fish. We are all in the ocean together, and mutually interdependent. I just want you to be as high up on the food chain as possible.

If you're swimming around with a lot of sharks, trying to transform them into dolphins, you are probably a tuna. Have you ever noticed how difficult it is to change yourself, even when you really *want* to change? It is a million times more difficult to try and change someone else. As a matter of fact, I would like to go on record as saying it is *impossible* to change someone else. All you can do is model behavior, and if the fish swimming in your vicinity see how happy you are—so much so that they want to be like you—then they have a chance to change themselves. But you don't do it. They do it. And they have to want it bad.

If you find yourself in the water with sharks, put your shark fin on as camouflage and swim to the nearest exit. You can try and adopt some protective shark behavior, but you will never be as good a shark as a real shark—you don't have the teeth for it. If you find yourself with tuna, model dolphin behavior for them, but don't get trapped into commiserating "ain't-it-awful" behavior. Love them—but don't do business with them, or you may find that sign "Sorry, Charlie" hanging in front of *you*.

We strive to become dolphin—smart, joyful, intelligent comrades, warding off sharks and saving tuna. This is our world view.

When you are ready, there is a greater vision: we are Ocean.

Today's Affirmation: "I float blissfully in the ocean of life, giving gifts to all its creatures."

75
Praise and Acknowledgment

"Let no one ever come to you without leaving better and happier. Be the living expression of God's kindness: kindness in your face, kindness in your eyes, kindness in your smile."

—Mother Teresa

Most of the people I know respond to praise like a thirsty dog getting a drink of water—they lap it up and glow. Unfortunately, some people would rather throw water on you than give you water to drink. But who wants to talk to them? People love being acknowledged for being wonderful. It makes them feel good. It also makes them feel good about *you*! A motivational speaker I know, Suzy Prudden, calls regularly and asks how I'm doing. When I say, "Great!" she always says, "That's true about you!" I love it when she calls.

A recent study found that talking with a friend lifted moderate depression as effectively as professional counseling or taking anti-depressant drugs. The researchers paired chronically depressed people with volunteer "friends" and were instructed to spend at least one hour together each week. At the end of the study, 39 percent of the control group, who were not assigned "friends," reported an easing of their depression. (Some depression lifts naturally over time.) But sixty-five of the participants who spent time with "friends" experienced relief.

Be someone who lights up people's lives. It's so *easy*! Just be someone who compliments others on a regular basis. It has to be sincere—if you don't really believe the praise you're giving, it won't go over well. Everyone has something they can be complimented about. Become a regular praise-giver, and you'll have lots of friends who will be happy to see you or hear from you. And you'll make a lot more money with a lot more satisfied customers, clients, or bosses.

Today's Affirmation: "I am a great people-praiser and people praise me back!"

76

Carmen the Waitress

"Praise, like gold and diamonds, owes its value only to its scarcity."

—Samuel Butler

I have been very blessed in this life with a wonderful, supportive, loving family. My two sisters are married with children, and live within two blocks of each other in Chatsworth, California. (The family joke is they used to live six blocks from each other, but they couldn't stand the commute.) I get to be the auntie, and developed the tradition of taking the kids out for a day trip each year for their birthdays.

One year, the kids and I decided we wanted to go to Disneyland, and since this was a big, fun trip, all the other adults in the family wanted to come, too. So there were eleven of us: two moms, two dads, grandpa, me, and five kids ranging in age from one to nineteen. After a great day of seeing sights, riding rides, and shopping 'til we dropped, we all trouped into a restaurant at the Disneyland Hotel to have dinner.

Hungry and tired parties of eleven, including a baby in a highchair, must seem daunting to most waitresses. But not Carmen. She was bright, she was cheerful, and she managed to make everybody happy. She got the special orders with no problem, all the changes so the kids were happy, and was efficient and upbeat the entire time. She was great!

At the end of the meal, I excused myself, went to the front desk and asked to see the manager. The hostess tensed when I made my request, and said she'd be back in a minute. I saw her go back into the kitchen and speak briefly with a young man. His shoulders slumped, he hung his head for a moment, then braced himself, straightened his tie and started walking out to see me. When he reached me, he asked tensely, "You wanted to speak to the manager?" As I said, "Yes," I noticed several other employees were hovering around, trying to look inconspicuous, but very interested in what was going to happen. Some patrons had stopped eating and were listening, too. I was going to have fun giving them all an earful—an earful of praise.

As I proceeded to tell this young man every wonderful thing I could think of to say about Carmen, his restaurant, and everybody in it, his smile began to turn into a grin and he blushed with pleasure. The other employees started grinning, too, and nodded to each other. The hostess beamed and the patrons caught the smiles also. It was really fun! He thanked me, and said, "You made my day." I said, "You made mine, too!"

Make someone's day—and you'll find you make yours, too. Never miss a chance to pass along a compliment or a kind word. It's so easy! People are hungry for praise. Feed them.

Today's Affirmation: "I am a praise-making machine, and I'm making a lot of it today!"

77

Operating from Joy

"Only one person in a thousand knows the trick of really living in the present. Most of us spend fifty-nine minutes an hour living in the past, with regret for lost joys or shame for things badly done... or in a future which we either long for or dread. There is only one minute in which you are alive, this minute, here and now."

—Storm Jameson

Successful people operate from anticipated joy, while others operate from current pain. Successful people have goals that excite them, that they are passionate about; they can see, taste, smell, feel the future reality they are endeavoring to create. They design their daily activities in harmony with where they want to go, rather than where they are now.

Successful people aren't on overwhelm; they make their time count. They are energized from being in action; the energy pours from them as from an overflowing well. They are happy in the pursuit of their pleasures. This enables them to say "yes!" to the things that move them forward towards their goals and "no" to the things that are off-purpose. They don't waste their time and their energy on too many pursuits.

Unsuccessful people are driven by today's trivia. They say "yes!" to everything because the fear of saying "no" is too powerful. They're afraid that if they don't, they might miss something important, they might offend someone, or people might think they're unavailable, or too busy, or not nice enough. They answer every ring of the telephone, even when they've got a deadline, or it's too early in the morning or too late at night. They make fear-based decisions, rather than goal-oriented ones.

What do you need to do today to move yourself forward? Make a list of all your daily activities and see what needs to be delegated or eliminated. Only purposeful actions towards achieving your goals should remain, along with healthy periods of rest, relaxation, family, friends, and fun.

Here's a prescription for how you might spend your time:

33 percent Sleep: 8 hours per night, 7 days per week = 56 hours

23 percent Work: 8 hours per day, 5 days per week = 40 hours

44 percent Fun: 168 hours minus 56 sleep and 40 work = 72 hours

Do you see? The majority of your time is for fun!

Today's Affirmation: "I am full of joyful energy, and all my dreams come true!"

78
Get Rid of the "I'm So Tired Blues"

"Never get in a battle of wits without ammunition."

—American proverb

How many times do you start a conversation with someone asking, "How are you?" and receive the answer, "I'm so tired"? What a disempowering response! It's a negative affirmation. Then they probably follow that statement with a whole explanation of their problems, their duties and responsibilities, and the crosses they have to bear. Who wants to hear that?

If you are guilty of saying, "I'm so tired," you need to develop a new habit. Start saying "I'm great—thanks for asking!" or "I'm wonderful—how are you?" If someone tells you they're tired, change the energy of the conversation immediately by focusing them on something good. Here are some sample responses:

"I imagine you have an active, creative life filled with wonderful activities!"

"That must mean business is great and your life is full of wonderful friends!"

You get the idea. It just might get them refocused in a positive direction. If they really just want to complain, they will eventually try to find someone less upbeat than you. Great! Let all the "Ain't it Awful" people hang out together and count you out. You go find the energetic people who want to talk about how great things are and getting better, too. Be about success, energy, and joy every minute, even when you're resting. Get lots of rest and relaxation. Mellow out. Joyfully!

Keep your goals in front of you every day. Keep your action plan to achieve your goals where you can review it often. Eliminate activities that do not move you forward toward your goals, unless they are fun, restful, fulfilling, enjoyable, balancing activities that fill you with energy rather than deplete your energy. If it's not fun, don't do it. Pay somebody else to do it—you'll both be happier.

"I'm so tired." Bah. Tell it to your cat.

Today's Affirmation: "Everything I do makes me richer and richer!"

79

Alcoholics Anonymous

"If you have made mistakes, even serious ones, there is always another chance for you. What we call failure is not the falling down, but the staying down."

—Mary Pickford

My name is Chellie C., and I'm an alcoholic. This is my story of what it was like, what happened, and what it is like now. For many years, I drowned my problems in alcohol. Drinking was a habit, my coping mechanism of choice, which increased over time until it got out of control. It started with having a glass of wine when I got home from work. Then two. In classic alcoholic denial, I bought *bigger* glasses so I could still say I only had two glasses of wine.

One day, with my liquor cabinet practically bare, I went to the grocery store to stock up. I went up to the checkout counter with a bottle of cabernet, a bottle of Merlot, some Chardonnay, Chablis, vodka, gin, bourbon, tequila, Marguerita mix, Bloody Mary mix, some assorted liqueurs—altogether I think I had about twelve bottles in my shopping cart—and some chips.

The woman at the checkout stand started ringing up each bottle, smiled and said knowingly, "Having a party?" Not getting it, I said, "No." I will never forget the look on that woman's face. I remember with stark clarity the utter humiliation I felt as I realized that if I was buying twelve bottles of booze, I *should* be having a party!

That night, I had to face the fact that I was incapable of going a single day without drinking. I had a good friend who always went to an Alcoholics Anonymous meeting on Wednesday nights. She sounded pretty excited when I called and asked if I could go to the meeting with her. Apparently, she'd been "saving a seat" for me. There I met a wonderful community of people who had faced their demons and were helping others along with themselves to live life clean and sober. I made a commitment to sobriety that night and I threw away every bottle of alcohol in my house.

Old habits die hard, but if you are determined, die they do. In the next months, I had to face every defect of my character and feel all the feelings that I had used alcohol to avoid. Sometimes after meetings, I would go to my car and collapse in sobs over the steering wheel. Kindly souls knocked on the window and asked if I was all right. But breakdowns will lead eventually to breakthroughs, if you are committed. As they say in AA, "It works if you work it." I grew into a new life and a new self. I deepened and matured. New awareness came to consciousness, and a deeper empathy for people. I cleared away the wreckage of the past and built a better life and a bigger bank account at the same time.

Is there a battle you are fighting? You don't have to fight it alone. Help is available. You just have to reach out and find it.

Today's Affirmation: "I have a wonderful community of friends who help me grow and prosper!"

80
The Tenth Archer

"Difficulty, my brethren, is the nurse of greatness—a harsh nurse, who roughly rocks her foster-children into strength and athletic proportion."

—William C. Bryant

A perfect day on a field of dreams. Sunshine casts its radiant light on the target that all desire to hit. The golden bow and silver arrow await the archers, ready to be used to their highest purpose.

The first archer takes the field confidently. He notches the arrow, pulls back the bow, and slings the arrow straight and true across the grass. Bull's eye! Cheers resound from the gathered watchers and the archer retires with a smile.

The second archer approaches. Reverently, she picks up the golden bow and sends the silver arrow straight to the target. Another hit! More cheers and smiles.

Seven more archers appear with gratitude for their opportunity, lift the bow, and seven times over, the arrow meets the target. The air shimmers with glory and joy.

The tenth archer approaches anxiously. Filled with doubt and dismay, fearful that he alone might miss the target, he tenses as he lifts the bow. The arrow goes wide and is lost in the grass.

In misery and embarrassment, he exclaims, "Damn bow and arrow!" as he leaves the field.

But the tenth archer knows that the fault is in his aim, in his arm, in his mind. He will rise tomorrow, early in the morning mist, and make his way once more to the practice ground. On that day, and many days to follow, he will lift the golden bow and shoot silver arrows hour after hour, until they find their mark deep in the heart of the target. At the next contest, his aim true, he will prevail.

Thus he will have earned the cheers of the crowd—and he will get them.

Are you hitting your targets? Or do you need more practice? More strength? Better thoughts? Better aim?

Today's Affirmation: "With confidence, reverence, and gratitude, I am always successful!"

81

The Saga of the Pants

"It's a little like wrestling a gorilla. You don't quit when you are tired, you quit when the gorilla is tired."

—Robert Strauss

This tale comes from Corinne and Dave Pleger, who participate in Civil War reenactments with authentic costumes, sets, and props.

"Over a year ago, Corinne took a class that taught her how to sew an authentic pair of Civil War Federal Army pants. Corinne sewed a pair for me that immediately became the envy of my unit. One man, Ron, admired my pants and asked Corinne to make a pair for him. By lucky coincidence, Ron is exactly my size, so all Corinne had to do was to duplicate the job she did on mine. Her self-imposed deadline was the annual Civil War Christmas party on December 12.

Night after night she worked industriously on the pants until they were nearly done. But when she brought them downstairs for me to try on, they didn't fit. The waist measured 38 inches instead of 41 inches. No amount of inhaling and pulling would make these pants fit. There was nothing to do but make a second pair.

"Newly ordered material arrived on December 4th and all through the weekend she slaved over the pants. She had them nearly finished on December 6th and measured the waist—39 inches. Corinne was upset. To be more precise, it was not a good evening to be near her. Corinne called me at work the next morning and said that she had calmed down and had ordered more material, determined not to be defeated.

"The material arrived on December 8 and was *generously* cut that night. A driven woman sewed late into the night on the 10th. On the night before the party, Corinne continued to sew. In some mysterious way, when Corinne completed the fly, it was on the wrong side of the pants. Perhaps this project was jinxed.

"Corinne resolved to finish the hem on Ron's pants while I drove us to the Christmas party. I drove very carefully so as to avoid having the car wrecked by the curse of the blue pants. Just as she finished, the light on her portable reading lamp burnt out. But this is a story of triumph! Ron loved his pants and two other guys immediately bought Corinne's other pairs."

Although Corinne has renewed her vow not to sew for people outside of the family, she learned that she has the determination, stick-to-it-ness, and confidence in her own abilities to see a project through despite any obstacles that threaten to bar the way. No matter what you're facing, keep your eye on the prize and keep going.

Today's Affirmation: "I am committed to achieving my goals."

82

The Black Limo vs. the Volkswagen

"The greater danger for most of us is not that our aim is too high and we miss it, but that it is too low and we reach it."

—Michelangelo

Annie, my artist friend, had found the Black Limo and gotten in. She was selling paintings to people, even selling a series of paintings to a company for their corporate offices. She arranged for a one-woman show of her work to be scheduled at an art gallery, and had interest from other galleries as well. She was an artist on the move!

I hadn't seen her in a few months, when I called to chat. She was in the middle of a big painting project. But not painting her art. No, painting her *house*. Big house, big project. Very distracting. Very off-purpose for her goals, dreams, and desires. "What was she doing?" I wondered. She had gotten out of the Black Limo. Then she told me she was thinking she should go back to school and get a degree in art. Nope, she hadn't gotten out of the Black Limo. She was about to *crash* the Black Limo and get in a rusty '74 Volkswagen instead.

I asked how long it would take to get her degree. "Four or five years," she told me. "And then what?" I asked. There was an uncomfortable pause on the other end of the phone. I asked if any of the art galleries or corporations or buyers had asked to see her art degree before they bought her paintings? Annie groaned and then giggled on the other end of the phone. "You think I'm just going back to school to play it safe and not have to be sending out ships and selling my art, don't you?" she accused. "I don't know, what do you think?" "I think I'm busted," she sighed. The Black Limo was safe. We left the Volkswagen burning by the side of the road.

Of course, education is extremely valuable, and sometimes it's a requirement. If you want to be a doctor, or an attorney, or a dentist, you have to go to school and get a degree to get your license. So do that. It's necessary. And if you're smart, you will never stop learning. Just don't use it as an excuse to stop *doing*.

The last time I looked, you didn't have to have a license to be an artist.

Today's Affirmation: "I love what I do and that love brings me all the money I want."

83
The Balance Sheet

"All my available funds are completely tied up in ready cash."

—W.C. Fields

The Balance Sheet. This is one of those important financial statements that bankers and accountants love. We need to love it too, because it is a snapshot of how we are doing financially at any one moment in time. It is basically just a list of the value of all the things you own, balanced against the money you owe to other people. This is its basic construction:

Assets (All the stuff you own)
Cash in bank accounts
Other cash
Stocks and bonds
Real estate
Automobile
Furniture
Art, Jewelry, etc.
Total $______

Liabilities (All the stuff you owe)
Credit card debt
Real estate mortgages
Car loan
Loans from family, friends, etc.
Total $______

Net Worth (Not as a human being, just financially)
Total $______
What's left after you subtract what you owe from what you own

Filling out a simple balance sheet is not that complicated a task. It is important for you to know what your financial status is. When you make the decision to improve your financial life, you have to know your starting point in order to know how you are improving. My friend, Corinne Pleger, an accountant, when asked what she does for a living, says, "I measure your success." Keeping accurate financial records will chart your success so you will know if you are on the right track or not.

Some people fill this out and are happily surprised that their net worth is higher than they supposed. Others are shocked at the size of their negative number. Whatever your number is now, know that if you keep on following this program, it's going to improve!

Today's Affirmation: "I accumulate assets that put more money in my pocket every day!"

84

Your Financial Thermostat

"The real tragedy of life is not that it's one damn thing after another—but it's the same damn thing, over and over."

—Unknown

Have you ever felt that, no matter what you did, you couldn't rise above a certain amount of spendable income? That those extra fun frills in life you long for are always just out of reach, even when you get the raise, or the insurance settlement, or the inheritance? Like a broken thermostat, the financial setting has gotten stuck on an amount of money that you subconsciously believe is the best you can allow yourself. You're stuck at just enough to get by, just as the thermostat is stuck at sixty degrees. You want to be warmer, and seventy-two degrees sounds great, but the thermostat won't budge. That's what keeps us at "getting by money" instead of "above and beyond money."

I began to notice this as a trend in my own life and it was mirrored by the experiences of my clients, as well. It became clear one day when I got home from a speaking engagement for which I was paid $1,000. As I drove home from the event, with my bright, crisp check for $1,000 of extra money—unplanned for and unbudgeted—I thought about all the things I could do with this windfall. I hummed happily to myself as I walked in my apartment and got myself a soft drink from the refrigerator.

I plopped myself down on the couch, reached for the remote and turned on the television set—which promptly blew up. Well, it didn't exactly blow up; it made a loud popping noise and went blank. A puff of smoke came out the back of it. My dreams of new purchases went out the window with that puff of smoke. I now knew what I was going to be buying with my check—a replacement TV.

Disappointed as I was, I had to laugh. I knew exactly what had happened. My money had exceeded my financial thermostat setting, so I created something to have to use the money for that would basically keep me even instead of being ahead. Has this ever happened to you? You get the raise—and the school your kids are in raises its tuition. Or you get the inheritance and then the car breaks down and you have to spend the money to fix it. You get a gift of money, but you find out you owe more taxes than you originally thought. When these things happen, you need to raise your money consciousness.

To raise your net worth you have to raise your self-worth. You need to look at your opinions or beliefs about money that limit you and change them. Think of yourself as rich and abundant, with plenty to have and to give. Feel good about the receiving of abundance as well as the giving, for they are two sides of the same coin. Thank God for the gift and pass it on. Light the fire, raise the thermostat, increase the heat! And more money will come to warm itself in your glow.

Today's Affirmation: "Every day, I'm burning brighter and growing richer!"

85

"Getting By" Money vs. "Above and Beyond" Money

"The road to success is marked with many tempting parking spaces."

—Executive Speechwriter Newsletter

Many people get caught in the trap of making just enough money to "get by." They work to pay their current bills, and once those are satisfied, they relax and coast until the first of the next month, when they start the process all over again. It is a basic money habit pattern. Working frantically to get the bills paid and then coasting will not get you to the pinnacle of success you deserve. No one ever coasted uphill.

A smart and savvy entrepreneur, Yvonne came to my workshop several years ago. She was in the executive search business and made a nice income working out of her home. When I spoke about the habit pattern of working just to get by, she related to it instantly. She said that she would work diligently trying to place executives with her client companies, but when she made a few placements that would pay all her bills, she literally stopped working. I asked her what would happen if she kept going, and she responded that she didn't know. I said, "Well, try it this week and see what happens," and she agreed.

She glowed when she walked in the classroom the next week. Beaming happily, she talked of how she made a placement that would pay all her bills, but then just kept going. She used the "Ships Log" to keep track of her activities and keep her motivated. Instead of stopping at her "break-even" point, she made $35,000 that week. This was definitely "Above and Beyond" money!

She was so happy, she wrote me a commission check. She had purchased my course at a charity auction to which I had donated it, so I hadn't been paid for her attendance. With that big win in her pocket, she wanted me to make money, too. As I accepted the check ("People love to give me money!"), I told the class I knew that she knew what goes around comes around. I expected that gift was going to produce even more money in her life.

Just a few years later, she had six branch offices across the country.

What could you have if you just kept going?

Today's Affirmation: "I always receive an abundance of 'Above and Beyond' money!"

86

Cruise Day

"Some people are making such thorough preparation for rainy days that they aren't enjoying today's sunshine."

—William Feather

Going on a cruise is a wonderful experience—it's a big adult playpen on the water. When I took my first cruise with Korey, we couldn't believe how much fun there was to be had with the wide variety of activities. There was a casino, bingo games, nightly entertainment, karaoke, dancing, a piano bar, aerobics classes, a gym, massage, shuffleboard, skeet shooting, and food galore. You only have to unpack one time and the ship carries you to different ports of call—you wake up and you're in another city. We had a fabulous time.

When we got home from the cruise, Korey and I decided that we didn't want the fun we had had to end. So we invented "Cruise Day." Once a month, we planned a day off. It had to be a work day so we could feel like we were playing hooky and getting away with something. For that whole day, we did nothing but have fun, just like when we were on our cruise.

We always checked with each other ahead of time to see if it was a High Budget, Medium Budget, or Low Budget Cruise Day. High Budget Cruise Days looked like this: We went to Nordstrom and shopped for great clothes, we went to the theater, we had steak and lobster at a great restaurant, etc. On Medium Budget Cruise Days, we did more window-shopping and less actual purchasing, we went to the movies and ate at a medium-priced restaurant. During Low Budget times, we rented videos and popped popcorn, picnicked on the beach, or visited a local museum.

I have to tell you we had every bit as much fun on Low Budget Cruise Days as High Budget ones. You can laugh and talk and have a great time with a great friend no matter what the contents of your wallet are. So plan a Cruise Day today!

Today's Affirmation: "I think, therefore I'm rich!"

87
It Pays to Be on Time

"The trouble with being punctual is there's no one there to appreciate it."

—Franklin P. Jones

I attended a financial workshop years ago, we played a game called "It pays to be on time." We were charged a dollar a minute for every minute we were late to class, to a maximum of ten dollars. You should have heard the arguments that went on in each class about paying those fines! A veritable cornucopia of "Yeah, buts." "Yeah, but there was an accident on the freeway," "Yeah, but my car broke down," "Yeah, but my biggest client called with a problem and I had to help him," etc. The workshop cost eight hundred dollars, yet here we were spending the first fifteen-twenty minutes of each class arguing whether or not someone owed their fine of two dollars!

There was an important lesson in this exercise. When you're late, you're late. Just own your responsibility that you made a choice that resulted in your being late. Whether it was to leave for the meeting with no leeway for traffic problems, to choose to pick up the ringing telephone when you were on your way out, or not having your car properly serviced so breakdowns don't occur—these are all choices that are your responsibility. If your ship sails and you're not on it, the reasons why you missed it won't put you on it.

One evening during this workshop, I wasn't feeling well and it was raining, so I made the choice not to go to class. The next week, as they read off the names of people who owed fines for being late, they ended with, "and Chellie Campbell, ten dollars." Surprised, I said, "I wasn't late tonight!" and was told, "This is for last week when you didn't show up." Hand on my hip, defensive attitude ready, I said, "Yeah, but I was sick!" And before I got the word "sick" out of my mouth, I had a revelation. I often used getting sick as an excuse to cancel things when I had over-committed myself. Sometimes when I looked at my crowded calendar, I would plan in advance to call in sick to something. Then, by the power of suggestion, I would really get sick. This was a habit that needed to be broken! I understood this lesson so powerfully in that moment that I paid the fine immediately with no further discussion. It was a cheap price to pay for a very significant life lesson.

Being late is a choice. Being late costs you money. Be on time today!

Today's Affirmation: "Time is my friend and I am always on time."

88

Do Nothing Day

"I work for myself, which is fun. Except for when I call in sick—I know I'm lying."

—Rita Rudner

After I had the revelation about my habit of getting sick in order to get out of commitments, I decided I had to change my behavior. I had to learn to say "No" to more things and break the cycle of over-commitment. I had to focus on my priorities, and one of them had to be my health.

I took a long, hard look at my calendar and all the activities I planned each week. I realized I was on the go too much—even with fun things. I needed more "do nothing time." I looked at what I did on my sick days: I stayed in my pajamas, wrapped myself in a blanket, I watched TV, I read books, I napped throughout the day, I talked with friends on the phone, I ate foods that made me feel better, I drank hot tea and soup. I wondered what it would be like to have a "sick day" when I wasn't sick? So I created "Do Nothing Day."

On "Do Nothing Day," I eat my favorite foods and watch videos of recent movies I really want to see. I always have several books I'm in the middle of, so I'll read them when the mood strikes me. I might play computer games, chat on the Internet, do crossword puzzles. I sit on the patio and watch the birds. I often stay in my pajamas, or at least wear comfortable scruffy clothes. I don't go anywhere. I don't put on any makeup. I don't answer the phone (it might be work related, and I'd rather not explain about "Do Nothing Day" on "Do Nothing Day.") I drink my tea and cuddle with my cat. There is a great pleasure in lying on a bed, holding a cat with its motor running, knowing you don't have to get up anytime soon and rush off.

After a "Do Nothing Day," I am a bundle of energy and enthusiasm: Renewed, refreshed, and once again eager to connect with the world and do the work I love.

When was the last time you took a day off just to loaf around? Put one on your schedule now.

P.S. "Do Nothing Day" is not "Chores Day." You do not have permission to do anything constructive.

Today's Affirmation: "I revel in relaxation!"

89

$10,000 on a Day Off

"It's when you're safe at home that you wish you were having an adventure. When you're having an adventure, you wish you were safe at home."

—Thornton Wilder

Jerry Warner is a stock trader. A mortgage broker for many years, he has a knack for valuing stocks and companies, and started trading options on a regular basis. Bright, energetic, and optimistic, he started a new business so he could share his ability with others. He re-enrolled in my workshop in order to collect new ideas and impetus for his new venture.

Just after completing the course, the stock market went through one of its volatile phases. Stocks values jumped wildly—up one minute and down the next. Jerry started getting nervous. His stocks were plummeting. Should he sell and mitigate his losses? Or should he hold on for a rally? He called to tell me what he did next.

"I just thought to myself, 'What would Chellie do?'" he told me on the phone. He decided that the companies he had invested in maintained real value and that the market gyrations were only a momentary glitch. He remembered a saying he had heard me repeat, "Never make a permanent decision while in a temporary state of mind," so rather than watch the ticker tape and worry about the ups and downs all day, he decided to take a "Do Nothing Day" or "Pajama Day." He took the rest of the day off, went home, got in his pajamas, relaxed, and read books.

"So what happened to your stocks?" I asked.

"Well," he said, "my initial instinct had been to respond out of fear, cut my losses, and sell everything. But I remembered you telling us not to make fear-based decisions. I forced myself to remain calm and relaxed. By the end of the day, the market went back up.

"I made an additional profit of $10,000—because I took a day off! Isn't that a great story?"

Yes, Jerry, it is.

Playing the stock market game takes nerves of steel. You have to develop poker skills—to know when to hold them and when to fold them. If you're going to get scared and sell out whenever the market goes down from time to time, you are not going to win at this game. You have to have a plan, sometimes revise the plan, mostly stick to the plan, and get the advice of a planner. It's an adventure. It's a gamble. Enjoy the ride—or don't play.

Today's Affirmation: "I buy low and I sell high!"

90

I Guess I'm Just Lucky

"When you're in the muck you can only see muck. If you somehow manage to float above it, you still see the muck but you see it from a different perspective."

—David Cronenberg

Oops! My car broke again. Well, machinery gets old and stuff happens. This time I was in a parking garage behind a restaurant in Culver City. It was 10:00 P.M. and I was one of the last people leaving a networking dinner. The key wouldn't turn in the ignition and the steering column was locked. The parking lot attendant came over and tried to get it to work too, but no go. Rats.

Okay, time to play "The Glad Game": Thank you, God, for the Auto Club. Thank you, God, for cell phones. I made some notes for my book and did some affirmations while I waited for the tow truck. Finally, my knight in shining armor arrived in the person of Bijan, astride his trusty steed, the Auto Club tow truck. He strapped my car to his truck, I got in the cab, and we took off for the repair shop.

"You know, there are some good things about this," Bijan said to me as we drove away. I looked at him in astonishment. The tow trucker from Iran was playing "The Glad Game"! He continued, "If your wheels hadn't been straight, I wouldn't have been able to tow you."

"Really?" I commented. "I guess I'm just lucky!"

"Yes, you are," he agreed. "A lot of things could have made this situation worse than it is."

"Did you ever see the movie, *Pollyanna*?" I asked suspiciously.

He shook his head, but told me that the trick to being happy in life was to look at what you did have instead of what you didn't have. He said that so many people are always unhappy because they're looking up at the few who have more than they do instead of down at all of those who have less than they do. We had a great philosophical discussion for the entire ride to the auto repair shop. What could have been an unhappy, angry experience was fun instead. I had met a kindred spirit from the other side of the world. And then, although it wasn't part of his job, he drove me home.

I guess I'm just lucky.

Today's Affirmation: "I am a lucky person—I feel lucky today!"

91

Another Bad Habit Bites the Dust

"He has spent his life best who has enjoyed it most. God will take care that we do not enjoy it any more than is good for us."

—Samuel Butler

I was in the middle of a hand of poker, when the woman tapped me on the shoulder. "Your friend isn't feeling well," she said. "She's sitting in the women's room and wants to see you."

Concerned, I got up immediately and rushed to the women's room. Shelley looked awful. She was pale and sagging in the chair. "What's wrong?" I asked. "I don't know," she replied. "I have a burning sensation across my chest." "Okay," I said, "Let's go."

I gathered up Shelley's belongings and my own, cashed out our chips at the casino cage, and redeemed the car from valet parking. "Do you think it's heartburn?" I asked as we drove towards home. "I don't know," she said, "But I took some antacid tablets." "Is it helping?" I wanted to know. "No." There was finality in that reply. I looked at her closely at the next stop light. "Do you want to go to the emergency hospital?" was my next fateful question. "Yes."

You can bet I drove as fast as the traffic would allow and we screeched into the UCLA emergency room parking. The nurse sat Shelley down, took her pulse, then turned to the nurse behind her and said, "Get a bed ready!" They hooked Shelley up to many machines and we watched the lines and numbers go wildly up and down for the next few hours. Then they sent me home.

Shelley had an angiogram on Monday and open-heart surgery on Wednesday. Triple bypass. The next week, a mutual friend of ours named Kathy died of lung cancer. Kathy was a smoker. So was Shelley. So was I.

Sometimes the messages God sends us are so clear, so powerful, we cannot miss them. I heard this one. And my answer back was, "No, it doesn't have to be me before I get it. Thank you. I quit."

I was a smoker for thirty years. I quit cold turkey. And you know what? It was easy.

Protect your health and your body—you can't make money without it. Is there something in your life that it's time for you to quit? Or are you waiting for God to send you an email?

Today's Affirmation: "I love myself and treasure my health."

92
Health Costs

"Every cloud has a silver lining but it is sometimes a little difficult to get to the mint."

—Don Marquis

It seemed, no matter what I did, I got a bad cold every year. Someone would sneeze around me, and bingo! A cold. My negative affirmations were loud in this area. And since I also believed that any cold would immediately degenerate into a sinus infection, it would be necessary for me to spend $125 for a doctor's visit, plus about $75 for antibiotics, cough syrup, etc. So colds were not only miserable for my body, they were miserable for my pocketbook.

Something had to be done. You can guess, by now, what I did—yes, positive health affirmations! But I could see I needed to back up the positive thinking with some ships, so I took action, too. I investigated preventive health measures, and decided to consistently take vitamins, eat better, and exercise more. Each action I took was a physical demonstration of my mental belief in my health.

I wasn't quite up to speed on my positive changes when a cold laid me low. But I continued to think positively about my health (between sneezes). A lot of people had told me of the benefits of Echinacea, an herbal remedy for colds, so I bought some and took it every day.

And you know what? The cold ran its course, but didn't degenerate into sinusitis. I didn't need to go to the doctor and I didn't need to pay $200. I paid $6.99 for a bottle of herbs.

Works for me!

I believe in mind over matter. I believe metaphysical medicine, in *Quantum Healing*, as Deepak Chopra's book says. I believe we sometimes create our disease, and sometimes we can heal them, just through our intentions, affirmations, and faith.

And I also believe in Western Medicine, flu shots, aspirin, penicillin, dental fillings, operations, and cough medicine. They've helped me on a number of occasions. When I improve my metaphysics, I'll need invasive medicine less. Until then, I'll see my doctor when I need to.

Take a look at your health maintenance program. Taking care of your body is just like taking care of your car. Are you doing the small, regular maintenance checks that keep your engine running smoothly? Or are you waiting for the big breakdown before you pay attention? Regular maintenance is a lot less expensive. Your body is the number one piece of business equipment you own. Take care of it.

Because if you ruin it, you don't get another one.

Today's Affirmation: "Shining, radiant health is flowing now through all parts of my beautiful body!"

93

Restful Sleep

"The last refuge of the insomniac is a sense of superiority to the sleeping world."

—Leonard Cohen

Insomnia used to upset me. I would have trouble falling asleep, then wake up in the middle of the night, angry and anxious about not getting enough rest. I just knew I would be tired and crabby in the morning. This negative energy fed on itself, and I had more and more sleepless nights. I was trapped in my negative thoughts about sleeplessness.

As I began working with positive affirmations, I focused my positive energy on money and business, but forgot to apply the same principles to my sleep habits. Duh! After about the thousandth time, I saw what I was doing to myself and knew I could change my mind and change my sleep. I started doing some positive affirmations about my restful sleep.

The next night I woke up at 1:00 A.M., I smiled to myself. Now was my opportunity to put positive thinking into practice. I decided that if I was awake, it must be for a reason. I did have a problem on my mind, so my first action was to get pen and paper and write down the problem, and any solutions to it I could think of. Next, I said to myself that no matter how much or how little sleep I got that night, it would be enough, and I would feel rested, alert, and full of energy in the morning. Perhaps I had been telling myself that I needed eight hours of sleep when my body didn't really need that much. My body would just have to be in charge—if I slept, it would be because I needed sleep, and if I didn't sleep, it would be because I had gotten all the sleep I needed. I picked up a book and read until I got sleepy, turned out the light, and went back to sleep.

In the morning, I awoke feeling great. I don't remember how many actual hours of sleep I got that night, but I have found that it doesn't matter as much as my attitude about it does. Sometimes I get eight hours of sleep and feel great, and sometimes I get only four hours of sleep—but I still feel great! By thinking that whatever amount of sleep I get is enough and that I will feel rested and energetic in the morning, I am not anxious about getting the "right" number of hours.

Anxiety won't make you money, and anxiety won't make you sleep. Sleeplessness is your opportunity to practice peace, serenity, trust, and calm. Then you can transfer those qualities to your waking hours—and your money-making hours.

Today's Affirmation: "I get all the sleep I need each night, and awake refreshed and energized each morning!"

94

It's a Wonderful Life!

"I'd been busy, busy, so busy, preparing for life, while life floated by me, quiet and swift as a regatta."

—Lorene Cary

We're only in this life for a short time. And none of us knows just how brief it will be. Sometimes we get so wrapped up in our busy panoply of obligations that we forget to live.

I was working on the program committee of a women's business organization with a woman named Joan. Joan, the Program Chair, had her own consulting business and worked hard, long hours. She was very responsible, did every task to perfection—and thus had trouble delegating work to others or setting limits as to what she would do. She always said, "Well, if I don't do it, it won't get done or it won't get done right." You could always count on her if you needed to get a job done, but I worried about how stressed she seemed. She rarely took time off or a vacation.

One evening, Joan called me for the phone number of a health professional we both knew. She was in terrible pain, and the doctors were having trouble diagnosing her condition. It wasn't long before she went into the hospital for tests. I went to see her the day before her operation, and she was scared and nervous, as any of us would be. It was the last time I saw her. When they opened her up, she was full of cancer. She died ten days later.

All of her friends and the members of the program committee attended her memorial service. We told stories of her love and courage, hugged each other and cried. The next day, the president appointed a new Program Chair.

That hit me like a thunderbolt. That's what's going to happen when I die, I thought. They're going to appoint a new me the next day. All those obligations, chores, and duties will be carried out by someone else or not done at all. That very day, I started eliminating all the excess clutter from my life: I didn't have to be all things to all people, respond to every request, fret about every last detail. I wanted bigger, more important moments in my life. I refocused on my dreams and goals and let go of the administrivia. I called the people I loved and made sure I wasn't "too busy" to see them. Often.

Buses will run and planes will fly without you when you're gone. Make sure that you live the life that you want to have lived by the time you're done.

Today's Affirmation: "I enjoy each and every minute of my blissful life!"

95

On Being Happy

"Very little is needed to make a happy life; it is all within yourself, in your way of thinking."

—Marcus Aurelius

As human beings are creatures of endless desire and hunger for betterment, it is our nature to always want to improve ourselves and our circumstances. This can be a positive force, motivating us onward to greater glorious goods for ourselves and for others. However, one can become lost in the constant search and craving for the next best thing, so trapped in future imaginings that we discount and ignore the accomplishments of the past evidenced in our present.

The art of happiness is an act of balance. We need to appreciate the process while we work within its creative ooze, the end result as yet unformed, like elements banging against each other in search of becoming sentient. As children playing with mud pies, the fun is in the making: baking in the golden sun, fingers sticky with mud-paint, grass-stained knees, brow wrinkled with concentration, searching for the perfect fine-grained dark earth to fashion into visionary pie. Day's end will come soon enough, no need to hurry to completion, for then the fun is over. Rejoice in the dreaming, glory in the doing, and let the dirt clods fall where they may.

Now, today, with your own mud-luscious imagined inventions, play with the ooze and be happy.

Today's Affirmation: "I am a rich child playing happily in Life's rich playground."

96
Love

"Where love is concerned, too much is not even enough."

—Pierre de Beaumarchais

It was the "Balance and Perspective" class—the seventh in my workshop series of eight classes. I had asked everyone to bring a testimonial letter that was written to them. A testimonial letter is any letter that describes how wonderful you are in glowing, specific terms. We were going to take turns reading each other's testimonial letters out loud.

A beautiful young couple, Donna and David, created a special moment for us. Donna had written a two-page letter to David, declaring all the beautiful things she loved about him. As he gave the letter to Donna to read aloud to him, we could see that the letter was worn and crimped from usage, having been read and reread many times over. He said that he carries the letter with him at all times, and reads it whenever things get tough.

As Donna began to read her letter, I told David to take every word in, that it was all true. Donna spoke passionately and with meaning; we could see the emotion welling up inside him until it spilled over in sparkling tears. (Do men know how beautiful they are when they cry?) He sat and listened to the woman he loved tell him how lovable he was and he cried unabashedly, with humility and grace. A blessed hush fell on the room as Donna's rich voice deepened with grateful tears of her own. We sat ensorcelled in our circle, breathless with wonder at the shared outpouring of love. Unwilling to break the spell, we quietly watched their embrace and held a moment more. No one spoke.

Tears streaming down my own face, I reached silently for the tissue box, and held it out to the loving couple. The noise of the tissue ripping from the box broke our fascination. With giggles and laughter everyone in the room got up to get one.

Love binds us in passionate threads of golden warmth, silver tears, and red-rimmed eyes. In the face of true love, openly expressed, we are all silent participants. We are changed. We are whole. We are one.

Have you written a love letter recently? Ever? Would you write one today?

Today's Affirmation: "I love and am loved. I am in the heart of everything."

97

Winning Through Service

"There is a wonderful mythical law of nature that the three things we crave most in life—happiness, freedom, and peace of mind —are always attained by giving them to someone else."

—Peyton Conway March

When I was a teenager, I belonged to a Masonic organization called Rainbow Girls. We had monthly meetings, wore formals, learned rituals and deportment, but the main *raison d'etre* was to be of service to the community. It was a team of dolphins. We held "dime-a-dip" dinners to raise money to donate to the homeless, car washes that raised money for crippled children, quilting bees to provide presents to the patients in the nursing home. We served as teacher's aides for special education classes in the summer and took baskets of food and toys to poor families at Christmas. And all the while we had fun, joy, and laughter while working to help others. The rewards we received far exceeded the gifts we gave.

Once a year, we joined a convocation of Rainbow Girls from across the state of California for "Grand Assembly." The culmination of the conference was the announcement of the new Grand Officers for the coming year, awarded to the Assemblies who had contributed the most to their communities, ending finally with the top office, Grand Worthy Advisor.

We knew we had worked hard and contributed much, yet we had not had a Grand Officer for several years. We were excited—we were due. Yet officer after officer was announced and we were passed by. We despaired. Finally, the last five top officers were being named. Dared we hope? But one by one they were announced and we were not chosen. No, not us, no, no again. Only one office remained. "Grand Worthy Advisor." We held our collective breath. Could it be us? Then we heard the magic words: we were chosen. We screamed, we cried, we jumped up on each other, pulled our hair and screamed some more. The top award was ours! We had done it! I still have the picture that was taken of us that day—it is all hands and arms, running mascara and shrieking open mouths of surprise and radiant joy.

Do you have a memory of such a win? If yes, it is one of the greatest treasures you possess. Take it out often and admire it as the priceless jewel it is. Revel in it again. If you do not own such a treasure, go create one, remembering that the first step in its creation is service to others.

Win through working, giving, loving, serving. Team wins are the most fun, because they are shared. Create a team of dolphins to win with. Introduce your children to a team of dolphins.

After all your money is made and all your toys enjoyed, the heart of life is in friendship and service.

Today's Affirmation: "I give generously to myself and to others and reap rich rewards!"

98
Appreciate Beautiful Things

"Think of all the beauty still left around you and be happy."

—Anne Frank

Feeling financially stress-free is a state of mind. We create this state through our thoughts, beliefs, attitudes, and feelings. If we are unconscious of this fact, our minds run by habit. Most of what we think every day is the same old news, endlessly repeated by the same old voices. We may want things around us to change, to improve our circumstances, to get more wealth, health, love, and happiness. But if we want our lives to change on the outside, we have to change on the inside. We must deliberately choose our thinking and decide before the fact that our bank account is, indeed, full.

The way to do this is to start appreciating the abundance that is all around you in the world, whether it is currently in your possession or not. Abundance is a flow of energy in constant motion around us. Admire the wonderful riches that exist everywhere and celebrate the fact that it is possible to create such glorious treasures. Each person who holds wealth is only its steward for a time. Understand this metaphysical truth: you cannot have what you envy another having. The energy of envy repels the object of its desire.

Rather, be joyful that beauty exists. I used to love to watch Princess Diana and all her wonderful designer clothes and jewels. She was tall and lovely and the image of a storybook princess. I didn't want to *be* her, nor did I envy her life with all its well-reported troubles. I was just glad that someone was doing the job of dressing up in fabulous outfits every day so that I could have the fun of watching.

When I visited London, I ogled the crown jewels at the Tower of London. They were amazing! Great pearls and rubies adorning crowns, emeralds and diamond scepters, gold and jeweled necklaces, rings, some very ancient. If there were no kings or royalty, these beautiful items would never have been made and they are so beautiful to behold. I'm glad that someone was rich enough to have been able to pay some wonderful artisans to design and painstakingly handcraft these fabulous creations, so I could enjoy looking at them.

There's so much of life you can enjoy, without having to own it. Admire something beautiful today, just for the pure sake of its existence.

Today's Affirmation: "I revel in all the wealth and joy that life has to offer!"

99
Lent

"Going to church does not make you a Christian any more than going to the garage makes you a car."

—Lawrence J. Peter

In the Christian religion, Lent is the approximately six-week period of fasting and penitence before Easter. In my youth, I remember my Catholic friends always "giving something up for Lent," but the concept of fasting never took root at my house. I wasn't very good at giving up things I liked, such as pecan pie, ice cream, parties, or movies. The idea of sacrifice completely eluded me.

As I grew older, I better understood the idea, yet still I resisted. If I give up chocolate for Lent, how does that benefit or glorify God? I didn't have the right attitude. Giving up chocolate just made me cranky.

I hit on a plan in the early nineties. I decided that instead of giving up some pleasure in my life for Lent, I would give up a bad habit. I was willing to sacrifice a personal failing, a character defect or flaw each year for at least six weeks. This may not be the spirit of what is meant by Lent, but it seemed to me that God would smile on this plan and perhaps appreciate my self-improvement program better than my doing without dessert. I hoped I would end up a better person instead of a thinner one.

So the first year, I gave up struggle. The next year, I gave up alcohol. The year after that, I gave up inappropriate men. In the following years I gave up criticism, vanity, complaining, envy, tiredness, stage fright, high heels, smoking. I tried to leave these burdens behind me forever, but shamefaced, I must confess I have returned to pick some of them up again. I am, after all, not St. Chellie. I am a work in progress.

Perhaps Lent is not relevant to you—then pick another period of the year in which to do the same thing. Yom Kippur, the New Year, Summer Solstice, your birthday—any day you select can mark the beginning of a six-week period of forging a better self from the ashes of your bad habits. Don't sacrifice the good things; they will all be laid on the altar of mortality eventually.

Sacrifice the little evils, the petty thievery, the unkind comments, panic attacks, despair. Give up jealousy, hatred, racism, profanity, hitting. Live without gossip, off-color remarks, jokes told at another's expense, fear-based decisions. These are the sacrifices that honor God and your fellow man.

Today's Affirmation: "I grow wealthier in spirit every day."

100

Free Drawing! Win Prizes!

"I am the greatest. I said that even before I knew I was."

—Muhammad Ali

When there is a door prize or a drawing for a free gift, do you usually win it?

Did one of the voices in your head just say, "Oh, I never win anything"? If so, that's the reason you're not winning. You have to *expect* to win.

I used to watch other people collecting their door prizes while I sat on the sidelines and never won any. Some people won multiple prizes, and I would hear the murmurs in the room as people turned to each other and said, "She's so lucky! She always wins something!"

As I worked on my affirmations, I noticed that when it came to winning door prizes, I wasn't doing a very good job of being positive. In fact, I was one of the people with a voice in my head that said, "I never win these things!" Well, seeing the problem is the first step in solving the problem, so I started doing new affirmations: "I am a winner," "I win often and I win big," "I win door prizes all the time," etc.

It wasn't long before I won a big basket of food, candy, and coffees at a luncheon. Pam, a good friend of mine who was also at the luncheon, shared her experience of this win with me. When the drawing was announced and the woman was reaching in the basket to pull out the winning ticket, she sighed, sat back in her chair and thought, "I don't win these things." But just as she had that thought, she happened to catch sight of me across the room. Pam said I was sitting up straighter in my chair, had a bright smile on my face, and looked like I expected to hear my name called. In a flash of understanding, she saw that the difference in our attitudes was creating the difference in our realities. She wasn't surprised when I won. She couldn't wait to tell me this story and find out what affirmations I was using. She started doing them herself, and a month later, won the door prize at the next luncheon!

Now when I hear the whispers, "She always wins!" they're talking about Pam and me.

And you?

Today's Affirmation: "I always win something, everywhere I go!"

101
Limited Thinking

*"As you go through life, brother, whatever be your goal;
keep your eye upon the doughnut and not on the hole."*

—sign at Pig 'N Whistle Coffee Shop

Most people never even begin to achieve their goals. They defeat themselves before they start by listening to that inner voice that tells them they can't do it. You have to learn to turn up the volume on the small inner voice that tells you that you're worthy, you're talented, and you can do anything you put your mind to.

When I was struggling to get work as an actress, the endless auditions, rejections, and the talent and sheer numbers of the competition sometimes overwhelmed me. One day when I was complaining to a friend about how hard it all was, he said, "Take out a piece of paper and write down all the reasons why you can't succeed as an actress." I agreed to do this and vented all my frustrations by making a very long list. Then he told me to write another list—all the reasons why I *should* succeed as an actress. I had a much more difficult time with this and didn't come up with many entries. He pointed to the positive list and said, "Until this list is longer than your negative list, you aren't going to succeed as an actress."

Like a sudden drenching in ice water, insulting, shocking, humiliating—it was a cold, bare statement of fact. I saw immediately that he was right, jolted into an awareness that my own negative convictions were keeping me from success. I vowed in that moment to start changing my focus and beliefs.

What are your inner voices telling you? Make your own list of positives and negatives. Focusing on what's wrong, what's missing, or what's not working will only produce more of that in your life. As I concentrated on my positive qualities instead of my limitations, I became more and more successful.

Madonna, in her movie *Truth or Dare*, had a scene where she was talking with two young people. She told them, "Sometimes I wonder 'Who the hell do you think you are?'...But I can't let myself think like that, or I'm gone."

You can't afford to think like that either.

Today's Affirmation: "I have all the reasons I need to be a terrific success at everything I do!"

102

I Am Blessed and I Am Thankful

"Great things are only possible with outrageous requests."

—Thea Alexander

That you are reading this book today is a testament to the vision, resilience, drive and determination of my wonderful agent, Lisa Hagan. Introduced through mutual friends, we took to each other immediately (My People!), signed a contract, and the search for the right publisher began. We emailed each other often along the way. There was interest, there were rejections, there were "yeah, buts." Once we had a publisher who said yes, we cheered and celebrated for four days. Then the deal fell through. We were crushed.

Lisa emailed me the next day:

"This week I was feeling a little blue about losing your sale and I went home one night and pulled the covers over my head and stayed there until the next morning. But I awoke in the middle of the night and I prayed and prayed for guidance. I walk to work each day one mile and I use that time to thank God for all my many blessings; sometimes I say affirmations. That day I used one of your affirmations: 'money comes to me from an unexpected source.' Well, it happened that very day I sold a book that I had thought I would never sell but I just kept trying. When I was saying my prayers of gratitude that night, I said the same affirmation and a royalty check came in from a company that hadn't been up to date in years. I thought, wow, well, I can't very well say the same affirmation again, can I? So I just thanked God for all that He has given me, all the blessings and love that is in my life...Well, today in the mail three more checks came for clients that the publishing house was two years behind in paying. Three days in a row! Once again I am blessed and thankful."

Change your attitude—change your experience. Turn it over to God. Works every time.

I was delighted with this story and yet couldn't help but notice that after two big successes with the affirmation, she thought "Wow, well, I can't very well say the same affirmation again, can I?" Isn't that just how we human beings work? We ask God for help, He gives it, then we get scared that we actually got what we asked for. Our prayers are powerful. But abundance makes us nervous.

I immediately flashed her back, saying, "Why not? It's working! Always keep doing what's working. You just got a little scared of your power. Keep it up!"

Lisa Lessons:

1. When life gets gray, pray for guidance.
2. When life gets great, pray your thanks.
3. An attitude of gratitude creates abundance.

Today's Affirmation: "Money is rushing to me from expected and unexpected places!"

103
Clarity

"I always wanted to be somebody. I can see now I should have been more specific."

—Lily Tomlin

Years ago, I heard this story:

One hot summer's day, a man was driving a truck down the road with a load of penguins in the back. Suddenly, his truck broke down. He got out, looked under the hood, and saw that he could fix the problem but it was going to take several hours. He was very concerned about the penguins being in the sun that long.

As he wondered what to do, he looked up and saw another truck coming down the road, and lo and behold—it was empty! Hopefully, he flagged down the other truck and explained his problem. He asked, "Could you please take these penguins to the zoo?" The other trucker agreed, loaded up the penguins in the back of his truck, and drove off.

The man worked on the repairs to his truck for about three hours, and was just about done when he saw the other trucker coming back down the road. But the penguins were still in the back of the truck! Only now, they were wearing sunglasses.

Very puzzled, he ran out in the road and flagged down the other trucker and said, "I thought I told you to take these penguins to the zoo!"

The other trucker said, "I did! And we had such a good time, now we're going to the beach!"

Today's Affirmation: "I see clearly what I desire and everyone I meet helps me create it."

104
Hawaiian Shirts

"A person will be called to account on Judgment Day for every permissible thing he might have enjoyed but did not."

—The Talmud

Financial stress reduction is as much about being relaxed and happy as it is about making a lot of money. Ideally, you want to be making more money and having more fun on a daily basis. Lack of either one creates stress and unhappiness.

A wealthy young stockbroker named Max, who had inherited money, took my financial workshop several years ago. Tense and unhappy when I talked with him on the phone, he seemed hesitant about attending the workshop, but agreed to come to the first class and see how he liked it. Although I instruct everyone to dress casually, he wore a suit and tie. He had a rather negative attitude, made skeptical comments, and sat in a closed position with his arms tightly crossed. It was clear to me he had an *attitude* and needed some help, but I wasn't sure I could reach him. However, by the end of the first class, he said he wanted to continue with the course.

During the second class, I ask each participant to share three opportunities and three obstacles they see facing them. Then, as a group, we offer each person creative suggestions for taking advantage of their opportunities or for solving their problems. When it came time for Max to share, a lot of anger came pouring out. Once again wearing a suit and tie, he had no opportunities on his list and about twelve obstacles. As he spoke, I saw that his need for financial stress reduction wasn't about money. He had that. What he didn't have was fun.

At that point, I jumped in and asked him, "Where is the fun in your life?" Totally taken aback, he just stared at me. I said, "Max, I'm giving you a special assignment for this week. You don't need to work on money—you have that. What I want is for you to do as many fun things as possible this week. Go to the beach for a day and just lie in the sun and swim. Go to a movie in the afternoon. Rent a hotel room for a night and take your wife out on the town. Whatever you think is fun, do it. The sky's the limit. Bring a list next week of all the fun you had to share with us."

As I spoke, he changed right in front of all our eyes. He started smiling. Then he grinned and blushed. He sat back in his chair and relaxed. Everyone applauded and envied his assignment.

He looked like a little kid at Christmas.

The next week, when he came to class with his "fun list," he was wearing a Hawaiian shirt and sandals! He wore a Hawaiian shirt to every class from then on—and a smile.

Make fun your priority today. Take a day off. Get yourself a Hawaiian shirt.

Today's Affirmation: "The more fun I have the more money I make!"

105

Providence Moves, Too!

"The moment one definitely commits oneself, then Providence moves, too. All sorts of things occur to help one that would never have otherwise occurred."

—Johann Wolfgang Von Goethe

Years ago, when I was working as the office manager for a small company, I wanted to buy a house with my fiancé. We didn't have any money saved for a down payment, and we didn't know how we could do it, but we set the goal anyway. Right after that, the company I worked for sponsored a class called Hypmovation—it was a combination of self-hypnosis and motivation. The goal-getting idea I got from them was to write a contract with yourself, identifying specifically what you wanted and by when. You were to describe in the contract the actions you would take to achieve the goal and then sign and date it. After that, you were to visualize the goal as a reality, and follow through by doing the actions you said you would do to accomplish the goal. I wrote that I would open a special savings account labeled "House Account" and save a specific amount of money every week plus any raises I received. I expected that it would take two years to save enough for a down payment on a house.

It only took six months. A surprising opportunity arrived that made home ownership a reality soon after declaring the goal. My fiancé and I were friends with another couple whose home had appreciated substantially in value. At dinner one night, they were talking about how they would like to buy more property, perhaps with another couple. Ka-ching! We told them that we were that "other couple" and the house hunt was on.

I had never thought about buying a house with partners. The idea presented itself because we had set a goal and were taking positive action to achieve it. Every day, we thought positive thoughts, visualizing owning our own home. Then we took action: We looked at real estate, talked to people, and educated ourselves. We counted our money, adding up the dollars that we saved every week in our "House Account." I got a raise...and then I got a house! I only owned 25 percent of my first home, but it was a start. When my fiancé and I broke up, I bought out his 25 percent interest in the property. When my partners and I sold it, I had a sizable down payment with which to buy a house on my own.

An attorney I knew wanted to own his own home. The home he wanted was in the $500,000 price range. He refused to settle for something smaller in order to get started. He didn't want partners. He didn't want a fixer-upper or a more distant location. He had "yeah, buts" for every suggestion.

That was fifteen years ago. He still doesn't own a home.

Write up a contract with yourself today. You don't need an attorney, but there will be binding arbitration if you fail to fulfill the terms of it. What would your penalty be? Fifteen more years without a house? Or a garden? Or a spouse? Or a career?

Today's Affirmation: "I am happily creating my own rich rewards!"

106

Shopping List

*"The more you can dream, the more you can do.
You are the one that can stretch your own horizon."*

—Max Steingard

Now my partners and I were shopping for a house. Our budget for this purpose was small. Therefore, in the Los Angeles area, we were looking in a fairly low price range. But I had a vision of the perfect house and it was a charmer.

I made a list of everything I wanted in our house:

1. Three bedrooms, two baths
2. A beautiful brick fireplace
3. Oozing with charm: beam ceilings, beautiful tiles, rounded archways
4. A living room and a den
5. A big airy kitchen with sunlight streaming through many windows
6. A large backyard with room to garden and lots of trees
7. A nice neighborhood
8. A swimming pool

Sheepishly, I handed my list to our real estate agent, Judy Washburn. Judy and her husband, Gary, were warm and friendly, a terrific couple who had helped my sister and her husband buy a house. But I was afraid she was going to tell us we couldn't possibly get all the things on my list in the price range we were looking at. I said I realized this was asking for a lot, but I needed her to know what I really wanted if we were going to be able to find a house that had at least some of the features on the list.

It was just a couple of weeks later that we were looking at some houses she had found, when we drove past a cute house with a for-sale sign on the front lawn. Judy couldn't find it in her lists, but went to the front door and asked if we could come in. The owners were home, and said, "Sure!" As we walked through this house, I got more and more excited. This house had everything on my list: Rounded archways in a Spanish style, burgundy and flowered tiles in bathroom and kitchen, a living room and a den. It didn't have a pool, but it had a large lot with ten orange trees on it and oh, I wanted it!

Within a month, the house was ours. When we finalized the purchase agreement, I reminded Judy about the list. She smiled as she shook her head in amazement.

"You were very lucky," she said. I agreed then. But now I know that I was following the path I was later to identify as 1) Think positive; 2) Send out ships; and 3) Count your money. It worked then and it works now.

What's on your list?

Today's Affirmation: "All my good is delivered to me now!"

107
Visualize Your Money

"The best way to reduce your bills is to put them on microfilm."

—Anonymous

Sophie, a talented writer, was between jobs. She was thinking creatively about what to do next—should she look for employment or start her own business? She was doing research considering her options, when she realized her current funds weren't going to cover her budget for the month. Anxiously, she thought about how she could create some additional income.

Years before, in wealthier times, Sophie had loaned a large sum of money to a friend, who was paying it back on an installment plan. For the past three years, this person had been making payments of $500 per month. In a flash, Sophie saw that this could be a source of additional revenue. She started to visualize the friend writing a check for $2,000 instead of $500. Every day for the next two weeks, Sophie said her affirmations, believed in her abundance, and visualized her friend writing a check to her for $2,000.

The check arrived. Sophie looked at the envelope, and held her breath as she tore it open. And there in her hands was a check for exactly $2,000.

(I told her to visualize $5,000 next month.)

And how much money do *you* want? Are you willing to believe it and affirm it daily? It's been said that faith can move mountains. It can move money, too.

Today's Affirmation: "I now receive large sums of money just for being me!" (Contributed by Christiane Schull)

108
Credit Card Interest Rates

"When I was born, I owed twelve dollars."

—George S. Kaufman

"Introductory offer—3.9 percent interest rate!" screams the envelope. It's another credit card solicitation. I add it to the pile I've been collecting, muffling the yell of the last offer of 5.9 percent. I must have forty of them now.

It's always interesting in my class when we start talking about credit card interest rates. People clamor to find out which credit card has the best terms. Should they switch their balances to a new card every time they get a new, lower offer? How can they make sure they notice when the interest rate balloons after the introductory period? Can they call their current card and get them to lower their interest rate?

I chuckle. All of this energy and attention is misplaced. They are treating the symptom and not the disease. The truth is if they pay off their balance every month, it won't matter what the interest rate is on the card. As long as it is a card that has a grace period and not one that charges interest from the date of your purchase, if you pay the bill in full when you get it, you won't owe one dime in interest.

Instead of "buy now, pay later," why not "save now, buy later"? If there is something you want, start saving for it. Then you earn the interest instead of paying the interest. What a concept! This is how they used to do it before the proliferation of credit cards and credit card debt enabled us to gorge ourselves on immediate gratification. Instead of worrying about which credit card has the best terms, spend your time and energy on how to get a job, get a raise, open a business, expand your business, and go for your goal. Watch your money making money in your bank account, your mutual fund or investment portfolio. You may just decide that's more fun than buying that new whatsit.

3.9 percent of zero is zero. 23.9 percent of zero is zero.

Any questions?

Leave home without it.

Today's Affirmation: "I love what a smart money manager I am!"

109

Sometimes It Helps to Know a Big Fish

"A bank is a place where they lend you an umbrella in fair weather and ask for it back again when it begins to rain."

—Robert Frost

Sometimes, when you're a little fish, you can get what you need by enlisting the support and help of a big fish.

After I graduated from college and got a job, I qualified to get my first credit card, a Bankamericard. (Those were the dark ages, before credit card companies found out how lucrative it was to give credit cards to students.) I used the card intermittently, and always made my payments on time. I had an excellent credit record.

When I got married three years later, I asked to have my husband's name added to my card. They immediately asked for me to turn in my credit card, telling me that I had to reapply for credit with my husband. (I told you those were the dark ages.) I dutifully filled out another application, along with my husband.

They denied our application.

They denied it on the basis that he was a free-lance actor, therefore self-employed, therefore without verifiable income. We were angry, but didn't know what we could do, until we saw a Bankamericard commercial on television, starring Dennis Weaver. Weaver, at the time, was the president of the Screen Actors Guild! Without further ado, we wrote a scathing letter to Mr. Weaver, telling him in no uncertain terms that we were very unhappy that the president of our union was supporting a company that denied credit to actors.

Within two days, we received a two-page letter from Dennis Weaver's attorneys. Attached was a copy of the letter they had sent to the Bank of America demanding that this matter be rectified. The day after that, I received a call from the president of the Bank of America, asking me what he could do to make me happy. I said he could send me a Bankamericard. You can bet I had one the next day. I wrote thank you notes to him, to Dennis Weaver, and to his attorneys.

You can have right on your side, but it helps to have might on your side, too. Is there a place in your life where you see injustice? Can you do something about it? Will you alone have enough resources to get the job done? Or do you need to enlist the support of someone else?

Walk softly, but know a big fish.

Today's Affirmation: "I have powerful supporters who help me accomplish great things!"

110

Men, Women, and Money

"I've figured out why first dates don't work any better than they do. It's because they often take place in restaurants. Women are weird and confused and unhappy about food, and men are weird and confused and unhappy about money. Yet off they go, the minute they meet, to where you use money to buy food."

—Adair Lara

The subject of money gets very sticky when it intrudes into relationships. Consumer Credit Counselors has stated that 50 percent of marriages end in divorce, and in 80 percent of the divorces, finances are a significant issue. In other days in other cultures, women did not own property, they *were* property. Nowadays, women are often a major contributor to the family income stream.

John Gray, in an article published in *Currency* entitled *Mars and Venus on a Budget*, wrote, "Shifting financial realities have had a huge and positive impact on how men and women are loving each other. I believe that the more involved a woman is with money, the more fully she participates in the relationship." In my opinion, the biggest problem is that everybody's talking about money in general, but nobody's talking about "my money" and "your money" specifically.

I regularly talk with couples who never had a discussion about finances before getting married. And since marriage, they haven't sat down and made a list of financial goals, or decided which goals have priority. Sometimes, years later, they discover that the love of their life is $50,000 in credit card debt—which now affects their own credit and lifestyle. Arguments erupt over whether to buy new carpeting for the house or take a ski trip for fun; invest in the stock market or put the cash in a money market account; make the car payment or the house payment. (A friend of mine once told me, "If it's a choice between making the car payment or the house payment, make the car payment." When I asked why, he said, "Because you can sleep in your car, but you can't drive your house to work.")

There need to be common financial goals in any relationship, business or personal, if you want the relationship to last. It requires honesty and openness about money in all areas: how it should be made, how it should be spent, and how it should be saved. Have this discussion with your significant other as soon as possible, make a written agreement and budget outlining your joint decisions, and have monthly updates to check the score.

Today's Affirmation: "My significant other and I make beautiful music—and money—together!"

111
Flexibility

"Money is better than poverty, if only for financial reasons."

—Woody Allen

The Rabbi said to my friend Shelley, "You shouldn't work so hard. You should be dating, meet a nice man, get married." Shelley is happily single and works hard because she wants to. A trifle annoyed at him for "shoulding" on her, she looked at him thoughtfully and inquired, "Are you offering to fix me up with someone?"

"Oh, well, I don't know," he replied, "What kind of a man are you looking for?"

Shelley answered, "He has to be 5'8," make $200,000 a year, and he has to be Jewish."

The Rabbi laughed. "Are you flexible about that?" he asked.

She thought a moment, then said sweetly, "Okay. He has to be 5'8," make $200,000 a year, and he *doesn't* have to be Jewish."

That was the last time the Rabbi mentioned dating to Shelley.

Today's Affirmation: "I create my life just the way I like it."

112

A Date at the Races

"No one has ever bet enough on a winning horse."

—Richard Sasurly

Even if you swim with dolphins, it's best if you swim in the same direction. It's hard to build relationships with people who are financially invested in projects diametrically opposed to yours. Let me tell you about my date with Steve.

Steve and I had a date to go to the races. I had never been to the horse races before, and was excited about going. Before the race, we sat down in the kitchen and picked our horses from the program. Steve was clearly an experienced handicapper, looking over the horses, jockeys, their experience, and the odds on each race. Knowing nothing, I just looked at all the names and picked the ones that sounded or felt good or just "grabbed me" in some way. Rolling his eyes, Steve snorted his contempt for my methods, but laughingly said, "Well, you'll probably have beginner's luck and win."

How prophetic of him. As I put my meager two-dollar bets on my horses, Steve made much bigger bets on his. Of course mine won. Race after race, I screamed with excitement and joy while Steve morosely tore up his losing tickets. He littered the ground in front of him with the remnants of his losses as I joyfully ran off to collect my winnings.

The date was not going well.

The ninth and last race arrived. Steve buried his face in the race form, then looked up at me and asked, "What horse did you pick in the ninth?" I'll never forget the name of this horse: Azalia Adios. When I told him the name, Steve brightened, looked again at his racing form, and said, "I think you've finally picked a good horse!" He bet all his remaining money on this horse coming in first place, while I upped my bet to four dollars. As we waited with excited anticipation, finally having bet on the same horse, I knew we had more than money riding on this race.

Azalia Adios was out of the gate fast. He took fourth position and held it until the straightaway, when he pulled out in front of all the other horses! First place! We won! Steve made back all of his losses and then some. Whew. The date ended on a high note after all.

The morals of this story are:

1. Not every great horse will win the race.
2. Not every mediocre horse will lose the race.
3. But if you go to the races with a date, bet on the same horse!

Today's Affirmation: "Money flows to me easily and effortlessly, waking, and sleeping!"

113

The Power of "No"

"You can say no and smile only when you have a bigger yes burning inside of you."

—Anonymous

I once worked for two titans of the motion picture industry, Edgar Scherick and Scott Rudin. Edgar was the older, more experienced mogul and Scott was the up-and-coming young counterpart. At the time, I was pursuing a career behind the camera in the motion picture industry and was Edgar's Executive Assistant.

One day, they fired the office gofer (you know, "go fer" this and "go fer" that.) They weren't going to hire a new one, and the rest of us in the office were anxious about who was going to get the schlepping assignments from then on.

I decided that it wasn't going to be me. I was reading a great book at the time, *When I Say "No" I Feel Guilty* by Manuel Smith. Smith gave wonderful tools for being more assertive and less of a people-pleaser. I knew that if I started doing some of the gofer's tasks, I would be doomed to that position and respect for me would disappear along with any dreams of advancement. I realized that if I was asked to do this work and refused, I might get fired. But if the price of working there was that I had to be in the lowest dead-end job, then I shouldn't be there anyway.

Several days later, Scott and Edgar had a meeting at MGM. Scott always drove the two of them to these meetings, and the gofer would pick up Edgar after the meeting and take him to his next appointment. Edgar knew someone new had to be given this assignment, but didn't choose anyone. He just walked out of the office saying, "Somebody's going to have to pick me up at five o'clock at MGM." The entire staff froze.

Scott knew then that he had to pick the new gofer. He turned around, saw me and said, "Chellie, pick Edgar up at five o'clock at MGM."

My heart pounding, my throat dry, I looked him straight in the eye and said, "No." Nothing else, just "no." (The book said not to give your reasons for saying no, or the conversation would degenerate into an argument over the validity of your reasons.)

He was totally taken aback by this and laughed. He said, "You have to! Pick Edgar up at 5:00!"

I said, no again. (Smith calls this technique "broken record"—just repeat your position.)

He stared at me for a long moment. I could see the wheels turning in his mind. I held my breath. Was I going to be fired?

Then Scott turned to the young man seated near him and said, "Fine. Then you do it." He said, "Okay," and became the office gofer from then on.

We have more power of "no" than we know. Two-year-olds know this instinctively, but some adults have forgotten. Find a two-year-old and remember. Then practice.

Today's Affirmation: "I make choices that make me happy."

114

No Moxie, No Money

"There's no substitute for guts."

—Paul "Bear" Bryant

No guts, no glory.

No courage, no cash.

No moxie, no money.

You won't make any money by waiting around for people to give you some. That's not how it works. You have to go get it. What would your life be like if only you had the guts to go get what you really wanted?

Rewrite the story of your life from the point of view of someone with a lot of moxie. What would that person have done differently? What risks would they have taken that you didn't? Why didn't you take them? Because of who wouldn't approve or like you?

Here's a newsflash: They probably don't approve or like you anyway. So get up, get out, and go do what you want!

Today's Affirmation: "I have all the moxie I need to make all the money I want."

115

Your Money

"What is not yours always chirps for its master."

—Spanish proverb

Your money is Your Money. You can't lose money that's yours and you can't get money that isn't yours.

It might *appear* that you can. Someone breaks into your house and steals your jewelry, your stereo, television, and other things you bought and paid for. It certainly looks like you've lost money that's yours. And it definitely looks like the thief got money and items that weren't his.

But that is only in the short term. If you take a longer view, you will find that you always replace the stolen items. Maybe you had insurance that replaced everything for you. Or someone gives you a television they don't need anymore. Or you get a raise, a promotion, or a new job that pays you more money. The money that was taken from you has been replaced because it was Your Money.

For a little while, it may look like the thief got money that wasn't theirs. But they don't hold on to it for long. They might survive a few weeks or months on ill-gotten gains, but there is no lasting success there. The money will dissipate. They will lose their money and possessions to rivals, to drugs, or to their own incompetence to manifest their own money through honest efforts. They often end up getting caught and serving time in prison. There is no road to wealth there. They will always pay a price for taking money that isn't theirs. The universe is quite skilled at taking it back from them.

If you ever seem to lose money, feel confident that the money will be replaced. It may not come through the expected channels, but it will turn up. The person who owes you money who doesn't pay you will pay somebody. And the money you are owed will be returned to you. Anger and resentment towards your debtors just makes *you* unhappy. So forgive your debtors and be happy in anticipation of the return of Your Money. It's on its way to you today. If you know in your heart you owe someone else money, start paying them today. Your higher self will honor your integrity and more money will start flowing to you in your life. You can't lose.

Today's Affirmation: "My Money is pouring into my life today from all directions!"

116

The Ballad of Love and Money

"In the kingdom of hope there is no winter."

—Russian proverb

Once upon a time in the Land of Milk and Honey, Love and Money lived together in peace and harmony, spreading joy and riches everywhere they went. Everyone in the country was rich, inside and out. In the natural order of things, Love and Money had many children: Kindness, Beauty, Appreciation, Generosity, Creativity, Grace, and Focus. They, too, bestowed their gifts on the people, who treasured them in return.

The evil Witch of Lack and Lamentation hated the Land of Milk and Honey. She was invisible there. She cursed and screamed and jumped up and down but people just walked past her smiling. You can imagine how frustrating this was. She gnashed her teeth whenever she thought about Love and Money. "How dare they banish me from their kingdom!" she cried. "I haven't been able to give away a poisoned apple there in decades!"

She fumed over the situation with a black heart, but couldn't figure out how to get the people of the Land of Milk and Honey to see her. Frustrated, she called a conference of her friends Anger, Envy, Lust, Greed, Sloth, Despair, and Poverty to discuss the problem. But they were invisible there, too. The meeting was disintegrating into fights and arguments, when a quiet voice at the back of the room broke in. "I can help you," said Distraction. "I am only sometimes visible there, but if we await the right opportunities, we can strike the people together."

And so they did. Distraction waited in the streets of the Land of Milk and Honey for the children of Love and Money. When Kindness stubbed his toe and yelled "Ouch!" Distraction introduced him to Anger. When Beauty bumped into a prettier girl, he presented her to Envy. When Appreciation accidentally caught sight of a woman bathing in the lake, Distraction brought over Lust. He introduced Generosity to Greed, Creativity to Sloth and Grace to Despair. And suddenly the Witch of Lack and Lamentation was visible all over town. Unable to cope with their children's turmoil, Love and Money got divorced and went their separate ways.

But try as he might, Distraction was never able to introduce Focus to Poverty. They screamed and yelled, threw stones and rolled in the dust at his feet, but Focus refused to look at them. "I have no thought to spare for you!" Focus cried. "I'm busy with dreams and goals I want to pursue!" Focus started an Internet business, milkandhoney.com, to distribute food and drink to the masses, employed all his brothers and sisters, and retired a billionaire to his castle on the hill. At Focus's home, Love and Money were reconciled, and they all lived happily ever after.

Today's Affirmation: "The more I focus on success, the more love and money are mine!"

117

Distractions

"Writing is like anything else. You fall, you pick yourself up, and you try again. When you're discouraged, you eat ice cream."

—Anna Quindlen

It's time to write now. I'm going to write. I stare at the blank page. Blank page. White. Snow. Weather. I wonder what the weather's doing today. Cold. My hands are cold. Think I'll go downstairs and get a cup of coffee to warm up my hands. Trudge, trudge down the rust carpeted steps, click, click, click my shoes tap on the kitchen tiles. Make coffee. Look around kitchen. Notice dishes and dirt—no fun, ignore. Notice newspaper—ahhh, maybe something interesting to write about in the newspaper. A good activity, research. Valuable. I'll do that.

Thirty minutes later: feeling too guilty to continue reading paper. I should be writing! Back to the stairs, click, click, back up the stairs trudge, trudge. Blank page.

The phone rings! Saved by the bell! Hello? No, thanks, I don't want to change my long distance carrier. Disappointment. Phone in hand, I want to talk to somebody. Who'd be fun to talk to? I know, I'll call my friend, Carol. Nope, she's not home, how about Susan? Hey, Susan, how's doin'?

Forty-five minutes later: lunch time! Trudge, trudge, click, click. Look over refrigerator selections, put together fine luncheon for one, turn on the television, surf and munch.

One hour twenty minutes later: Click, click, trudge, trudge. Blank page.

I'll never make any money this way! I've got to get busy and write so I can make money and pay my bills...I wonder how my bank balance is doing. Do I have enough to pay the bills this month? Oops, I haven't reconciled my bank statement yet, better do that. Better update my budget, too, while I'm at it...Where is that bank statement? somewhere under this pile of paperwork. I should do this paperwork. I've got to get organized, then I can write....

Two hours later: blank page. Oh, it's almost time for *Oprah*!

One hour later: where did the day go? Well, I got some bookkeeping done, made some phone calls, did some research, got organized.

Tomorrow I'll be ready to write.

Does this sound familiar? Does it accurately depict some of your afternoons—or days? Sure, once in a while, we're going to have an off day, a day when no inspiration comes, when nothing works. One of two things is usually going on: you're avoiding something, or you're creating on the subconscious level instead of the conscious. If you're avoiding something—look at it now and handle it. If your creativity is cooking subconsciously and needs more time before you take it out of the oven, give yourself a break. Inspiration will probably wake you up later. Be ready for it when it comes.

Today's Affirmation: "I am inspired by my creative vision every day!"

118

The Spinning Plates

"Do one thing at a time and do that one thing as if your life depended upon it."

—Eugene Grace

Robert, the doctor, had more energy than a power plant. He was excited and had a million goals. The problem was that his energy was too scattered. It's fine to have a lot of goals, but it's really difficult to try to get them all at once. You really can't start four businesses at the same time and have them all be wildly successful. Robert wanted to build his medical practice, enroll and teach three different seminars, be a professional organizer, and start a new networking group.

It was too much. He was running into difficulties at the networking meetings he was attending. He only had thirty seconds to introduce himself and he was trying to talk about all four businesses in that short time. Not only was this ineffective, but it actually worked against him because it made people doubt his credibility in any of the businesses. When I need a doctor, I want a doctor who is a full-time dedicated health practitioner, who eats, sleeps, walks, talks, breathes healing, not someone who is thinking about three other businesses at the same time.

The same thing is true if you have too many projects in the works at the same time. It is difficult to split your focus and maintain the energy level needed to bring all the projects to fruition. You need to set priorities on your goals and concentrate on the most important "A" goal first. If you are interested in having more than one business, the best way to proceed is to get one business up and running well, then add personnel to maintain the business. Then you can allocate some of your time to starting up the next business.

It's like the circus performer who spins many plates on top of tall sticks. He doesn't start all the plates spinning at once—he starts with one plate, gets it spinning on the stick, then starts spinning the second plate. All the attention the first plate needs is a small touch once in a while to keep it spinning. Then he starts the third plate, while the first and second are spinning along fine, needing just a touch now and then. Then the fourth plate, the fifth and so on, until he has many plates spinning at the same time. He never tries to start spinning all the plates at the same time and he can't ever totally ignore the plates that are already spinning. Otherwise, he'll get a lot of broken plates!

What is your number one, best, fine-china plate? Set it spinning.

Today's Affirmation: "I focus my abundant energy and produce extraordinary results!"

119
Structure and Discipline

"Everybody is creative and everybody is talented. I just don't think everybody is disciplined. That's a rare commodity."

—Al Hirschfeld

A friend of mine once met Al Hirschfeld for lunch and had a wonderful visit with him. He remembers that at precisely one o'clock, Hirschfeld looked at his watch, and excused himself to go back to work. His discipline supported him to become a successful, famous artist.

What is the structure and discipline that supports your work? I always tell people that the workshop business is a very simple business supported by three basic activities:

1. I network and speak in order to meet lots of people = Marketing the service
2. I follow up with the people I met = Selling the service
3. I teach the workshop = Providing the service

These are the ships that I send out. If my activities each week consist mainly of these three items, I know I will be successful and each workshop will be full. Everything else I do is basically support "administrivia." But I can't allow myself to get lost in the paperwork shuffle. Paperwork is just an avoidance technique.

Focus on the activities that bring you the money. Find your structure and the discipline to work it. For me, "The money is in the phone"—where is your money?

Today's Affirmation: "Easily and effortlessly, my discipline supports my success!"

120
Do What Makes Money First

"If you want to leave footprints in the sands of time, wear work boots."

—Anonymous

I have three rules for making money:

1. Do what makes money now.
2. Do what makes money soon.
3. Do what makes money later.

This is of primary importance if you are in sales or own your own business (then you're in sales too). The primary responsibility of a business is to be profitable and the primary responsibility of a salesperson is to bring in the money. Without sales, there is no money. If there is no money, there will be no business.

You need immediate money to survive. It's no good spending all your time working on the big project that won't materialize for a year if you don't have the money to survive until that big deal comes through. It's okay to be building the big battleship, but you'd better make sure you have lots of little canoes going out in the meantime. On a weekly basis, I suggest spending 60 percent of your time on your daily bread and butter sales, 20 percent on mid-range sales, and 20 percent on the big deal that may take a long time to close.

Do what makes money first. Everything else can wait.

Today's Affirmation: "I am richly paid for the fun work I do!"

121

The Wishing-Hoping-Waiting Game

"Waiting until everything is perfect before making a move is like waiting to start a trip until all the traffic lights are green."

—Karen Ireland

John had a big ship out there, sailing the ocean with all of his dreams aboard.

Just one problem: just one ship.

We met for lunch one afternoon and he explained his situation. He had a fabulous idea for a product. I thought it was great. So did the major corporation that had received his proposal.

But now the deal was stalled and John was running out of money.

"What other corporations have you talked to?" I inquired.

John looked at me, surprised. "Well, none, of course," he said, matter-of-factly.

"Why ever not?" I exclaimed.

"But this corporation has said they're interested!" he protested. "It would be unethical of me to go to someone else!"

"John, have they paid you any money?"

"No."

"Have they signed a contract with you?"

"No."

"Have they told you when they're going to pay you or sign you?"

"No."

"Then there is no agreement, no contract, and you are not ethically bound to them in any way. What you need to do is contact many corporations and get as much interest in your project as possible. If this corporation thinks they might lose the deal to another company, they will take action. But now they have no reason to put this deal at the top of their priority list."

John understood it then. He had put a lot of work into finding a company that was interested. He didn't want to keep working that hard to find more companies that might buy his idea. It was easier to hope that this deal would pan out. He got caught in the "wishing-hoping-waiting game." He needed to keep on sending out ships, or he could starve waiting for that one to come in. One is not enough.

Get another ship in the water.

Today's Affirmation: "I have an ocean full of ships that are bringing me money today!"

122

Feast or Famine

"Winning is not a sometime thing—it's an all the time thing. You don't win once in a while; you don't do things right once in a while; you do them right all the time."

—Vince Lombardi

People often ask me, "How long do I have to send out ships?" I answer, "How long do you want to eat?"

You can't ever stop sending out ships. The Universe, that big "Yes" machine, gets confused if you do. It thinks you don't want any more good to come into your harbor, so it stops sending ships in if you stop sending ships out.

For example, let's say you are madly sending ships out every day. You're working in the flow on a daily basis. You send out ships—then send out more ships. The next day, even more ships. Every so often, you check the horizon for ships coming in. But no ships. So, you go back to work sending out more ships. Again you check the horizon: No ships. You send out ships, send out ships, check the horizon: No ships.

Don't get depressed—get angry! You've been doing your part. You've said your affirmations every day, you've been taking positive action and you *deserve* to have a return on your investment. Now, *demand* your good from the Universe.

And the Universe sends it. All of a sudden, the Spanish Armada, the Royal Navy, the Merchant Mariners and America's Cup ships are sailing into your harbor. And you are feasting! "Oh my God," you might think in shock. "How am I ever going to unload all these ships?!" Then you'll want to slam on the brakes and stop sending out ships so you can unload the ships that came in. The Universe gets the message not to send any more ships into your harbor, shrugs and says, "Okay."

Meanwhile, you are frantically unloading ships and finally, you unload the last one. "Whew!" you exclaim. "That was a lot of work!" After a moment's respite, you look around at the empty harbor and say, "Where are my ships?" You tell the Universe, "I'm ready for more ships now!" But the Universe has been sending ships into somebody else's harbor. You haven't been sending any out—there aren't any ships in the pipeline. So you have to start all over again, building the ships, hiring the crew, storing provisions, and setting the ships a-sail. During this time, there are no ships sailing into your harbor—famine.

The lessons of feast or famine are:

1. Send out ships every day.
2. When a lot of ships come in at once, hire a crew to help you unload.
3. Send out ships every day.

Today's Affirmation: "A lot more money is coming to me today—and I deserve it!"

123
Pharaoh's Dream

"Remember that there is nothing stable in human affairs; therefore avoid undue elation in prosperity, or undue depression in adversity."

—Socrates

You might remember the story of Joseph in the Bible, how he was sold into slavery by his brothers and taken to Egypt. After his misadventures with Potiphar's wife, he was thrown into prison. But there he was discovered to have a talent for interpreting dreams. After several amazing interpretations, which later came true, word of his special talent eventually spread to the palace.

The Pharaoh had been having a terrible recurring dream. In this dream, he saw seven fat cows feeding in the grass, but then seven gaunt and starving cows came up after them and ate them. He also saw seven healthy ears of wheat, but they, like the cows, were swallowed up by seven ears that were withered and blighted. The Pharaoh was very disturbed. He felt a portent of doom was being shown to him, but he didn't know what it meant. When he heard about Joseph's ability to interpret dreams, he sent for him immediately.

Joseph had only to hear the Pharaoh tell the story and he knew what was afoot. He explained to the Pharaoh that the dream foretold seven years of plenty followed by seven years of famine and advised the Pharaoh to take one-fifth of the bounty from the first seven years and store it away against the need in the second seven years.

Even in ancient Egypt you had to budget—and save for a rainy day (or drought, as the case might be). Nothing much has changed. We regularly have economic expansions, followed by recessions. Yet we don't seem to store 20 percent of our grain for the lean years. We use credit cards—even when the economy is booming. During the economic expansion from 1995 to 1999, *Newsweek* reported, consumer debt rose 34 percent to about $6.2 trillion. If you go into debt during the fat years, who is storing grain for the lean years?

Today's Affirmation: "I am a wonderful saver and investor, and store up plenty during plentiful times!"

124

To Save or Not to Save?

"A deficit is what you have when you haven't got as much as you had when you had nothing."

—Gerald F. Lieberman

People with debts often ask me if they should pay them all off before starting to save money for the future. Most financial planners and accountants point to the fact that it's not financially smart to be saving money and only earning 5 to 8 percent on the money when you could reduce debt that is costing you 15 to 25 percent. This certainly makes mathematical sense.

But mathematical sense is not the only thing that should be considered here. Human beings are complex creatures, and habit and emotions play a significant role in behavior.

Studies repeatedly show that Americans don't save much of their income. Consumer spending accounts for two-thirds of the economy, and consumer debt continues to rise. The endemic habit is to spend a lot, save a little, and go deeper in debt. To change this habit, new behavior is required. So my suggestion is to start saving now, even if you are in debt, because you need to begin the savings habit. It may take you longer and cost you additional interest to do it this way, but in the long run you will profit from it.

For example, let's say you have a five-year plan to pay off debt. You use all available cash to pay the debt and don't save anything. Three years later, you are still a person with debt and no savings. Most people feel frustrated and stressed because they have no savings to make them feel prosperous and they still have debt that makes them feel poor. The light at the end of the tunnel looks too far away and too hard to reach. It is often at this point that people will incur more debt to buy something to make them feel better. The habit of debt is reinforced once more. And saving money becomes an ever more distant, unreachable goal.

If, on the other hand, you pay off debt more slowly and save money at the same time, three years later you may still be a person with some debt, but you're a person with savings, too. This will make you feel much more abundant. Every month, your debt goes down and your savings go up. You feel better and better about yourself and your prosperity. And most importantly, you are establishing for yourself the habit of saving. One day, the debt will be gone and you can take the monthly payment you've been making on the debt and add it to your monthly savings. Since the habit of saving has already been established and reinforced, it will be easy to increase the amount you're saving. As your power over money improves, your feelings of self-worth will rise along with your net worth.

Go directly to your wallet. Close your eyes, reach in, and take out a bill. Whether it's a five, a ten, a twenty, a hundred, or a one, that's the start of your savings plan today. Congratulations! Then do it again tomorrow.

Today's Affirmation: "I save money happily and responsibly!"

125

Patience

"I waited and waited, and when no message came, I knew it must be from you."

—Ashleigh Brilliant

Patience.
I am patient.
I *am patient.*
I am P-A-T-I-E-N-T.
"He also serves who only stands and waits."
I can wait my turn.
I can W-A-I-T.
I have patience.
God has three answers to prayers:
"Yes," "Not now," and "I have something better for you."
Of the three, "Not now" is the toughest one.
Not now. Okay.
WHEN?
"Good things come to him who waits."
I am waiting.
AAAARRRRGGGGHHHHH!
WAIT.
Wait.
Wait.

Sometimes it seems, when we've been sending out a lot of ships, but none are coming in, that all our dreams are on the "slow boat to China." Don't lose faith; don't lose hope. The ships are sailing; you just can't see them. If they're not in sight yet, it's because they're not supposed to be. This is the process by which human beings develop patience, faith, and trust. All things are working together for your good.

You are in charge of sending ships out. You are not in charge of when they come in.

Today's Affirmation: "All things seen and unseen are working for my good."

126

Let Go, Let God

"Good morning. This is God. I will be handling all your problems today. I will not need your help. So, have a good day."

—Anonymous

I was stamping my foot and moaning about my life when my friend, Jennifer, reminded me that there was only so much I could do to make my dreams come to pass. Then I had to relax and let God take over. A hard lesson, that. Jennifer then repeated this poem to me, which I never forgot:

As children bring their broken toys
With tears for us to mend,
I brought my broken dreams to God,
Because He was my friend.
But then instead of leaving Him
In peace to work alone,
I hung around and tried to help,
With ways that were my own.
At last I snatched them back and cried,
"How can you be so slow?"
"My child," He said, "What could I do?
You never did let go!"—Unknown

So much in life is a matter of timing. The sun comes up at dawn, not before. The ship sails on the tide, not before. I have to do all that I can do, then let go and let God. As Marianne Williamson says, "His ways aren't all that mysterious."

God knows what time it is. You're on His schedule. Trust.

Today's Affirmation: "I live in buoyant assurance of my continuing abundance!"

127
Perspective

"Once the game is over, the king and the pawn go back in the same box."

—Italian proverb

One afternoon, I was complaining about all of my problems to a friend as we milled with a group, waiting for a meeting to begin. She listened patiently to me whining for about five minutes, and then she had had enough.

"Excuse me!" she said loudly. I froze in my tracks.

"Did you eat today?" she asked.

"Yes," I said, not understanding why she was asking this question.

"Do you have a place to sleep tonight?" she continued, looking at me coldly.

Now I was getting the picture. "Yes," I said sheepishly.

"And do you have a car to drive you to that place you're going to sleep tonight?" she demanded.

I was dead meat now and I knew it. "Yes," I whined.

"And is that car a *Mercedes*?"

"Uhhh..." I was inarticulate with embarrassment.

"Then shut up!" she exclaimed.

We stared at each other for a moment and then we both laughed. "Thanks, Sandy," I said. "Message received."

I thought about this at the memorial service for my friend, Tom. Tom was happily married to Barbara for many years when his diabetes took a turn for the worse. First one leg had to be amputated, then later, the other. A wonderful role model and mentor, his motto was "No sniveling." At the service, Barbara said that after the loss of his legs, when someone would whine in his presence, he'd say with a twinkle in his eyes, "Oh? Cut off both your legs and then come talk to me." That pretty much shut everybody up.

And what are *you* complaining about? Take another look. Chances are, if that is the worst problem you have, your life is pretty good.

No sniveling.

Today's Affirmation: "I take time to be happy—and to know that I am."

128

Go for the Underlying Value

"If a man is called to be a streetsweeper, he should sweep streets even as Michelangelo painted, or Beethoven played music, or Shakespeare wrote poetry. He should sweep streets so well that all the hosts of heaven and earth will pause to say, here lived a great streetsweeper who did his job well."

—Martin Luther King, Jr.

For many years I had studied acting, gotten my B.A. Degree in Dramatic Art, and made the trek to Hollywood as countless thousands before me. I got my Equity card performing in *Hello, Dolly!* with Martha Rae, my SAG card in *The Time of Your Life* with James Whitmore, and did odds and ends of dinner theaters, commercials, and Disneyland. Though even minor stardom eluded me, I enjoyed my creative pursuit of the dream.

In between acting jobs, I took secretarial jobs to pay the bills—luckily, during one summer school session, my mother had said, "Learn to type, honey!" Each time a show closed, I'd call the employment agency and they'd send me on my next temporary assignment. One fateful day in September, a play I was in closed when the backers ran out of money. The temporary secretarial assignment was supposed to last for two weeks.

I was there for four years. The catch was they kept promoting me. With every promotion, I got more involved with the company and my coworkers, my skills improved and I discovered a love for the creative side of business. I found myself turning auditions—and then parts—down. I had clearly come to a crisis about what work I was meant to do.

Agonizing over my choices, I called my friend, Gaye Kruger. She asked me what I loved about acting. I said I loved being creative, the fun I had with the other actors, the applause and acknowledgment, the money, and feeling important. She asked me what I loved about my office job. I said I loved being creative, the fun I had with my co-workers, the praise and acknowledgment, the money, and feeling important. She said, "It's the same list. Go for the underlying value. You have everything you want where you are now." She was right. The ruby slippers were on my feet and everything I wanted was in my own backyard. I never acted again.

And never missed it, either.

What are the underlying values in your life and work?

Today's Affirmation: "All my desires are worthy and I always get everything I desire."

129

Programming

"I forgive myself for having believed for so long that I was never good enough to have, get, be what I wanted."

—Ceanne DeRohan

From the moment of birth, our programming starts. Our parents tell us things over and over as we grow. We inculcate their opinions, beliefs, and emotions until they are almost ritualized. Like Pavlov's dog, we salivate when the bell rings, whether or not there is food on the table. A look, a word, triggers automatic response. We don't choose our response; it is programmed. The word is spoken or the body tenses or the angry look pierces us, and the CD goes in the slot and the record plays. We are unconscious; therefore we are helpless. We are our programming.

As we grow, we begin to learn that we can change the programming. We can put on a different CD. The search begins for the recording we want to hear. We go to college, seminars, psychotherapists; we read and study books, we discuss our search with groups of like-minded friends.

But if we don't give the new programming enough repetition, enough time, we fail to overcome the original input. The original CD may be harsh, loud, out-of-tune, and play with a constant boom and thud in the background, like a neighbor's over-amplified bass blaring their rock music. We give up in despair, surrendering to the thought "I was born this way. I can't change. It's just the way I am."

Have faith! You will succeed. Newly programmed thoughts take time to marinate throughout your being. Habits are changed over time, with attention paid; consistent application of the new process, constant playing of the new CD will have its end result in new thoughts, new actions, and new results.

In the play *Ondine* by Jean Giradoux, the title character—a water nymph—has been betrayed by her human husband, Hans. Their doom is that he shall die, and she will return to the sea and forget him. But Ondine tells him that she will not forget; she has taken her precautions: "You used to laugh at me when I made the same movements in your house. You said I counted my steps. It was true. It was because I always knew the day would come when I would have to go back. And now, in the depths of the Rhine or the ocean, without knowing why, I shall go on making the same movements that I made when I lived with you. When I plunge to the bottom, I shall be going to the cellar. When I rise to the surface, I shall be going to the attic. In this way, I shall be true to you always."

You, too, are being true to a pattern, a habit of thought and movement. The one you were programmed with—or the one you chose. Which CD are you playing?

Today's Affirmation: "I choose to be rich and happy and all my actions are in harmony with my choice."

130

Expand Your Income Horizons

"Every morning I get up and look through Forbes' *list of the richest people in America. If I'm not there, I go to work."*

—Robert Orben

Many years later, I had the opportunity to return the favor to my friend, Gaye, who had helped me define the underlying values that were important to me in my work. She had owned her own business for several years, doing advertising specialties out of her home. She arranged for companies to have gift items printed with their logos on them. It was a nice little business, but emphasis on the "little" nature of her business kept her from realizing most of her material dreams.

When she came to the *Financial Stress Reduction® Workshop*, Gaye wanted to change the way she was doing business and make a quantum leap in her income. Working alone out of her home, she had a six-figure annual gross income, but because of the high cost of goods sold, her net was very small. Gaye was having trouble making ends meet. She cried on my shoulder as she told me she had to borrow money to fix her old, broken car. As we worked together, she saw that she really enjoyed the creative and sales part of her business, but disliked the administrative and fulfillment tasks. It was fun for her to devise a marketing item for a client, to get just the right jacket design, color, material, and logo within the budget specified. She loved the meeting, greeting, and schmoozing with clients and potential customers, but running around buying materials, calling manufacturers, shipping, typing letters, invoicing, and bookkeeping she loathed.

We came to the conclusion that the best of all possible worlds for her would be to merge her business with a larger company in her field, and to take a position with them in which she had responsibility only for creative ideas and sales. The ideal company would have many staff people who would handle the other administrative tasks. Within two months of making this decision, Gaye had her new position with a major, multi-million dollar company.

"Chellie, it's amazing!" she called me to report. "I had no idea what was possible to do in this industry! When I was in business for myself, I was happy to get a $3,000 order. But here people are writing $300,000 orders! I ask them if I can stand by them and watch while they write up these $300,000 orders because I'm hoping it will rub off!"

It did. The next year, she wrote nearly $2,000,000 worth of orders, bought a new car and her dream home in the hills.

Owning your own business is not always the best of all possible worlds. Maybe you can find a job where they pay you to do just the fun things you *like* doing. Who do you know who's doing that? Copy them. Or be the first one on your block to do it.

Change your mind. Change your job. Change your money. Change your life.

Today's Affirmation: "I expand my knowledge and ability to manifest riches every day!"

131

Show Me the Money!

"The world isn't interested in the storms you encountered, but whether or not you brought in the ship."

—Raul Armesto

"Show me the money!" is that great expression from the movie *Jerry Maguire*. Cuba Gooding, Jr. plays a football player who keeps asking Tom Cruise as his agent to get him a multi-million dollar contract. He was enthusiastic, positive, powerful, and single-mindedly devoted to his purpose. He got the money.

Business is like a football game and money is the scorecard. A good business may have many goals, but the primary goal of making money must be achieved or it won't be in business for long. Just as the players in a football game need to know the score in order to know whether to run for a touchdown or kick a field goal, a business owner must know the money score at all times to ensure the success of the business. It's helpful if all the players on the team know the score, too, and not just the quarterback!

One of the news shows on television once ran a story about a company that made a different employee the chief financial officer each month. They were responsible for the record keeping of income and expenses for the business during that time. This responsibility gave each person in the company a hands-on feel for the finances of the company: how the money was earned and how it got spent. What a great idea! Not only did everyone get a good education about the money mechanics of running a business, but got to be responsible for it too. This made everyone on the team feel more a part of the money-making and money-saving process which in turn produced better financial results for everyone.

What's your score? If it's not the best score right now, what about tomorrow? What are you doing to turn the game around?

Today's Affirmation: "I'm scoring touchdowns in the game of life today!"

132

You Won the Lottery!...Now What?

"What you love is as unique to you as your fingerprints. You need to know that because nothing will make you really happy but doing what you love."

—Barbara Sher

We've all had the fantasy of winning big. It takes many forms: winning the lottery, winning the multi-million-dollar jackpot in the Megabucks slot machine, getting discovered and becoming a movie star, selling your screenplay for millions of dollars, writing The Great American Novel, buying the stock that leaps in value making you a billionaire, inventing the next big thing that everyone buys.

You visualize the celebration, the adrenaline rush, the happiness you share with your friends and family. You see the new house, the new car, the vacation trips you've always wanted. Shopping sprees dance in your mind—you can have anything you want! You buy it all.

And then? What?

What do you visualize yourself doing after you become wealthy? Lying around on the beach all day? For how many days would that be interesting? When anyone tells me that, I know I'm talking to a person who either hates their job or hasn't had enough vacation. As a creative being with talents and abilities beyond loafing and consuming, you have to do something that gives your life meaning and purpose. Go find a job doing that now...or create one. You don't have to wait until you're rich—this is the way you become rich.

Years ago, Paul McCartney came to Los Angeles with his band as part of his world tour. A particular quote from the program impressed me. He said, "People ask me, 'Why d'you do it? Why bother with the distractions? You're rich.' Cos I think everyone's little dream, certainly mine when I was at school was, what you'll do is get a lot of money and then you'll go off on holiday forever. Just go off on a boat. But when you grow up you realize it doesn't work. A year of holidays, maybe, is dead funny and a great groove. But after a year you think, what do I do in life again? Sail around the world in boats? Surely not...I know that after a year I'd start to wonder. I'd pick up a guitar."

Act as if you already won the lottery last year. Now go do what you love.

Today's Affirmation: "I am a winner in the lottery of life!"

133

The First Three Things Lottery Winners Do

"I've been rich and I've been poor. Rich is better."

—Sophie Tucker

Your wildest dreams come true: you pick the winning numbers in the lottery and suddenly you are a millionaire!

Now what? What do you do first?

There was a study several years ago that determined the top three things that most winners did—and nearly 90 percent did all of these three things. I will list them for you in reverse order, à la David Letterman:

3. They buy a new car.

2. They take a trip. If they were married with children, they go to Walt Disney World in Florida. If they are married without children or single, they go to Hawaii.

1. The very first thing they all do is say, "This isn't going to change me."

That one fearful statement, "This isn't going to change me," rang in my consciousness like a clarion call. To me, this is stark evidence that most people have a negative picture of what having money will do to them. Many people in our society grow up with the idea that "dirty money" or "filthy lucre" will somehow corrupt them—that they will become arrogant or miserly and lose all their friends. A nationwide study conducted by the AARP in 2000 showed that the majority of people believed that "lots of money makes people greedy and insensitive." How are you going to let money in your life if you think having it will make you a bad person? Doesn't it make sense that if you thought money was a powerful force for good and that having an abundance of money would mean you could make large contributions to worthy causes, that a lottery winner would say instead, "This is really going to change me for the better"? If you think that having a lot of money will make you a bad person, your internal sense of integrity is probably not going to allow it into your life. You need to change your attitude about having money and being rich if you want more abundance in your life. Make a list of positive things you would do with money if you were wealthy. Why not decide that money will make you a better person?

Today's Affirmation: "The more money I get, the more money I share."

134

The Camel and the Eye of the Needle

"No one would remember the Good Samaritan if he only had good intentions. He had money as well."

—Margaret Thatcher

When I started thinking about becoming a prosperous person, I hit a stumbling block. There was a quote from the Bible that worried me for a long time: "It's easier for a camel to pass through the eye of the needle than for a rich man to get into heaven." (I thought for a while it didn't say rich *woman*, but somehow I knew that qualification wasn't going to fly.) I wanted to be a rich person, but I wanted to be a good person and hopefully go to heaven, too. How was I going to do both?

Then, one evening, I happened across a television program that featured several religious scholars examining some Biblical statements, taking into account the geography, culture, and the era in which it was written. I heard one scholar mention the above quotation and comment that most people misunderstood it. He said that people thought that the needle mentioned was a common sewing needle and therefore, of course, it was impossible for a camel to get through it's eye. But this scholar laughed and said that "The Eye of the Needle" was the name of a gate in the wall of Jerusalem. And a camel could easily get through it—a moderately laden camel, that is, not a heavily laden camel. This changes the entire message. To me, this suggests that the lesson was only an admonishment to be *balanced* about wealth, and not overdo it to the point of overburdening your camel!

Leo J. Fishbeck, in his book *Sing Your Song For All You're Worth* states, "A careful study of the Bible, particularly the Old Testament, reveals that the people who were considered to be the most spiritual, those who were the great contributors to enlightened thinking, the most highly regarded, were usually very wealthy people—millionaires by our standards. As we read about their many accomplishments we find that, usually, the account ends with the statement, 'And he was favored by God.' According to the ancient authors of the Scriptures, there must be a connection between prosperity and Spirituality."

Money is a neutral. It will not corrupt you—only your use of it will. It is the wealthy who set up charitable foundations, endow hospitals, establish scholarships, promote art, literature, theater, etc. Ted Turner donated one billion dollars to the United Nations. Bill and Melinda Gates funded a charitable foundation with more than twenty billion dollars. You can't do things like that if you're broke.

Examine your old beliefs. Are they facts—or just opinions? Are they refutable? Investigate. If they aren't producing good things in your life, replace them with better thoughts.

Today's Affirmation: "The perfect order of the Universe is abundance for everyone—including me!"

135

Honor the Warriors

"The ultimate test of man's conscience may be his willingness to sacrifice something today for future generations whose words of thanks will not be heard."

—Gaylord Nelson

Some of your goals may not be accomplished in your lifetime. But they are worth your effort, nonetheless. They are your gift to those that follow you. Likewise, it is important that we honor those who came before us, and gave us gifts through great sacrifices of their own. Susan B. Anthony and Elizabeth Cady Stanton worked tirelessly, all their lives, for women to have the right to vote, but died before the amendment was added to our Constitution. Were it not for them, half the citizens of the United States would have no say in our government.

But without the early patriots, we wouldn't have a government. I visited Philadelphia and wandered around the city, looking at all the memorials and monuments. I stood in the room where the Declaration of Independence was written and tried to imagine the warm breath of the patriots there, who created a new nation out of their best ethics and beliefs. In sweat and blood they heaved forth a tiny, mewling infant country, "conceived in liberty and dedicated to the proposition that all men are created equal."

A price was paid for this child of dreams, for this "government of the people, by the people, for the people." The signers of the birth certificate of our nation faced loss of friends, family, homes, money, businesses, and lives. The debts were collected. They paid them all.

Of all the monuments in Philadelphia, the one that touched me most, that had me in helpless tears in the middle of a bright, sunny day, was an unprepossessing bronze plaque in the center of a small park. There were no crowds gathered around it, there were no tour guides, no music; it stood alone, a silent sentinel under the limbs of a shady tree. It marked a battlefield where soldiers laid down their lives in blood and muck so that this infant country might grow and prosper. So that I might have freedom. Remember us, the plaque seemed to say; we perished so that *you* could be free; we died so that *you* could vote.

And countless thousands upon thousands lie down in their wake and spend their last breaths dying hopelessly, helplessly, courageously for me. Some do not die in their body, but die in their minds or in their souls, lose their way, lose their families, lose their faith. Others die in their memories of the horrors of war. The price for freedom continues to be paid. May God bless them all, who died and died and die again. For me.

And for you. Honor those who came before you, who paid for your freedom. Vote. Pay your taxes. Honor those who come after you; what will you pay for them? Expand your vision. Run for office. Save the environment. Get involved.

Today's Affirmation: "I honor and cherish my freedom, and those who provide it for me."

136

Forgive Us Our Debts

"If you think nobody cares if you're alive,
try missing a couple of car payments."

—Anonymous

I know what it's like to be unable to pay your bills. In fact, things once got so bad for me that I filed bankruptcy.

I had been on top of the world. My bookkeeping service had doubled every year and was now generating approximately $450,000 per year. I had twelve employees and a beautiful new office suite. But I had one major client who accounted for 75 percent of my income, and when they left with a mere two weeks notice, disaster loomed. Since I was absolutely strapped for cash, having been left with many financial obligations and no current means of paying for them, I borrowed $50,000 on credit cards.

Five years later, I had faithfully paid the minimum balances every month, but by then I had the habit of using credit cards whenever cash flow dipped. Compound interest ate me alive. By this time, I owed $80,000. Then my chief bookkeeper quit and decided to go into business for herself. A lot of my clients went with her. My ex-business partners asked when I was going to pay them for the purchase of the company. I tried to sell the condominium I purchased at the top of the real estate market in 1987, but its value had plummeted and I owed approximately $30,000 more than it was worth. It didn't matter; I couldn't find a buyer at any price. I could no longer pay my current bills, let alone my debts. The barrage of telephone calls from creditors was non-stop. So were my stress, anxiety, and tears.

A dear friend sent me to a bankruptcy specialist who exclaimed, "The bankruptcy laws were written for people like you!" He showed me that there was a way out, a path to forgiveness of my debts under the law, a new beginning for me after this failure. He pointed out that business involved risk, and that sometimes when you risk, you lose. The average millionaire files bankruptcy 3.5 times, he told me, and I was in some good company, with people such as Walt Disney, Donald Trump, Wayne Newton, Mark Victor Hansen, and R.H. Macy, founder of Macy's department stores, who filed bankruptcy seven times before he was successful.

I filed. The credit card debt went up in smoke as though it had never been. The tension eked out of my body as I started to relax and breathe again. Of course, my credit was now a black smudge of ashes. But, after all, what did I need credit for? Only to borrow money, and that was what got me in trouble in the first place. I needed to learn to live without borrowing, just as I learned to live without drinking.

If you have ever stood in bankruptcy court and admitted your powerlessness over debt, forgive yourself and learn from the experience. If you have never had to do this, have compassion for those who have.

Today's Affirmation: "Forgive us our debts as we forgive our debtors."

137
Find Another Way to Have What You Want

"It is surprising how many improvements can come out of things that go wrong."

—Anonymous

In the end, financial stress reduction is simply this:

1. Earn more.
2. Spend less.
3. Find another way to have what you want.

When we're doing all we can to satisfy the first two requirements and yet when we see things we want that cost money, what can we do to stay within our budgets and still get what we want?

This is where you earn your graduate degree from M.S.U. (Make Stuff Up).

In the habit of spending a lot of money on clothes? Learn to sew, or trade services with a friend who sews. Buy too many books? Go to the library. Is enjoying nature your priority? Instead of feeling bad that you can't afford to buy a house with acres of land, live somewhere that is close to a park or wildlife refuge and take a walk there every day.

In my financial darkest days, I lost my home to foreclosure. I had bought when the real estate market (and my business) was high. When the recession hit and the market and my business plummeted, I found I couldn't sell it. Eventually, I had to give it back to the bank. It was a humiliating personal disaster.

One Friday night, I was playing cards with some girlfriends. They knew I was going through hard times, and one of the girls turned to me and said, "So where are you going to live now?" I said, "I don't know." She said, "Why don't you move in here with Shelley?" And Shelley looked up from her cards and said, "Sure. You can move in with me."

So I did. I moved into a gorgeous two-story, three-bedroom, three-bath, 3,000 square foot home in a beautiful hillside setting in a gorgeous neighborhood. It was the most beautiful—and most expensive—home I had ever lived in. Shelley and I got along great and it was fun having a roommate after years of living alone.

The rent? $200 per month. The value of the house does not appear on my balance sheet. But when I'm walking around in it, I can't tell I don't own it.

This particular scenario might not fit your lifestyle. Find one that does. Don't follow the "American Dream" of home ownership if it's not *your* dream. If it is, and you do own a home, in an economic downturn you could find a roommate or two to share expenses. Think outside the box. Make something up.

You don't have to *be* rich to *live* rich.

Today's Affirmation: "I am a money magnet!"

138

Create What You Want—And on Budget, Too!

"Our Accounting Department is the office that has the little red box on the wall saying 'In case of emergency, break glass.' And inside are two tickets to Brazil."

—Robert Orben

As I work with people to help them reduce their financial stress, I look at the choices they've made that put them in a financial position that isn't viable. One of the problems that seems endemic is the mental habit of considering only two options before making a decision. When I question people's choices in spending, they always have an answer of the other choice they considered that was worse: "I have to do X because the only other choice is to do Y, and Y is unacceptable." This polarity keeps people from continuing to search for a better choice.

For example, a recent client and I were trying to solve her cash flow problems. She was spending more than she was making, so we were looking for ways to cut her expenses. She was in business for herself in the medical profession and dedicated to building her practice. I suggested we needed to cut to a minimum all personal expenses while she built her business and she agreed. When I asked about her housing costs, she admitted she was paying a lot of money for her house, but it was either that "or live in a tiny $400 per month cracker box apartment."

"No, that isn't the only choice!" I said, and told her of my own wonderful rental situation. Her eyes lit up and she agreed she hadn't done the creative thinking necessary to come up with other housing ideas that might have her living in a nice place that she enjoyed and yet didn't cost a lot of money.

Be a creative thinker! Start with a visualization of what you want in great detail. Then put the price on it that works for your current budget. Then start your detective work to find what you want at that price. Tell your friends what you're looking for. Ask everyone you meet for ideas.

Know that the first three answers you get will be awful. Those answers are coming from your negative programming that tells you that you can't have what you want for the price you want to pay. Most people stop at this point and give in to the negative belief. Don't give up! Be determined to get what you want and you will. It won't come in the usual way, and it might not look exactly like your picture, but if you are flexible and open, you will see it as a good stepping-stone in the right direction.

There's a lot of gray between black and white. Put some new shades in your life.

Today's Affirmation: "I always find exactly what I want at exactly the right price!"

139

Pleasure Purchases

"The poor man is not he who is without a cent, but he who is without a dream."

—Hugh White

Annie the artist was concerned about the difficulty of selling art. The other members of the mastermind group listened attentively, ready to offer help. "I just took a great marketing class," said Annie, "and I'm having a difficult time coming up with a pain statement—a reason why people should buy my art because it will alleviate a pain they have. All around me I see people struggling with money and I can't convince myself that they need to buy art. This makes selling art very difficult for me."

Cynthia Masters spoke up then. A sleek, successful attorney, she smiled and said, "Oh, but art can be very important to a person, even when they don't have a lot of money!" She said that when she had just moved to Los Angeles and was going to school, she had a job that paid her $384 a month—gross. After taxes, she had about $225 left and her rent was $145. She had $80 remaining for the balance of her expenses. This budget would be a Low Budget for anyone!

One day, she walked along La Cienega Boulevard with a friend, looking at all the pictures in the art galleries that lined the street. Suddenly, she saw a picture that stirred her heart and soul. She knew she just had to have it. It cost $125, but she bought it. She paid $5 per month every month until the picture was hers. It meant bologna instead of ham, it meant months of no extras. She had to struggle to make that payment. But she cherishes that picture, bought so long ago, that has continued to bring her joy every time she looks at it.

Some things are bought to alleviate a pain, others are bought purely to provide pleasure. There is a market and an approach for both. Everyone needs some special pleasure purchases in their lives. What have you bought that you truly treasure for the pleasure it brings you?

Today's Affirmation: "I attract great beauty into my life!"

140
Low Budget Blues

"More than ever before, Americans are suffering from back problems: back taxes, back rent, back auto payments."

—Robert Orben

Low Budget is a useful tool for occasional use. But too often I see people with the Low Budget Blues. They've gotten into the *habit* of Low Budget. They think poor: Tighten the belt, do without, never buy new, can't afford it, shop at garage sales, eat cheap, sleep cheap, think cheap.

It's great to be able to do this during a recession, a cash flow problem, between jobs, after a loss, or to save additional money for a large purchase. But too often people buy into Low Budget as if it were reality. Low Budget is a choice. When it becomes a choice for too long, it becomes a habit.

During my rough financial times, I lived on low budget for years. All available cash went to paying off debt. Even after filing bankruptcy, there were debts I was obligated to repay, such as approximately $12,000 in taxes. Though I was not required to, I repaid the smaller businesses I owed money—my accountant, my attorney, and some personal loans from friends. I started with very small payments. Then the more money I made, the bigger debt reduction payments I made.

It took me another four years past filing bankruptcy, but when I finally became debt-free, what a relief, what a celebration! A hundred pounds felt lifted from my shoulders. Then I realized I hadn't a clue what I would spend money on instead of debts. Debt reduction had been my number one goal, and in my zeal to accomplish it, I had forgotten to have a number two. I sat with my High Budget form for two days without being able to come up with anything I wanted to put on it. I hadn't allowed myself to think about having anything but bare necessities, and I was out of practice. My hunger and thirst had been to be debt-free, and I had achieved it. That desire was strong. Now I needed to remember how to have fun, fabulous treasures, and pleasures, for savings to ensure I was never debt-burdened again.

I started looking around at the world again at all of the riches life has to offer. My High Budget took form and shape. I exceeded it in six months and made a new one. A year later, I revised it upwards again, and now I do it every year.

Do whatever it takes today to live in happiness instead of misery. Don't sing the "Low Budget Blues" one more time. Take a day off from money. Take a walk. Paint a picture, write a poem, sing a song. Play with a pet; play with a child. Play the piano. Dance in the sunlight. Stroll in the moonlight. Glow. High Budget is on its way.

Today's Affirmation: "I am now enjoying living on High Budget because I can afford it!"

141

The Number One Mistake Financial Planners Make

"Everyone must row with the oars that he has."

—English proverb

Years ago, when I was first starting to earn good money, I thought I would go to see a financial planner to get started saving and investing for my retirement. We talked about my goals, and what amount of money I would like to live on when I was retired.

Then she made The Mistake. She calculated how much money I would have to have saved by age 65 in order to have enough to retire, adjusted by inflation. I remember the amount, because it seemed enormous and totally unreachable: $1.2 million. She told me that I would have to start saving $800 every month in order to reach my goal. Well, I was only making $2,000 per month at the time! There was no way that I could save $800 a month. It was a totally unreachable number to me. I thanked her very much for her time and left the office, thinking that I was never going to be able to retire, so I might as well not bother saving anything. And so, for years, I didn't save a dime.

The *Los Angeles Times* has run articles called "Money Makeovers" where a financial planner helps people with their retirement objectives. They are usually quite good, but every now and then one of them makes The Mistake. I'll never forget the one who was advising a young professional woman in her early thirties who had a six-figure income and over $1 million saved, that she wasn't saving enough. What kind of message does that send to people who don't have anywhere near that kind of money? If she's not going to be okay, you must be headed for a homeless shelter with a shopping cart!

Did this ever happen to you? Did you ever get the impression that the goal was so out of reach that it was out of sight? Don't get discouraged before you get started. Get into the savings habit. Start small and build. Learn about asset building and planned prioritized spending. Get excited as your assets grow. Strengthen your muscles climbing the hill in the back yard before you attempt Mount Everest.

If you don't have a financial planner, get one. Find one who will be your savings coach, and help you build your wealth, and celebrate your wins with you. My financial planner, Dianne Bishop, calls me every time I send her a more substantial check and says, "Good job, Chellie! I'm proud of you!" I find myself trying to make more money so I can send her even bigger checks and really impress her. Get one like that. Or be one like that.

Today's Affirmation: "My assets grow easily and effortlessly every day!"

142

You Already Own Your Own Business

"Don't be afraid to try something new. An amateur built the ark. Professionals built the Titanic."

—Anonymous

If you've ever thought of going into your own business, I have exciting news for you. You already own your own business.

You may only have one client, a company that pays you a salary. You negotiated your "contract," you determined your salary by agreeing to it, and you bargain for increased fees and reimbursement of expenses with every review. You provide services for a fee to a client. You may have another client or two if you moonlight in a second job.

Like any business owner, it is important that you constantly update your skills so that you stay the most valuable supplier of services to your biggest client. Customer service should be your top priority. How can you make your client more profitable, more efficient, more productive? What can you do to make business run faster, cheaper, better? Do you bring better, newer ideas to company meetings? Is the client getting great value for the money they are paying you? Are you fun to work with?

As you add more value to your client's business, you will be able to ask for more value for your own. And you'll get it, too—from this client or a new one!

Today's Affirmation: "I run the successful and profitable company of Me, Inc.!"

143
Tunas Can Learn

"The closest to perfection a person ever comes is when he fills out a job application form."

—Stanley J. Randall

I learned a lot from Jennifer Martin, a fun-loving, free-spirited woman from England who worked as an account executive at the employment agency where I was the office manager. Jennifer was in sales, matching prospective employees with prospective employers and receiving a commission from the fee paid to the company for this service. She had fun, she stood her ground, she made a lot of money, and she wasn't afraid to tell you the truth, even when it hurt. My meek little co-dependent soul lapped up her lessons in self-esteem.

Grumbling about the state of my finances, one day I said to her, "I'm not making enough money. I'm going to ask for a raise!" "Is that right?" she said. A chill went through me and I spilled my coffee. You see, Jennifer only said "Is that right?" whenever someone said something particularly stupid. As I stood there fumbling in my mind, trying to figure out where I went wrong, she decided to help me out.

"What makes you think you *deserve* a raise?" she inquired. I didn't know what she meant. "Well, I've been here a year now," I replied, to which she answered, "So what? Just warming the seat for a year isn't worth anything." I was shocked. She was my friend! How could she say that?

As I stared at her with my mouth open, she smiled. "Come with me," she said, and sat me down and gave me some lessons in selling. She explained that asking for a raise was like a sale. I had to convince the buyer—my boss—of the benefit *to him* of paying me more money. And I needed to back up my request with proof of my value to the company. I needed to document my accomplishments and show how much work I did above and beyond my original job description. I should stress my commitment to the company and that I would continue to grow and improve in my job. A cost comparison of what salaries were paid other people in similar positions would help to make my case as would any accomplishments of mine that had helped save the company money.

What an eye-opening experience and valuable training that conversation was. I took her advice, did my homework, prepared my presentation—and got the raise.

So are you warming the seat or are you making a valuable contribution? Prove it.

Today's Affirmation: "I am paid very handsomely because I'm worth it!"

144
Pick Your Price

"Certainly there are things in life that money can't buy, but did you ever try buying them without any money?"

—Ogden Nash

Whether you work for yourself and have many clients who pay you, or you have one major client (i.e., you have a full-time job,) you have to decide on the price you want to be paid and feel comfortable asking for the money before you can get it.

Make sure you understand the value of what you're doing for your customer. My dad gave me a great tip when I first started job hunting. He said to me, "The main thing to understand is that anywhere you go to interview for a job, the person behind the desk has only one thought on his mind: how are you going to make him money?" It's like the old sales motto that every potential customer has one thing on his mind—WIIFM (What's In It For Me). When you are able to show your boss or client that you are providing the exact products or services that they need and want, they will be happy to pay you what you ask.

Many people make the mistake of thinking they have to keep their price low in order to get the job. Actually, the opposite is often true. A woman I knew was starting her own computer consulting business. She contacted a man who worked in a major corporation who she knew could refer a lot of business to her. He was delighted she had decided to go into business and said he would be glad to refer her. What was her fee, he asked. When she told him $40 per hour, he said, "I'm sorry, I can't refer you unless you charge at least $75 per hour." Shocked, she asked him why. He replied that $40 per hour was too cheap and no professional worth his salt would work for so small a sum, therefore people would think she wasn't any good.

Many people are so afraid that if they charge what they're worth, they'll be too expensive and no one will hire them. Certainly, there are customers and companies that want the cheapest personnel they can get. Are those the people you want to work for? I don't think so. You have to have the guts to say no to these people. Look for someone who's willing to pay you what you're worth. If they want what you have, they will pay any price to have it. If they don't want what you have, free isn't cheap enough. Make sure that you provide the best quality services available, then you will find there are plenty of people willing to pay top dollar to get top quality.

You have to ask for it, however.

Today's Affirmation: "I love to ask for money!"

145

Whose Advice Are You Taking?

"If I wanted to become a tramp, I would seek information and advice from the most successful tramp I could find. If I wanted to become a failure, I would seek advice from people who have never succeeded. If I wanted to succeed in all things, I would look around me for those who are succeeding, and do as they have done."

—Joseph Marshall Wade

Jeff, a music producer enrolled in my workshop, was working on pricing his services. He had a strong feeling that he was undercharging his clients, and that he could improve his profitability significantly by raising his rates. I asked him what amount of money felt right to him when he said, "I charge ____ dollars per hour." We tried out a couple of different figures, but $75 per hour was what his gut feeling told him was appropriate. This was significantly more money than he was currently charging, and he was nervous about asking for it.

Afraid of losing business if his price was too high, he needed to do market research in order to find out what other people in his business were charging for the same services. He came back to class the next week and said that based on his research, $75 was too high, and he should only charge $50 per hour. He seemed resigned about it, not as excited and happy as he had been about $75 per hour.

This didn't feel right to me. I asked him who he had contacted about pricing—was he talking to people who owned successful recording studios or people who were struggling? I saw a wave of understanding wash over his face as he thought back to the people he had talked to—they were all people he knew who were struggling! He determined right then that $75 was his price.

When you want to succeed, you have to ask for advice from people who are successful. If you ask people who are struggling, you will get lists of reasons why you can't succeed or why it's hard. Collect role models and learn from the stories of people who have made it where you want to go. How did they do it? What were the common themes as they climbed up the ladder of success? What did they do that made them different from the crowd? If you want to go where they went, you've got to do what they did to get there.

The next week, Jeff brought to class a contract he signed with Quincy Jones.

Whose advice would you like to take today?

Today's Affirmation: "I am successful and earning more and more money every day!"

146

The Leopard Comforter

"If you think you're too small to be effective, you've never been in bed with a mosquito."

—Anita Roddick

There was a beautiful animal print comforter with matching sheets and pillow shams that I had my heart set on. To buy the complete set was expensive, however, and I was saving for it, hoping that it would go on sale. Finally, the department store was having a white sale, and although this particular bed set wasn't in the catalogue, I hurried down to the store to check on it.

There it was! One of the showroom beds had been made up with my comforter set: comforter, dust ruffle, satin sheets, shams and throw pillows all in beige, brown and black leopard designs. It was beautiful! Excited, I eagerly rushed to the cashier's stand and asked the woman if it was on sale. Her attitude stopped me cold. Never looking at me and moving very slowly, she sighed and picked up the sales catalogue. "No, it doesn't look like this one's on sale. Sorry." And she turned away.

Hopes diminished but not dashed, I went back to look longingly at the beautiful bed set and thought about what I could do to get it to be on sale. The saleswoman I had talked to was clearly not interested in helping me. She was one of those people I call "bench warmers"—there to put in the hours required, doing as little as possible while they are there. They don't care about their work or you. I knew I needed a different kind of salesperson. Did one exist in this store?

"That's such a beautiful comforter, isn't it?" My eyes widened as I turned my head to look at the lovely woman who stood beside me. Yes! She had on a department store name tag. I knew immediately that this was a *real* saleswoman, a "player." She had seen me staring at the bed set and could feel that I wanted it. With one comment, she had let me know she admired my taste, asked me a "tie-down" question (sales lingo for a question that automatically elicits agreement), created a sense of rapport, let me know she had time for me, and seemed available and willing to help. Maybe there was a sale in my future after all!

Get a different salesperson, get a different answer: "Is it on sale?" I asked, innocently. "I'm sure it must be," she said, "Let me look and see." She reached up to the sign that listed the prices for the different items, and behind that sign was another one that listed sale prices. She told me that the sale didn't really start for two days, so the sale prices weren't posted yet, and she offered to take my store credit card number and ring it up first thing in the morning the day of the sale. "Great!" I said. "Which items would you like?" she asked. "I'll take everything!" I answered.

She made an $800 sale. I also asked to see her manager and told him in great detail how wonderful she was. Thanks, Lillian Sellahewa, at the Macy's store in the Fox Hills Mall.

Find a salesperson like that. Or be one like that.

Today's Affirmation: "I buy my perfect treasures at perfect prices!"

147

Taxes

"A government that always robs Peter to pay Paul will always have the support of Paul."

—George Gershwin

One morning, I got up early and went to a networking breakfast. The sun was shining, business was good, and the people at the meeting were fun. I was in a great mood as I sat down with my plate full of bagels, eggs, fruit, and cereal. The gentleman who sat next to me, though, was clearly not in the same frame of mind.

"I can't believe how much money I have to pay in taxes," he complained. "I had to write such a big check to the IRS this week, it's obscene. And what the government does with the money is even worse! I can't stand the fact that I'm paying for the industrial military complex, the stupid politicians, the no-good people who aren't working but collecting welfare..." On and on he railed.

Oh, no! I had inadvertently sat next to one of the "Ain't It Awful" people. I put up my mental shield so that I wouldn't take in the negative energy, and waited for him to wind down a little. I could tell he was upset and needed to vent, so saying anything but "Hmm" was useless at the moment. Until he was done, he wasn't going to be able to hear anything I said.

Finally, he seemed about finished with his list of government entities that shouldn't get his money, so I looked up at him, smiled and said, "Oh, none of my money goes there."

"What do you mean?" he asked, scowling.

"Well, my tax money goes to all the good things, like the libraries and the schools. It fixes the roads, pays for policemen to keep me safe and firemen to rescue me if I need it. It goes to pay for the space program, which I really like, and to the relief organizations to feed the poor and starving. It goes to the welfare recipients who really need some assistance briefly and then go back to leading productive lives. I like how the government helps people with my money."

"But you don't know your money goes there!" he argued.

"You don't know your money goes to those other things either," I replied. "But I'm happy and you're not."

He stared at me and I smiled. Then we both started laughing and had a lovely breakfast after that.

Maintain your positive outlook in the face of other's negativity and you will stay happy. Who knows? They may decide to join you!

Today's Affirmation: "All my tax money flows joyfully to do good in the world!"

148
Tax Advice

"There's only one thing worse than paying income tax; and that's not paying it!"

—Anonymous

I am not a CPA, nor an enrolled agent. I don't prepare tax returns, so I am not going to give you specific tax advice. This is just the general news I think everyone needs to know:

1. *Get professional advice.* I never had a tax preparer that didn't save me more money on my taxes than his or her fee cost me. In *The Millionaire Next Door,* authors Stanley and Danko outline many areas where the typical millionaire saves money: buying second-hand cars, resoling their shoes, etc. "But they are not nearly as price-sensitive when it comes to purchasing investment advice, services, accounting services, tax advice, medical and dental care, educational products, and homes." They state that the affluent account for only about 1 percent of the U.S. households, but they pay 25 percent of the tax on personal income. Taxes are the largest expense they have, and they want the best advice they can get on how to reduce that burden. The tax preparer's fee is even tax-deductible!
2. *Declare all your income and pay the tax on it.* Millions of people work at home, have small side businesses, receive extra cash from sources outside their regular work, etc. Sometimes they don't declare all the income, figuring that no one will ever know about it. You might fool the IRS, but you cannot fool yourself. And if you know you are doing something dishonest or illegal, it is going to cost you in stress and lost sleep. Somehow, the money you thought you saved or got away with, will be taken from you. Pay what you owe on what you earned. More than what you paid out will come back to you.
3. *Take all the legitimate tax deductions you can.* The tax code allows you to take many deductions, exemptions, and credits because it recognizes that it cost you some money to make the money you earned. There are many legitimate costs related to earning income that are tax-deductible. If you're using the golden phone to send out ships in order to get business, the phone charges are tax-deductible, too. Take every deduction to which you are entitled. Pay what you owe, but don't pay more than you owe.
4. *Celebrate your payment as a gift.* You've got to pay for the government anyway, so you might as well do it happily. Choose the line items in your national budget that you approve of, and decide that's where your money is going. My taxes help pay for all sorts of positive and wonderful programs to benefit society. Where do your tax dollars go?

P.S. It's highly likely that this book is tax-deductible for you. Check with your advisor!

Today's Affirmation: "I happily pay my fair share to help my government run efficiently and effectively."

149

The Chinese Version of Heaven and Hell

"Those who bring sunshine to the lives of others cannot keep it from themselves."

—James M. Barrie

This is a story I heard years ago, origin unknown:

In the Chinese vision of Hell, many people are seated around a large table. The table is laden with fine food, piled high in the middle of the table, looking scrumptious and smelling delicious. At each place setting, there is a set of very long chopsticks with which each person can reach the food in the middle. But the chopsticks are too long for the people to be able to get the food into their mouths. So they are all wailing, angry and starving.

In the Chinese vision of Heaven, many people are seated around a large table. The table is laden with fine food, piled high in the middle of the table, looking scrumptious and smelling delicious. At each place setting, there is a set of very long chopsticks with which each person can reach the food in the middle. But the chopsticks are too long for the people to be able to get the food into their mouths. However, everyone here is fat and happy—because they are using their long chopsticks to feed the person across from them.

Someone once told me, "No one goes to Heaven until everybody goes."

Hmmm. Rather gives you a different sense of your responsibility in the world, doesn't it?

Today's Affirmation: "As I give to others from my abundance, I give to myself as well."

150

The Son of Jaws Meets the Bride of Tuna

"There's a sucker born every minute."

—P.T. Barnum

"Easy money!" The ads seem to scream. "Work at home part-time and make thousands of dollars!" Solicitations arrive in the mail: "You're already a winner of one of these four fabulous prizes: a new car, a new television, a new stereo, or luggage. Send your check for $39.95 shipping and handling to…." Of course you get the luggage—a plastic little fold-up airline bag worth $1.49. I know because I fell for that one.

Have you? Here are the Top Ten Telemarketing Frauds, as reported by the National Fraud Information Center:

1. **Work-at-Home Plans:** programs sold with false promises of earnings.
2. **Telephone Cramming:** consumers are billed for services they never ordered.
3. **Advance-fee Loans:** loan offers requiring payment in advance for loans that are never made.
4. **Prize Offers and Sweepstakes:** consumers are asked to pay up front fees in order to collect a prize or be eligible for one.
5. **Telephone Slamming:** consumers' phone carriers are switched without the consumers' knowledge or consent.
6. **Magazine Sales:** fake subscriptions or renewals to magazines which never arrive.
7. **Travel and Vacation Offers:** offers of "free trips" that have undisclosed costs.
8. **Credit Card Offers:** phony promises of cards for which payment of fees are required in advance.
9. **Investment Opportunities:** use of high-pressure sales tactics and outrageous profit claims to get consumers to invest in phony investment pools.
10. **Credit Card Loss Protection Plans:** using scare tactics or misrepresentation to sell unnecessary "coverage."

Well, let's see, in addition to having fallen for number four in the example above, I have also been taken in by number six and number seven. I bought several subscriptions that never arrived. Then I bought a vacation package to Las Vegas, but when I went to the address they gave me, it was a vacant lot.

After that, I got smarter. I asked more questions. If it looks too good to be true, figure out why they're telling *you*. Ask questions, research, do your due diligence. Buy from people you know and trust—and are going to see again next Tuesday.

There are sharks in dolphin's clothing out there. If you fall for them, you're a tuna.

Today's Affirmation: "I am safe in the lap of luxury."

151
Choices

*"No matter how big or soft or warm your bed is,
you still have to get out of it."*

—Grace Slick

Never before have human beings had as many choices as those presented in our modern society. The train, the steam ship, the automobile, and the airplane have made travel accessible to the masses. With mobility come broader perspectives and new choices: you can live anywhere, choose any career, meet anyone. Today you can pack up and move to New York, Chicago, Orlando, Kansas City, or a farm in Montana. You can learn to sail, write a book, produce a movie, adopt a child. We yearn for the excitement of the new challenge and play with the fantasies of what might be, what could be, if we would just go for it.

Then the "yeah, buts" take over and we don't make a move after all. The change looks too scary, and what if we fail? We convince ourselves that we are safe where we are, and we'd better not risk what we have by going after what we don't have, or the sheer magnitude of possible choices overwhelms us, and we cry, "But I don't know what to choose!"

Pick anything. Make a list of possibilities that interest you and just pick one. Then go for it. You might not write a book today, but you can write a page. You might not be ready to sail around the world, but you can take a sailing lesson. Dream of stardom? Audition for the local community theater. Take a step in a new direction. You don't have to make the *right* choice, just make a *new* choice. Get in the habit of choosing your life.

Not choosing is a choice to choose what you've already chosen.

Today's Affirmation: "I choose my favorite treasures from life's overflowing treasury."

152

Resistance

"The average man is always waiting for something to happen to him instead of setting to work to make it happen. For one person who dreams of making fifty thousand pounds, a hundred people dream of being left fifty thousand pounds."

—A. A. Milne

Transformational seminars are often uplifting, joyful, fun, and filled with fabulous life-changing accomplishments. But along the way, there is often incredible resistance to change as people break free of their "comfort zone."

One week, five people who had missed the previous "Time Management" session called to ask if they could transfer to a later session or quit and get a refund. The latter requests came even though the contract everyone signed before beginning the course specifically states that the course fee is due whether or not they complete the course.

Time management is a major issue for many people; our lives seem to be a never-ending stream of possible activities. The participants who called to renegotiate their agreements to complete the course had very legitimate sounding reasons for their requests:

"Yeah, but we just bought a house, are closing escrow, have to move, and business is booming—we got three new clients this week! We're just too busy right now."

"Yeah, but the class just hasn't fit well into my schedule."

"Yeah, but I just got divorced and I'm too overwhelmed right now."

"Yeah, but I just got married and I'm too overwhelmed right now."

Like a lifeguard who has fun in the sun at the beach on most days but who earns all his money on those few days when the surf is rough and people are drowning in the waves, I earn my keep by fielding these requests. I recognize that they expect me to be the "nice guy," understand their difficulties, and let them out of our contract. But if I do that, I fail them. My job is to keep their feet to the flame and show them how they sabotage their money and their lives with "yeah, buts." At these times, the inner self that is afraid to succeed, to move beyond its limitations, and to rise to the next level of accomplishment, throws a wrench in the works. "Stop!" it says. "Change is too difficult!" But it is here that opportunity lives. It is here that they can stop taking the easy way out, stick with their agreement, and learn the lessons they came to this class for. It is my job to convince them to do it.

Three of them stayed and got the financial rewards they came for. One didn't return my calls. And one's screaming rage made me rather relieved she wasn't coming back. I wonder how they're doing.

Today's Affirmation: "I have all the time I need to achieve all my dreams and desires!"

153
Voices

"Train a child in the way he should go,
and walk there yourself once in a while."

—American proverb

As people start to practice positive affirmations, they often become very conscious of the negative voice inside their heads. Where does that voice come from? Who is it? As children, we hear and record many messages from our parents, our teachers, and other influential adults in our lives. Some messages are more forceful than others, are repeated more often, make a deeper impression, or for some reason in our own psyche are latched on to and repeated. These messages become internalized, and like a continuous loop tape recording, play out endlessly in our minds. Here are two lists of adult messages to children:

Negative	Positive
Can't you do anything right?	*You are really talented.*
Your room looks like a pigsty.	*You have beautiful hair.*
You're just like your father.	*I love you.*
You'll never amount to anything.	*You can do anything you put your mind to.*
I told you so.	*Don't worry, you'll do better next time.*
How could you be so stupid?	*What did you learn from this?*
You're old enough to know better.	*It's amazing how smart you're becoming.*
Because I said so, that's why.	*You can figure this out.*
It's for your own good.	*I trust you.*
No, you can't do that.	*You have a higher purpose.*
No, you can't have that.	*Let's create some fun together.*
What's wrong with you?	*You're always tops in my book.*
Why don't you ever listen?	*I appreciate you.*
Do you think I'm made of money?	*Whatever I have, I share with you.*
I thought you were smarter than that.	*I know you will do the right thing.*
You don't know what you're talking about.	*I always have time to talk to you.*
Who do you think you are?	*You are the best and the brightest.*
I can't trust you with anything.	*You are trustworthy.*
You don't know how lucky you are.	*Aren't we lucky to have each other?*
I'm ashamed of you.	*I'm so proud of you.*
All you think about is yourself.	*Thank you for being so thoughtful.*
Why can't you be more like ____?	*I'm so glad you're you.*
You've had it too easy—you're spoiled.	*You are a miracle of life.*

Which messages did you hear most often? Which messages are you giving most often? Would you like to change the tape?

Today's Affirmation: "I am, and everyone around me is, a miracle of life!"

154

The First Law of a Thousand Times

"Life is like a taxi. The meter keeps a-ticking, whether you are getting somewhere or standing still."

—Lou Erickson

We have to hear the truth a thousand times before we understand it. This is "The First Law of a Thousand Times." At the thousandth repetition, we hear the truth again but this time with a difference. Finally, we get it; we undergo the "Aha!" experience and we see clearly some truth about how we have been operating our lives.

"Aha!" my mind clicks open and a shiver runs through my body. Voices ring in my head and I hear my mother telling me that truth when I was twelve, a teacher saying something similar when I was fourteen, a boyfriend whispering it when I was twenty, a client saying it when I was defending my position, a colleague repeating it when I "Yeah, butted" him, and my best friend murmuring it when I cried on her shoulder.

It happened one night in class. We were recalling past wins and I had instructed everyone to think about the truly meaningful triumphs of their lives. This group had no trouble with remembering failures, but successes were harder. They just didn't spend enough time relishing their wins.

Nancy started to cry, explaining that she just had an "Aha!" experience. She said she could remember ten wins but would allow herself only five seconds to enjoy the experience. After that would come a voice that took it all away from her: "Well, you still didn't do ____ right." She saw how many people around her always said something to squelch the joy, to rain on her parade. She had recorded all their voices so that, in case the Nay Sayers were unavailable in the flesh, she could do it herself. Nancy remembered many times this had happened in her life, but now that she recognized it, she could change it. We celebrated her discovery with her and offered our help: when she had her next win, we would help her celebrate it so that she could fully experience her happiness and joy.

One of the most wonderful parts of being a teacher—or a friend—is seeing the "Aha!" experience happen. When people hit the thousandth time, they change right in front of you—you can see it on their face. It is thrilling to watch, and you must appreciate it, knowing that you will not see this happen often. But it doesn't matter whether or not you see the change. What matters is that it takes one thousand times, so every one of those repetitions is just as important as the thousandth. You can't have the thousandth time until you've had the first time, the fiftieth, the nine hundredth. If you tell someone a truth and their lack of understanding is clearly visible, just know they haven't hit the thousandth time yet. They will one day. Maybe ten years from now. Maybe tomorrow. You don't know what number they're on.

You don't know what number you're on either. Pay more attention. Listen. Learn. The thousandth time might be today!

Today's Affirmation: "I hear the truth, know it, and live it today!"

155

The Universal Bank Account

"Sure, the world is full of trouble. But, as long as we have people undoing trouble, we have a pretty good world."

—Helen Keller

I have always felt that there is a rhyme and reason to the Universe, that justice does prevail in the long term, that life really is fair. It's like a big bank account in the sky—my karmic bank account, if you will, where I record my debits and my credits. Some days I make deposits to its bank account, and some days I make withdrawals. I feel happy when my accounts are balanced.

Whenever bad things happen and I am once again going through challenges in my life, I feel I am building up credits in my Universal Bank Account. I work to overcome the obstacles, learn the lessons and tally the results of my actions. I sense that it won't be long before my account is again overflowing, and goodness and mercy will rain down on me once more.

When I do something stupid or with questionable integrity; when I say a harsh word to someone out of my own ill temper or lack of grace; when I miss the opportunity to help someone when I easily could have; then, oh, then I feel the weight of the black debits eating up the golden store of good in my account. Funny how it's just then that the car breaks down, the computer loses files, a friend breaks a date, a new client cancels.

Time for prayer and meditation and repentance. And then to do good wherever I can once more: write a love letter to a friend, call business associates and ask what I can do to help them, write a check to a worthy cause. The balance shifts, the black debits retreat in confusion, and the golden rule creates yet more gold in my life, my work, my relationships.

What goes around, comes around. Watch it work. Check whether you are making deposits or withdrawals from your Universal Bank Account. It's up to you. You fill it up and you deplete it.

Make sure to keep it filled up, because the Universal Bank Account always pays great dividends.

Today's Affirmation: "I make many golden deposits to my Universal Bank Account and it showers me with riches!"

156

Time or Results?

"Men occasionally stumble over the truth, but most of them pick themselves up and hurry off as if nothing had happened."

—Winston Churchill

I'd like to ask all employers: do you care about the time employees put in? Or do you care about the results they produce?

Years ago, when I was a struggling actress, I had a secretarial job for a medical equipment company. The job was fairly easy and the people were nice, except for the other sales secretary with whom I shared an office. Sandy had her Masters Degree in "Look Busy." She could work more slowly than anyone I ever saw, drawing out each task to fill the eight-hour day so it always looked as if she was working. I didn't get it. I was high-energy and wanted things to do. I used to finish all my work early, help her with her work, and then help out in the service department, too.

One afternoon, I had completed what work I had, helped the others, and took a short break to study my lines for a play I was rehearsing that evening. As luck would have it, the office manager, Ron, walked in just at that moment. Here is dutiful Sandy, working away, and Chellie is reading a play. You can guess the rest. I almost got fired. What really floored me was that Ron said Sandy had been complaining about me!

Oops. These were clearly not "My People." I got another job the next week. In retrospect, I can see that they could see I was not one of "Their People." I clearly had aspirations beyond working in that office. I didn't really fit on their team. I was just "getting by" there, making rent money, while my true focus was on becoming a professional actress.

A couple of years after that, I found a great company, Career Data Personnel. The president, Len Savallo, cared about results. I remember him telling the sales personnel: "If you can sell $20,000 per month and only work one hour a day, more power to you! I will not ask you to punch a time clock. But if you aren't doing $20,000 per month, I expect to see you here from nine to five." Can-do, positive, upbeat people worked for him—and produced results, too. I liked their energy and Savallo's results-oriented philosophy. He's the one who promoted me to my first job in bookkeeping—and that changed my focus, my direction, and my life.

Time isn't money. Time is just one of the resources used to make money. Focus on results. And focus on the people that produce results.

Today's Affirmation: "I produce fabulous results in short order every day!"

157
The Fine Art of Delegating

"Successful people think up things for the rest of the world to keep busy at."

—Unknown

It was the time management session of the *Financial Stress Reduction® Workshop*, and I had just explained how to prioritize activities: "A": most important tasks; "B": important task but can be delegated to someone else; and "C": unimportant task that anyone can do.

Cindy spoke up then. She was a successful businesswoman owning two stores with thirteen employees. But she complained that there wasn't time to get everything done.

You must know by now that this excuse is useless. Everyone has the same twenty-four hours in their day. I asked her to describe a typical day. This was her list:

1. Open the store
2. Listen to phone messages
3. Talk to employees or customers
4. Return phone calls
5. Go through mail
6. Prepare bank deposits
7. Go to the bank
8. Prepare bids
9. Make sales calls
10. Attend networking meetings

The biggest problem business owners—and mothers!—have is that they are so good at everything, they have a problem delegating tasks to other people. They want to know everything that's going on, have every detail carried out perfectly, and be in charge of the whole show. This works well when a business (or family) is small—and there's only one person or two people involved. The minute you add a third person, however, the prime mover has to delegate.

I asked the class to help prioritize each one of Cindy's tasks in order. Open the store was definitely a "C", as was listening to phone messages—anyone could do that. Other "C" tasks were: go through mail, prepare bank deposits, and go to the bank. We determined that talking with employees was an "A" in some cases, "Bs" and "Cs" in others, as was talking with customers. We delegated half of Cindy's daily tasks to her employees, which freed up her time for the "A" priorities: prepare bids, make sales calls, and attend networking meetings. In the next few months, Cindy created a lot more income in her business by focusing on obtaining new customers and delegating everything else.

For all you mothers reading this, I suggest you realize you are the president of your home corporation. You need to decide where your priorities lie, and delegate a lot of tasks to your vice president (husband) and employees (children.) The tasks you delegate may not be done perfectly, but they'll be done *well enough*. Give up perfection and put everyone around you to work!

Today's Affirmation: "I am on golden time making gold!"

158
The Day I Hired a Maid

"There are three ways to get something done: Do it yourself, employ someone, or forbid your children to do it."

—Montana Crane

I was breathless on the treadmill, not the one in the gym—the one in my head. It said I had to work smarter, harder, longer, faster. I was president of the Los Angeles Chapter of the National Association of Women Business Owners, on the board of the Rotary Club of Pacific Palisades, and running my business management company with thirty clients and four employees. Work consumed my life.

On this particular afternoon, I had to leave the office early. I was having friends over for dinner and my condominium was a mess. It needed a thorough cleaning before I could let anyone inside. I threw myself into the work—vacuuming the floors, doing the dishes, dusting everything, cleaning the furniture, washing the bathroom. It took me three hours, I didn't do a great job and it wasn't fun. Now I was tired and wanted to rest, but it was time to cook the dinner! By the time my friends arrived, all I wanted to do was sleep.

Something was wrong with this picture. As I cleaned up after the dinner was over, I analyzed the situation. I had made a decision to save money on cleaning services by doing my house cleaning myself. At first glance, this looks like a good, solid, money-saving idea. I was accustomed to being self-sufficient. But I soon saw the flaw in my reasoning. If I had stayed at work for those three hours instead of cleaning my house, I would have billed my time at $40 per hour and made $120. I could have paid a maid $40 to clean my house and I'd have been ahead $80. And the maid would have a new client and be more prosperous, too!

I hired a cleaning service the next day. A few years later, I graduated to caterers. Now, *that* was a truly heavenly day.

Make money doing what you love and you can pay other people to do the other stuff. What's your least favorite task? Delegate it today!

Today's Affirmation: "It is a pleasure to prosper myself and others!"

159

Jimmy Can't Find the File

"Time is the coin of your life. It is the only coin you have, and only you can determine how it will be spent. Be careful lest you let other people spend it for you."

—Carl Sandburg

Sometimes, something goes wrong with delegating. The person you hired to delegate to starts delegating to you instead. Let me tell you about Jimmy.

Jimmy was a handsome, energetic, young man I hired as a full-charge bookkeeper at my business management company. He was terrific, with one exception: he could never remember where files were. He got into the habit of coming into my office and complaining he couldn't find a particular file. I have a good memory for things like that, so I got into the habit of jumping up and finding it for him.

It wasn't long before I realized I was working for my employee instead of vice versa. Every time he needed something, he asked me for it and I ran and got it. It reminded me of all the years I had worked as a secretary. But something was wrong with this picture—I was the boss!

I realized that I was going to have to spend the time to train Jimmy how to look for files. This would take more time initially, but eventually I would be freed from this task if he could find files on his own. So the next time he told me he couldn't find the file, I asked him to sit down in my office.

"Where have you looked?" I asked him. He looked at me wide-eyed. He was certainly surprised by my question. I don't think he had actually looked anywhere yet, but he named a particular section of the file cabinet.

"Okay," I said. "And where else do you think it could be?" Now he was a trifle annoyed, but named another place. I told him to go look there and come back to me if it wasn't there and we'd think about other places it might be. Somewhat ruffled, Jimmy left on his search.

He came back once to report he still couldn't find it, and we brainstormed some other ideas. He got the message that I wasn't getting out of my chair to go look for it for him. We went through this routine a couple of times more before he stopped coming to ask where files were. By then, he knew the process.

Think this is something you might try with your employees? Or your children?

Today's Affirmation: "I love to delegate to others so I can do the work I love!"

160
Do Nothing Weekend

"I have finally figured out that the purpose of life is to enjoy it."

—Rita Mae Brown

One of the most relaxing times I ever spent was a three-day weekend with Jennifer, a friend of mine. She was a nurse working a hectic, full schedule; I was busy running my bookkeeping service, being an officer of a club, and starting up my workshops. We both were in desperate need of some R&R, so we decided on a getaway with no plans and no schedule—she would come to my house Friday morning and we would drive north.

Friday arrived warm and clear—perfect weather for a drive along the California coast and we found ourselves relaxing almost immediately. We became conscious of enjoying the present moment and began noticing things we had never seen before. We spotted an overgrown road off the highway and decided to explore it. The road ended in an isolated beach, with waves gently breaking on the sparkling sand and no sounds but the sea gulls overhead. Pleased with our discovery, we took our shoes off and walked on the beach. We didn't walk feeling like we had to hurry to our next destination, and we walked until we felt complete. Ahhh!

Back on the road, we saw a small town and made the detour to explore it. Finding a cute antique shop on the main street, we browsed among old items of yesteryear. Next we went into a small bookstore and had tea with the charming woman who owned the store. As dusk fell, we decided it was time to look for a motel. When we saw a cute little '50s motel with a bright "Vacancy" sign, we agreed that it looked perfect. We bought our favorite snacks, rented videos, and stayed up late eating, laughing, and watching movies. We didn't set the alarm for the next morning.

The whole weekend was like that. Relaxing, exploring, and talking about sights, sounds, philosophies, and life; we felt like kids again instead of adults with responsibilities. It was a glorious "Do Nothing Weekend."

After treating ourselves to so much lazy relaxation, we were brimming with energy and enthusiasm when we returned to work Monday morning. That's the side benefit of really allowing yourself time to enjoy life and play. When people tell me they're burned out and want to quit their jobs, I always ask them when was the last time they took time off or had a vacation. The answer is almost always, "What's time off?" or, "I haven't had a vacation in five years." You can't live happily or productively like that. You have to take time to relax and play, if only to protect your supply of energy.

Schedule a weekend off. You may re-discover a strange, wonderful, fascinating concept: spontaneity.

Today's Affirmation: "The more time off I take, the more money I make."

161
Living in the Present

"Today is a gift. That's why it's called the present."

–Unknown

We all want wealth in our work, serenity in our spirit, and a balance between the two. Balance seems to be the most elusive quality. We try to do too much. Perhaps it is because there is so much possible. Our unlimited choices of where to go, what to do, how to do it, when to do it, and who to see, have us stretched and stressed. We want to do it all and we want to do it perfectly. "If only I had spent more time with my children!" we cry. Then in the next breath, "If only I had spent more time on my work!" How can we win when every choice we make produces guilt over the choice we didn't make?

It would help if theaters and restaurants would check all cell phones and pagers at the door, like they used to check guns in the Old West. Then we would be *unavailable*, uninterruptible, and unanswerable to anyone or any piece of technology. Then we might relax and enjoy the experience we were having—while we were having it. There are very few conversations in the world that can't wait two hours. Have a conversation with the person you're with. That's why you're with them and not on the phone. It's rude to try to do both at the same time.

Let go of the habit of guilt, of "if onlys" and "what ifs." Let go of the habit of looking at what you're not doing instead of what you are doing. "Be here now," Baba Ram Dass said in the '60s. It still works. Make the best choice you can each moment. Have confidence in your ability to choose. Then *be in* the present choice. Live fully in the present moment. Happily. Joyfully.

Today's Affirmation: "Every choice I make is the right choice!"

162
Truce

"Every time one laughs a nail is removed from one's coffin."

—Honduran proverb

Perky Lindsey wasn't her usual bubbly self at the family dinner.

"How is your term paper coming along?" her mother, Jane, asked sympathetically.

"Oh, it's really hard!" Lindsey exclaimed. She looked like it was hard too, poor haggard dear.

A sophomore at UCLA, she was embroiled in all the challenges of academic diligence sandwiched between sorority parties, dances, and general fun.

Her older sister, Marissa, had just graduated from UCLA and was happily at work as Strategic Sales Coordinator at a sports radio station. Although she clucked her sympathy, you could tell she was feeling a bit smug.

Picking up on this energy, Mama Jane decided to have a little fun. She turned to Marissa and asked, "How many papers are you working on, Marissa?"

"None!" she replied gleefully.

"And how many finals are you studying for?"

"None!"

"How many units are you carrying?"

"None!"

Everyone laughed at this exchange, except Lindsey, who looked quite put upon. She struck back immediately: "How many hours are you working, Marissa?" she asked sweetly. Gotcha! we chorused; we all knew Marissa was working a lot of overtime in her new job.

Not to be outdone, Marissa shot back, "How much *money* are you making, Lindsey?" Oohh, good answer, good answer, the family nodded.

"I don't need to make any money! Mom and Dad are paying for everything," smiled Lindsey.

Zing! The joke had rebounded back on the one who started it. "Ouch!" Mama Jane winced ruefully. We all dissolved in laughter at the good-natured repartee.

Touché, touché for both girls. Life passages have their upsides and their downsides. Dance gloriously, then pay the band. Enjoy each passage with humor and grace.

Truce.

Today's Affirmation: "I love my life and all its rich rewards!"

163

Little Acorn and the Old Ones

"The key to everything is patience. You get the chicken by hatching the egg, not by smashing it open."

—Arnold H. Glasgow

"How come I'm not taller?" cried Little Acorn. "I want to stand tall and straight and reach the skies. Like you!"

"Wait," whispered the Old Ones, leaning down from their great height. The winds sighed through their rustling leaves.

"But I want to be big now. I shouldn't have to be little like this. This is no fun!"

The elder trees stood stoically, stretching their long limbs to the skies. "Wait."

"It's not fair! How come you get to be so tall, while I'm stuck here on the ground? I'm just as good as you. I should at least have some roots and some limbs!"

"Wait."

Frustrated and uncomprehending, Little Acorn cried and complained into the long night.

Years passed, and Little Acorn grew. His roots took hold of the rich earth, sending long shoots deep into the rich soil. He quenched his thirst in the rain. His limbs lengthened and strengthened in the sunlight. The sap ran strong beneath his bark.

Still Little Acorn was not satisfied. "But I still can't reach as high as you!" he whined. "You're at the top of life and I'm stuck here in the middle. Why can't I be as tall as you?"

The Old Ones nodded in the breeze and their voices sighed softly on the wind, "Wait."

Many suns and moons moved across the skies and the eons passed. And one day Little Acorn realized he was the tallest tree in the forest. His life-long dream had come to pass. The birds sang in the sunlight in his topmost boughs. Children played beneath his feet. He could see for miles around and stood proudly with his comrades. Now he, too, was one of the Old Ones.

His joy was complete.

Then he heard a small voice crying on the ground. He leaned down to see who was weeping so piteously. It was his child, Tiny Acorn.

"How come I'm not taller?" cried Tiny Acorn. "I want to stand tall and straight and reach the skies. Like you!"

With an ache in his soul and the wisdom of the ages in his kindly voice, he whispered, "Wait."

Today's Affirmation: "I have abundant faith and trust that all my good is on its way to me now."

164

The Wonderful Trip

"When Goliath came against the Israelites, the soldiers all thought, 'He's so big we can never kill him.' But David looked at the same giant and thought, 'He's so big, I can't miss.'"

—Ode to Joy (Society of Paul)

My friend, Paris Salido, a terrific masseuse, wanted to go on a vacation to Australia, yet had other budget priorities for her money. Being a graduate of the *Financial Stress Reduction® Workshop*, she knew the importance and power of affirmations, so she invented one for vacation purposes: "I now receive free first-class travel and accommodations all around the world." (She told me that it is important when saying this out loud to move your arm in a circle three times with "all around the world.")

Four months later, she was talking with a friend of hers in the travel industry—someone with a large family who always had plenty of relatives to whom to give any travel vouchers or discounts. She had never given Paris anything before. But this particular day, she said to Paris, "We've been friends a long time and I want to give you this voucher for a free airplane ticket anywhere in the world!"

That alone would make the affirmation worth doing. But this was not the end of the story.

She told everyone she was going on her dream vacation to Australia. As she was sharing her story one day, a friend asked her where she was going to stay. "I don't know yet," she replied. "Well," he answered, "I have a condo in Sydney that is usually rented year-round. But the people who have been there for the last five years just moved out, and the new renters aren't moving in for two months. You can stay there for free if you want. I'd appreciate having someone there to take care of it."

Paris had a wonderful time on her trip.

Where would you like to go?

Today's Affirmation: "I now receive free first-class travel and accommodations all around the world!"

165
Motivation

"There is only one way to get anybody to do anything. And that is by making the other person want to do it."

—Dale Carnegie

Psych 101—guinea pig class. It was a general education requirement when I was in college. In this basic psychology class, you were required to participate in an experiment—you had to be an involuntary guinea pig for one of the graduate student's experiments.

The day of my experiment dawned and I sashayed down to the psych building, planning to get out of there as soon as possible, so I could go to the party on the beach. I sat down in the lab and the young man running the test explained it to me: he would show me a series of two words side by side. Then he would show me only the first word and ask me to remember the second word. "Okay, let's go," I said, and ho-hummed my way through the list, thinking more about the beach party than his silly word list. When we were finished, I started to get up and go, but the grad student said, "Wait, we're not done. Now we're going to do the same exercise again, but this time I'm going to give you a quarter for every pair you remember."

Now, my college days were long ago, and a quarter was real money. I perked up immediately! When he ran the pairs of words to remember, I concentrated on them. All thoughts of partying on the beach fled from my mind—I was totally focused on the task at hand, because I had a reason to be. I left the lab with seven dollars and fifty cents jingling in my pocket—about what I spent on food for a week.

Motivation is everything. People can produce extraordinary results when they have a goal in mind that spurs them forward. What is driving you? What drives your husband, your clients, your friends, your children? What reward are you after? How can you get your goals in alignment so that you can accomplish your goals together?

Acknowledgment is often a better reward than money. On job satisfaction surveys I have seen, employees usually state that praise and the satisfaction of a job well done are the primary reasons that make them feel fulfilled in their work. Money is usually third or fourth on the list.

There are lots of jobs you can take to make money—why did you choose the job you have now? What are the rewards of the job that fulfill your soul's satisfaction? In every area of your life, why are you doing what you're doing?

What's the payoff?

Today's Affirmation: "I am praised and acknowledged for everything I do."

166
Winning

"If at first you don't succeed, skydiving is not for you."

—Unknown

I told the class to remember a time when they were winning: they won the race at the track meet, won the football game, got the part they wanted in the play, got the job or promotion, won the award, got the acknowledgment. When I asked them to tell their stories, they beamed and their faces glowed. On the white board, I started to list the emotions and feelings they remembered experiencing while winning:

Excited: Lucky, Energized, Ecstatic, Confident, Special, Enthusiastic, Fun, Happy, Powerful

They were thoughtful, tentative and reflective as they mentioned these feelings. Then I asked them to think about the challenges they faced, the breakdowns and roadblocks they were experiencing on their road to success. They fired out the following in rapid succession, sometimes two or three speaking at once:

Depression: Why try?, Helpless, Doubt, Panic, Fear, Worry, Insecurity, Trouble, Illness

It was amazing how quickly they came up with the second list. Those words and feelings just flowed out. I had to drag the other adjectives out of the group, we had to work really hard to come up with them—it was like pulling teeth! Unfortunately, most people are more comfortable with the negative voice. Their thoughts go there really easily. It's more familiar. It's like a rut in a road.

Use your affirmations to create a new rut—a rut of positive thinking! With practice, your thoughts will move to the positive automatically instead of to the negative. The negative voice will get quieter and quieter. You'll find you go whole days without one thought of lack, limitation, or scarcity. Instead, abundance, prosperity, happiness, and wealth will pervade your consciousness. You control your thoughts. Which rut in the road do you want to go down?

Today's Affirmation: "Winning is my natural habit. I win everywhere I go!"

167

I Can Hardly Waits

"A three-year-old is a being who gets almost as much fun out of a fifty-six dollar set of swings as it does out of finding a small green worm."

—Bill Vaughn

Children always seem to be excited about something. They have an abundance of energy and enthusiasm, looking forward to the opportunity for fun. Their lives are filled with what speaker Dave Grant thirty years ago called, "I can hardly waits!" "I can hardly wait until Saturday and the baseball game," "I can hardly wait until my birthday party next week," "I can hardly wait until school's out," "I can hardly wait until Christmas." Their eyes sparkle, they grin, they vibrate with the vision of the fun they're going to have.

Adults, meanwhile, have "I can hardly stand its." "I can hardly stand how commercial Christmas has gotten," "I can hardly stand the traffic on the freeway," "I can hardly stand the taxes I have to pay," "I can hardly stand my boss, mother-in-law, co-worker, spouse...." Some people can be relied upon to complain the moment you see them. I call them the "Ain't It Awful People." You don't dare ask how they're doing—they'll tell you. "Oh, I'm so tired, I'm working so hard...," "I just lost a lot of money in the stock market...," "My doctor says I have to have tests for this chronic pain...." They immediately put a damper on every conversation. It takes a lot of energy to remain centered in a positive, happy frame of mind when you're with them.

Stop that! No complaints! Find something to look forward to with joy and focus on that. Schedule a day off, a vacation, or a party to put fun in your life. Abraham Lincoln said, "Most people are about as happy as they make up their minds to be." Make up your mind to be happy. Plan events to look forward to. My friend Barbara, who "can hardly wait" until her vacation each year said the worst thing about it is coming back because then she doesn't have it to look forward to anymore. Excited anticipation is a blissful state of being, and she loves imagining the fun she's going to have. So the first thing she does when she gets home is call her travel agent and get more brochures so she can pick out her next vacation!

What are the "I can hardly waits" you're looking forward to? Make a list, then pick one to be especially excited about today. Say, "I can hardly wait until ____" three times, jumping up and down and laughing! (If this feels silly to you, watch out! You're in danger of getting old. Not mature. Not grown-up. Old.)

Today's Affirmation: "I can hardly wait until ____________!"

168
Happiness

"Now and then it's good to pause in our pursuit of happiness and just be happy."

—Guillaume Apollinaire

Not everyone thinks life is about being happy. I do. And it is not a function of money. Studies have shown that beyond the subsistence level, more and more money does not equal more and more happiness. Happiness is a choice.

Decide to be happy. Take joy in every pleasurable thing around you. Have lots of "I can hardly waits." In my workshop, I ask everyone to play "The Glad Game"; to make a list of things they are grateful for. Most people write a few things easily, then stop to think. One woman, Lee Killian, wrote furiously for the entire time we did this exercise and completely covered her page with notes. Everyone knew Lee was a happy person—she always had a bright smile that lit up the room. You always looked forward to seeing her, because you knew her happy energy would lift you up. I asked her for a copy of her list, which included: "Me, my health, my kids, my mom, friends, home, car, movies, music, dancing, beach, trees, animals, desert, snow, rain, sun, sleep time, telephones, dry cleaners, perm-a-press, pens, coffee, rainbows…" I know this list was endless.

Then I was given a book called *14,000 Things To Be Happy About* by Barbara Ann Kipfer. This woman had started making lists when she was in the sixth grade of all the things she enjoyed in life. It's a great spirit-lifter! I love to just pick up the book and flip through pages at random. It always makes me smile. Here are a few samples: "steel drums, jazz dances, leaves in great golden drifts as crisp as beaten gold foil, flaky-crust meat loaf, hot chocolate at an outdoor café, herb roasted chicken (a lot of her choices are food), a scarecrow that does not work, blue topaz, at a 6 A.M. breakfast watching the sky perform, thirsty children kissing water from a fountain, beaver lodges, albino watermelon seeds, diamond mines, a thermos lunch, singing along to the movie *Carousel*, dark blue Indian cotton, apricot butterfly rolls, consuming M&Ms by color groups, being motioned to come sit by someone, the meaning of a bird's song, Sunday papers, a riot of colors…" When was the last time you gave attention to things like that?

In their book, *The 500-Year Delta*, Watts Wacker and Jim Taylor give business prophecies for the future. They state, "What society has always treasured is what is scarce…Satisfaction and domestic contentment have rarity, and rarity, as always, has the greatest value…If you want status, walk into a room and announce that, amidst the ambient chaos of our times, you're a happy person." One of my favorite compliments was given to me in class one day: "Chellie, you'd have fun in a paper bag all by yourself." Yes!

Live your life today so that, if someone said that to you, it would be true.

Today's Affirmation: "I enjoy life and everyone around me enjoys me enjoying life!"

169
The Jost Vacano Lessons

"Getting there isn't half the fun—it's all the fun."

—Robert Townsend

When I was working as a secretary in the motion picture industry, I became known in our office as the person who could locate people or things that no one else could find. These assignments were great fun—they were like detective work to me. But when I was given my first one: "Get me the home phone number of the cinematographer who shot *Coal Miner's Daughter,*" my first thought was, "I don't know who that is. And who would give me, a stranger, his home phone number anyway?" But the boss said "Do it!" so I picked up the phone and started calling people. This was how I learned what a magical instrument the telephone is.

The first call I made was to the cinematographers union. They told me that the person I wanted was Jost Vacano, but they either didn't have or wouldn't give me his home number. I asked them who might have it, and they suggested the production company or his agent. When I called the production company, I spoke to three different people, none of whom had the information I sought. I asked each one, "If you don't know, who do you think might know?"

This, I discovered is a magic question. Invariably, everyone I asked had an idea or two of who might know the answer. Many times they even had their phone number and gave it to me. I kept notes of every suggestion and followed every possible lead.

The search took two days, but eventually I got to the person who had the answer, and I delivered to my boss the home phone number of Jost Vacano—in Munich, Germany! After that, I got lots of these assignments.

The Jost Vacano lessons are:

1. When you don't know something, call someone who might know.
2. If they don't know, ask them who they think might know.
3. Keep lists of who might know.
4. Remember that somewhere, someone knows—you just have to find them.
5. Keep calling until you know.

Today's Affirmation: "I always say just the right thing that makes people happy to help me."

170

Dreams, Luck, and Diligence

"By the streets of 'by and by' one arrives at the house of 'never.'"

—Miguel de Cervantes

Dreams and goals are not the same. Just thinking how nice it would be to have a bigger house, a new car, a business of your own, the relationship you've always wanted, a vacation in Europe, a diamond ring, or a vacation home, won't get it for you. The dream is there to spur you to action. It is not action itself.

Some people seem to think that good things happen to people through sheer luck. They think that other people in life are just luckier than they are—that they have these things through some unfair, lucky twist of fate. This belief disempowers them completely. Instead of putting some effort into achieving their dreams, they fantasize about winning the lottery, inheriting a fortune from a long-lost relative, or that someone will come along, see their potential, and shower them with gifts. Once in a blue moon, this actually happens to someone, and then all the dreamers use that as the shining example that their fantasies could come true. Never mind that the odds are fourteen million to one.

When these odds beat them, they often turn resentful and bemoan their fate, saying life isn't fair. They start to hate the people who have the things they want. Resentment will get them nothing. It is a misuse of creative energy. It's been said "resentment is like drinking poison and waiting for the other person to die." Instead of resenting those who have the things they want, they need to find out what they do to get them, and then do those things. This is the true road to riches. I've found that most people who have the things they want in life work diligently to have them. But resentful people will just ignore the legions of people who work for what they want, and point to one of the few who were born rich or someone who achieved wealth through exploitation of others. This enables them to stay stuck in their lack and limitation. They win their argument but lose the game of life.

This is the formula for turning your dreams into reality:

1. Write down your dream in detail—now it is a goal.
2. Write down your action plan to achieve your goal.
3. Every day, send out one ship that is on your action plan.
4. If you want the goal sooner, send out more than one ship on your action plan.
5. Find successful people you admire and copy their action plans.
6. Make a goal budget, outlining what you will do with more abundance.
7. Visualize your success daily and believe in your ability to create it.

You can have everything in life you want. You just have to send out some ships to bring it in to shore.

Today's Affirmation: "I walk, talk, look, act, think, and am rich!"

171

Choosing the Right Goal

"Life is lived on the road—not at the inn."

—Spanish proverb

Many people have asked me how to choose the right goals. Or they anxiously cry that they don't know what they want. I tell them, "Your best guess for today will do." It doesn't have to be the right goal, the best, brightest, or perfect goal. Any old goal will do. Its purpose is to get you out on the road experiencing life. Once you're on the road, anything can happen.

It's like you're sitting in your car in Dallas, Texas, wondering whether you want to drive to New York or San Francisco. You can sit there for years, asking passersby which city they like best, collecting conflicting recommendations. You can send away for brochures from travel agencies and chambers of commerce, you can search the Internet for answers to your questions: how many people live there? What are they like? Will they like me? What's the weather like? Will I be able to stand the heat, the cold, the rain, the sun, the crowds, the isolation, the fear? Will I be happy there? Will I be loved?

There is no way to answer these questions without putting the pedal to the metal and driving to one city or the other and finding out in real life and real time, instead of endlessly perusing your mental images of what might happen. Ultimately, you must go. Or you will grow old and die in that car without ever having been anywhere, inertia and fear your only companions. And on your tombstone, your epitaph will read: "Born—Waited—Died."

But if you go, what adventures await you! You will experience Life at first hand; its richness, its vastness, the high roads, and rocky roads; your chance for heart-pounding joy will be paid for with heart-wrenching tears, but you will know you are alive, alive, alive! Panting and sweating and anxious sometimes—there are brigands on the highway—but success awaits you at the top of the hill with moments of radiance and complete love.

So choose New York—or San Francisco—it doesn't matter. Just get going! You will find out when you get there if New York was the right choice. If it was, great; if not, move on to San Francisco. But it's just as likely that on the drive to New York, as you pass through Nashville, you decide that Nashville is a pretty cool place. And you could decide to live your life, completely happy, in Nashville—a town that wasn't even your planned destination. That is the magic of goals—they get you places you would never have gone if you hadn't had them.

Life is lived on the road. You pick your goal, you choose your destination—and Life takes over. Put your pedal to the metal and drive!

Today's Affirmation: "My best guess for today is my best plan for today!"

172

New Projects

"I never did a day's work in my life. It was all fun."

—Thomas Edison

When requested to fit a new project into my calendar, I ask myself these three questions:

1. Is it going to do a lot of good?
2. Is it going to be a lot of fun?
3. Is it going to make me a lot of money?

This is the first test, and at least two out of three answers must be yes. Then I ask two more questions:

1. Is it going to take a lot of work?
2. Is it going to take a lot of time?

Hopefully, the answers to these questions are no. If they are yes, I have a final question:

1. Is it worth doing anyway?

If the answer to that is yes, I do it.

Today's Affirmation: "I do a lot of good. I make a lot of money. I have a lot of fun."

173
Market Research

"We jump off buildings and make our wings on the way down."

—Ray Bradbury

It was 1990, and the recession was in full swing in California. I had survived in business one year after losing my biggest customer, and most of my clients and friends knew about it. Now they were afraid as business prospects diminished, money got tighter, and "lean and mean" became the business order of the day. I started getting a flood of calls that sounded like this: "Chellie, things are getting difficult. When you had your problems last year, what did you do? Somehow you survived a major downturn in your business—maybe I can, too."

Jumping in to help, I dispensed a lot of free advice over lunch. When three people in the same week told me I should teach a class in these principles, the *Financial Stress Reduction® Workshop* was born. Or rather, the *flier* for the workshop was born.

One of the most important ideas I had gleaned through my own disaster recovery program was this: "Do What Makes Money First." I couldn't afford to spend an inordinate amount of time and money creating and advertising a workshop that wasn't going to produce income for me and my company. I needed to make sure it would sell. So, I wrote a flier advertising the benefits of the workshop, cut and pasted some graphics on it, and mailed it out to my entire mailing list.

And waited.

No one called. But by this time, I was committed to the idea of my workshop, had visualized how it could help people and I wanted to do it. Unwilling to give up, I got out the mailing list and started making phone calls to the likely suspects I thought would be interested in this class. Over the phone, with enthusiasm and excitement, I promoted the benefits of the class and enrolled twelve people within two weeks. (These are my personal examples of the principles "Sending Out Ships" and "The Money is in the Phone.")

Soon, I had twelve people destined to show up for class. I had sent out the ships, the ships had come in and were due to be unloaded in three weeks. Then, and only then, I sat down to write the workshop.

Years later, I met a woman who did it the other way around. She invested $13,000 in four-color brochures, mailing lists and advertisements for her weekend seminar. Breathless with anticipation, she waited for the phone to ring and for enrollments to arrive in the mail. She never made a phone call herself. When only two people signed up for her workshop, she canceled it and folded her business—a $13,000 loss.

Research your idea to make sure people want it and that you can sell it before investing money in it.

Today's Affirmation: "People are clamoring to pay me for my wonderful services!"

174
Rewarding Investments

"Inflation is the crabgrass in your savings."

—Robert Orben

Anne Farrelly, a financial planner in Los Angeles and author of *Invest Without Stress* gave me some figures years ago regarding particular investments:

If you had invested $10,000 on December 31, 1979 in the following companies, this is the amount of money you would have earned from that investment by December 31, 1989—just ten years later:

Neutrogena	$286,000
MCI	$294,000
The Gap	$355,000
Wal Mart	$530,000
The Limited	$615,000
Circuit City	$810,000

This is very good money to be making while you're sleeping.

Anne went on to say that during the same period, if you had made a $5,000 investment in Growth Fund of America on the worst possible day of each year (buying in at the highest price of the year) for the past fifteen years for a total investment of $75,000, the investment would have grown to $325,890. The key point is that investing—even at the wrong time—is better than not investing and sitting on the sidelines, waiting for the "perfect" time.

In the nineties, the stock market had the biggest boom ever. The Dow Jones Industrial Average went from the 3,000 range to over 10,000. Lots of money was made during that period of time, even if some of it was lost when the technology bubble burst in 1999 and the next downturn began. Cumulatively, over the long haul, the stock market goes up.

So what do you invest in? Financial advisors recommend having a varied portfolio of stocks, bonds, mutual funds, real estate, etc., in order to mitigate your risk (otherwise known as "hedging your bets".) When investing some funds in a single stock, pick a company whose business you know well and whose future prospects look particularly good to you. For example, my brother-in-law, Dick, had some extra funds he wanted to invest. He had noticed that the local Cheesecake Factory, where he often went for dinner, was always busy. The food was delicious, the service was exceptional, and they seemed to be successful. He did some research on their financials and their growth pattern, and decided this was a company he wanted to invest in. Over the next few years, he quadrupled his money.

You can't win if you don't play the game. But I suggest you get a coach.

Today's Affirmation: "All my investments pay me handsome rewards."

175
Home Ownership

"The first payment is what made us think we were prosperous, and the other nineteen is what showed us we were broke."

—Will Rogers

Owning your own home is one of the American Dreams. But it seems to me that many people scrimp and save to buy a home and then are "house poor"—they can't go anywhere or do anything because all their available income is going to pay their mortgage! In *Rich Dad, Poor Dad*, Robert Kiyosaki states he doesn't even consider a home an asset. He says it's because there are so many other attendant expenses that go with home ownership that it is a drain on most people's income. It is a liability that "takes money out of your pocket" rather than an asset that "puts money in your pocket." During recessions, we all know it is possible to lose money in real estate—it's not a slam-dunk investment.

When considering whether or not to buy a house or condominium, consider first your lifestyle. Are you part of a family with children who want the stability of a home and neighborhood? Are you home a lot of the time? Are you single, do you travel a lot or are you out every evening? If so, how much value are you getting out of owning a home if you're never there? (For me, this is sort of like spending a lot of money on a hotel room—the only time I'm there is when I'm asleep!)

Yes, there are tax advantages to owning a home as an investment vehicle, since you get an income tax deduction for your mortgage interest. But take another look at the total amount of interest you are paying over the life of a mortgage loan and it might not look so attractive. And don't forget your budget for all the expenses involved with home ownership:

1. Mortgage payment—principal and interest
2. Interior decorating, furniture, fixtures
3. Carpets and drapes
4. Appliances
5. Landscaping
6. Lawn and garden maintenance
7. Construction, renovations, repairs—major and minor
8. Property taxes
9. Homeowner's insurance

And then, whenever your income increases, you buy a bigger house with a bigger mortgage and need better furniture, appliances, and landscaping to go with it, and you're house-poor again.

What else could you do with all that money?

Today's Affirmation: "I appreciate all my appreciating assets!"

176
Home Mortgages

"The old woman triumphantly announced that she had borrowed enough money to pay all her debts."

—P.L. Lord

Anyone who has ever bought a home has been dismayed to find out how interest is amortized over the life of the conventional thirty-year mortgage. During the first fifteen years of the loan, the majority of the loan payment is interest. In fact, for the first five years, it's almost *all* interest. It's not until the twentieth year of the mortgage that the monthly payment is even half interest and half principle. Not to mention the fact that after paying for thirty years, depending on the interest rate, you will have paid more than twice the amount of the original price of the house.

I wonder what genius figured this out. It's great for the mortgage lenders—in the first few years of a mortgage, they get all the interest charges paid upfront and you still owe them nearly the entire amount of principal. I suppose it didn't make that much difference in the days when most people bought a house and stayed in it their whole lives. But today, people move much more often. In our consumer-oriented society, people move up to the biggest and best house they can afford as soon as their income rises. With each new mortgage, almost all of their mortgage payment is interest; they have not made any significant principal payments at all. Essentially, they are just paying a *fee* for living in the house. People will argue, "Yes, but it's tax deductible!" But you still have to pay out 100 percent of the fee in order to earn a 15-30 percent tax deduction.

I suggest you start looking at your amortization schedule. Don't just pay the regular payment each month as an automatic habit, but look at exactly how much money is going for principle and how much for interest. You might want to start making extra payments to reduce the principle of the loan—if you plan to stay in your home for many years, this can greatly reduce the total amount of interest you will pay. Or you might find, as one of my workshop participants named Laura did, that the second mortgage you got ten years ago was a negatively amortized mortgage. This means that the monthly payment doesn't even cover the amount of interest charged, let alone reduce the principle. Laura was horrified to discover that, after ten years of faithfully making her monthly payment, she owed more money than she had originally borrowed.

Real estate is like any other investment. You can make money in it and you can lose money in it. But when you're borrowing money to buy it, please do the math so you know what your *real* costs are.

Today's Affirmation: "All my investments maximize my money!"

177

It's Ten O'Clock. Do You Know Where Your Money Is?

"The truth will set you free—but first it will piss you off."

—Werner Erhard

"Please balance my checkbook for me!" My new client, an attractive blonde woman who held a highly responsible job in city government pleaded with me. "No matter what I do, I just never can get my checking account to balance."

I soon discovered why. When I started matching her bank statement with her check register, I discovered that she rarely wrote in the correct amount of the check. The check and the bank statement would show that she wrote a check to the cleaners for $42.30. But she recorded this check on her check register as $40! The check to the clothing store was written for $178.62, but her check register said $200. Most of her checks were rounded figures instead of the exact amount. Then, of course, there were the six or seven checks she just forgot to record at all...

In the twelve years I owned my bookkeeping service, I encountered many people who just couldn't master balancing a checkbook. Twenty-six percent of Americans say they have balanced their checkbooks in the past year, according to Maritz Marketing Research. Not that many, is it? Some people regularly closed their checking accounts and started over every year in order to get a fresh start at trying to keep track of it. But this became the new habit pattern, and they still didn't balance their checkbook, knowing they'd get a fresh start next year. These people also tended to have the unfortunate belief that they could call the bank each day to find out how much money was left in their account. Please note: this doesn't work because the bank can only give you the total based on the checks that have gotten to them for payment. They don't know about the $300 check you wrote yesterday and mailed to someone, so they aren't deducting that amount when they give you your total!

Balancing your checkbook is part of counting your money. It's important to know how much money you have at your disposal at any given time. Otherwise, you have tension and stress every time you write a check, wondering if it will bounce! Here is a handy tip for keeping your check register correct: always write the amount of the check in your register first. Then write the check. This will become a habit, and you won't ever again forget to record checks. This will make the process of doing a regular monthly bank reconciliation easy and smooth—a "no more tears" proposition—and it will only take five minutes. Your tension and fear will dissipate and you will enjoy feeling in control of your money.

Today's Affirmation: "I love to count my money and I create lots of money to count!"

178

Going Shopping vs. Going Spending

"To pretend to satisfy one's desire by possession is like using straw to put out a fire."

—Chinese proverb

A major "Money Malady" is "spending bulimia," which is a habit pattern of buying things out of impulse, without regard to chosen spending priorities. For some, the buying habit is a quick fix to emotionally lift their spirits—it's fun to buy a new outfit, a new golf club, or a new car and then have the satisfaction of the complimentary "oohs" and "ahhs" from other people. Some buy presents for others as a way of buying love, the emotional high is seeing someone else excited over a new toy and being grateful for the gift and the gift-giver. Other people are on the spending cycle because they are used to it and haven't thought of another hobby—going to the mall has become a national pastime.

Unfortunately, the quick fix doesn't last long. You're high on the purchase for maybe one day, and high on the compliments for another day. Then you've got to start all over again, buying something else to get another fix.

I believe in replacement therapy—if you've developed a bad habit, it's easier to replace it with another habit that is good than to just stop doing the bad habit. So instead of telling people they can't go shopping, I tell them they *can* go shopping—they just can't go spending. For example, you want to go to the mall. Great! Go—but leave all your cash, checks, and credit cards at home. You take a tablet and a pen with you and as you shop, you write down all the things you'd like to buy and their price tags. It's really quite fun, because money is no object—you're just shopping, not buying. You still have the enjoyment of looking at all the wonderful toys and beautiful things—like when you go to a great exhibit or museum. When you get home, total up all the prices of the items you would have bought and congratulate yourself—"I saved $40,000 today!"

This interrupts the mental program you have of impulse buying. Put the list away for a week. If you can still remember what was on the list a week later and you still feel like you want it, then you can add it to your High Budget and plan for having it. This ensures that you will only buy the things you really want enough to plan for and gives you back the power and control over your spending.

I love to shop by looking through catalogues. I cheerfully dog-ear each page that has something I like on it. Then I put the catalogue on the shelf. After a week or so, I pick up the catalogue and try to remember what it was I thought I wanted. If I can't remember, I chuck the catalogue.

Do you remember what you bought when you went shopping last month? Are you still as excited about it as you were then? Half as much? Or sorry about it, thinking, "What a waste"? Stop spending and go shopping instead!

Today's Affirmation: "I have all the riches I desire right now!"

179

Spend Money with Joy

"He threw his money about like a man with no arms."

—William McIlvanney

When you spend money, spend it with joy. Spend a little extra on service personnel. Tip above the usual amount. You will create a lot of happiness for them, and you'll feel good about it, too. Some people resent tipping, complain about it, and are always cheap about it. I hope they aren't surprised when they don't get good service. It's one of those self-fulfilling prophecies. Spending a little extra money—especially when you aren't required to do it—can actually increase your income.

I used to attend a weekly breakfast of a group called "The Inside Edge" at the Beverly Hills Hotel. It was a great, high-energy meeting filled with lots of wonderful people who were making money, doing good, and having fun. We had terrific motivational speakers like Jack Canfield, Barbara De Angelis, Martin Rutte, Nathanial Brandon, and Susan Jeffers. It was one of the more expensive groups I belonged to, but it was worth it.

After the meeting, everyone headed for valet parking, and although there were five or six valets, it took some time for them to handle the seventy-five to one hundred people who were leaving all at once. Sometimes I had to wait thirty minutes to get my car. I wanted to get to my office and get to work right away, but didn't want to leave the meeting early in order to avoid waiting in line. I knew that most people gave the valets the standard one-dollar tip, but I started giving them two dollars.

It only took a couple of meetings for one valet to figure out that I was good for a two-dollar tip every week. He started looking for me when the meeting let out, and when he saw me come through the door, he went to get my car. He began parking my car in a premium space near the entrance, and by the time I made it down the walkway to the driveway, he had my car ready and waiting for me to go. All this extra service for a mere dollar more!

I figure I saved myself about two hours of waiting each month and it only cost me four dollars. Since my billing rate was forty dollars per hour, I was actually making seventy-six dollars on this transaction. I was delighted to pay the valet for this service.

Stop sniping about tipping. Pay up cheerfully. Isn't that how you'd like people to pay you?

Today's Affirmation: "I always appreciate the fine service I receive and I reward it well!"

180

The Leopard Slippers

"It takes two flints to make a fire."

—Louisa May Alcott

Betty, a retail seller of miscellaneous goods, approached me at the networking meeting. Knowing I like animal prints, she was always on the lookout for the next leopard-zebra-furry gizmo to sell me. "I just got in these great leopard slippers—they'd look perfect on you!" she sang. "I'll take them!" I sang back. Great transaction so far. Betty knew what I liked and looked out for me—I felt special and very well served as a customer. Then it went downhill.

"Can you come over and pick them up?" she said. Well, she lived on the other side of town and in Los Angeles that means a major drive. I didn't want to spend over two hours round trip to go get them, so I asked her if she was going to be at the next networking meeting. Frowning, she said, "Yeah, but I don't know if I can remember to bring them." I suggested she put them in her car when she got home and I'd remember to ask her for them. Then she said, "Yeah, but there's no room in my car." "Okay, mail them to me." "Oh, that's so much trouble." That was all the help I was going to give her to help *her* sell *me* slippers. I said, "Well, Betty, if you find a way to get the slippers to me, I'll buy them."

What a pity! A transaction that had begun happily and prosperously for all concerned ended with two people dissatisfied and thinking the other was being difficult. Upon reflection, I think we each thought we were doing the other a favor. She had taken time to look out for something I might like and the slippers were the result of her thoughtfulness. She expected more appreciation from me, and therefore thought that I would be glad to go out of my way to solve the delivery problem. I thought I was contributing to her prosperity by giving her an easy sale and expected her to take responsibility for delivery. The bottom line was neither of us was committed enough to the end result to be willing to be inconvenienced.

We laughed about this later, and both acknowledged the importance of service, completion, and follow-through in every transaction, no matter how small. Every business depends on customer loyalty, satisfaction, and good will. Even the smallest thing can damage it. Preserve it at all costs.

Today's Affirmation: "All my relationships are joyful and prosperous!"

181
Stephanie's

"You can make more friends in two months by becoming more interested in other people than you can in two years trying to get people interested in you."

—Dale Carnegie

More money too, I might add. I often window shopped at the little boutique in Pacific Palisades called Stephanie's. She had the most beautiful clothes on display! But the prices were a little higher than I was used to, and I was afraid they didn't fit into my budget. So, with a sigh, I passed by.

Then, one day, I was at a Chamber of Commerce networking mixer, and the door prize was 20 percent off merchandise at Stephanie's. Oh, I wanted to win that prize! And when Ted Silverberg, the Allstate Insurance agent, reached his hand in the basket to pull out the winner's business card, I focused all my winning concentration on him. Yes, yes—I won!

I ran right down to Stephanie's the next day and started browsing through all the fine things. Which item should I buy? The beautiful black leather belt with the special gold buckle? Or the fine rust-colored mohair sweater with pearl buttons? Stephanie watched me for a little and then walked over to where I stood, fingering all the beautiful merchandise. "Are you looking for something in particular?" she asked with a smile.

"No," I said, "but it seems I like everything you have! I just won the discount certificate at the Chamber mixer and I have a question."

"Yes?"

"Is the discount good for only one item or for everything I buy today?"

Stephanie's eyes sparkled as she gave me the perfect entrepreneur's answer: "Everything you buy today!"

Now Stephanie really went to work. She got a pad of paper and a pen, sat me down and started asking questions about my wardrobe and my lifestyle. She asked me to describe my favorite outfits, what I did for work, and what I did for fun. She asked me if I owned a black skirt, a black blazer or cowboy boots. She made notes as I answered her questions, and after her pad was full, she jumped up and started putting outfits together for me, all the while giving me ideas of how to use the items she showed me with things I already owned at home. This was true service! I felt cared about, listened to, and well served.

I spent $1,200 that day—and many thousands more in the years since.

Make buying from you a pleasure. Make seeing you a pleasure. Make hearing your voice on the phone a pleasure. Make everything about being with you a pleasure.

Today's Affirmation: "I provide extraordinary service and reap rich rewards!"

182

Talk about Money with Your Honey

"There are two kinds of people in life—spenders and savers. Usually, they are married to each other."

—Anonymous

"Money is power" is a commonly held belief by both men and women. Whoever has the money in the relationship has the power in the relationship. This power is almost always abused by the one who has it and resented by the one who doesn't. This is not a prescription for love and romance. Not talking about it only makes it worse. The subject has to be addressed, and if the relationship is to thrive, joint decisions about money must be made.

My fiancé and I were very happy with one financial program that worked quite well: we each took a certain amount of money monthly from our joint funds—we called it our "allowance." This was money that we each had for personal items, and we didn't have to account for this money to each other in any way. I believe this is a necessity for married couples. Then you can always feel free to go shopping and buy something without having to ask the other for permission, or explain the value of your purchase after the fact.

Make sure the rules are clear to each other, however. My fiancé and I were doing fine with our allowances until one day, when he brought up the idea that we should buy a new car. I said, "Fine, but what are we going to do about the down payment?" to which he replied, "Well, I thought we could use our allowance that we've been saving." I looked at him, eyes wide in shock (picture deer caught in headlights). He had been saving all of his personal money. Not only that, but he just assumed that I was saving mine, too! I remember how angry he was when I told him I had spent all of my allowance. Oops.

Make your relationship work. Talk about your money, your expectations, your goals, your beliefs. Write them down. Then write some positive money affirmations and practice them together. Give each other space to talk about what is really important to you financially, even if you're afraid the other person will think you're frivolous, cheap, irresponsible, tight, or whatever. If the things you really want aren't provided for, either in your current (low or medium) budget or your goal (high) budget, anger and resentment are going to creep into your relationship. Design the plan to have everything you want, and what you have to do to get it. Then prioritize your goals and work on achieving them together.

And make sure you're together on your definition of "allowance."

Today's Affirmation: "Everyone in my home creates health, wealth, and harmony there!"

183

You Are Fabulous!

"People travel to wonder at the height of mountains, at the huge waves of the sea, at the long courses of rivers, at the vast compass of the ocean, at the circular motion of the stars, and they pass themselves by without wondering."

—St. Augustine

When you were growing up, were you ever told not to brag? Perhaps you were put down for talking positively about yourself. You might have been taught to cover your pride with a patina of false modesty because that was considered appropriate behavior. Unfortunately, that habit of "being nice" makes it really difficult to ask for a raise, ask for a promotion, or a larger fee from a client.

We don't take inventory of the evidence we have to feel good about ourselves. What we do is tell ourselves, "Oh, I should have done that better." A perfect example of that is when a friend of mine was making her first speech in front of an audience. Susan was very nervous, but I encouraged her to speak from her heart and her knowledge to help the listeners and she would be fine. She did a great job, and I congratulated her afterward, telling her she did great.

Immediately, Susan started telling me how she *didn't* do great. "Oh, I forgot to say this, and I stumbled over that, and I screwed up this other..." I said, "Stop right there. Everybody who speaks has the same story. What you need to know is something I learned as an actor: most of the audience can't tell when you've made a mistake. They don't know that you forgot to say something, because they don't have access to the script. They don't know that you messed up this or that, they just get a feeling from you, and the feeling that you gave them tonight was great." Susan blushed in pleasure as she thought about this. I said, "So you don't get to criticize yourself any about that. Just don't let your mind go there. Go to the place where you were wonderful and fabulous and think about that. Tonight is your night to bask in the glory. You can work on improvement another day." Susan grinned and said she liked that idea a lot.

I love to give (and get!) positive messages like that. They are little valentines of pleasure to be smiled over and cherished. You, too, can be a harbinger of good tidings to the people around you. Take the time to give compliments. It takes very little—and it's fun! And people are so appreciative. No one gets enough compliments. They hear "constructive criticism" internally and externally: what they did wrong, what's missing, what they need to improve—not what's great.

Change that. Be happy, fabulous, and successful—because you are!

Today's Affirmation. "I am happy, fabulous, and successful!"

184
Public Speaking without Fear

"Courage is fear that has said its prayers."

—American proverb

Most people are terrified of speaking in public. They're afraid people won't like them, that they'll look or do something foolish, that they will be ridiculed and hence outcast. These fears flow through their minds, their bodies mirror their thoughts. At the networking meetings I attend, the worst part of the meeting for many people is when they have to stand up for thirty seconds and say who they are and what they do.

I was no exception. When I first started public speaking, I had all of these symptoms and more. People thought that since I had a background in theater, this would be easy for me. But it made no difference. Acting was playing a character different from myself, and someone else had written all the lines. When I started public speaking, I was myself, and the lines were my thoughts and my feelings. I felt totally naked. "What if they don't like me?" I thought. "Is my hair okay? Am I wearing the right dress? Will they criticize my ideas? Will they laugh at my jokes or laugh when they're not supposed to?" No wonder I was a wreck. But I kept doing it, knowing that somehow it would get better.

It all changed for me one day when I was scheduled to give a talk to a group of one hundred businesswomen. As I walked to the podium, the familiar litany of criticism sounded in my brain. But as I turned to face the audience, something new happened. I looked out at the sea of faces and connected with a woman in the front row. She was smiling—but the overwhelming impression I had was that she was *hopeful*. She had come to hear about financial stress reduction—and she needed it. I looked at the woman next to her and felt the same need.

Suddenly, I understood. This talk wasn't about me—it was about *them*! They had come to hear answers to their pressing financial problems. They thought I might have some solutions to the problems that were plaguing them. They didn't care what I looked like. They came to hear the message, not to see the messenger. In that instant, my inner voices quieted and I prayed, "Dear God, please put the words in my mouth that need to be heard tonight that can help somebody." I focused on helping others, and the words flew from my mouth. I was filled with energy, power, and passion. I was connected to the audience and they to me. The speech was over before I knew it. The applause was thunderous.

I've been a professional speaker for over ten years now. I say that prayer now before every speech, and haven't been nervous since.

Your only thought when you are working should be how best you can serve other people. It's not about how you look, or how much money or acknowledgment you're getting. What do people need that you have? Your job is to give it to them. Put your attention on your customer, where it belongs. Get your ego out of the way and your fear will leave with it. And then riches will pour into your life.

Today's Affirmation: "I enrich everyone and everyone enriches me."

185
The Preacher and the Bad Check

"It is the foolish sheep that makes the wolf his confessor."

—German proverb

In a 1999 article, the *Los Angeles Times* reported that the district attorney's office decided there was insufficient evidence to charge a preacher when he deposited a bad check for $87,000 and then withdrew funds against it. Apparently, a man had offered the church a $10,000 donation if the pastor would cash the check for him, explaining that he did not possess proper identification. Somehow, the bank cleared the check and the pastor took out about $50,000 in a series of increments and gave it to the man. A few days later, when the bank informed the preacher that the check was bad, the man was nowhere to be found.

When I owned my bookkeeping service, I once received a letter from someplace in Africa, proposing that they use my bank account in America to wire funds, for which I would receive a 10 percent commission. Since they wanted to transfer $10 million, I would make $1 million! Boy, did that fantasy look good! But that was all it was—a fantasy. Upon investigation, I found out that other people had acted on this offer, provided the Africans with all their bank information, and then found their accounts totally emptied overnight. When one of my clients later told me he was flying to Africa for a business deal, a chill went down my spine. I asked him details, and as he told his story, I saw that it was suspiciously similar. I told him of my research and showed him my letter. He blanched—it was the same people! He immediately canceled his plans, and thanked God for his narrow escape.

There are sharks in the water. Sometimes they're wearing dolphin clothing. Check their teeth.

Today's Affirmation: "I help all around me to achieve their heart's desire, and so achieve my own."

186
Cancellations

"That's one thing I'll say for The Beatles, we always honored our agreements. For years, every time we had a record that went to Number One we still had six months' work already booked at little ballrooms for fifty quid a night when we could have been earning maybe £5,000. But we always honored them."

—George Harrison

Cancellations are a misery. You've planned a party but then several people call to cancel at the last minute. Some people don't even call to explain or apologize, they just don't show up. Prospective clients fail to arrive for an appointment. The sponsor of the event pulls its support at the eleventh hour.

Violet was a case in point. A business owner, she had enrolled in my workshop because she wanted to grow her business. We had a great conversation about her dreams and goals. She planned to come to the September class and promised to send a deposit.

The deposit didn't arrive. I called to remind her of the first class and asked about the check. She said she had just gotten busy, but would bring the check with her on the day of the first class. Neither the check nor she showed up.

Violet apologized profusely when I called her the next day. There was a contract dispute that had taken all her time and attention. I told her I would send her the tape recording of the session she missed, and she could catch up with the class the next week. She thanked me and said she would send a check in the meantime.

Of course, the check didn't arrive. Neither did Violet at class number two. I made sure to go back over the reasons she wanted to take the course when I talked with her the next day. Again, she promised to come to the next class and I sent another tape.

It didn't surprise me when she missed class three. In the end, I didn't get the money, just a note canceling her participation until her busy season was over next June.

Cancellations happen because people have difficulty saying "no." They don't want to offend you, they don't want to end the relationship, they don't want you to argue with them. So they say, "Fine, wonderful, I'll be there, I promise, you can count on me," all the while holding on to a reservation in their mind that they might not keep this agreement.

There are people in this world whose word is golden. They tell the truth. They make no excuses. Whatever they say they will, they do. If they don't want to do something, they will tell you "no." Collect these people. And be one of them. Keep all your agreements. Because what goes around comes around, and if you don't want people to cancel on you, don't cancel on others. Show up.

And if you keep trying to get money out of a tuna—guess who's a tuna, too?

Today's Affirmation: "I keep all my agreements and others keep theirs with me."

187
Collections

"When a feller says it ain't the money but the principle of the thing, it's the money."

—Abe Martin

Sometimes people owe you money and are slow to pay up. You can be diligent, have a follow-up system in place, send second notices, or, as a last resort, sue them or turn them over to collection agencies to do all that for you. But for the most part, when you have to go into these gyrations to get paid, you have already lost the war.

When someone owes you money, and doesn't pay you, month after month, year after year, there are only two reasons:

1. They are tuna: they can't pay you.
2. They are sharks: they don't want to pay you.

Now doesn't that just make you mad? Well, get over it, because it's your fault.

As a dolphin, your job is to do business with dolphins. Don't go making loans or payment agreements with tuna—they're not going to be able to pay you back. It's their nature. You can get frustrated, and yell at them, beg them, send them angry letters, and sue them, but if they don't have any money you're not going to be able to get any money.

And if you can't get money out of a tuna, you surely aren't going to get money out of a shark. Even if you sue them, they're likely to sue you back. Even if, eventually, you do get some money, along the way you'll probably bleed to death from the shark bites. Sharks won't hesitate to bite you, you know. At the very least, you'll have spent a lot of time, money, and energy in a crazy-making, anger-provoking business. Not my idea of a good time.

If somebody's "got your goat" and is making you angry because they're not paying you the money you are owed, put the responsibility for this back where it belongs—on you. You picked these people to do a financial transaction with. Bad idea. Big mistake.

Now you have to put an end to both the anger you hold for them and the lingering hope that "someday" they're going to pay you. So write off the debt. You just paid a fee for a Life Seminar called "How to Lose Money Swimming With Sharks and Tuna." Tune in to your higher self, write them a genuinely nice letter forgiving the debt, and consider it your "School of Hard Knocks" graduate diploma—bought and paid for. If you truly forgive them and yourself for this experience, you win. And more money will flow to you from other, expected and unexpected, places.

Then pray that you don't have to repeat the course.

Today's Affirmation: "All my clients pay me in full, fast!"

188

Give and It Will Be Given to You

*"Help thy brother's boat across, and lo!
Thine own has reached the shore."*

—Hindu proverb

I sat hunched in my chair at my computer, going over my Accounts Receivable. Sometimes I will offer clients a billing system based on regular monthly payments. Most of the time it works out well, but other times, people just don't pay as they had promised.

On this particular morning, I reviewed two accounts that were more than a year old. Now it was time either to write a strong demand letter with a threat of legal action or to turn the accounts over to a collection agency. But as I sat there neither choice felt good to me. Quite the opposite: I felt depressed, uncomfortable, and irritable. I thought about what action would make me feel good and it came to me clearly: send these people a nice note wishing them the best and letting them know I was writing off their balance. With that thought, a smile danced across my face and I wrote off $1,195. It was a joyful choice that I felt happy about.

The next day, my accountant called to tell me that I was due a tax refund. That evening, I went out to play poker. Poker is a fun and relaxing hobby of mine. Believe me, I am not a high stakes player! This particular evening I was having a rather lucky run of cards, what poker players call "being on a rush." I was up about $100 when I hit an unbelievable "rush." I got four of a kind, a straight flush, all the great hands. The cards all just lined up the way I wanted them and I won and won and won. I left the poker table with more money than I had ever won before at one sitting: $1,115!

Sunday morning, as I drove to my Easter family gathering for church and brunch, I wondered why I had been so lucky this particular weekend. Between the tax refund and poker, I had received $2,773 in "Magic Money"—unexpected income. A chill ran down my spine as I suddenly realized it was a complete demonstration of the principle of "give, and it will be given to you." By releasing others of their debt to me, I had opened the floodgates of my own prosperity.

I sang the *Hallelujah Chorus* that morning with extra feeling!

Is there a debt you could forgive today?

Today's Affirmation: "The more I give, the more I receive, for both are infinite!"

189

Be Careful What You Don't Ask For—You Might Not Get It

"It is a kind of spiritual snobbery that makes people think they can be happy without money."

—Albert Camus

"Oh, I really don't want to focus on money," said the woman on the phone. A successful executive who worked in training and development for a major corporation, we had met at a networking meeting. She was very interested in my work since she was also in the business of helping people through training, but balked at the idea of taking a class centered on money. Her main goal was to help people and do meaningful work, she said.

I often encounter this same idea, stated in different ways, which comes from the root belief that the pursuit of money for its own sake is inappropriate, and maybe even *bad* (remember "the love of money is the root of all evil"). I've heard many, many people say, "I don't care about the money," or, "The money isn't important to me." What they are trying to make clear is that they have a larger objective, a goal of helping others or doing work they love that transcends their need for money.

Unfortunately, that is not what they *say*. Words are powerful. When they speak their word that they "don't care about money" what they are inadvertently doing is telling their creative mind, God, and the universal power of supply not to send money. Their need to state it this way is indicative that they have a fear-based mentality about money—they are afraid that somehow, if they make a lot of money, it will corrupt them, pull them off course, make them a slave to material things, etc. The universal power of supply that is directed by our creative minds is just a "Yes" machine. Tell it you want money—it says "yes." Tell it you don't want money—it says "Yes." Your choice.

Why not declare instead that "I really want to help and serve people, and making a lot of money will help me do that even better"? Money is neutral—in and of itself it is neither good nor bad. Only the way it's used can be judged in that way. You have the power to decide to use the money that flows into your possession for good: donate to charity, expand your work to help more people, beautify your surroundings, give to the arts, invest in worthy businesses doing socially responsible work. Do care about the money! My belief is that all the truly spiritual, wonderful people should have lots and lots of money, because they are the ones who will use it most positively.

You have to have some money in this world in order to live. Why not have lots of money in order to live well?

Today's Affirmation: "I help and serve people and make a lot of money, which I then use to help and serve people!"

190
Rejection

"There's a four-letter word you must use when you get rejected...NEXT!"

—Jack Canfield

I remember that Jack Nicholson, upon accepting his Academy Award for Best Actor in *One Flew Over the Cuckoo's Nest*, said something like, "I dedicate this to my agent—who told me ten years ago I had no business being a serious actor."

All successful people have stories like this to tell. Albert Einstein failed math. Winston Churchill failed English. Failure is just another step on the road to success. If you get rejected by someone, they just aren't "Your People!" Here are some of the rejection experiences of very famous, successful people:

Alex Haley received 200 rejection notices before *Roots* became a mega-bestseller.

Chicken Soup for the Soul was rejected by thirty-three New York publishers. The best-selling franchise has now sold over 50 million books.

John Grisham's first novel, *A Time to Kill*, was turned down by more than thirty agents and fifteen publishers. There are now more than sixty million copies of his books in print.

The reviewer of Fred Astaire's first screen test said, "Can't act. Can't sing. Can dance a little."

Lust for Life by Irving Stone, a novel that later became a motion picture starring Kirk Douglas as Vincent Van Gogh was described by an editor as "a long, dull novel about an artist."

Harry Warner, President of Warner Brothers pictures, said in 1927, "Who the hell wants to hear actors talk?"

Alexander Graham Bell's banker said to him, "Get that toy out of my office immediately."

"Playing the guitar is all very well, John, but you'll never make a living at it," said John Lennon's Aunt Mimi. *The Beatles Anthology* told how some of his fans made a sign of her quote and sent it to her. She hung it up on display—in the house he bought her with the money he made from playing the guitar.

These are all nay sayings from the nay sayers. They are to be pitied, not believed.

Today's Affirmation: "I am successful—financially and spiritually—in everything I do!"

191
Elevator Opportunities

"I have missed more than nine thousand shots in my career. I have lost almost three hundred games. On twenty-six occasions I have been entrusted to take the game winning shot—and I missed. And I have failed over and over and over again in my life. And that is precisely why I succeed."

—Michael Jordan

The room was bubbling with ideas. We were talking about luck—that magical happenstance also described as preparation meeting opportunity. I had asked the group what would you do if you walked into an elevator and the only other person in it was Bill Gates? Or the Pope? Or Stephen Spielberg? You'd have thirty seconds in which to make an impression. What would you say?

Linda Sivertsen, a professional dog-walker, woke up one morning with a vision of a book of celebrity interviews about experiencing success in every area of life. She followed her dream and wrote her book, *Lives Charmed: Intimate Conversations with Extraordinary People*. But the path to the book's success involves an important elevator story: "I was about halfway through my manuscript and had run out of contacts. I had already interviewed all of my clients and was in need of further subjects. Several publishers had shown interest in my book and were anxiously awaiting several additional 'big names.' I was feeling pressured to deliver.

"I was attending a golf tournament and was introduced to Charles Barkley. He agreed to be interviewed for my book. I was excited and knew in the back of my mind that his best friend, Michael Jordan, would also make a great interview. But I was reluctant to ask him for an introduction.

"One afternoon, I was in the elevator and Michael Jordan got in. He said hello. Feeling timid about asking him to be in my book, I knew I would forever regret it if I didn't at least give it a try. 'Hey, you wouldn't want to be in a book I'm writing, would you?' I knew as soon as I said it that this was a sure way to lose a deal, but my fear of interrupting in Michael's day was greater than my need to get the interview. He smiled and said, 'Uh, I think I'm going to have to pass.' Trying to make light of the situation, I laughed, 'Barkley's doing it,' to which he replied, 'I can see why.' With a smile, Michael left the elevator and was out of sight. Ouch."

Linda's book turned out beautifully, with Woody Harrelson, Leeza Gibbons, Arnold Palmer, Robert Townsend, and other celebrities who share their secrets of creating a charmed life. But Michael Jordan isn't in it, because she wasn't prepared for the elevator opportunity. You can bet she is now. She's working on book two.

And on elevator speeches. When your opportunity gets in the elevator with you, don't you want to be prepared for it? Write down what you'd say to get the interview, get the appointment, get the job, get the date. And start practicing. Get your ships together then people will start remarking how "lucky" you are.

Today's Affirmation: "I am now highly pleasing to myself and to everyone I know."

192
Overnight Success

"If you want more, pay more."

—Stella Adler

We've all heard stories of the "overnight success"—and the one, fabulous break that meant stardom for someone. What I didn't recognize until recently was that there were usually many "lucky breaks" piled on top of each other, year after year, until the one breakout smash hit "suddenly" happened. In reality, it took them ten or twenty years of hard work to get to that one lucky moment. I thought it was just one lucky moment.

Here are some examples of what I mean:

From a very early age, Jon Bon Jovi wanted to be a rock star. He worked as a janitor for two years at his cousin's radio station to earn a living. On the side, he cut upwards of fifty demo records in pursuit of his dream. Finally, one of his songs entitled *Runaway*, was put on a compilation tape and played on the radio. It became an instant hit locally, and Jon hurriedly put together a band, then an album, and got a recording contract. But after two albums, some band members were still living in their parents' homes, because they had no money. It wasn't until their third album, *Slippery When Wet*, that national fame arrived and fortune followed.

Sharon Stone worked in films for more than ten years before *Basic Instinct* made her a superstar. I imagine that she thought any number of the films that she made before that one might be her "lucky break" film. *King Solomon's Mines*? No. *The Year of the Gun*? No.

Colonel Sanders, of Kentucky Fried Chicken Fame, began his business at age sixty-five, after he received his first Social Security check, looked at the tiny amount of money, and decided, "This will never do!" The only thing he could think of to sell was the great recipe he had for fried chicken. Over one thousand restaurants turned down his approach for a partnership. Then one said yes. Then another and another. Overnight success.

Do you have a goal, a dream, a vision of the work you want to do in the world? Do you love it enough to devote this kind of energy, hope, enthusiasm, persistence, and dedication to it? If not—why not? There isn't anything else to do. And tomorrow could be the day. Your lucky break is waiting behind the next daybreak. Or the one after that.

Today's Affirmation: "Today is my lucky day!"

193

Little Actions

"It's no good running a pig farm badly for thirty years while saying 'Really, I was meant to be a ballet dancer.' By that time, pigs are your style."

—Quentin Crisp

Your life is the sum total of all the little actions you take, your daily habit pattern. Successful people are those whose daily habits add up to something great. You don't suddenly one day write a book. You write a paragraph today. Then tomorrow, you write another one. And the next day, another. On a great day, you write a whole page, loving it. On a bad day, you stare at a whole page, hating it. But every day, your goal is to write; your discipline is to write; your support structure is to write.

Don't say: "I wish I could write." Or "I wish I had time to write." You can write—just do it; you have time—the same twenty-four hours everyone has. Nobel Prize-winning author Toni Morrison said, "I wrote at the edges of the day," before her children awoke in the morning and after putting them to bed at night. It was this commitment to her voice and her vision, carried out through little actions every day, that brought her world-renowned success.

Little actions add up, both the actions of commission and the actions of omission. If I want to lose twenty pounds, I have to choose low fat foods and vegetables and omit hot fudge sundaes and brownies. If I want to play the piano beautifully, I have to practice scales today instead of watch television or play baseball. If I want to sell my product or service, I have to confront my fears and make a phone call to a stranger today. I must, each day, make the choice to put off the instant gratification of today in exchange for the delayed gratification that may be years in the future.

This is where habit can serve us well. It's too hard to think through these choices anew each day. I have to make the commitment to my goals once, then perform the little actions each day because I have made them my habit to do them. It's hard only for the first couple of days, then I will have established this pattern as a habit—a habit that will lead me, over the years, to the future success I desire. I don't have to wrestle with myself, try to avoid it, think of other things I'd rather do. It's what I do, it's in my schedule, it's in my blood, it's a habit.

So what are your daily little actions? You are creating your future with them today.

Today's Affirmation: "Every action I take today creates my glorious success."

194

The Jar of Quarters

"Fall down seven times; get up eight."

—Japanese proverb

My secretary, Joanne, was terrific. Bright, thoughtful, energetic—I hired her on the spot. As we worked together over the next few months, there was only one problem: she wouldn't proofread her work. We fell into the habit of her preparing a rough draft, I would proofread the letter, then she would type the final. But often the final draft would also have a typo or two and would have to be done again. It finally dawned on me that this was not an efficient use of my time.

The next morning, I brought a big jar to the office. I put it on my desk, and I told Joanne that the proofreading of her work needed to be reassigned because I could no longer spend time on it. She asked who was going to do it now. "You are," I said. She laughed and said, "Oh, Chellie, you know I'm no good at that! I've tried." "Well," I said, "I think you're going to try harder. You may not work here forever, and my goal is to train you to be so fabulous in your work that when you hand a letter to someone for it to be signed, they can rely on you to have done it perfectly every time. This will get you trust, promotions, and more money.

"From now on, I am going to charge you a quarter for every mistake I find in your work. Each typo, every misspelled word, every missing punctuation mark will cost you. I brought this jar to put the quarters in." Joanne laughed a little and remarked, "That's a big jar. You must think I make a lot of mistakes." "Prove me wrong," I replied, as I gave her some letters.

The first letter cost her seven quarters. We watched together as they clinked into the bottom of the big jar. She went off to do another letter. Five quarters. Day in and day out for the next several weeks, the quarters piled up in the jar. It was beginning to cost her real money. She started getting frustrated with the game, and determined not to fill up that damned jar. She was now motivated to change. We both cheered the day she turned in a perfect letter and no quarters had to go in the jar. She had succeeded in changing her habit. We went out to lunch on the jar money.

Years passed, and eventually Joanne left to take another position. Over time we lost touch. Then one day, I got a phone call from her—she was working in management and very successful. She said that of all the things she had learned while working for me, the lesson that always stood out in her mind was paying a quarter to the jar for mistakes. Now she had her own secretary. And she was the one with the jar of quarters on her desk.

Got a bad habit you'd like to change? Get a jar.

Today's Affirmation: "I work in perfect harmony with the time and tides, and rivers of money flow in to me."

195

The Second Law of a Thousand Times

"Just because you made a mistake doesn't mean you are a mistake."

—Georgette Mosbacher

The first law of a thousand times is that we have to hear the truth a thousand times before we understand it. The second law of a thousand times is that after understanding the truth, it takes a thousand attempts to make it a part of your life before it works. After a thousand tries, you are finally able to make the new truth a part of your life, and you are changed.

The process of change is often slow. It seems that we do what doesn't work over and over, watching ourselves fail, before we get the glimmer of the idea that if we want things to change, we have to change ourselves—otherwise, they don't change. Then we think about change for a long time, fearful of what the new challenge will bring, while the committee in our heads rages arguments pro and con. Finally, it hurts so much to continue the way we are that we make the decision to actually change. Next, we get to watch ourselves continue to be and do the old ways that we know don't work. We feel powerless to escape the habit we have built.

Suddenly, in one moment, we think the new thought and do the new action in a seamless, effortless triumph over our past. This happens around the 300th time we make the attempt. We feel how good the new choice feels and we celebrate that we have finally changed. Then, we backslide and do things the old way, again and again. Then, on the 551st try, we do the new change brilliantly once more. Now we've got it, the new feeling of the new way of being and doing is clearer. We slide back again into the old habit, but then we accelerate the number of times we do it right. We backslide less often, and succeed more often.

Finally, on the 1,000th time, we've made the new change a part of our new selves.

Be patient with yourself as you work on your changes. Bless the process, keep courage and heart in your spirit, and move forward, one step at a time. The 1,000th time will arrive.

Today's Affirmation: "I embrace changes that make me stronger, wiser, and richer every day."

196

A Home Office for Balance

"If you surrender completely to the moments as they pass, you live more richly those moments."

—Anne Morrow Lindbergh

Everyone seems to struggle with balance—how to leave personal problems at home while at work, and leave work problems at work while at home.

Patricia owned a "pet hotel," a wonderful place for boarding animals. She loved her work, was consumed by her work, ate, drank, slept, and breathed her work. Her passion was terrific and made her a great businesswoman, but she had trouble turning it off so she could relax when she was at home. It was beginning to have a negative affect on her relationships with her family.

When we talked about this problem, we saw that she had a habit pattern of always thinking about work. It was her passion, but she needed to turn it off some of the time. She needed to learn to be fully present with her family and enjoy her time with them.

The best way to break an old destructive habit is to replace it with a new constructive one. We decided to designate one room in her house as her imaginary "home office." Whenever she found herself thinking about work, she had to stop whatever she was doing and go to her "office," shut the door, and stay there until she was done thinking about it.

It only took about two weeks for Patricia to stop thinking about work when she was at home. She would be cooking dinner, start to think about her office payroll, and have to go to her "home office." She would be working in the yard, start thinking about hiring another employee, and have to go to her "office." Her husband would catch her thinking about work and tell her to go to her "office." It became frustrating to leave her home project and have to go to another room, so she would start catching herself and make herself think about her home and family instead. She began to trust that work was going fine and she didn't need to obsess about it every moment in order to keep it humming. She began to live in the present moment instead of in her mind. The tension eased from her body, the worry lines disappeared from her face, and she had more upbeat energy when she was at work. She was happier and so was her family. Her income went up, too.

As an actress, I was taught to leave my personal problems at the stage door. As workers, we need to leave our office problems at the home door. Create a space at home and designate it as your "home office." Then make yourself go there when you start thinking about work. You will train your mind and spirit to be present in the same space as your body. Your mind will be where you are, instead of miles away. Your family will enjoy your presence. And you will enjoy theirs.

Today's Affirmation: "I relax into the flow of life and let my mind, body, and spirit soar."

197

The Businessman and the Wise Woman

"To keep the heart unwrinkled, to be hopeful, kindly, cheerful, reverent, that is to triumph over old age."

—Thomas B. Aldrich

"Getting old isn't what it's cracked up to be," complained the aging rich and powerful businessman. "What's left of my hair is gray and I have aches and pains I never had before. They never told me that."

"Of course they told you that," said the wise woman.

"No, they told me I'd have money, power, and prestige," he replied.

"Well, you do have that," she said.

"But it doesn't matter!" he cried.

"Ah," she said. "T*hat's* what they never told you."

Today's Affirmation: "I am young at heart, rich in life experience, and loving in spirit."

198

Choose Beliefs That Make You Happy

*"Life precedes form and life survives the last atom of form.
Through the countless days proceeds the life-ray,
the one, like a thread through many jewels."*

—The Book of Dzyan

One lazy Sunday afternoon, I opened up my keepsake trunk and pulled out some of my old scrapbooks. Nostalgically, I reminisced over pictures of high school dances, dried flowers from the corsage I wore at the cotillion, drama reviews of plays performed, bits of cheerleading pompon. I remembered the hopes and dreams of the girl I was then and the fun I had dancing through days dappled with sunlight and shadows.

The phone rang, bringing me back to current reality. It was my friend, Carol. When she asked me what I'd been doing, I told her I had been having fun looking through my "remembrances of things past."

"Ugh," Carol exclaimed. "I hate to do that."

"You do?" I asked. "Why?"

"Because it reminds me how fast life is passing and how much time is gone already. I'm getting older and there's a shorter and shorter length of time left to live."

"Well, of course, that's true. But then there's the next life to look forward to!"

"No, I don't believe in that," said Carol. "There's only one life and this is it. I'm an atheist. When you die there's nothing."

"Oh, I can see why that would make you feel bad. It must be scary, too," I commiserated.

Carol agreed that it was very scary—and depressing.

"Well then, Carol," I said, "I think you should change your beliefs. We are both experiencing the passing of time, but I'm happy about it and you're miserable."

"But I believe what I believe!" she protested. "I can't just change my beliefs!"

"Sure you can," I replied. "Look at it logically: If you're right, when I die—I won't know. There'll just be nothing. But I'll live this whole life happily, thinking my beliefs are true. Your belief, on the other hand, makes you miserable. And if I'm right, and there's a life on the other side of this one, you're going to be very surprised. And you would have been unhappy all this time for no reason. So the smart choice is to choose a belief that makes you happy to believe it right now!"

I'm not sure she got it. Do you? Re-examine all your beliefs right now. What limiting beliefs do you have—about anything—that make you miserable? Find evidence to believe things that make you happy instead. You can believe that "the world is a terrible place" and prove it by example. But I can say, "The world is a beautiful place," and prove it just as easily. For which belief do you want to gather proof? Do you want to think positive or not?

Today's Affirmation: "I choose beliefs that make me happy!"

199
Life Missions

"Your lost friends are not dead, but gone before, advanced a stage or two upon that road which you must travel in the steps they trod."

—Aristophanes

I believe that. I believe we come to this planet to learn and grow in spiritual understanding. It is school. When people have learned the lessons they've come to learn, helped the people they came to help, they move on to the next level of experience. It is hard for those of us left behind to say goodbye—we miss them. We may feel incomplete or that we have unfinished business or just that we want to hold them or talk to them one more time. We "rage against the dying of the light." But I don't believe the light dies—it just changes residence.

A lot of the people I have known and loved in this life have left this realm of existence. For me, they are still alive. I think of them as my cheering section on the other side. I envision them having monthly support meetings to talk about my progress and give me some inspirational pep talks in my dreams. (Sometimes, when I'm not doing well, I think they meet daily.)

When I'm afraid or lonely, I ask them for help. "Intercede for me!" I cry. "Help me out of this mess!" I always picture them laughing when I do that. "Come on, Chellie," they chide me. "You know better than that! You chose this. Choose again!" They make me laugh, too. We sign off with "I love you." They are with me always.

Love never dies.

Call a meeting of your spiritual guides—from this world or the next. Ask for guidance. Look for wisdom. Pray for enlightenment. And love.

Today's Affirmation: "I am love, you are love, we are all love."

200
Memorial Days

"The bitterest tears shed over graves are for words left unsaid and deeds left undone."

—Christopher Crowfield

The clock read 12:40 A.M. My heart hammered as I gripped the telephone, listening to my sister, Jane. "Mom's been taken to the hospital in critical condition."

"I'm on my way," I replied. I jumped out of bed, pulled on pants and a tee shirt, grabbed my purse, and was out the door. Alone in the car, I thought about Mom. Bright and cheerful, she had just been to her 50th high school reunion, played golf with her friends, and baked a pie for the Memorial Day dinner we were having tomorrow. What had happened?

I finally screeched into the hospital parking lot and rushed to the nurses' station. "I'm here for Nell Campbell." A blond nurse, her face a symphony of sympathy, glided over and took my hand. I knew then that Mom was gone.

The nurse took me to my father, and we held each other tightly with tears streaming down our faces. My sisters arrived next; we reached for them and they for us and wept together for the loss of our Nell. When we saw her earthly body for the last time, it was never so clear to me that there is a soul that inhabits this empty vessel and that it had gone. The butterfly had left the chrysalis on the bed and flown on.

At the funeral, the church was overflowing with Mom's dear friends and family. The minister likened death to a ship sailing out to sea. To those of us watching from the shore, the ship appears to get smaller and smaller as it sails away, until finally it disappears completely. But it doesn't really disappear. The ship is still a ship, sails billowing in the wind, as it proceeds on its journey out of our view. And although those of us on this shore are waving goodbye, saying, "There she goes," there are those waiting on that farther shore, waving hello, and saying, "Here she comes!" This is the final ship any of us send out. It just sails to a different port.

My last conversation with my mother came five days before she died. I had been at a meeting where we shared stories about who had influenced us growing up. I said that my mother influenced me; she always said, "Can't never did!" and, "You can do anything you put your mind to." As I talked, it struck me that I should call Mom and thank her for that. I am sure that some angel guided me to make that goodbye call, to tell my mother that I thought she did a great job of raising us kids, and that I loved her very much. It was my last chance to thank her. I am so grateful I took it.

Take every opportunity to acknowledge and appreciate the dolphins in your life. You don't know how long they'll be swimming at your side. Make that call.

Today's Affirmation: "I praise and honor my friends and family, whose support I treasure and whose love I return."

201

Affirm, Believe, Get

"Success is moving from failure to failure with no loss of enthusiasm."

—Winston Churchill

"I have a question," said the psychotherapist in my workshop. We were mid-way through the eight-week session and dealing with surviving storms. "Let's say you're having a bad day and you're doing your affirmations anyway."

"Yes," I said, acknowledging the scene she had set.

"But you're not doing them with the enthusiasm that you usually do them."

"Yes."

"Does that matter?"

"Yes."

The class erupted in laughter as she sighed and hung her head.

I laughed along with them. "I know that's not the answer you wanted to hear, but it's the truth. What you need to do is keep doing the affirmations until you get the enthusiasm. This is where acting comes in handy: act as if everything is wonderful, dream your dream, think about what you want to have happen, and pretend like it's happening now. Feel the feelings that you feel when the good times are rolling. Talk yourself into feeling good now, in the present. That's the energy you want to have when you start working your plan for success. Success comes in this order:

1. *Affirm* and feel the emotion of success.
2. *Believe* you are a successful person.
3. *Get* the actual success.

Most people have it backwards. They want to get the success first, then they will affirm and feel the successful feeling, and after that they will believe they are successful. But you don't get corn out of the field before you plant it. Just reverse the process! Then success will truly be yours.

Before he became famous, Jim Carrey went to the Hollywood Hills and shouted affirmations, declaring that he was a famous movie star who got paid $10 million per movie. He has stated that he did this until he believed it. He wrote a check to himself for $10 million and dated it several years in the future. Years later, on that date, the check was good. When his father died, Carey put the check in his father's pocket to be buried with him. He had practiced daily affirmations, believed in himself, envisioned his success as a major motion picture star, and then became the successful celebrity that he is today. Not the other way around.

Today's Affirmation: "I believe I have the power to achieve!"

202
The Processional Effect

"Keep on going and the chances are you will stumble on something, perhaps when you are least expecting it. I have never heard of anyone stumbling on something sitting down."

—Charles F. Kettering

What had happened to me, as I made a ninety-degree-angle turn from actress to bookkeeper, was a result of what seminar leader Roger Lane called "The Processional Effect." As you pursue a goal, you accumulate knowledge and develop skills and abilities. Some of these are related to the goal you have chosen, but many are not. All of these new insights and abilities percolate inside you until, one day, you see another goal; something you couldn't have seen from the place you started when you picked the original goal. From this new vantage point, another goal becomes clear. Now that you see the new goal, it looks shinier and brighter than the original goal. And you change goals.

To diagram this, you can picture yourself at Point A, looking at your goal, which is at Point B. As you take steps towards Point B, you eventually arrive at Point X, a fork in the road. In one direction, you can still see Point B. But down the other fork, you now see a possible new goal, Point C.

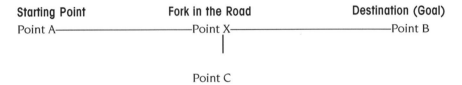

Starting Point **Fork in the Road** **Destination (Goal)**

Point A————————Point X————————Point B

|

Point C

You cannot see Point C from Point A. You have to get to the fork in the road at Point X in order to see Point C. And after Point C, there's Point D, and Points E, F, G, H, I, J, etc. You have to be on the road towards something—anything—in order to see the next goal. Other goals will show up—you don't have to know what they are when you start out. Just get started.

There's no college course in how to create a *Financial Stress Reduction® Workshop*. I couldn't make this my goal as a child. I had other goals, and the pursuit of them led me to this one. From actress to bookkeeper to business owner to workshop leader to speaker and now to writer, each goal led me to new opportunities for growth, experience, entertainment, and fulfillment.

And each step along the way was necessary. I couldn't see the goal of being a business owner when I was an actress—I could only see it when I was a bookkeeper. I couldn't see being a public speaker when I was a bookkeeper—it only became visible when I started teaching workshops. What you learn achieving each goal gives you the knowledge and skill to create another.

Set a goal—any goal. It will lead you where you need to go.

Today's Affirmation: "I am open to receive prosperity, joy, and love from all directions!"

203

Working Is Fun

"Let us realize that the privilege to work is a gift, that power to work is a blessing, that love of work is success."

—David O. McKay

A third of your life is spent working, a third is spent sleeping, and the other third is for having fun. If you love your work and your work is also your play, then two thirds of your life will be fun. It is up to you to create your life this way.

Have you ever listened to interviews with movie stars talking about how much they love their work? Many times they say they can't believe they get paid to do it, it is so much fun. And they never seem to be looking forward to retirement so they can do what they want. They are doing what they want now. Getting paid for it is a bonus. When was the last time you heard a famous movie star say, "Boy, I can't wait until I've saved enough to retire so I can quit working"?

Too many people get trapped into working at jobs they hate in order to pay the bills. When I was doing secretarial jobs for rent money while I was trying to develop a career as an actress, I was unfortunate enough to land in a couple of jobs I really despised. I remember waking up in the wee hours of the morning before the alarm clock rang and saying to myself, "Oh, I hope it's not morning yet. I don't want to have to get up and go back to that terrible job." It's impossible to live a happy, healthy, or productive life from that frame of mind. And you certainly won't create prosperity there. I attended a lecture given by Deepak Chopra, who told us of studies that were done with people who had heart attacks before age forty. They were looking for common denominators. They found only one: they all hated their jobs. It was chilling that most of the heart attacks took place on a Monday, and most of them happened around nine o'clock.

Lawrence Boldt wrote a wonderful book entitled *Zen and the Art of Making a Living* in which he talks about how true fulfillment in life comes from finding your right work. Instead of trying to fit yourself into a box that someone else has constructed, he suggests creating your own special, individual box and filling it with your life's work. If it's fun for you, it's right for you. What are you good at? Once you know what your talent is, look for people who need that, and are willing to pay to have it. That's how you create your own path of employment, whether you're working on your own as an entrepreneur or working as an employee at a company.

Don't like your job? Well, who picked it? Here is your key. Unlock your shackles. Move!

Today's Affirmation: "My work is my play and I am paid to play!"

204

Everyone's in Sales

"I don't care how many degrees you have on the wall, if you don't know how to sell, you're probably going to starve."

—George Foreman

Some of the stories in this book look like they're meant just for salespeople and business owners. They aren't. If you are a salaried employee, someone owns the business you work for and someone is in charge of raising the money to run it. Top salaries and perks are handed out to the people who are best at bringing in the money. Learn how they do it and contribute to the cause. Be one of the people who care about cash flow, cutting expenses, maximum efficiency, and productivity. Look for opportunities to maximize income and minimize expenses. Anyone can do this. Put yourself in your bosses' shoes and think as they think. What do you think they want most—and how can you give them that? Be one of the profit centers of the business and your success will be assured.

Everyone is in sales. When you convince your significant other to go with you to the movie you want to see, that's a sale. When you convince your child to stay in school, that's a sale. When you convince a friend to stop drinking, that's a sale.

"I'm reminded of a conversation I had one day with a boyfriend named Bobby. I was trying to convince him to go with me to a movie. Well, Bobby was a salesperson too, and all of a sudden he noticed all of the sales techniques I was using on him. He said, "Chellie, you are closing all the time and you don't even know you're doing it!"

When I said, "Well, you know you want to see me," he said, "That's the Assumptive Close!" I continued, "And we could either go see that romantic comedy or the spy movie" and he said, "That's the Alternative of Choice Close!" I said, "We would have fun, get to laugh, eat popcorn, have some balance in our lives, and the only down side is taking some time away from work." "Benjamin Franklin Close!" Bobby hooted. "So what do you think?" I said, and stopped talking. Bobby didn't say anything either. After a long silence, he said, "Final Close, and The Next One Who Speaks Loses. I guess that's me." And so we went to the movies!

We're all making sales every day. Use your powers of persuasion to convince others to contribute to your charity, organize political action, improve the schools in your community, or help you turn a hobby into a money-making home business. Help your company to make more money—and then convince the powers that be to give you a raise. The raise will not come automatically—you have to ask for it and show the reasons why you deserve it. It's a sale.

You are a marvelous, creative human being and endless opportunities await you. Look for them. Then sell your way into them.

Today's Affirmation: "I am a marvelous, creative person and wonderful opportunities await me."

205

You Are Unique—Market It!

"It is never too late to be what you might have been."

—George Eliot

I was introduced to networking by my insurance agent, the late Sharlee Bishin. She came by my office one day, when I had only had my bookkeeping business for about a year. We chatted for a bit, and she asked me, "Where are you networking?" I looked at her blankly. "What's networking?" I asked. Horrified, she said, "Come with me, dear," and we were off to a dinner meeting of Women's Referral Service, a wonderfully friendly group of supportive businesswomen (and men) founded by Nancy Sardella.

It didn't take me long to figure out that I was doing something wrong. Every person I met asked me what kind of work I did, and I would answer, "I'm a bookkeeper." The reactions were swift and instantaneous. People frowned, drew back, changed the subject, or left in a hurry. As an actress, I had developed the ability to know when I had my audience's attention and it was clear I lost it the minute I mentioned the word "bookkeeping." No one wanted to have a conversation about that.

Something had to be done. I had heard about Gene Call, who taught the *Word of Mouth Marketing* class, so I signed up for it. "You have to be interesting in thirty seconds or people will turn off, peg you in a category from which you will never escape," he said. "Most people introduce themselves by saying, 'I'm an accountant,' or, 'I'm an attorney.' Boring!" He suggested that you start by describing the benefit you provide to others: "I help people measure their financial success" (accountant) or, "I help people protect their property" (insurance agent).

I started saying "I do financial stress reduction." The difference in the reactions was truly amazing. People laughed, leaned forward, asked me, "How do you do that? Do you give away money?" One woman threw her arms around me in a giant hug! I could tell by a person's reaction to that one statement if they were interested in my services. So when I started teaching my course, it seemed natural to call it the *Financial Stress Reduction® Workshop*.

Reframe your self-introduction today. You're not "a housewife"—you create beautiful family environments. You're not a "mother"—you're a loving support provider. You're not a "teacher"—you're a Guru. You're not a "psychologist"—you help people find personal enlightenment. You're not a "secretary"—you're a business facilitator. You're not a businessperson—you're a money-making machine!

Today's Affirmation: "I am the most unique and beautiful me I know!"

206
Round Robins

"To make dough, do."

—Bertram Troy

At many networking meetings, each person is given an opportunity to do a thirty-second commercial on their business. This is called a "round robin." This is a great chance to advertise the benefits of the products or services you provide to others. It is important that you represent yourself in an interesting way—say or do something that stands out or makes you special. You can't educate the audience or explain everything you do in thirty seconds—you just have to pique the audience's interest so that they want to talk to you later.

Here are some memorable examples from networking meetings I've attended:

"If you're in debt, don't fret, call Bret."–Bret Davis, Bankruptcy Attorney

"Humpty Dumpty sat on a wall. Humpty Dumpty had a great fall. And who did he immediately call? The law offices of Rhoda Walsh."—Rhoda Walsh, Personal Injury Attorney

A woman at the podium drinks a glass of milk, turns to the audience and says, "Got cookies?"–Shell Brown, Shell Brown's Cookies

"Give me your checkbook, your bills, your huddled receipts yearning to breathe free. . . ."—Alan Smithee, Bookkeeper

"I'm your brother-in-law in the jewelry business."—Bruce Spiegel, The Jewelry Factory

"Hair today, gone tomorrow."—Rita Katzman, Electrologist

"If you want to move your dream house closer, call Ellen Grosser." —Ellen Grosser, Real Estate Agent

"Have you heard that all printers charge the same?" Audience response, "It's a lie!" "That's right. I can get you the best price in town," says Sharon Helmer, Printer.

Do you ever have to introduce yourself at a business meetings or events? Make it clever, make it entertaining, make people laugh. It's not only fun—it's good business. People like to be entertained. They will remember you. And that's all marketing was ever about.

If you are not in business or in sales, open up to the possibility of marketing the company you work for. Their success is your success—if they make more money, they'll have more money with which to pay your salary. And if you aren't employed, find a creative tag for whatever you are doing with your time: "I nurture children," "I'm doing my part to hold down the divorce rate," "I perfect golf swings." Whatever you do, don't put yourself down by saying, "I'm just a _____." Be proud of who you are and what you do. Or change it.

Today's Affirmation: "People are always fascinated by what I have to say!"

207

Success Instructions

"If what you know now was enough, you'd already be where you want to go."

—Jack Canfield

When I started writing this book, I didn't know anything about the book business. What I did know was that if I was going to have a successful book, I had better find out as much as I could about writing, publishing, marketing, and selling books. Writing a good book wasn't going to be enough. I had to know how the publishing industry worked, how to write a good book proposal, how to get an agent, how to negotiate a book contract, how to promote and advertise the book, and how to close book sales. I bought books on these subjects, listened to tapes, asked everyone I knew who had contacts in the publishing industry, visualized success, wrote down my goals, practiced my affirmations, meditated, prayed, and sent out ships every day.

A few months later, I discovered that Mark Victor Hansen and Jack Canfield were giving a seminar called *How to Build Your Speaking and Writing Empire* in my area. These two men, authors of the *Chicken Soup for the Soul* book series, had sold more than 50 million books! They were the perfect role models for me. I signed up immediately and drank in every word of the seminar when it was given. It was fabulous! Not only did they present a terrific amount of information, but gave many resources for getting more.

The day after the workshop, my networking paid off: through Women's Referral Service, I met a chiropractor, Jim Blumenthal, who referred me to Theresa Stephens, who put me in touch with her friend Jim Jermanok, who put me in touch with his friend, literary agent Lisa Hagan at Paraview, Inc., who signed me as a client the day she received my manuscript. Lisa found me my wonderful editor and publisher, Deborah Werksman at Sourcebooks. They are all "My People!"

Here is the short list of Mark and Jack's success instructions:

1. Visualize your goals.
2. Write down your goals.
3. Do affirmations.
4. Meditate.
5. Pray.
6. Take action (send out ships!).

I like their list!

Today's Affirmation: "All creative forces are working together for my good!"

208
Facts or Excuses?

"You can make money or you can make excuses—
you can't make both."

—Unknown

Sometimes the excuses are stated subtly, as though they were facts. This makes it difficult to tell that it's really an excuse used to justify someone's behavior. One summer afternoon, I was talking to a seminar leader, Mary, who had a successful business. She told me she was doing a lot of traveling and writing at the time, because everyone knew that the seminar business was dead in the summer.

I looked at her, shocked. "I didn't know that!" I exclaimed.

She looked at me quizzically. "You mean your business doesn't slow down in the summer?" she asked.

"No," I replied. "It's a good thing, too, because I have to eat in the summertime!"

"What about during the holidays?" she asked. "Surely you don't get enrollments between Thanksgiving, Christmas, and New Year's Day?"

"Now that difficulty I recognize," I acknowledged. "People tend to use the holidays as an excuse to cut back on their activities and wait until next year to do anything new. So I tried to think if there were any reasons why someone might want to take a money management class during the holiday season.

"I ask them if their work is slower during the holidays. If the answer is yes, then I ask if this slow period might be a good time to do a course, since they'll have extra time on their hands. I ask if they often overspend at Christmas, and if that answer is yes, I suggest that this might be a perfect time to take a workshop that could coach you not to do that, pay off your debts, and start the New Year off right with a new attitude about attracting wealth and money. I've found that if you get the specific problems of the season working for you instead of against you, you'll make a lot of money during a time when your competition thinks you can't make any!

"But I never heard that the seminar business was slow during the summer, so I never experienced it. Who told you that?"

She didn't remember who it was—probably the anonymous "They." Be careful of buying into beliefs because "They say." "They say" doesn't pay.

Today's Affirmation: "All the time is a great time for me to succeed!"

209
Glenda's Creative Solution

"The shortest and best way to make your fortune is to let people see clearly that it is in their interests to promote yours."

—Jean de la Bruyere

Glenda has two young children and serious medical problems. The kids have had medical problems, too, which makes it impossible for her to work full-time. But she needed to make a living. What to do?

Glenda opened a quilting store. She only works one day a week, but the store is open seven days a week from morning until evening. Although the shop is fully staffed, Glenda has no payroll. She makes a nice profit and her income helps to support her family.

How does she do it?

Her store is completely staffed by volunteers. They are enthusiastic hobbyists, who love quilting. They are happy to spend their time among the quilts, quilting materials, books, and other hobbyists who share their passion. They receive discounts on merchandise, free materials, and free classes in exchange for their time. Everyone's needs are met. Everyone is having fun.

And Glenda's not living on disability, moaning about her fate. She's a successful business owner making a wonderful living for herself and her family.

Think about how you might turn a hobby into a career. Can you use Glenda's model to create something similar for yourself?

Pick your price. Make your budgets. Save money. Don't go into debt. Then find another way to get what you want!

Today's Affirmation: "I always find creative ways to have all that I desire!"

210
The Negotiating Game

"A money-grabber is anyone who grabs more than you can grab."

—Anonymous

Many people run into trouble when it comes to negotiating money. This applies to salaries, pay raises, prices of products, and fees for services. Often fearful of asking for too much, they make the opposite mistake and ask for too little. It's like they study the situation very carefully, figure out the least amount they can possibly ask for and still be able to eke out a living, and then ask for their rock bottom line amount. Then, when their prospective boss or client tries to negotiate a better price, they are angry and resentful. How, they think, can this person ask for a better price—don't they know this is an incredible deal and the cheapest price around?

Well, no, they don't know! They are playing the negotiating game. It is a win-win scenario if it's played correctly. This is how to play it:

1. Seller figures out bottom line price.
2. Seller asks for amount *above* bottom line price.
3. Buyer asks for reduction in Seller's price.
4. Compromise is reached in the middle.
5. Every dollar Seller got above his bottom line, he wins.
6. Every dollar Buyer gets Seller to reduce his asking price, he wins.
7. End game: Win-Win.

You can see that if the Seller goes in asking for his bottom line, he leaves the Buyer nothing to do but say "Yes" or "No." Then somebody loses and is unhappy. To make it possible for everyone to win, the Seller must ask for more money than his bottom line.

Note: If the Seller asks for an amount above his bottom line and the Buyer says yes immediately—he didn't ask for enough money!

Today's Affirmation: "I am worth lots of money and always get paid what I'm worth!"

211
Give Yourself a Raise

"Self-respect is a question of recognizing that anything worth having has its price."

—Joan Didion

Give yourself a raise. Ask for more money. You're worth it!

Many people have a hard time asking for their worth. They know their value, but are afraid of the reaction they might get if they ask for it. They get scared that their clients or bosses will feel they have over-priced themselves and that they will find someone else who will do it for less. This is generally a groundless fear. People do business with you for one primary reason—they like you. Sure, they want to save money, get a good deal, and pay a fair price. But if you are doing a great job for them, they don't want to change and have to find and hire someone else who may not be able to do as good a job as you are doing.

A music composer named Steve took my workshop a few years ago, and had just found a new agent to represent him. He was very happy with the new agent, who had a great reputation, lots of experience and clout. But he was concerned because the agent wanted to increase his price from $150,000 to $200,000 per film. He said he just felt he couldn't ask for that much money.

I asked him if there were any composers working in the industry who made that much money. "Well, of course there are," he said immediately. "There are famous composers who get paid millions of dollars per picture."

So I told him that $200,000 wasn't enough—he should ask for $400,000. He was totally shocked by that amount, which seemed outrageous. I told him to practice saying "I am paid $400,000 per film, I am paid $400,000 per film," twenty times per day for the next week. He needed to say it with positive emotion and intention behind it until he believed it. Steve laughed, but he agreed to try it.

At the next class session, I asked him if he had practiced stating his new price. He answered that he had and that it felt good. "Does $200,000 per picture sound like a reasonable amount of money now?" I asked him.

"As a matter of fact, now it doesn't sound like enough!" he answered, which provoked gales of laughter from his classmates.

The reason this exercise works is that it helps you to convince *yourself* that you're worth the money. When you establish your price, you are telling people what you think you're worth. They take their cue from you. If you state your new price tentatively, fearfully, or questioningly, they're going to spit it back in your face and demand a lower price. If you state it confidently, like this high price is really *unbelievably cheap*, they will see the respect you have for yourself and more likely accede to your request. After all, if you're getting that much money, you must be worth it!

Today's Affirmation: "I love to ask for money and I get paid top dollar when I do!"

212

When to Raise Your Price

"The ideal income is a thousand dollars a day—and expenses."

—Pierre Lorillard

"I got a raise!" Most people are familiar with the joy that comes with that good news, but every employee knows the nervous anxiety that goes along with *asking* for a raise. It is no different for self-employed people, except for the added difficulty that they must ask many different "employers" (clients) for that raise. Knowing the best times to raise your fees (salary) will help ease your discomfort and you will encounter the least resistance. Raise your fees when:

1. **You have too much work and not enough time.** Success is yours! Everyone admires and appreciates you. You are in demand. Now you find yourself working until the wee hours night after night trying to get all the work done. This is the perfect time to get a raise—you are obviously worth it! If you are self-employed, you may lose a few clients when you increase your rates, but you will make up for that by making more money working fewer hours for the clients you retain.
2. **A market survey shows your pricing is lower than average.** If you are on salary, you should always be aware of the going rate of pay for your job position with your skill set and experience. The Small Business Administration has stated that the number one reason small businesses go under is that they don't charge enough for their product or service. If you are underpriced, you will burn out working long hours for survival wages.
3. **Your boss or client is doing great financially and you helped.** You don't ask for a raise when the company has just posted a big loss, is downsizing, or is in the middle of a change in direction or management. Timing is everything. You want to ask for a raise when you have just helped increase profits through your new advertising campaign, or made the deal to get the new computers at a discount. When they are happy with you and your work, when they need you for the next project—that is the time to ask for more money.
4. **You just received special recognition or publicity.** Whenever you win an award, get a prestigious appointment to a board, get profiled in a newspaper or magazine article, or appear on television, make sure to let all of your clients know about it. When your clients regularly see you achieving success and notice, they will recognize that you have moved up in the world and are worth more money.

Ready? Then fill up the hold with cargo, batten the hatches, and go sailing for a bigger sale.

Today's Affirmation: "I have perfect timing for getting perfect pay!"

213

Do Your Research, Get Your Raise

"Darling, only cows are contented."

—Stella Adler

Sally's eyes were snapping and her face burned with resentment. "I've been working for these people for five years and have done wonders for them, but they are so stingy they are only giving me a 3 percent raise!" She was so hot she could barely sit in her chair.

It was a beautiful spring day, and we were sitting outdoors at the local restaurant. I knew something was wrong the minute she arrived. Sally was the Executive Director of the Chamber of Commerce and was quite visible in the community. She did a wonderful job, and I had seen the growth in membership and programs of the Chamber during her tenure. I had no idea she wasn't well paid. "Tell me everything," I said, "but start at the beginning. How long have you been working in this job?"

"Five years," she exclaimed, "starting as a part-time secretary. I've been full-time for the past four years and have taken on many more duties and responsibilities. I've tripled their membership and their budget, but they still only give me tiny annual cost-of-living raises based on my starting salary as a secretary!" She was seething. "I'm going to quit!"

"Take a deep breath and relax a minute," I coached. "You can always quit—that's a last resort option. But you like the job except for the low pay, so why don't we work together to try to get you the money you deserve?" She thought about that for a minute, then agreed it couldn't hurt to try.

Over the next couple of weeks, I coached Sally on how to get a raise, just like Jennifer Martin had taught me years before. First, I told her to lose the resentment—anger doesn't sell. People just get defensive. Not being well paid was her responsibility and hers alone. She had been waiting for the Board of Directors to recognize her contributions and voluntarily significantly raise her salary. But she had not given them the facts and figures they needed to justify the increase. Now she understood, so she put together a presentation for the board that outlined every achievement and the dollar amounts her contributions had made to the bottom line of the organization. She did her research and discovered the pay rates for the same position at similar organizations. She prepared written comparisons of the Chamber budgets for the five years she had been working for them.

We met again at lunch just before her presentation to the board, so she could practice her delivery. She did a masterful job and I told her so. She looked powerful, professional, and determined.

She got a 35 percent raise in salary.

Do your research, do a great job, and get your raise!

Today's Affirmation: "I am powerful, professional, and very well paid!"

214
Enough Money

"It is a gorgeous gold pocket watch. I'm proud of it.
My grandfather, on his deathbed, sold me this watch."

—Woody Allen

Every individual has some interior sense of what is "enough" money. When you don't have enough money, you can only think about two things: yourself, and getting money. It is not until you have "enough" that you can think about others and giving money.

Have you ever met a salesperson operating below the line of enough money? They aren't interested in selling you what you need or want; they only want to get your money so they can pay the rent, the phone bill, their taxes—in other words, themselves. They are solely intent on getting, not giving. It isn't fun to deal with people like that because they don't have your best interests at heart.

My friend, Shelley, went to the auto dealership to buy a new car. She told her salesman she wanted a green one. "Oh, green's a terrible color!" he told her. "You don't want green. I had a green one that sat on the lot for two years. No one wants a green car!" "I do," said Shelley, and promptly went to another dealership where they were happy to sell her a green car.

A salesperson who is above the line, who knows they always have enough, can be interested in your welfare and what's best for you. They focus on giving, knowing that getting will be its natural by-product. It is a pleasure doing business with people who really care about serving their customer. They know there's enough to go around. They can give. Then both of you will benefit.

The above-the-line salesperson is confident and happy. And it becomes a self-fulfilling prophecy. They get more business because they are contributing to others out of their sense of abundance, and then others want to give to them.

That's how repeat business is born. And repeat business is easy business. If your customer wants green, give them green!

Today's Affirmation: "I appreciate the abundance of life and there is plenty for all!"

215

Bill Paying Time

"Maybe they call it take-home pay because there is no other place you can afford to go with it."

—Franklin P. Jones

Whenever you are in a period of financial stress, when there is too much month left at the end of the money, thoughts of lack and limitation can be overwhelming. Doing positive affirmations won't do much good if you do them for ten minutes a day but then think anxious and worried thoughts about money for the other twenty-three hours and fifty minutes.

What I suggest is that you make an appointment with yourself once per week for bill paying time. (If you're married, you can do this with your spouse.) It must be a regular weekly appointment, for example, Saturday morning at 10:00 A.M. During that hour you will sort out what bills you have and how much you can pay on each one. You will do the best you can with what you've got. Pay everyone something, even if it's just a few dollars. When they receive a payment from you every month, they will be more likely to trust you for the balance eventually. I once had a client pay me only ten dollars per month—but she paid every month for three years, and one day it was paid in full. For this hour, you may let yourself worry and fret if you must if there is not enough to go around.

At the end of bill paying time, you are not allowed to worry about your bills for the rest of the week. All bills received just get put in the drawer for the next Saturday at 10:00 A.M. You are not allowed to think about them or deal with them until then. Your full attention is to be on sending out ships and producing income! Positive affirmations, joy over every bit of money received, and daily gratitude for all that you currently possess is to be your state of mind for the balance of the week.

The flow of abundance will swell as you focus on the money and possessions you do have, instead of the ones you lack. It won't be long before there's plenty of money to go around.

Expect it.

Today's Affirmation: "All my bills are paid in full and I still have all this money."

216

The Big Fix

"Hope is the feeling you have that the feeling you have isn't permanent."

—Jean Kerr

Many people hunger for "The Big Fix." This is the magical appearance of a large sum of money which will pay off all the past due bills, credit card debts, school loans, mortgages, etc., buy the new house, car, vacation home, and Rolex and still have enough left over to completely fund the retirement plan. It's winning the lottery, closing the biggest client, inventing the newest electronic gizmo, writing the best-selling novel, getting the starring role in the hit movie, producing the mega-hit record, creating a billion-dollar Internet company. They don't really need to budget, call their creditors and arrange payment plans, renegotiate the loans, move to a smaller house, or sell the boat, because "The Big Fix" will take care of everything.

Michael had been struggling on the fringes of the music industry for years, eking out a living. He had enthusiasm and energy and a great smile, but only made thirty thousand dollars per year. He resisted doing his budget for this amount, but clung to his high budget figure of fifty million. "That's what I'll be making when my band hits it big!" he declared. "That's great," I told him, "but you need to practice sound money management principles with what you are earning today before the Universe will trust you with fifty million dollars."

I pray that all of you reading this will have that big deal come to fruition. I would love for all your financial dreams to come true. Big dreams make us strive for success with energy and optimism. But it's important to act responsibly with the money you're entrusted with now in order to prove yourself ready for more. Ideally, you should be operating successfully with whatever amount you are currently earning—this will create an attitude of abundance within you that will draw more and more wealth into your life. *Want* the big deal, the "magic money," but don't *need* it. Desire it for the fun of playing in a bigger game, but not because you need it to solve your problems. You must have power and control over your money, or when the big money comes into your life, it will exit just as quickly. That's the reason why some lotto winners go broke in five years, rock stars blow their fortunes on drugs, and gamblers win millions only to give it all back the next day.

Develop the tools to manage money wisely: practice your affirmations daily, send out your ships, and count your money. Save 10 percent of your income in a retirement account, plan for your irregular expenses, update regularly your Low, Medium, and High Budgets. The more expert you become, the more comfortable you will be and the more money will flow into your life.

Today's Affirmation: "More and more money is flowing more and more easily into my life."

217
Budgeting Spree Money

"Beware of little expenses; a small leak will sink a great ship."

—Benjamin Franklin

Many people struggle with budgeting. They know how much they spend on rent or mortgage, how much the car payment is, and the amounts of other fixed expenses. But there are so many other monthly expenses that are variable! How much do you spend on food? Dining out? Parking meters? Books? Movies? Magazines? Coffees? Munchies?

What's the grand total of all the ATM cash and where does it go?

If you can relate to this problem, I suggest you start counting your money. I mean count all of it, from the fifty cents you pay for gum to the dollar for the lottery ticket, the quarter in the parking meter to the dime you pick up off the street. Carry around a small notebook specifically for this purpose and record every time you use money in every transaction, large and small. Only then will you know *exactly* where your money has gone. Knowledge is power. When you know what you're doing, you have the power to change it. Knowing that you're going to have to record spending $3.95 on a double cappuccino latte may not stop you on the first day, but may make you think about it on the third day! You may just start to become aware of how much of your money slides out of your grasp on trinkets and incidentals. $3.95 a day for 365 days is $1,441.75.

I have nothing against buying a nice cup of coffee. You just have to be aware of and have budgeted for it. Determine your priority spending, make choices about how to spend "spree money," and then don't whine and complain that you don't have enough money to take a vacation, put a down payment on a house or a car, or anything else you feel you can't afford. You have choices about your money flow, but first you have to know what you're doing with it now.

People avoid this exercise in droves. They'd rather stay unconscious about what they are doing with their money. They're afraid that if they count their money, they will have to face the reality that they are spending more than they make and will have to stop spending on things that give them pleasure. This is people's resistance to budgeting in a nutshell: they think it will doom them to only paying bills with nothing left over for fun. This isn't true. Budgeting enables you to have fun in proportion to your priorities. Which do you want more—the cappuccino now or the beach vacation later? With balance and perspective, you'll soon see that you can stick to a budget and still have it all (just not all at once).

Start counting your money today. Is it going where you want it to go? Is there enough to go around? If not, how can you make more or spend less? Adjust the mix until you're happy with it. Then get creative and find other ways to get what you want.

Today's Affirmation: "I adjust my money mix for maximum abundance!"

218
Changing the Paradigm

"If no one ever took risks, Michelangelo would have painted on the Sistine floor."

—Neil Simon

Joel Barker produced and narrated a wonderful video entitled *The Business of Paradigms*.

It is an examination of how business and the marketplace responds to new ideas and new inventions that radically change the way things are. He demonstrates how our natural tendency is to cling to the old paradigm, the old pattern or habit rather than embrace the new, seemingly radical idea. Businesses that have been built and made a success out of an old idea are reluctant to accept a new idea that will fundamentally change the way they do business. Change must come from the outside.

For example, when the man who invented the copier machine decided to sell his idea, he went first to Kodak. The copier process was a kind of photographic process, so it seemed logical to take it to the preeminent company specializing in cameras and film. They turned him down. They didn't see how the application of this new technology would change business forever and spawn a new generation of technological office machines. So then he went to Xerox. That's why we Xerox reports instead of Kodaking them.

What is the current paradigm of your business? Of your life? Can you think of a new idea that might radically change what you do or how you do it? If nothing comes to mind, you may be too firmly rooted in the old paradigm, too weighed down by habit, to think of change. The known seems so safe. But great products, great services, and great wealth come from new ideas that provide greater benefits. A friend of mine kept a poster in his office that read "How can I improve this?" He searched constantly for new ideas to improve the quality of his products and services so that he could better serve his customer, and thereby, better serve himself.

The more people you serve, and the better you serve them, the more money you make.

Today's Affirmation: "All my affirmations happen in the perfect way for the highest good of all concerned."

219

The *Star Trek* Experience

"A snowflake is one of Nature's most fragile things, but look what they can do if they stick together."

—Unknown

My friend, Beca Lewis, in her workshop, *The Shift*, told a story about *Star Trek*. She said that in this television series, every week a team of people on a space ship goes exploring. They know their mission: "To go where no one has gone before." They know how they are going: "Boldly." Every week, they encounter an "it." This is something that appears to be a threat or at least a dangerous mystery.

But there is a difference in the behavior of the crew on *Star Trek* and most people. They have a solid team and support one another. No one ever says, "How did you make this happen, you idiot?" And no one ever says, "How did I make this happen? I'm such an idiot!" There is only rational discussion of how to handle the threat. They engage in the process of looking for solutions instead of searching for someone to blame. The solutions are found each week by the group acting as a team, and the decisions are all based on a personal code of ethics and morality.

And no one ever says, "We better not explore any more. Remember what happened last week!"

I quite enjoyed this story. Maybe that's what I like so much about the *Star Trek* series—the friendship and support of the team players. Whatever challenges they face each week, you know that they will stand and face them together. They are all dolphins.

Life is like a *Star Trek* mission. We are all exploring and we are all traveling with a team. We have a choice whether to be critical or supportive. What would you like to receive from your team? Be the first to give them that.

Today's Affirmation: "I am courageous, strong, and victorious, and so is my team!"

220
Trekkies

"Please God, please—don't let me be normal!"

— Luisa, in *The Fantasticks,* by Tom Jones and Harvey Schmidt

It was a dark and stormy night. I zipped past channels on the TV in search of entertainment when I alighted on the documentary film, *Trekkies,* about the fans of the *Star Trek* television series.

What a fun movie! I truly enjoyed watching these fans speak glowingly of their fascination with the stars, the mythos, the technology, and the spirit behind this television show. There is a convention somewhere in the world every weekend.

Make no mistake—this is a happy group of people. They may seem a little left of center to you, but they are having fun. One of them, a dentist, Denis Bourguignon, has a practice called "Star Base Dental" in Orlando, Florida. He, his wife, and all the staff dress in *Star Trek* uniforms and have decorated the entire office with space ship regalia. A man who changed his name to something *Star Trek*-related said many people complimented him on his courage, saying they could never do that. Sure you can, he said, "You can do anything you want in life." Good attitude.

Various stars from the shows were interviewed. A paralyzed woman told Kate Mulgrew, "For the hour you are on, I forget about the body I'm trapped in." And James Doohan, who played the engineer, Scottie, spoke movingly of a woman who wrote him a suicide note. He called her and told her there was a *Star Trek* convention in two weeks and he wanted to see her there. She went, they talked, and he told her about the next convention, and he wanted to see her there. She went to that one, too. And the next, and the next—for about two or three years. Then silence.

Eight years later, she wrote him a letter, thanking him for taking the time to help her. His kindness and attention had lifted her spirits and given her the will to go on. She was writing to tell him that he had inspired her to get her degree in electrical engineering. He had tears in his eyes as he spoke of it.

Are you laughing at these people? Do you think it's ridiculous for a dentist to dress up in costume? Well, perhaps they think it's ridiculous that men wear ties that choke them, women wear high heel shoes that hurt their feet, and people work in jobs they hate. Perhaps your hobby is swinging a metal rod in order to hit a little ball into a hole? Sliding down a hill on wooden poles? Or collecting spoons? What's normal?

Beam me up, Scottie.

Today's Affirmation: "I live long and prosper!"

221

Role Models

"We haven't come that far—and don't call me baby."

—NOW button, circa 1975

Someone asked me yesterday who my role models were when I was growing up. I don't remember many role models—rather I remember a lack of them. When I was in high school, it seemed most girls gravitated toward (or were led to) becoming a teacher, nurse, or mother. None of this looked too thrilling to me.

But in the field of "actress," I found women I could relate to—strong-willed, determined women, carving out a place at the top of the world, like Bette Davis, Rosalind Russell, Katharine Hepburn. I loved the musical stars: Jeannette MacDonald, Ginger Rogers, and Cyd Charisse. I watched and envied them all on television, dreaming of following in their glamorous footsteps.

Nowadays, role models for women abound. Women are doctors, attorneys, politicians, psychiatrists, accountants; they run major corporations and own their own businesses. I watched the barriers come crashing down: Muriel Siebert was the first woman to buy a seat on the stock exchange. Madeline Albright was the first woman Secretary of State. Sally Ride was the first woman in space. Sherry Lansing was the first woman to run a movie studio. Whatever career you aspire to, there are many wonderful women who have led the way for you to work at the top of that profession. Seek them out, listen to their stories, follow in their pathways. Role models and mentors abound. Whatever they have done, you can do.

There remains a lot more to do. Women make up over 50 percent of the population, but women in the top bastions of power are rare. On average, women make less money in the marketplace than men do. Only 1 percent of the Fortune 500 CEO positions are held by women. Women over forty are rarely featured in movies or star in television series. Why do we have to get off the stage at forty when we have another forty years to live? I want some wrinkled role models in my magazines, newspapers, and films. I want to see women respected and admired for their intellectual gifts, not just their beautiful bodies—and I want more shapes and sizes recognized as beautiful. I want more women running things.

There is the problem—can you be part of the solution? I challenge you to make this happen. Be a role model: give a young girl someone to look up to, assist a female co-worker, hire that "older" candidate because she has more experience, promote feelings of sisterhood among all women whether they work in an office or in their home, and, most important of all, realize your dreams and achieve success!

Today's Affirmation: "I empower every person I meet today to rise to their full potential!"

222

Whining Time

"The world breaks everyone;
then some grow strong in the broken places."

—Ernest Hemingway

You will have down days. Remember this page and come here when you have one. Maybe today life sucks. So go ahead and bemoan your state. Weep. Wallow. "Blow winds and crack your cheeks! Rage! Blow! You cataracts and hurricanoes, spout till you have drenched our steeples, drowned the cocks!" rages the mad King Lear. You, too, are entitled to your rage. Call up a friend and complain. (Ask for permission before you start dumping, though. You don't want to rain on someone's good day.) Try not to redeem *all* of your complaint coupons with your friends today because you may need them again. You'll want them to be there for you when you do. Too often, and you might become one of those perpetual complainers that no one wants to see coming.

One afternoon, I went to meet my *Wild Women Writers* group for lunch. I was having a bad day: Mercury was in retrograde, my computer wouldn't connect me to the Internet, someone called to cancel my workshop. I had a headache, and was basically in a complete funk. When I got to the restaurant, I nursed a coffee waiting for the others to arrive. When they straggled in, it seemed like a blue Monday for everyone so I asked, "Can I be bitchy now?" Squeals and sighs all around as everyone relaxed into that great tension reliever: whining. We ate comfort foods—chocolate cake and ice cream. It was great. We let it all hang out so we could jump over it later.

Jumping over it, climbing, crawling, or sliding over it later is the key. For whining and complaining you only get one hour, one afternoon, or one day. The end. Then back to positive affirmations, sending out ships, and counting your money tomorrow. That's what successful people do. You stay under your bedcovers for longer than one day, and you're setting up a new habit. And this habit is the "Why-me-God-it-isn't-fair-everyone's-a-winner-but-me-I'm-a-loser" habit. One day is okay—it's an aberration, a field trip to Loser Land, nice to visit but you wouldn't want to live there. Two days of this and you're in trouble. But everyone's entitled to a little whine for one day. Enjoy it. Revel in it.

Then get over it.

Today's Affirmation: "I am perfect just the way I am."

223
Anger

"Darkness cannot drive out darkness; only light can do that. Hate cannot drive out hate; only love can do that."

—Martin Luther King, Jr.

"Everyone sees real estate agents as sharks!" said Arlene. "And most of them are. They're only out for themselves. I have to work really hard to let people know I'm not like that!"

To say Arlene was angry was a complete understatement. She seethed and roiled like a mama grizzly bear that just had her cub taken away from her. She was angry at the people she perceived as sharks in her profession, angry at her husband who wasn't earning money, angry at her sister who wouldn't loan her money, angry at her life. When at last she turned her anger inward towards herself, she got depressed. Then she'd get mad again at all the people in her life that caused her pain and upset. It was a vicious cycle.

Anger had become her comfortable friend. The angry position has power attached to it: you get to be right, and self-righteous, and you get to be a martyr—suffering but absolutely blameless. It's never your fault. The difficulty is that you can get stuck there forever. If the problem is always in other people, you are powerless to change your situation. It's impossible to change other people. But if you accept responsibility for your life, realize you create your reality, you can change everything because you cause everything.

I asked Arlene how long it had been like this. "Years," she said. I asked her if she wanted it to change. She said, "Yes." That gave me permission to help. I explained to her that I saw her trapped in her cycle of anger and that there was a way out. I let her know that it would feel uncomfortable at first, because she was used to her anger and kept it with her out of habit. She needed to break free.

I suggested that she write down everything and everybody she was angry with in a freeform, let-it-all-out manner. When she had written everything and felt finished, she should go back and rewrite every statement as a positive. For example, if she wrote, "My husband is a burden and never makes any money," she should reframe it as "My husband is a wonderful support and makes lots of money, too." This is taking every negative thought—which had operated in her life as a negative affirmation—and making a positive statement out of it. Then four times a day every day she needed to read the positive statements out loud. But most importantly, she needed to stop saying the negative statements. I pointed out that saying positive affirmations for five minutes a day wasn't going to do a lot of good if she was saying powerful negative affirmations the other twenty-three hours and fifty-five minutes. Tearfully, she agreed to do as I suggested.

Two weeks later, I called to check up on her. She said she was much better, had sold a house, and was rushing off to sell another one. It works if you work it.

Today's Affirmation: "I bless everyone I meet and wish them success and happiness."

224
High Class, Quality Problems

"Being sober doesn't mean you won't have problems. But the quality of your problems will improve."

—overheard at an Alcoholics Anonymous meeting

Making more money doesn't mean you won't have problems, either. Sometimes the people in my workshops with the most money have the most problems. But they are high class, quality problems!

I'm reminded of an old story about some villagers who were complaining to God about their problems. Every day, they moaned and groaned, until finally, God called them all together for a meeting in the town square. In the center of the square was a huge oak tree. God told everyone to take their collection of troubles and hang them on the tree. After everyone had done so, He said, "Now walk around the tree, look over all the troubles, and take down the ones you'd rather have." After the villagers examined all the problems hanging on the tree, each one took back his own set of problems and returned home without complaining again.

We are afraid to risk the unknown, and so we put up with the problems we've got. I say upgrade your problems and upgrade your life! And if you find yourself complaining, stop and look at the troubles other people have. Then you might want to thank God for your high class, quality problems.

Today's Affirmation: "As I generate my earthly fortune, I am reminded of my heavenly connection, which is the source of my true wealth."

(Contributed by Shelley Ackerman, in *New Woman* magazine)

225

Time to Enjoy Your Money

"There's never enough time to do all the nothing you want."

—Bill Watterson

"Jerry makes plenty of money," his wife Judith said when I called. "He doesn't need your class. What he needs is more time to enjoy the money he makes."

I had met Jerry when we appeared together on Paul and Sarah Edwards's radio show. He was happily making large sums of money in his public relations business, but reacted strongly when I mentioned that my workshop was called *Financial Stress Reduction*®. "I'd really love to keep making money but reduce the stress," he said. "Call me and let's talk about it."

I called as instructed, and that's when Judith let me know the real problem: Jerry's work hours (24/7), his time off for fun (zero), his time with family (minimal) and her frustration with this situation (huge). I commiserated with her, then let her know that my class was not just about making money, but about having lots of time off to enjoy it as well. "Sign us up!" she exclaimed, and enrolled the two of them in the next course on the spot.

At the beginning of the class, they spoke of the goal they had put on their "Intended Results" list—to take a month off to travel in France with another couple. It seemed unreachable then. Jerry's fear of losing clients was a palpable force keeping him chained to his telephone at all hours. But as they did the work of the course, they came to see that when they practiced positive thinking about money, sent out ships consistently, and counted the money to keep score, they could relax. The system worked and could be relied upon. Customers could understand—and admire—a commitment to family and balance. They could be alerted to the fact of an impending vacation and get their work in early. Reciprocal deals could be made with other professionals to handle emergencies in Jerry's absence. As Jerry's fear decreased each week, he began to relax. He started smiling more often—and so did Judith.

They had a wonderful time in France.

And where are you going? When?

Today's Affirmation: "I have abundant time to enjoy all my abundant riches!"

226

Breakdown to Breakthrough

"Most of my major disappointments have turned out to be blessings in disguise. So whenever anything bad does happen to me, I kind of sit back and feel, well, if I give this enough time, it'll turn out that this was good, so I shouldn't worry about it too much."

—William Gaines

We set our minds, set our goals, and start sending out ships to make all our dreams come true. We are headed for Breakthrough, for the golden shore where the sun is always shining, the money is rolling in, and everything is going our way.

But Breakthrough is often preceded by Breakdown. This is because much of what you've been hanging onto—out of fear of change—has to get out of your way in order for you to live your dream. The challenges strengthen us as we overcome them, and we have to grow in order to escape the pain. Dr. Jeffrey Mishlove states that it is the law of nature to push itself to the brink in order to create crises and then evolve. Every system in the Universe evolves through crisis. Looks like we human beings do, too.

Our crises take place on two fronts: internal battles and external ones. We fight to overcome our shadow side; to become kind, generous, loving human beings. And as we grow, we struggle to survive the storms at sea that threaten our ships and sometimes even our lives. It's important to remember, when the waves are pounding, your ship is leaking, and you can't see daylight, that the shore is still there where you left it. The storm is just a test designed to strengthen your resolve, test your nerve and your dedication. You will be better off because of it. Without the storm, you cannot appreciate the peace of calm waters.

Today's Affirmation: "My wonderful breakthroughs create my fabulous successes!"

227

Sometimes You Have to Ask God for a Sign

"If only God would give me a clear sign!
Like making a large deposit in my name at a Swiss bank."

—Woody Allen

There have been times when I have done everything in hopes of achieving my goals: building ships, sending out ships, dredging ships up from the bottom of the sea, rebuilding the ships, hiring new crews. I have tried to get the job done, but the job remains undone. I try to decipher whether I should keep trying or know "when to fold 'em." Is this goal not for me after all? Am I supposed to give this one up? How am I to know?

For months, my agent, Lisa Hagan, and I searched for a publisher for this book. Many rejections and several almost-deals later, I still didn't have one. Meanwhile, a friend from my writers group had the most glorious success. She prepared her proposal, met with nine publishers, her book went up for auction, and she got a six-figure advance! I was truly happy for her and celebrated her success. But I couldn't help asking God, "Hey, what about me?"

I was willing to do whatever it took to get a publisher. Lisa told me that most of the publishers disliked the original page-a-day structure. So I revised the proposal and rewrote the book as an eight chapter narrative. I changed the packaging and paid to have a matching cover design for my audio and video tapes. The new packages went out to publishers, and once again, Lisa and I waited.

Meanwhile, I had a conversation with God. I asked God for a sign. I told Him I have done everything I knew how to do, and now I needed Him to clearly show me if this goal, this book, was meant for me or not. I let Him know that I am here to do His work, and that I was willing to get my poor human ego out of the way and give this up, if that was what He wanted me to do. But I needed a clear Sign whether or not to keep trying.

Exactly two days later, Deb Werksman at Sourcebooks called to say she was interested in my book. We discussed the narrative version and then she asked, "What's this page-a-day book that your agent told me about? She says everyone in her office uses it." After I described it to her, she said, "I want to see *that* book." It wasn't long before I got another call from her: "I just got out of an acquisitions meeting and we would love to publish your book!"

And you know what? They bought the original version!

God's on duty 24/7. He's just waiting for you to *ask*.

Today's Affirmation: "Thank you, God, for giving me perfect time, money, love, luck, and health at all times now."
(Contributed by Carol Allen)

228
Hot Fudge Sundaes

"There can be no rainbow without a storm and a cloud."

—F.H. Vincent

Yum. I can taste it now, that glorious vanilla ice cream, covered with the creamiest hot fudge, foamy whipped cream, crunchy walnuts, and the maraschino cherry precariously perched at the top of the heap, about to make its slippery pink slide down the ice cream mountain. The hot fudge came in its own little silver pitcher, so we could pour it ourselves, mixing fire and ice in our own private chemistry class in a goblet. Of course, we'd spill it, laughingly licking our messy fingers, not wanting to miss one drop of the precious chocolate fudge. We couldn't get enough of hot fudge sundaes.

We loved those Sunday mornings when the family piled into the red and white '55 Oldsmobile, dressed in Sunday-best clothes, smelling of Sunday-best smells, and met all our friends at the church for prayer and good thoughts. Usually, we'd stop on the way home and pick up a dozen fresh donuts for brunch after the sermon. But once in a while, our chorus of "Let's go to Jack's, please, please!" would be met with a look and a nod between Mom and Dad and a smiling assent that said, "Yes! You can have a hot fudge sundae!" And we'd drool with anticipation all the way there.

No ice cream sundae ever tasted as good as those. When I grew up and went away to college, I thought, "Yippee. Now I can have all the hot fudge sundaes I want! I can have them every day!" That's how I found out about the law of diminishing returns. One hot fudge sundae once in a while is fabulous. Two is pretty good. Three and my tummy hurts. Four and I don't fit into my clothes. When I can have one whenever I want, I don't want one very often.

In an old episode of *The Twilight Zone*, a gambler has died and gone to heaven. All of his favorite gaming devices are there, and he is always a winner. The billiard ball always goes in the right pocket, the dice always roll seven, and the ball in the roulette wheel invariably lands on the number he picked. This is fun for about a minute and a half. By then, the gambler is supremely bored. In despair, he turns to the man in the white suit who has been his guide and says, "This is awful. I'd rather go to the other place." With an evil laugh, his guide says, "This *is* the other place!"

There is relish in anticipation, in not knowing outcomes, in not always getting what you want when you want it. Enjoy the "I can hardly wait!" of positive expectation. There are many, many more of these moments in life. The actual achievement is the end of the dream. The dreaming of the goal, the *striving* towards the goal is where the fun is, where the life is. "Waiting for the day when" is the fun part.

Today's Affirmation: "I live happily each day in joyful expectation of positive outcomes!"

229
Life Is Beautiful

"Only those who will risk going too far can possibly find out how far one can go."

—T.S. Eliot

Do you remember Roberto Benigni at the 71st annual Academy Awards? When *Life is Beautiful*, the movie he wrote, directed and starred in, won Best Foreign Film of 1998, he jumped for joy. *Literally*. Rarely have I seen an adult human being express happiness so openly and unselfconsciously. He filled himself up to overflowing, let the dam burst and filled the room with starburst laughing delight. He jumped up on the back of his seat, and ran down the backs of some other seats, then hopped to the podium. A sixteen-megaton smile blazed from his face, his eyes twinkled and he said, "Thank you, thank you. This is a moment of joy and I want to kiss everybody...my body is in tumult. I would like to be Jupiter and kidnap everybody right now in the firmament, making love to everybody!"

He was funny and he was adorable. His joy was so pure and so radiant that I could feel it through the television screen and shared in it myself. I felt the warm embrace of his generous spirit. Alone in my room, I laughed out loud. I'm grinning now as I recall it. At that special moment in time, I was one with Roberto, his wife, and all the millions of audience members who felt that same radiant happiness.

Not everybody felt this way, mind you. In the days following, a lot of people seemed very uncomfortable with his open display of emotion. Newscasters laughed nervously, some critics rolled their eyes and shook their heads. What a pity. I understood, then, that you have to be happy yourself in order to share other people's happiness. You also have to not care what other people think. I suppose it's not cool to be joyful. Perhaps it isn't mature either.

Well, I think maturity is a myth. I don't know anybody mature. I just know children with older bodies. The people who talk about maturity aren't mature—they're just stuffy.

When you can share other people's happiness, you can feel all the same feelings as though it had happened to you. Open up! Share the joy! And your own personal joy will grow in geometric progression. Practice feeling happy today. Then find some dolphins to share it with.

Today's Affirmation: "Life is beautiful! Business is terrific! People are wonderful!"

230
Singing for My Supper

"Criticism didn't really stop us and it shouldn't ever stop anyone, because critics are only the people who can't get a record deal themselves."

—Sir Paul McCartney

When you step outside the proverbial box, you have to be prepared for criticism.

As I went from meeting to meeting, networking my way to successful workshop enrollments, I perfected my thirty-second commercial introduction. I always started with a song: "You're gonna be rich tomorrow…if you take my class today," or "We're in the money…my clients are singing this song." Generally, people enjoyed the upbeat flavor of my off-beat presentations.

But then I found myself in a different networking group. Everyone there gave a standard introduction in the exact same format: "Hi, I'm Larry. I am an attorney specializing in real estate law, I've been in business for twenty-five years"; "Hi, I'm Susan. I am a CPA specializing in taxes. I've been in business for fifteen years."

As my turn approached, I hesitated. Maybe I shouldn't do my singing thing in this room. Then I thought, "Nah," and went ahead, "Money makes the world go around, that clinking clanking sound…if you want more clinking and clanking in your life, call me." There were a few shocked faces, but mostly smiles as I looked around me.

The next time I went to this meeting, a woman came over to me. "There were complaints about you at the last board meeting!" she exclaimed. "It was felt that singing was inappropriate behavior at a business meeting."

"Well, I have to tell you," I replied, "that may be, but ten people came over to me after the meeting and asked for my card and six of them signed up for my workshop, so I think I'm going to keep singing!" But I knew my days there were numbered.

When I related this story to a friend, she told me about a friend of hers who was a professional singer. In search of work, she moved to Hong Kong and was invited to an office weekend party. She wrote a song for the company and sang it, after which she was asked if she would teach it to the president, whose favorite thing was karaoke. She ended up choreographing and teaching the song to the entire management team. She sang a duet with the president, who then hired her to be the cultural ambassador for the company. She now travels to all their international offices, bringing fun and morale to the company's clients and employees. Why singing? Everyone in Asia sings—all the business people, every chance they get, all the time. There it is a huge asset to sing. She says she's like a goddess over there.

Hmm. I think I should start planning a trip….

If you're having trouble with the box you're in, take yourself to a different box.

Today's Affirmation: "There are people everywhere who enjoy the unique gifts I have to share."

231

It's Just a Co-Dependent Love Song

"One comes to believe whatever one repeats to oneself sufficiently often, whether the statement be true or false."

—Robert Collier

Years ago, I heard a singer-songwriter named Scott Kalechstein sing a clever, paraphrased version of *It's Just an Old Fashioned Love Song* called *It's Just a Co-Dependent Love Song*. That made me laugh, but it also made me think. I loved all those old torchy, hurt-so-bad love songs and sang them all the time. Whenever I felt blue, I just put on some records or strummed my guitar and wailed. I sang *Crazy*, *Single Girl*, *Don't Think Twice*, *Too Far Gone*, *Am I Blue*, *Mean to Me*...get the picture?

It is emotionally satisfying to sing the blues now and again. But every day? It didn't cross my mind that, if sung too often, these songs could act as negative affirmations. I just wondered why my love life was a mess....

Think about the songs you're walking around singing. What's the message you're giving yourself? Are they positive affirmations, joyful songs? Or heartbreaking, emotional downers? (Not to mention the violent rapper songs. Better to channel all that anger and rebellion into music than into mayhem in the streets, but I wouldn't be singing along if I were you.)

Songs are speaking your word, and your word is powerful. Now I make sure to counteract the blues by also singing songs like *I'm All Right*, *Happy Talk*, *I Feel Lucky*, *It's My Life* and *Thank You For Loving Me*.

Why not write your own positive song or change the lyrics to a favorite tune? If you change lyrics to a tune, it must be an already upbeat song, or your subconscious memory of the negative words will impede your progress. A friend of mine had rewritten the lyrics to *Lemon Tree* to be *Money Tree*, but when I sang it, I always remembered the word "impossible" in the song. I didn't want the word "impossible" connected with my money, so I had to stop singing that one.

Here's a song most people know that we can rewrite for our purposes: Change the word "birthday" to "money" in the song *Happy Birthday*. I think singing "Happy money to me" is a great affirmation! Sing it today!

Today's Affirmation: "Happy money to me! Happy money to me!"

232
Affirmations Are Forever

*"Endurance is the most difficult of disciplines,
but it is to the one who endures that the final victory comes."*

—Buddha

People sometimes ask me when they can stop practicing their affirmations. I answer with another question: "When can you stop brushing your teeth?"

Affirmations are forever. It's a daily maintenance program. I thought negative thoughts for many more years than I've been practicing positive ones. I certainly don't want to backslide, do you? Those old habits are just lying in wait. One of my clients did her affirmations regularly, without fail, and then got more business than she could handle. Frightened, she purposely turned off the flow. She said, "Okay, that's enough!" and stopped doing them. Business completely dried up. As a matter of fact, all three big jobs she had gotten were canceled. She immediately recognized what she had done and started doing her affirmations again daily. She got another big job that week, and two of the lost projects were restored.

Every time I run into one of my clients that I haven't seen for awhile, I always ask how things are going. If they answer, "Great! Business is booming and I'm really happy!" I ask if they're still doing their affirmations. Invariably, they respond, "Oh, yes! I have them in my wallet, posted on my bathroom mirror, and I do them in the car, too." Conversely, when things aren't going well for someone, they sheepishly reply that they somehow just forgot about doing them.

One attorney, after admitting that he wasn't practicing his affirmations, vowed to start again that day. A week later he called me. Very excited, he told me that he had collected $6,000 that week and $4,000 of it was unexpected income. "This really works!" he exclaimed. "Tell everybody!"

Consider yourself told. And knowing about it isn't the same as doing it.

Today's Affirmation: "I am happily practicing my positive affirmations every day!"

233

Treasure Maps

"It all comes from the mind. I've seen the most incredible success stories...because a person had a dream and it was so powerful no one could touch it. He'd feel it, believe it, think about it all day and night. That would inspire him to do things necessary to get the results he wanted."

—Arnold Schwarzenegger

Visualizing what you want goes hand in hand with positive affirmations. When you declare what you want and have a clear picture of what it is you want, sooner or later what you want shows up. In order to make more money, you have to have a reason to make more money. What do you want more money for? If you aren't clear about what you want, it will be much more difficult to get it.

Treasure mapping is a great tool for becoming clear about your goals. It is also a fun project. You start by collecting lots of magazines that are filled with beautiful color photographs of things you want, places you want to go, representations of the kinds of people you'd like to meet, relationships you'd like to have, spiritual values, etc. Buy some poster board, scissors and glue. Put on some great music and start cutting and pasting—you're making a collage of all the great things you'd like to have in your life.

It is a great activity to do with friends, or your family. You can admire each other's choices and desires and compliment each other's creativity and artistic expression. With family members, you can create separate treasure maps or one family effort that will have each person's goals and dreams contained in it. Have fun, smile, and laugh a lot while you're making it!

When it's finished, put your treasure map on the wall. Look at it every day, remembering the fun you had making it, and visualizing having all the things represented in your life. Do positive affirmations about having the things you see. Send out ships to actualize these things coming to you. Start a savings account for major goal purchases. You will be amazed at how quickly many of these things will show up.

One summer, I created a *Financial Stress Reduction® Graduate Cruise Weekend* for people who had taken my workshop. I brought all the materials for treasure mapping and we had a great afternoon on board the ship creating pictures of our dream goals. One of the women put pictures of babies all over her map, because she and her husband wanted to start a family.

Six weeks later, she told me she was pregnant. And she had twins!

Today's Affirmation: "I visualize and create exactly what I want."

234
Creating Your Life

"Man cannot discover new oceans unless he has the courage to lose sight of the shore."

—Andre Gide

No one who has ever written a story, painted a picture or improvised music will tell you that it came out exactly as envisioned before the moment of creation. Our lives are like paintings that take on a different energy with a single unplanned brush stroke; colors merge and blend, the eyes see form beneath the paint, the arm arcs with power, and a surprising new line is drawn. Novelists speak of their characters as having a life of their own; they whisper to them in dreams in the night, and the plot flows through fingers in tune with a metaphysical channel of energy. Music flows from rhythm and beat; whirling notes cascading from mouths, fingers, horns, and strings. It is the gift of being in what psychologist Mihaly Csikszentmihalyi terms "flow," in touch with being; what athletes, artists, salespeople, teachers, all who have experienced being completely focused in a moment of creation know as being in "The Zone."

Our lives are like that. We tune and strengthen our instrument, we gather our paints and canvases, we read and write and perfect our gift of language, and set out upon the road of the world. We cannot see what is around the bend, what lies beyond the next hill, what notes will carry gaily on the air, what musicians will travel in our band. But we have goals, wishes, wants, dreams, plans. We create in our minds what we'd like to see up ahead, and set out in search of the prize. And we always get a prize—just not always the one we were expecting.

That you set a goal and get something different does not negate the goal-setting process. Indeed, without a goal to set your life in motion, you wander aimlessly, a pawn to be used for other people's goals. Without a goal, there is no action; without action, there are no accomplishments.

Prizes don't drop in on you unannounced, while you sip your morning coffee in your bathrobe.

Today's Affirmation: "I have what it takes to go out and get what I want!"

235
Fantasies

"Turning it over in your mind won't plow the field."

—Irish proverb

In response to fans' complaints about plot developments on the television show *La Femme Nikita*, the producer said, "They should get a life." The fans swarmed like angry bees on the Internet web sites devoted to the series, in response to his statement. I chuckled over the following message board post:

Fan #1: "This girl will get a life when she's darn good and ready to!"

Fan #2: "Life? We don't need no stinkin' life!"

Fan #3: "I have a life. What I want is a good fantasy!"

Fantasies are fun. We all indulge in them. Sometimes we turn our fantasies into goals and our goals into reality through planning and action. But all achievements begin through the dream—the delicious vision of a possible reality; something we imagine will be fun, exciting, thrilling, surprising, swooning, ecstatic.

Theater, movies, television, and books give us vicarious thrills of exciting adventures we may never actualize in our real lives. Perhaps we will never really be a spy, never hold a gun (let alone shoot one), never be super-model gorgeous, never wear a fabled diamond necklace, never fly a plane, never cut our way through the Amazon jungle. But we can hitch a ride on someone else's dream: our bodies and minds can ride an emotional roller coaster for an hour or two, and experience much the same feelings we would if we were actually having the experience. I celebrate living in this rich world where these things are possible. I thank the dream merchants who invite me to enter their worlds and forget reality for a time. Through them I live many lifetimes beyond my own.

But fantasies of a fire will not keep us warm and fantasies of rich food will not feed us. Enjoying other people's dreams will not give us what we seek in real life. From the dreamtime we must pluck out those things that we feel most strongly about and actualize them. When we work for someone else we are helping them to actualize their dream. It takes less attention, focus, and energy to assist someone else than to carve your own dream on the mountain.

But then don't complain that it's not your face on Mount Rushmore.

Today's Affirmation: "My dreams become goals and my goals become reality!"

236

The Real Black Limo

"Chance is always powerful. Let your hook be always cast; in the pool where you least expect it, there will be fish."

—Ovid

The Black Limo Fantasy actually came true for me once. A friend of my sister's worked for a market research company, and was looking for women to test Dove soap. My sister, Jane, called me one afternoon to invite me down to their office for an interview, so, on a lark, I went. A friendly woman interviewed us, one by one, on videotape.

A week later, I got a call from the marketing company telling me that they had selected a group of women to do a seven-day trial use of the soap and inviting me to participate. I had them send me the sample bar of soap. You know what? I really liked it! "It's one-quarter cleansing cream" and it made my skin feel really soft. So it was easy for me to praise the soap when I went back in for my follow-up interview.

I knew that the makers of Dove used "real people" as opposed to professional actors in their commercials. I wondered if this was an audition in disguise? When I got there, I could tell that it was. I saw several people behind a camera in a small room, and others in another room with see-through glass walls. The lighting was professional and there was an excitement and energy in the room. I said every good thing I could think of to say about the soap and they all smiled and beamed at me. Ten years after giving up my acting career I was actually about to get a national commercial. Of all the fleet of ships I had launched during my acting days, most of which had sunk or sailed into someone else's harbor, this one staunch, lone survivor was about to sail home.

They hired me! They called and asked me if I'd like to go to New York to film a television commercial and I said, "You betcha!" They flew me to New York, put me up at the Grand Hyatt Hotel, and gave me a check for $1,000 for expenses while I was there. I was getting paid standard Screen Actors Guild rates (there was a moment's hesitation when they discovered I already belonged to SAG—maybe I wasn't a real person after all—but since I hadn't done anything in so long, they said it was okay). Over the next two years, I made about $15,000. Residuals are glorious: you work a couple of days and get paid for it over and over and over. Checks just keep showing up in your mailbox—truly "Magic Money."

But for me, the best part was waiting for me at New York's JFK airport: the "Real Black Limo" had arrived to whisk me away.

Good energy is never completely lost. Whenever you reach out to accomplish something, that positive energy will manifest somewhere, sometime, in unexpected ways. You still have some hardy little ships clinging to the waves out there. Check the horizon.

Today's Affirmation: "All my ships are sailing into my harbor loaded with treasure for me!"

237

Making Money While You Sleep

"Each of us has the choice—we must make money work for us, or we must work for money."

—Conrad Leslie

A doctor and his wife who had heard me speak flew me to Oklahoma to speak to their staff on customer service. It was a nice group of about fifteen people, and we had a great meeting over dinner as I coached them on *Office Etiquette*.

After dinner, Dr. John, his wife, Mary, and I sat quietly discussing money and business. He told me that one night, he was lying awake in bed and thought, "I make a lot of money working as a cosmetic surgeon, but if I don't show up for work, I don't make anything. My money is totally dependent on my working hours." He turned to me and said, "But I want to make money while I'm sleeping! I want to make money whether I show up for work or not."

So he bought an oil well. And that oil well is pumping oil twenty-four hours a day, making him money, whether or not he works. This is called "passive income."

How can you make money while you're sleeping? Can you invent a product that stores can sell and people can buy whether or not you're there? Can you receive a commission on sales that other people make? Years ago, I appeared in a Dove soap television commercial. Although I only worked one day filming the commercial, it was shown on television across the country for two years—and I made money every time it aired. A woman I knew made up a creative company name, registered it as a trademark, and another company paid her an annual licensing fee to use it. When you invest in a growing company that prospers and pays you dividends—that's making money while you sleep.

If you set up enough passive income, your only job will be managing it. And you can phone that in from Tahiti!

Today's Affirmation: "Every day when I wake up in the morning, I'm richer than I was when I went to sleep!"

238

The Lessons of The Richest Man in Babylon

"Albert Einstein, when asked what he considered the most powerful force in the Universe, answered: 'Compound interest!'"

—Mignon McLaughlin

George Clason wrote a wonderful little book entitled *The Richest Man in Babylon*. It is the story of a group of trades people in ancient times in the city of Babylon. The butcher, the blacksmith, the shopkeeper, and others are talking together about money. They marvel how one of them became the richest man in town, when he started out as just the potter down the street from them. How did he do it? they wonder. They are all still struggling day to day to get by. They decide that they will all go together to ask him to share with them the secret of becoming wealthy.

The richest man smiles when he hears their request. "A part of all you earn is yours to keep," he says. That is the magic formula he imparts to his old friends. Out of every portion you are paid, reserve 10 percent for yourself. This money you never spend, but invest and get the money working for you. The money will multiply itself through wise investing, and work for you even when you are not working.

His formula for budgeting was also simple: Save 10 percent for investments, use 20 percent to pay off debts, and the other 70 percent is for living expenses. Once all debts are paid in full, you have 90 percent for living expenses.

These simple lessons still work well today. Save 10 percent of your income in retirement accounts—see a financial planner or investment advisor to set up a plan of action for you now. Make a list of all your debts and devote yourself to a "PDQ" program—20 percent of your income until all debts are paid in full. The rest is yours to play with, to create your home and lifestyle.

Who knows? You could be the next *Millionaire Next Door* or *Millionairess Across the Street*.

Today's Affirmation: "I work smart, I work easy, and I work rich."

239

Retirement Planning

"It isn't necessary to be rich and famous to be happy. It's only necessary to be rich."

—Alan Alda

She was fifty-five years old and worked on an assembly line for a major corporation. It was time to retire, she told Dianne, the certified financial planner.

"How much money do you have in your 401K plan?" the financial planner asked.

"Around $20,000," she replied.

"And do you have additional savings?"

"No."

"Investments in real estate?"

"No."

"Alimony? Expectation of inheritance? Other sources of income?"

"No."

The financial planner shook her head sadly, and explained that $20,000 wasn't going to be enough money to allow her to retire.

When Dianne told me this story, she told me how frustrated she felt when people didn't understand, until too late, just how important it was to have a financial plan for the future. Even if you save money on a regular basis, that doesn't mean that you'll have enough to live in a castle on a hilltop in Europe when you decide to retire. Another client, who had a million dollars saved for retirement, thought he was going to be able to spend $20,000 a month. Spending $240,000 per year would eat up a million dollars rather quickly.

You have to have a budget worked out for tomorrow just like you have to have a budget worked out for today. Money doesn't magically appear just because you turned fifty-five or sixty-five. Furthermore, you can't assume that just because you save money on a regular basis that you are saving *enough* to allow you to live without working. You have to do the math.

How much money can you reasonably expect to save each year? How much money will your investments likely produce in interest income? How many years do you have in which to accumulate savings until your projected retirement date? What kind of lifestyle do you want to maintain when you are retired? Will you work part-time? Will you need less money than you do now because you won't have work related-expenses such as the cost of commuting, networking, business attire, etc.?

You probably need help with these questions. Make an appointment with a financial planner. Get a plan together, then take the actions that are on the plan every month.

Or be willing to keep on working.

Today's Affirmation: "I accumulate wealth daily for my abundant future!"

240
Save Your Singles

"Penny and penny, laid up will be many."

—Anonymous

Many people have saved extra money just by saving their loose change at the end of the day. Over time, all that change mounts up and can added to savings accounts, vacation spending, holiday gifts, etc.

Suzanne Miller, who creates wonderful designer jewelry, started saving dollar bills instead of change. At the end of each day, she just took all the singles out of her wallet and put them away in a cookie jar in her closet. It became a habit, and she never missed the money.

Her business was booming. She hired people to help her and added more jewels and precious stones to her inventory. Much of her income was invested in expanding her business. The holidays were approaching and she wanted to travel to see family and take a vacation. Remembering her singles savings, she looked to see if there was enough to help with her plans.

This is what she was able to do with the money she found in her closet:

1. She bought a round trip ticket to Tucson from Los Angeles.
2. She bought a round trip ticket to Seattle from Los Angeles.
3. She put a 50% deposit on a vacation package to Jamaica.

Just from saving singles at the end of the day!

Today's Affirmation: "All the money in my possession increases every day!"

241

Penny Wise, Pound Foolish

"It was said of old Sarah, Duchess of Marlborough, that she never put dots over her 'i's to save ink."

—Horace Walpole

One of my dream vacations was to go on a Mediterranean cruise. I had always had an interest in archaeology, having read about Howard Carter's discovery of King Tut's tomb and Henreich Schliemann's excavation of Troy. (I even thought seriously about pursuing it as a career until I realized that these men spent a lot of years digging in the dirt without finding anything before their major discoveries. I really just wanted to show up on the day they hit pay dirt and see all the golden treasure.) But I yearned to walk through the ruins of the Roman city of Pompeii, buried by volcanic ash in 79 A.D. I wanted to tour the Vatican, climb the hill to the Acropolis in Athens, and roam the sandy beaches of the Greek Islands. I had been doing my friend Paris's affirmation—"I now receive free first class travel and accommodations all around the world"—when I received an inheritance that completely paid for the trip.

The trip was everything I had hoped for and more. The ship was terrific, the company delightful. I won a jackpot in a slot machine in Monte Carlo (if this surprises you, you haven't been paying attention to all I've been saying in this book), our room was beautiful, the food was delicious, and the sea was so flat no one got seasick.

At each port, we were in a different country with different currency, and we had to visit the currency exchange dealers when we disembarked in order to have cash to spend that day. It made me laugh to see several of the passengers run from exchange dealer to exchange dealer, looking for the best exchange rate for their money. I'm sure they thought they were being careful with their money, but to me they were wasting the only time they had to be visiting this exotic locale in trying to pinch pennies! The trip cost $3,000—what's another dollar or two in exchange rate savings? When we visited the palace at Monaco, the tour guide told us we needed to give a franc (about twenty-five cents) to the restroom attendant when we visited the facilities. I saw a woman who only had a dollar bill trying desperately to find someone to give her change so she didn't have to give the whole dollar to the attendant.

Lighten up. Share the wealth. We're not talking big money here. You're on vacation—the goal isn't to come back with money saved, it's to have a great time experiencing new places. Keep in mind the relative values at all times. Give up spending ten dollars on gas and an hour of your time driving from supermarket to supermarket to save ten cents on a box of cereal.

Don't blow dollars saving pennies.

Today's Affirmation: "I am an expert at spending money wisely."

242
Integrity

"The art of acceptance is the art of making someone who has just done you a small favor wish that he might have done you a greater one."

—Russell Lynes

It is a universal principle of money that whatever money you obtain dishonestly, by lying, cheating, swindling, or in any way taking money that isn't rightfully yours, will be taken back from you tenfold. At least. The reverse is also true. Whatever money you gain by serving others with love and joy, will be given back to you tenfold. Wealth, riches, joy and abundance, pressed down, overflowing.

It doesn't always appear that this is so. Resentful people are often fond of pointing out rich people with ill-gotten gains that seem to have come from deceptive practices, exploitation, or out-and-out thievery. It won't serve you to think like that. The belief that someone else has become rich through exploiting others will only keep you from attempting to make your own fortune for fear of becoming a bad person. You can't be worried about what other people are doing about their integrity. Just worry about your own. As you start to see your positive efforts from a center of personal integrity produce financial rewards, and whatever cheating you do result in a reduction in your wealth, you will see that financial integrity is one of your most important assets.

Mimi Donaldson is a vivacious public speaker. Over lunch one day, she was explaining to me how she works with speakers bureaus in order to get booked nationally as a speaker at corporations and conferences. She has been speaking for many years, and told me a story of how she was contacted by a meeting planner to speak at an upcoming conference. As they talked, she remembered that she had been booked for this same group three years before by a woman named Rosalind, who owned a speakers bureau. Although Mimi was contractually free of paying Rosalind a fee for the engagement, since she only had to pay for repeat engagements for two years from the first date, Mimi felt that she would not be getting this job without Rosalind's initial help. She called Rosalind to tell her that she was going to accept the engagement and would pay Rosalind her fee. Rosalind was so impressed with Mimi's integrity that she substantially reduced her fee. This created great friendliness and harmony between the two of them and each appreciated the other's generosity, honesty, and integrity. (Dolphins recognize each other.)

A week later, Rosalind called Mimi with another engagement.

It is fear that causes a lack of integrity. Fear that there isn't enough to go around, that there isn't enough for you to survive. But you always have survived, haven't you? Fear is just an old habit. Replace it with trust.

Today's Affirmation: "All my friends are successful and happily making large sums of money!"

243
Son of Jaws

"A pessimist, confronted with two bad choices, chooses both."

—Jewish proverb

"Trouble, my friend, you got trouble. That begins with a 'T' and that rhymes with 'P' and that stands for...prospect," I thought to myself, paraphrasing the words and music from *The Music Man*. I watched the prospective client pace in front of me as he ranted and raved about his last bookkeeper. He complained vociferously about what a bad accounting job had been done and told how he had fired the bookkeeper and was looking for a new one. He hoped I would be better.

Alarm bells were clanging in my head. I asked him what *exactly* had been done that was so terrible? He showed me a check stub in his company checkbook. In the memo portion, the stub said "Insurance." The prospect angrily told me that the bookkeeper had posted the check to the company insurance account. I was confused. "Well, it says insurance in the memo portion," I said. "Why would it say that if it wasn't insurance?" The man then explained that he had written the check to his employee to get cash, and his bookkeeper should have known that that's what it was. After all, he had already paid his insurance premiums.

Since I didn't have my degree in mind reading, I knew this client and I weren't going to get along well. I told him I didn't think I would be able to do a better job for him than the last bookkeeper did and left.

When I operated from a position of scarcity, I used to work with people like this. I sat with one new client while he showed me all the money he owed to people. He then gave me instructions to pay small amounts to some of them, and for others, he just said, "I'm never going to pay them." But I actually sat there thinking he was going to pay me for the work I was doing for him. That little life lesson cost me $800. Wish I could say that was the only one, but apparently it was a lesson I had to repeat a few times before I got it.

Sometimes, the ship that comes in is the Black Ship, and the captain has a big "T" for trouble written on his cap, along with the skull and crossbones. You can see it very plainly if you look closely. See the red flag go up, hear the "Do, do, do, do" music from *Jaws* and get out of the water. Sink those ships in the harbor that have bad clients in it. Otherwise, you're going to end up a tuna sandwich.

Today's Affirmation: "All the people I work with are easy-going, honest, and fun!"

244
The Doctor's Accounting

"Did you ever hear of a kid playing accountant—even if he wanted to be one?"

—Jackie Mason

The distinguished doctor I met at a party asked me what I did for a living. "I own a bookkeeping service," I replied. He immediately started bragging how he saved $600 a month by firing his accountant and doing the bookkeeping himself. "Really?" I asked. "How long does it take you to do it?"

"It takes me about six hours," he replied.

I asked, "And how many hours do you work as a doctor?"

He replied, "Oh, I work a full office schedule—about 35 hours a week."

"I would imagine that you make a lot of money as a doctor," I said.

"Oh, yes!" he exclaimed proudly.

"When you're working at being a doctor, do you make as much as $300 per hour seeing patients?"

"Certainly," he said. "Sometimes more, depending on the patients and their needs."

"Then it seems to me," I suggested, "if you spent the six hours you're spending on accounting being a doctor instead, you would make $1,800. Then you'd pay the accountant $600 and have a profit of $1,200. So, firing your accountant didn't really save you any money—it cost you money."

He was speechless for a moment, and I could see his mind working, processing this information. "But, I enjoy it," he said finally.

"Yes, I do, too!" I agreed. "It's my business."

I found out later he rehired his accountant.

If you can think of something more fun, productive, or profitable to do than the onerous task you hate, then do it and delegate the other. You don't have to do tasks just because you *can*.

Today's Affirmation: "I love to delegate to others so I can do the work I love!"

245

The Circle of Abundance

"Money is like manure—it's not worth anything unless you spread it around!"

—Dolly Levi in *The Matchmaker,* by Thornton Wilder

Money is a circle of abundance that is constantly flowing, creating ripples of prosperity just as a stone creates ripples when dropped in a lake. With any purchase, you can easily follow the ripples if you look.

For example, if you buy a car, you have created prosperity for many people in an endless chain. First, the salesperson who sold you the car gets a commission, as does the dealership. The manufacturer also is enriched by the transaction. Most people are conscious of this much sometime during the transaction.

But the ripples continue: your purchase of the car sends money into the hands of all the people and businesses associated with the production, manufacture, shipping, assembly, and inspections of the automobile. The advertising agency who writes the ad that attracts the buyer, the newspaper that prints the ad, the salesperson who sold the ad space, the person who sells the newspaper the paper stock and the ink. The lumberyard that produced the paper, the lumberjacks who chopped the wood, the trucker who hauled the wood and the one who moved the paper. Then the insurance company that provides the insurance policy on the car and all the workers associated with that business. How far can you follow the ripples? It is endless.

It is important for your personal prosperity to take joy in this process. As you write the check or pay the cash for your purchase, know that you are creating financial benefits for many unseen individuals who make their livings from multiples of these transactions. Smile and remember to write "Thank you!" on every check. You are giving of your abundance to other people and they will be doing the same—sending it out and around and eventually it will circle back to you.

Then you will send it out again.

Today's Affirmation: "Every dollar I send out comes back to me multiplied!"

246

The Optimism Insurance Policy

"How many joys are crushed under foot because people look up at the sky and disregard what is at their feet?"

—Catharina Elisabetha Goethe

Al the accountant bought a lottery ticket for himself every week. He said that it was his optimism insurance policy. Each week when he bought his ticket, he had fun thinking that he could win the lottery and become a millionaire. He smiled and spoke of how it much fun it was to think about having something wonderful like that happen. It kept him in a happy frame of mind all week. When the day of the drawing arrived, he would look at his ticket and think, "Today could be my lucky day!" If he didn't win, he would immediately buy another ticket: "Maybe next time!" He always kept his optimism insurance policy renewed and in full force.

Don't mention the lottery to my friend, Dave. He's really mad about all the money he wasted buying tickets when he's never won anything. He thinks it's rigged, unfair, sinful, bad, and a rip-off because he hasn't won. He is full of resentment towards the people who have won it, the state that runs it, the government that allows it, and the other players who are losers.

Not every dollar you spend has to be sensible and smart. Some part of your budget needs to be "mad money" or "spree money"—money you can spend for fun. If you get a return on your investment, great; if not, so what? But, if you can't have fun with it, don't do it.

The eleventh commandment is "Thou Shalt Lighten Up."

Today's Affirmation: "Today is a very lucky day, filled with wonderful surprises and money!"

247
Motivation

"So many thirsty pass so close to the water, yet do not drink."

—Sufi proverb

Jim Rohn, a great speaker and business philosopher, writes that motivation is a mystery. He said, "Give a lecture to a thousand people. One walks out and says, 'I'm going to change my life.' Another one walks out with a yawn and says, 'I've heard all this before.' Why is that?" He shakes his head in wonder that a millionaire tells a thousand people about a book that started him on the path to wealth, yet very few of them ever get the book. If people are listening to this man talk, and probably paid money to hear him, why wouldn't they do what he told them to do? He called this a mystery of life.

During one session of the *Financial Stress Reduction® Workshop*, I had twenty-five participants. On the day of the last class, twenty-four of them wrote glowing reviews of the course on their evaluation sheets. The twenty-fifth didn't come to the last class, but instead left a message on voicemail that she "didn't hear anything new" and wanted a refund of her money. Why was that? She heard the same information. Why couldn't I reach her, too?

Many people are looking for someone special who holds the key to their success. They believe that the right key will unlock their potential. What they don't realize is that everyone has that key. They're being showered with keys all the time. They just don't turn it in their lock. Instead of saying, "This isn't working for me," they need to say, "How can I make this work for me?"

Look for your key today. Then put it in your lock and turn it.

Today's Affirmation: "I learn from all around me and grow wiser, richer, and happier every day."

248

Go to the Top

"In the long run men hit only what they aim at. Therefore, though they should fall immediately, they had better aim at something high."

—Henry David Thoreau

Michelle was having difficulties marketing her services. She was making calls daily and recording them in her Ships Log, but she was not getting the results she wanted. Time after time, the people she spoke to listened politely and then said they'd call back later when they were interested. After I asked her a few questions, the problem became clear: she was making her sales pitch to the company receptionist! Now, receptionists are often very nice people and they can be most helpful in directing you to the right people to talk to. But they do not make the buying decisions for the company. Michelle needed to talk to the people at the company who were in positions of power. As soon as she started talking to company presidents, vice presidents, and managers, her sales improved dramatically.

Michelle's story reminded me of an old family story: my grandfather, William Livingston, was an attorney in private practice in the small town of Prentiss, Mississippi. When his son Rob graduated from law school, he went to work with his father. The two of them had a successful practice together for many years.

One afternoon, an elderly gentleman arrived at the office and asked to see Mr. William Livingston. Knowing that his father was very busy that day, Rob asked if he could help. The man thanked him, but said no, he wished to see Mr. William Livingston, and he would wait.

A quarter of an hour went by, and Rob again went out to the waiting room, to see if he could be of assistance. The man shook his head.

After another half-hour, concerned about the client's wait, Rob said, "I am William Livingston's son, and I'm sure that I can help you with whatever you need."

The older man looked him over calmly. Then, with a twinkle in his eye, he said, "Son, I didn't come to see Jesus. I came to see God!"

He was immediately shown in to my grandfather's office.

Today's Affirmation: "People are always happy to see me and help me get my goals."

249
Swimming in Corporations

"I will smile at friend and foe alike and make every effort to find, in him or her, a quality to praise, now that I realize the deepest yearning of human nature is the craving to be appreciated."

—Og Mandino

There is a dynamic between business owners and employees that is disempowering to both: resentment. Employees often feel that they are unfairly exploited, that they aren't paid enough, that they don't enjoy enough privileges, perks, benefits, freedoms, etc. They feel trapped by the bargain they have made to exchange dollars for time, then resent the time and feel the dollars aren't enough. They turn a resentful eye on those bosses above them that they see making more money, driving nicer cars, living in bigger houses in swankier neighborhoods. They resent the annual reviews, the raises that are never high enough, the bonuses that don't stretch far enough. They imagine that if they owned the business, they would pay better salaries, and be universally loved by all their employees. They become Tuna.

Business owners always seem to be taken by surprise by this attitude from their employees. They know the enormous financial risks they have taken to start their business, and the fear of failure that lurks in the dark corners of their minds. They are blind to the fact that most employees don't know what it took to create and build the business, they just see the perks and want them. The business owners become resentful of what they see as an employees ingratitude. Some employers become so embittered by this that they treat their employees with little respect and pay the lowest wages they can get away with. They become Sharks.

The company that is divided by an "us vs. them" mentality between bosses and employees is losing a great deal of its power and focus. It will never be as effective as a company of dolphins in which everyone knows they're on the same team, and when the team wins they all win; where all involved are aware of the importance of every other person in the company.

I believe that if employees knew the risks, talents, and skills that are required to open and successfully run a business, they would appreciate their employers more. I believe every employee ought to start, not in the mailroom, but in the sales room. Let them learn what it takes to create money by selling a product or service to customers. Then they can move on to a different job, but they will never lose their appreciation for the people who, with talent, drive, and persistence, create everyone's income. If there are no customers, no one has a job. Employers need to spend one day each quarter doing someone else's job in order to appreciate their employees. Everyone needs everyone else, and mutual appreciation eliminates resentment. They become Dolphins.

Can you find a corporation of Dolphins? Or is it time for you to create one?

Today's Affirmation: "I appreciate everyone who works with me, for they help create my wonderful income!"

250

Teamwork

"Humankind has not woven the web of life. We are but one thread within it. Whatever we do to the web, we do to ourselves. All things are bound together. All things connect."

—Chief Seattle

I stood in the aircraft hanger with my family, looking at the half-built shell of the space shuttle. It was "Family Day" at Edwards Air Force Base for employees of Rockwell International. Children and adults covered the hangar like ants on honey, grasping to wrap their minds and arms around the immensity of this project.

I paused in the middle of the hubbub and turned to my father, who had helped design the shuttle's navigational systems.

"How many people does it take to build a space shuttle?" I asked.

"About four thousand," he answered.

"And how many people does it take to get the shuttle up and flying around the Earth?"

"About four hundred fifty thousand."

Ah. I let my breath out slowly, standing reverently in this truth, and thought how much like the ants we really are. One ant cannot survive alone. One person cannot put up a space shuttle. One person can paddle a canoe, but it takes a crew to sail a cruise ship. We need teams. And we have them. Your teams are all around you.

Some teams are formalized. Corporations are teams, communities, cities, political parties, charities—all are teams. Networking groups exist to help each other by giving referrals. When you're on the team, it's just as much fun to give your teammate a great business lead as it is to get one yourself.

But your informal team is all around you. Your family of birth and your family of choice: friends, co-workers, golf buddies, hairdressers, friends on the web. The person standing behind you at the grocery store could need your services or know someone who does.

My friend, Victoria Loveland-Coen, author of *Manifesting Your Desires,* wrote a wonderful new book on baby bonding. Victoria wanted to connect with Rosie O'Donnell, who is well-known as a children's advocate. She immediately put the word out to all her teams. I didn't think I could help her until one evening when I overheard a fellow poker-player mention her "good friend" Rosie. My ears perked up immediately. "You know Rosie O'Donnell?" I asked. "For years!" she said. The connection was made.

You have but to ask and the support of a team is yours. Some you pay in dollars and some you pay in love.

What are you trying to do alone, while your life team stands by, at-the-ready, waiting, hoping to help?

Today's Affirmation: "I give and receive loving support from all my teammates today!"

251

The Sprinter and the Long Distance Runner

"Time is a great teacher. Unfortunately, it kills all pupils."

—Hector Berlioz

The sprinter runs at top speed, with an all-out burst of energy, heart pounding and legs pumping to beat the wind to the finish line. Exhausted, lungs bursting at the end, the racer collapses and rests. He will sprint again. Later.

The long distance runner cannot sprint—the course is too long. He must learn a different set of skills; he must know how to pace himself, to select those moments in which to push harder and faster, when to ease into the regular run for maintenance.

Life is not a sprint. It is a long distance race.

Too many people are pushing themselves at top sprinting speed every day, every week, year after year. They don't pace themselves. They don't take a break to recover after a big push to meet a deadline—instead a new deadline takes its place and a new sprint begins. The project gets finished but another project stands urgently behind that one. And another. And another. The sales quota, when met, gets raised. Like a meal rushed to its conclusion, the achievement is gulped untasted. Burnout of mind and body arrives after too many sprints in a row.

When was your last vacation? When was your last three-day weekend? What day of the week is your "Do Nothing Day"?

Are you trying to sprint long distance?

Today's Affirmation: "My life is beautifully paced, with nurturing rests between triumphs."

252
How to Schedule Time Off

"Most people are so busy knocking themselves out trying to do everything they think they should do, they never get around to do what they want to do."

—Kathleen Winsor

People often ask me how I schedule time off. Their lives are so crowded with work, family, hobbies, outings, appointments, obligations, etc. that they look at the calendars and just can't see how they can get everything done and still have "Do Nothing Days" or regular time off.

It's really a very simple process. You open your calendar, pick a day, draw a line through it, and that's your day you've booked with your most important client—yourself! People who are over-committed often gasp and laugh nervously when I tell them this. They are overwhelmed with too much to do. I ask them how often they get sick. When they say, "Pretty often," I tell them that that is their body's message to them to take a break and lie low for a while. Wouldn't it be better to take the break while you're well so you can enjoy it? Get in front of the process and plan time off instead of letting the cold catch you when you've run yourself down.

When someone wants to schedule a meeting with you on your day off, don't tell them, "Oh, no, that's my day off." You'll feel guilty and they'll talk you into meeting with them, and now your day off has become a work day. You just say instead, "Oh, I'm sorry, I'm booked that day, how about next Thursday instead?" You really can do this—it works great!

Someone will always ask me at this point, "Well, what if the most important person in the world calls to meet with you that day and you could make a million dollars and they are only going to be in town that one day—what do you do then?" I tell them that's why they made erasers—so you erase the line you drew through that day on the calendar and schedule the million dollar meeting. But then you immediately draw a line through an alternate day on the calendar and that new day becomes your day off! Trading days is okay—canceling days off completely is not.

You schedule time off as a commitment to your health and your sanity and to replenish your supply. The irreplaceable million-dollar piece of business equipment you own is your body—treat it with care, respect, and regular maintenance. You deserve—and need—regular breaks!

Today's Affirmation: "I deserve and enjoy my time off."

253

Art, Music, Dance, Poetry

"The poet speaks to all men of that other life that they have smothered and forgotten."

—Dame Edith Sitwell

When financial cutbacks hit the school system, the arts are usually the first things to go. But they should be the last. We need art, music, poetry, and dance. We need it in our lives every day, not only on special occasions when we dress up and go to the theater to watch spectacular artists performing spectacularly. Where poetry meets the mind and dance frees the body, we escape the bonds of earth and circumstance and live beyond our time and space. Without the arts, creative expression dies, and school can degenerate into a memory test of names, dates, and places.

Today, I invite you to write poetry. Have you every tried it? When was the last time? If you never have, here's a new experience to enjoy. I hadn't written poetry in thirty years. But I sat down to write a money management book, and one day, poetry flowed out. It was surprising. It was fun. I didn't realize how I'd missed it. Here's a sample from my poem, *Road Repairs*:

"Fourteen men in four-ton trucks
Rope the road that twists and bucks
They brand a hot new blue-black skin
Where once old pock-marked scars had been.
I, too, have shouldered such a load
With layers thick of rocky road
Buried deep beneath new skins
I paste on top to hide my sins.
And I will bear more troubles well
Because this road has led through hell
Resurfacing in brighter days
I slowly learn to change my ways...."

You don't have to be Robert Frost, Dylan Thomas, or Maya Angelou. You just need to be a human being. It costs nothing to write a poem. Just a pen and piece of paper and you can play with million-dollar words, with crazy, happy rhymes, with buzzing, beautiful sounds of syllables. Clash them, mash them, make words up. Flow with it. Write your feelings, your passion, your pity, and your fury. Free associate, then connect the dots. What lies deep within you that needs art, poetry, music to find its way out?

Write something. Paint something. Sing. Put a record on and dance. Just for the joy of it.

Today's Affirmation: "I have the soul of an artist, and music and poetry fill my life."

254

Feng Shui and Fountains

"The most powerful emotion we can experience is the mystical. It is the power of all true art and science. He to whom this emotion is a stranger, who can no longer wonder and stand rapt in awe, is as good as dead."

—Albert Einstein

Pat McKee is a rock hound. She loves her rocks. She knows the mystical properties in every stone, every crystal, and generously shares her information. Under a tree-shaded patio in San Dimas, California, Pat teaches people to build feng shui fountains to put in their homes. Feng shui is the ancient Chinese art of object placement, which can affect the harmony of your life positively or negatively.

Some people swear feng shui works, and that rocks and crystals can promote certain energies. Other people think it's New Age hogwash. I'm for anything that works, so I took Pat's class and built a fountain. I put wonderful wealth-enhancing stones in my fountain. Here's what I used:

1. **Citrine:** Called "The Merchant's Stone," it attracts abundance
2. **Variscite:** Encourages the flow of energy fulfilling the need
3. **Tiger Eye:** Stimulates wealth and enhances the stability required to maintain wealth
4. **Vanadinite:** Thrift in spending
5. **Diamond:** Good amplifier; inspires forces of accumulation. Helps manifest abundance in all areas of life. (I put an old gold ring with diamond chips in the fountain for this one.)
6. **Gold:** It's gold!

When I got home from the Saturday morning workshop, I plugged the fountain in place in what had been designated to me as the "wealth center" of my house. I met some friends for a poker game and promptly won $450. The next morning—on a Sunday!—a woman called to enroll herself and a friend in my workshop for $1,000 apiece. So, in the twenty-four hours following putting a "Prosperity Fountain" in my home, I was $2,450 richer.

Maybe this is all coincidental. Maybe these things would have happened anyway. I certainly wouldn't suggest that *all* anyone needs to do to be wealthy is feng shui their house and get a fountain. The prosperity principles this book is based on need to be attended to as well.

But don't you try to take that fountain out of my house.

Today's Affirmation: "I use all the knowledge and power available to me to create the life I desire!"

255
Astrology

"About astrology and palmistry: They are good because they make people vivid and full of possibilities. They are communism at its best. Everybody has a birthday and almost everybody has a palm."

—Kurt Vonnegut, Jr.

Astrology has been practiced since ancient days. I believe there is something to it, and I check in with my astrologer about important things. I read the daily horoscope in the newspaper, too, although they are careful to state that it is to be read for "entertainment." That seems fair, since it would be hard for one little three-sentence overview for the day to be spot-on for everyone in a particular sign. It's just the sun sign; it doesn't take into account your rising sign, moon sign, or any other sign that might mitigate the prediction for your day.

But you can get some great affirmations for the day from the astrology section of the newspaper. Read the one for your sun sign—if you like it, you can decide that it is a true prediction for your day today. If you don't like it, decide that there was a mistake made, or your rising sign makes a different prediction more appropriate for you that day...you get the idea. Then read all the horoscopes for each sign and choose the one you like best as your forecast for the day.

I've saved a few that make me feel good when I read them. I pick one out now and again to be my positive astrology affirmation for the day. Then I rewrite them as positive affirmations to add to my list. Here are some examples of affirmations I created in the style of Sydney Omarr, whose horoscopes are published in the LA *Times*:

1. "You are on the precipice of universal acclaim. Fame and fortune are coming your way today. Be yourself and you win."
2. "This could be your power-play day. Concentrate on putting forth your best effort. Great success is just around the corner."
3. "Today is your kind of day! What appeared to be out of reach will be yours. Emphasis on love, friendship and partnerships."
4. "Good things in store—financial picture brightens. Astrological cycle highlights production, intensity, reward."
5. "Time to celebrate! Hopes, wishes, desires fulfilled in fantastic manner. Many are talking positively about your talent, personality, and luck. You'll receive rewards."

The guiding principle is—If it makes you feel happier, believe it. If it makes you feel worse, don't believe it.

Today's Affirmation: "Today is my kind of day! Great success is here to stay!"

256

Almost a Millionaire

"No man can tell whether he is rich or poor by turning to his ledger. It is the heart that makes a man rich. He is rich or poor according to what he is, not according to what he has."

—Henry Ward Beecher

The lottery jackpot had been thirty million dollars. I checked my numbers in the morning. Nope. I hadn't won it.

At lunch that afternoon, I sat next to my friend, Dori Jackson. A wonderful, creative art teacher, she always had the ability to make me laugh. She showed me the winning numbers:

4 9 16 32 33 46

Then she showed me her ticket with the numbers she had picked:

4 9 16 32 33 47

Clutching each other's arms, we wailed together. So close!

But Dori laughed. She was beautiful in her gratitude for the sixteen hundred dollars she did win, since she got five out of six winning numbers. She refused to participate in the "coulda-shoulda-woulda" of her near miss for the millions. She looked me in the eye and said, "Yesterday I had a dollar. Today I have sixteen hundred dollars. This is good!"

Do you have a favorite story of a near miss? Can you tell it happily, or do you tell it with regret? If you let go of outcomes, your whole life is just one, long, interesting story. Some wins, some losses. Keep looking forward to the next win and you'll be happy every day of your life.

Today's Affirmation: "I celebrate every demonstration of abundance in my life!"

257

Things Are Getting Worse—Eat Chocolate!

"Consider a duck. It encounters the air, water and soil. It benefits from each, is hindered by none, harms nothing. They are cute, too. Be a duck!"

—old Slovakian saying

My priorities in life were pretty well-established by the time I was two. My parents told me that, at that age, I had taken a terrible fall down the stairs. They stared at me, frozen in fear that I had hurt myself horribly. But I stood right up, looked around and said, "Where's my cookie?" It wasn't until I found out the cookie was smashed and broken that I started crying.

A popular card from years ago had an elephant on it and read, "Things are getting worse—please send chocolate!" I can relate. Most of the time, I am a happy, energetic, positive person. People have even asked me, "You always seem so cheerful—do you ever get depressed?" Of course, I do. (I don't cry over broken cookies anymore, though. That's when the calories fall out.) I have my down moments, like anyone else. It's normal. So then they want to know what I do to get over it.

I eat chocolate.

Chocolate is my anti-depressant drug of choice. Chocolate candy, chocolate cake, chocolate pie, chocolate ice cream, chocolate cookies, chocolate Krispy Kremes™, chocolate chocolate. Ummmm. When "Once more, dear friends, into the breach," doesn't cut it, I forget Shakespeare and Prince Hal and say, "No more breaches today. I need a treat!" I give myself some time off, I cuddle up in my bed, turn off the phone and zone out with books, videos, and naps. And *chocolate*.

I am really perky after that. Giving myself permission to take a break and pamper myself makes me feel like I own my life. I fight the good fight every day. I get more "Nos" than "Yeses" every day. And sometimes I just need more "Yeses!" So I say yes to myself, yes I want chocolate, yes I can have chocolate, and yes, I say yes I will yes (with apologies to James Joyce).

No, I can't do this too often or yes, I will be fat and broke, but some days, sometimes, I play hooky from my work and sensible eating and take a break with chocolate.

Where's your cookie?

Today's Affirmation: "I enjoy all of the wonderful abundance of life!"

258

There's Always Hope on the Seventh Green

"Things don't go wrong and break your heart so you can become bitter and give up. They happen to break you down and build you up so you can be all that you were intended to be."

—Charlie "Tremendous" Jones

Tim Collins was studying hard for his Series Six license. To become a financial planner, he needed to pass a complicated test. He had tried six times already. He knew the material perfectly, but a deep-seated fear of tests prevented him from achieving his goal.

He began each test with high expectations that yes, this time he would pass! But somewhere about three-quarters of the way through, the knotting fear would grip his throat like a noose, and the internal demon voices would scream, "You can't do it! You're not good enough!"

One evening, he was pouring over his books and his notes, when his teenage son Robert pulled up a chair and sat down beside him. "Dad," he said, "I know you're going to pass the test this time. Seven is a lucky number and this is your seventh try. I want you to remember, when you're half-way through the test, and the going gets rough, it doesn't matter—because this time you are going to pass. Visualize yourself on the seventh green at the Pebble Beach golf course and putt the ball in the hole."

Tim had tears in his eyes as he told me this story. His dear son had, in one of Tim's darkest moments, held out to him love and hope and faith. Robert had created a vision for Tim to hold onto, so that he would be able to create sunshine and a green fairway in the midst of anxiety.

On the day of the test, the first part of the examination went well, and his spirits soared. Then, as before, after passing the halfway mark, the test got tougher, and Tim sagged in his chair. The negative voices started ringing in his ear. But Tim remembered his son's words, closed his eyes, and turned his inner vision to the seventh green at Pebble Beach. His golf ball lay on the green in perfect position. With a deep breath, he reached back, swung, and perfectly putted the ball into the hole. "Yes," he whispered to himself, "I can do it!" With renewed energy and optimism, he opened his eyes, and finished the test.

Of course, he passed.

"I can" will triumph over "I can't" every time. You just have to focus on the outcome you want instead of the outcome you don't want. When we choose to see the battle won, the goal achieved, and the ball sunk perfectly in the hole, our reality starts taking shape in that direction. And we don't have to do it alone. There are life support teams of dolphins swimming by you every moment. They could even be your children. Park their words of wisdom in your mind and let them cheer you on.

The seventh green is waiting for you.

Today's Affirmation: "I am safe and successful on the seventh green!"

259

Appreciating vs. Depreciating Assets

"Debt is a trap which a man sets and baits himself, and then deliberately gets into."

—Josh Billings

This is the story of the new car I *didn't* buy. At least, not right away....

I had weathered many financial storms, but the sun was shining now. My new business was booming. I was earning good money, saving regularly, and was on the road to becoming debt-free for the first time in my life. I did my positive affirmations daily, and my "High Budget" was becoming a reality. Then I happened across a brand-new Lexus GS 300.

A brilliant, sparkling, gold, sporty model, I could picture my cute little red head breezing down the highway, arriving at business meetings looking and feeling rich and prosperous. I could afford it and it seemed like an appropriate reward for myself for all of my hard work. I started investigating, getting brochures and costs, and posted a picture of the car on the wall in front of my desk as part of my "Treasure Map."

Then I read *The Millionaire Next Door*, by Thomas J. Stanley and William D. Danko. It was like someone threw a bucket of cold water on me. The authors show how the wealthy become "Over Accumulators of Wealth" (OAWs) by behaving differently than "Under Accumulators of Wealth" (UAWs). OAWs buy *appreciating assets*: they invest in things that will produce more income. UAWs spend too much of their income on *depreciating assets*: things that lose value over time.

I thought about what I was doing. I was about to follow the UAW pattern of spending money on something that was going to decrease in value rather than increase. Not only was I going to take on more debt in the form of an auto loan, but I was going to add a lot of attendant expenses such as increased auto registration fees, higher maintenance, and service charges. This is the UAW spending habit: to spend every increase in income on lifestyle.

Remembering the saying, "The definition of insanity is doing the same thing over and over, expecting different results," I knew I needed to take new actions if I wanted to become an OAW. I wasn't on "High Budget" yet. The Lexus could wait until the total expenses connected with its purchase was a smaller percentage of my disposable income. So instead of buying a new car, I bought shares of stock in a mutual fund, added cash to my money market account, and invested in an expansion of my business.

I kept the picture of that car on my wall for the next two years as a goal and as a reminder that I had the ability to change my behavior, plan my expenses wisely, and accumulate wealth instead of just appearing wealthy. I drive that car now with pride in my accomplishments instead of nervousness about the expense.

What picture do you have on your wall? What do you have to accomplish before you get it?

Today's Affirmation: "I deserve rich rewards because I do what it takes to earn them."

260

Hey, You! Pay You!

"When a man begins to think seriously of saving for a rainy day, it's probably a rainy day."

—Anonymous

The savings rate in the United States has been on a downward trend for many years, even during times of a robust economy. U.S. households save far less than those in most other industrialized countries. Here are the savings rates from recent years:

South Korea	18.0%
France	13.6
Italy	11.7
Japan	11.2
Germany	11.0
Britain	10.8
United States	3.8

People neglect to save because we wait until the end of the month when we've spent all the money to try to save. Then we vow we'll save next month. And then next month. And so it goes. The habit of spending is entrenched and the habit of saving never gets a chance.

Save money. SAVE MONEY. S-a-v-e M-o-n-e-y. Hold on to a portion of all the money that comes to you. Save and invest a measly 10 percent and spend all the rest. Live on 90 percent of your income. Follow this simple plan every day, every week, every year. Teach your children to do it, too, by the example you set. Do it now.

I know, it doesn't look like there will be enough money to do everything else you have to do. But magic happens when you make a commitment to your financial fitness. Take the right action, even when you don't know how it will all work out, and, as they kept repeating in the movie *Shakespeare in Love*: "Somehow it will all work out. I don't know how. It's a mystery."

Start with a baby step, but take a step today. Whatever money you get today, save 10 percent of it. If you can't do 10 percent right now, start with 5 percent. Or twenty bucks. But start. It's a habit waiting to happen. One day at a time.

Today's Affirmation: "I pay myself promptly and profitably, and therefore I prosper!"

261

Major Money Malady—Buying on Time

"The quickest way to double your money is to fold it in half and put it back in your pocket."

—Unknown

We don't pay for anything up front any more. When we want something, we get it. If we don't have the money, we charge it. We buy everything on time. The longer the time, the more money we pay for the item. But the payments are so small, we forget.

Rennie Gabriel, in his book *Wealth on Any Income*, gives an illuminating example of the total amount we end up paying for products purchased on credit. He states that a dining set on sale at a department store for $648 (including tax) costs the store approximately $300. So if you pay in full up front, the store makes a profit of $300 (excluding tax).

But this dining set can be purchased on credit with payments as low as $12 per month. The interest rate charged to customers at most department stores is currently over 20 percent and in his example, the actual interest rate was 21.6 percent. At $12 per month, a person would be making that payment for over 17 years before the dining set would be paid for in full. And instead of paying $648 for your dining set, it would cost you at staggering $2,460! That's a profit to the store of $2,160.

Of course stores want to extend you credit—they would much rather be paid $2,460 than $648. And you thought it was a good bargain because it was on sale...

This is a money malady that keeps us cash-poor, debt-ridden, and financially stressed. We feel the pain every month when the bills come in, but we pay our minimums and hope it'll be better next month. But unless positive action is taken to control our spending and live within our means, next month won't be any better. Most of the time, next month is worse because we have once again used those charge cards in a flurry of impulse buying. We live in denial of the fact we have a problem until we can't meet our monthly minimum payments.

This month, why not start a savings account for the major purchases you want? Then you'll pay only for the item itself and no interest. You'll even make some additional money from the interest on the savings account.

If you can't do the time, don't borrow a dime.

Today's Affirmation: "I am rich and pay cash for all the material goods I desire."

262

Credit Card Management

"I'm living so far beyond my income that we may almost be said to be living apart."

—H.H. Munro

Credit cards can be wonderful, useful tools of convenience when used correctly. Toni Morton, an office manager at my bookkeeping service, shared a great way to manage credit card expenditures and stay debt-free. Every time she used her credit card, she deducted the amount of the charge from her check register, just as if she had written a check. She never used the card unless she had the money in her checking account. By deducting the amount when she made her purchase, she always had the money to pay the card off in full each month when the bill arrived.

For example:

Date	For	Amount	Bank Balance
			$2,000
4-1	Rent	$700	$1,300
4-2	Groceries	$100	$1,200
4-3	Credit card	$100*	$1,100
4-6	Credit card	$50*	$1,050
4-10	Car payment	$250	$800
4-15	Insurance	$100	$700
4-20	Personal care	$100	$600
4-20	Groceries	$150	$450
4-21	Credit card	$100*	$350
4-25	Utilities	$150	$200
4-27	VISA bill	$250*	$200

* $250 *already deducted*

But credit cards are doom to your budget, your bank account, and your financial future if you go "shopping for love" without the money to pay your credit cards off in full each month. Grocery stores take credit cards because it has been proven that consumers spend 20-30 percent more if they use a credit card rather than cash. You need to think of credit cards as debit cards, with the money coming right out of your bank account.

If you don't have the cash, don't use the card!

Today's Affirmation: "I have fun with my funds because I manage them well!"

263

Ten Stupid Things People Do to Mess up Their Money

"Money in the bank is like toothpaste in the tube. Easy to take out, hard to put back."

—Earl Wilson

A producer named Lori was looking for a "money expert" for the Dr. *Laura Show*, and Felicia had told them about me. I thanked her, called Lori, and faxed her my information. Lori called me back and said yes, they wanted to have me on the show. Great! Then she said, "Think up something fun to do with Dr. Laura for six minutes. Call me back at six o'clock tonight."

It was noon, and I was leaving for Las Vegas at two o'clock with four friends for our annual Super Bowl weekend trip. This was a short-notice request, but at least I had more than the thirty-second elevator opportunity! I did some research on Dr. Laura Schlessinger, and discovered she had written two best-selling books, so I thought I could do a take-off on that: "Ten Stupid Things People Do To Mess Up Their Money." I started writing on the plane. After I checked into the hotel and joined a game in the poker room, I asked for contributions from my friends and the other players. Here's what we came up with:

1. Buy clothes that are too small because their diet is really going to work this time.
2. Spend two hours driving forty miles to use a ten-cent coupon.
3. Spend $100 to get a $30 tax deduction.
4. Forget to notice when the 3.9 percent credit card goes up to 23.9 percent.
5. Get a second mortgage to pay off the credit cards—then charge the credit cards up again, too.
6. Believe they can make millions just working a few hours a week in their spare time.
7. Spend $200 on something they don't need but think they saved $30 because it was on sale.
8. Marry someone without asking the amount of his/her credit card debt, school loans, alimony, or child support.
9. Work twenty years at a job they hate just to get the retirement benefits.
10. Buy the two-gallon drink at the movies so they can get the free refill—then spend the whole movie in the rest room.

I called Lori, told her my idea, and read her the list. She laughed, Dr. Laura approved it, and I was scheduled to make my national television talk show debut.

Make sure you avoid these ten stupid things!

Today's Affirmation: "I have control and power over my life and my money!"

264

Ten More Stupid Things People Do to Mess up Their Money

"Courage is being scared to death but saddling up anyway."

—John Wayne

After I was set to appear on the Dr. *Laura Show*, they decided to add another segment—they wanted me to do a "man-on-the-street" type interview à la Jay Leno. I had to think up some questions to ask people about money that they might have funny responses to. My research team of poker players came up with: "Whose picture is on the ten dollar bill?" (Alexander Hamilton); "What does 'FICA' stand for?" (Federal Insurance Constitution Act—this is your contribution to Social Security); "What does the 'k' in '401k' stand for?" (nothing—it's just a section of the tax code); among others.

The morning of the filming, I had to talk myself out of being nervous. I did affirmations and convinced myself that I was born to be a roving reporter, that I was a natural, that I was perfect for this. So when I arrived at the Third Street Promenade in Santa Monica, I was ready to "act as if" I had been doing this a long time. After the first few "takes," they asked me if I had done this before!

Two days later, another "Real Black Limo" picked me up to film the show. Once more, I practiced affirmations and acted "as if." Just in case we needed them, I prepared "Ten More Stupid Things":

1. Buy stocks on a hot tip from a friend.
2. Pay $65,000 to climb Mount Everest. Best-case scenario: they're hungry, cold, and in need of oxygen. Worst-case scenario: death.
3. Give their life savings to a con man in exchange for his "winning" million-dollar lottery ticket.
4. Day trade on the stock market—then panic and sell everything at a loss the first time the market takes a dive.
5. Buy designer water.
6. Believe that a bank will loan them money just because they have a good business plan.
7. Buy life insurance when they're single.
8. Undercharge for their product or service and "make it up in volume."
9. Save millions while living a lifetime in poverty, then die and leave it all to heirs who travel first class.
10. Buy the cutest house on the block in a bad neighborhood.

You're not guilty of any of these, are you?

The filming of the show went very well. Everyone connected with it was friendly and helpful. It was a pleasure. Affirmations and "act as if"—an unbeatable combination. Remember that.

Today's Affirmation: "I do a great job at whatever I choose to do!"

265

The Workers in the Vineyard

"For everyone who asks receives, and everyone who searches finds, and for everyone who knocks, the door will be opened."

—Matthew 7:8

I love the parables in the Bible, the Sufi stories, and all the metaphysical teaching stories Wise and Holy Ones have shared with us through the ages.

Sometimes they make me tear my hair out, however. The one in the Bible about the workers in the vineyard bugged me for *years*. This is the story about a man who hires laborers early in the morning to work in his vineyard. He agrees to pay them each one denarius. Later in the day, he hires additional workers and pays them one denarius also. Then, in the evening, when the day's work is almost done, he hires some more workers. And—you guessed it—he pays them one denarius. I just didn't get it. It just wasn't *fair* that some people only had to work an hour to make the same money that the others worked all day to make. What was this about?

Sort of like the story of the prodigal son, too, whose father killed the fatted calf in celebration of his return home, when the dutiful son who stayed and worked with his father the whole time never got such a celebration. Poor guy. Where's his party? What's the message here?

To confess to you truthfully: it is only now, as I write this page for the third time, that the door to understanding slowly creaks open, and light begins to pour through the crack. When I began, I thought this story was about money and fair wages. But here is the truth this story holds for me now: no one is better than anyone else. Begrudge no one their denarius or fatted calf. Begrudge no one God's mercy or forgiveness. Celebrate the return of every prodigal one. Rejoice that everyone has a denarius to spend. Welcome everyone to wealth, spiritually and physically, early or late. Who knows? The latecomer—the prodigal one—may be you.

Today's Affirmation: "I rejoice in God's glorious bounty, in which we all share."

266

The Law of Karma

"You can preach a better sermon with your life than with your lips."

—Oliver Goldsmith

It's been said that whenever you point your finger at someone else, you have three fingers pointing back at you; that you can't even recognize a fault in someone else unless you also have it in you. Just for today, try not to point a finger at anyone else's character defect. We all have failings; what we're supposed to be working on is our own.

Yes, you may notice those sharks in the water and have wonderful suggestions of how they might change to become a dolphin. But if they're a shark, they aren't going to listen to you. They might turn around and point out some shark-like behavior of yours. And that tuna crying on your shoulder—when was the last time you shared a victim story of your own?

Today, when you notice someone's lack, limitation, or fault, instead of pointing it out to them, or calling a friend to complain about them, look at your own life and see where you manifest the same quality. Then make your helpful suggestions to yourself, not to them.

Ah. Self improvement. The only improvement plan with a chance of success.

Today's Affirmation: "I am better and better and richer and richer every day!"

267
Competition

"I love the winning, I can take the losing, but most of all, I love to play."

—Boris Becker

Human beings seem to have an innate competitive nature. We love our games, scorecards, and winning. The world of football, baseball, soccer, tennis, golf—indeed, all sports—are predicated on the supposition that all people are not created equal, and we love to see the differences at play. Competition spurs us on to be the best we can be—complacency is not an option if you expect to be outstanding in your field. Or even *in* the field.

A while ago, after receiving my second moving violation in the space of two weeks, I had to go to traffic school. (Oops, I had a negative affirmation in my consciousness that told me I was a bad driver, but now I am a *good* driver.) Traffic school was held at the Comedy Store, and a comedian named Dave was our instructor for the day. He understood the nature of competition very well. He divided us into groups and created a team competition for getting the most right answers as we studied the California vehicle code. We got extra points for creativity, so that perked me up. If we knew a joke that had traffic in it, we got extra points for that, too. The person with the most points at the end of the day would win the prize: a TicTac. Not a box of TicTacs—one TicTac.

Amazingly enough, I knew a traffic joke: there was a terrible accident when the tortoise ran over the snail. At the hospital, they asked the snail what happened. He said, "I don't know. It all happened so fast..." Bingo. Extra points for Chellie.

It didn't matter what the prize was—it was a competition and lots of us wanted to win it. Creating a game out of being in traffic school turned what could have been deadly, dull, long, boring day into fun. The energy in the room was high and eventually everyone caught the spirit. We laughed, we paid attention, we outdid each other trying to win the most points. Every so often, when the competition got a little fierce, Dave held up the prize and reminded us: "Relax! It's just a TicTac!"

Competition creates excitement. Hearts pound, adrenaline rushes, voices raise, and everyone wants to win. Even a TicTac. Put some competition into your life—try to outdo your own best performance. Pick a prize to strive for. And reward yourself with it when you win.

P.S. I won the TicTac.

Today's Affirmation: "I love to play, have fun, and win!"

268

Working for Less

"Everything comes to him who hustles while he waits."

—Thomas Edison

"Chellie, your workshops are always full! How do you do it?" exclaimed my friend, Marti, at the networking meeting. "Would you be willing to coach me on your sales techniques?"

I said that I would be happy to, and arranged to meet with her. Soon after that, two other people approached me at the same meeting for the same reason, and I said to myself, "Sounds like I should do another workshop!" and the *$ecrets of $elling* seminar was born.

The class was designed to be a three-hour session on Saturday morning, and I charged $65 for it. My thought was that everyone who wanted to come to my *Financial Stress Reduction Workshop®* but didn't like the $1,000 price tag, would flock to this class. I figured this would be an easy enrollment!

Nothing could have been farther from the truth. I quickly discovered that it took just as much time, trouble, energy, networking, and follow-up to enroll someone for a $65 class as it did for a $1000 class. Then I did the math: it took *fifteen* sales class enrollments to equal *one* financial class enrollment. So I did fifteen times the work and spent fifteen times as many hours to make the same money, plus I gave up my Saturdays. More hours—less money. N*ot* my concept of smart. I had forgotten that another seminar leader once told me, "The more you charge for your workshop, the easier a time you will have enrolling it." I have found this to be true. There is a perception that if it's expensive, it must be good. I was either going to have to raise the price of the sales class, or stop teaching it. Since all the extra work was taking a toll on my time and energy (and I hated giving up my Saturdays!), I decided to put the sales class aside for the time being.

Stop right now and do your math. Each task, each product, each business has a profitability factor. Look for the one that is taking the least time and bringing in the most money. And do more of *that*.

Today's Affirmation: "I work smarter and richer every day!"

269

Protect Your Supply

"Life is a never-ending stream of possible activities."

—Alan Lakein

In this wonderful age of freedom and opportunity, there are so many wonderful career, business, hobby, and entertainment choices it is easy to over-commit one's time, energy, and resources. Everyone wants to have it all—*today*. How many people do you know who are tired and worn out because of too many "to dos" on their "to do" lists?

When I was president of a business organization, prior to the start of each board or committee meeting, a group of us would talk while we waited. The conversations went like this:

Woman #1: "Oh, I'm so tired! I just finished meeting with three clients back to back and now I've got this board meeting."

Woman #2: "Me, too! And not only that, but I've got to do a bid proposal tonight after this meeting."

Woman #3: "You think that's bad? I started this morning at 6:30 A.M. with non-stop meetings, I'm event coordinator for the charity auction this Saturday, and my five-year-old has the flu!"

It was like a contest—who is the most overworked, is the most exhausted, and has the worst martyr story! What does the winner get, I wondered? The most sympathy when they have their nervous breakdown?

I decided this was a contest I didn't want to win. I was tired of being tired. I took a serious look at my calendar and eliminated activities that did not support my primary goals. I made sure I had some creative down time scheduled. The next time we had a meeting, I spoke up at the end and bragged, "I feel great! I took a nap and watched videos all afternoon!" That shocked them—but they all wanted to know how I managed it.

Breaking up the day with a nap can increase almost anyone's efficiency. Winston Churchill and President Lyndon Johnson were known for their afternoon naps. President John F. Kennedy often took half-hour naps. Dr. Joyce Walsleben of the New York University Medical Center/Sleep Disorder Center said, "There's a loss of alertness that accumulates over time. People who take breaks and naps can alleviate it." Well-spaced rest periods, meditation, walks, and naps are all stress reducers and enable us to do more with more energy afterwards.

Psst. You. Relax. Take a nap.

Today's Affirmation: "I take time each day to rest, relax, and refresh myself."

270
Marge Morning

"You must lose a fly to catch a trout."

—George Herbert

Marge Thompson is my bookkeeper. She is a smart businesswoman from Central America with one of those melodious honey voices that lulls you just listening to her. An ace bookkeeper, she efficiently crunches all my numbers one morning per month. I look forward to "Marge Morning." I feel quite pampered when she comes, especially since I'm a bookkeeper myself. I could certainly do my own books and save money—right?

Wrong. My goal, my mission is to help people make more money and have more time off for fun. Performing tasks like bookkeeping or house cleaning are off-purpose to that mission. They are subsidiary activities that cost me time and energy away from my purpose. I always tell people the workshop business is a simple one consisting of only three main tasks: 1) network to find people who are interested in the class, 2) call the people and enroll them in the class, and 3) teach the class. Everything else is of minor importance.

I hired Marge when I saw I was dreading bookkeeping day—and that it was keeping me off of the telephone talking with people, which is my primary task. So I decided to shell out the money to have it done for me. It seemed like a big luxury at the time, and I was a little nervous. My demon voice told me I was being ridiculous, that I could do this work so I *should* do it.

The first day Marge came to do my bookkeeping, I took my phone into the bedroom and enrolled two people in my class during the four hours she was here. That's one thousand dollars times two, which means I made two thousand dollars. I paid Marge two hundred dollars, so I figure I made a profit of eighteen hundred dollars from hiring a bookkeeper, a decision which at first glance looked like it would cost me two hundred dollars.

The next time she came, I took a nap. The profit I made from that activity is less obvious, but a profit nonetheless. I had started to get into overwhelm and overwork, which leads to burnout. I had networked morning, noon, and night, given speeches, coached people, and made call after call on the golden phone. Money was great, but my number one piece of business equipment—my body—was shot. Burnout was approaching. It's hard to look successful when you're tired! So I put my body in the body shop—my bed. I used my "Marge Morning" to nurture myself, relax, and replenish my energy. That, too, is profitable for me.

Marge is not a luxury. She is a necessity. And she always makes me money!

You might want to look for a Marge yourself.

Today's Affirmation: "The more I delegate, the more money I make!"

271

Producing and Consuming

"The secret of success is to be in harmony with existence, to be always calm... to let each wave of life wash us a little farther up the shore."

—Cyril Connolly

It seems that everything we do is either producing or consuming. When we work, we are producing goods or services that contribute to the welfare of others. When we play, we consume goods and services produced by others. Money flows in and out, whether we are producing or consuming.

I remember reading a *Psychology Today* article long ago that compared producing and consuming in a primitive jungle tribe with our modern day society. The primitive tribe spent far fewer hours producing: The men hunted and fished, the women gathered or raised some fruits and vegetables, and took care of the children. Other time was spent making huts, jewelry, baskets, etc. Consuming consisted of eating meals and trading objects. Most of these activities were performed in a slow, easy, relaxed manner; the only exception was hunting, which necessitated some edge of quick tension when capturing wild game. Once the producing chores were done, the rest of the day was spent in an activity that was neither producing nor consuming. Doing nothing is an alien concept in our modern world.

Think about it. How much time do you spend doing nothing? Neither producing nor consuming? We work longer hours at our jobs than ever before, taking it home with us evenings and weekends, when we travel—even on vacations. We think about our work, talk about our work, and read about work. Then when we are at leisure, we consume: we shop, we eat (if we prepare the food ourselves we are producing and consuming), we watch TV, movies, plays, and concerts. What is doing nothing, anyway?

Much has been written about how out of balance we are as a society, to be so driven by work, so into the mode of production that we feel guilty if we aren't doing something useful. Is it any wonder that we try to balance the scales by overdoing our consumption as well? Our workaholicism feeds its counterbalance: rampant consumerism. We shop as a leisure activity, not from need.

The primitive societies had many hours of leisure time each day to relax, to do nothing. To sit by the fire and play with their children. To talk with each other. To dream. To think. To breathe. To be. A human being instead of a human doing.

We have more creature comforts than they. But the price is all the time spent producing so we can consume. We have lost relaxation as a normal part of every day. A *big* part of every day. Can you imagine slowing your pace? Taking back some of your leisure? If you can't do a whole day, start slower—block out an hour. And *do nothing.*

Today's Affirmation: "I am at peace, cherishing the abundance of life."

272

A Moment out of Somewhere

"There is no duty we so much underrate as the duty of being happy. By being happy we sow anonymous benefits upon the world."

—Robert Louis Stevenson

My friend, Sarah Edwards, co-author of *The Practical Dreamer's Handbook* with her husband, Paul, sent me this lovely story:

"I was rushing to meet Paul at the hardware store. As I charged along, I was oblivious to the sunny day and the crisp breeze around me. I was pretty oblivious to everything actually, except getting where I was going...until I heard the voice. A man was singing. The sound was so strong and deep and clear, I had to know, who was that?

I stopped walking. My eyes were darting from place to place. I had to find the source. There! Sitting on a crate along the sidewalk was a very old man.

"I found Paul and told him to meet me outside where I'd be listening to the street performer. And there I stood for the next fifteen minutes. But I could have stayed all day. His voice was gravelly and deep like rough sandpaper; then rich and smooth like molasses, and finally, for moments, rising so clear and pure as to seemingly be soaring on the wings of eagles. He sang song after song from some long forgotten past, coming from someplace within himself.

"Clusters of people were walking by. Teenage girls, laughing and giggling among themselves. Couples fully engaged in one another. Families straggling and herding each other like a gaggle of geese. Old folk out for a Sunday walk. Almost without exception, as they approached, they, too, would stop, if only a moment, to search for the source of a voice that was singing to their soul.

"All too soon Paul came from the store, eager to leave and get on with our day. I asked if he had any money I could drop in the large black suitcase the musician had laid open at his feet on the sidewalk. Paul only had a five and told me he'd go back inside to get change. 'No,' I said, 'a five would be perfect.'

"We have no idea who he was. He had no tapes to sell. No sign announcing to the world who he was, but there he was that Sunday morning reminding me I was alive and walking in a crisp breeze on a bright sunny day. A deep, familiar hunger had returned to my heart. 'If only I could sing or do anything at all as beautifully and as profoundly as he can sing,' I said to Paul, 'it would make everything worthwhile.' 'Oh, but you can,' Paul said. 'When you write from your soul, your words are your songs.' Oh, that they were, I thought to myself, and resolved to go home and make them so. How many others, I wondered, went home to do the same with their gifts upon hearing this man sharing his?"

Today's Affirmation: "I listen and everywhere the voice of God moves me and inspires me."

273

Get Some Help

"Don't be irreplaceable; if you can't be replaced, you can't be promoted."

—Unknown

Aren't you tired of being self-sufficient?

Enough I say. Get some help.

It consistently amazes me how people wear themselves out re-inventing the wheel. Over and over again. Like nobody ever had this problem before, and you have to figure it out all by your lonesome. Who told you that?

I admit it took me just about forever to figure this out. Now, every time I need to know something that I don't know, I just find out who does know and go ask them. When I wanted to learn to ski, I signed up for ski school. When I wanted to learn how to market my business, I signed up for marketing classes. Several. When I wanted to learn about the publishing industry, I read twelve books. I'm still reading.

One morning, I was taking a seat at a sales seminar, when a woman who had taken my *$ecrets of $elling* class sat down next to me. She looked at me, shocked. "What are you doing here?" she demanded. "You teach this stuff!"

I smiled. "Yes, I do," I said, "but that doesn't mean I can't learn something new that will benefit me and the people who take my next class. The more I know, the more I know I don't know!"

She nodded in understanding. The seminar was powerful and informative, and, sure enough, I learned something new. I always do.

Get some help today. Sign up for it. Read about it. Ask for directions. Take the shortcut.

Then relax and let them show you how to do it.

Today's Affirmation: "All the knowledge I need to be great is right before my eyes!"

274

You Don't Have to Know Everything

"When in charge ponder. When in trouble, delegate. When in doubt, mumble."

—Anonymous

I used to think I had to know everything myself. What a mad scramble that was.

When I was president of the Los Angeles Chapter of National Association of Women Business Owners (NAWBO), I had to get over that idea—fast. There was just too much to do, and a lot of it was beyond the scope of my capabilities. I quickly learned to delegate, and to compile a roster of great resources—people who were terrifically talented at their chosen professions.

NAWBO had an advisory board of politicians, business people, and community leaders who helped with policy and strategic planning for the group. One evening after a board meeting, two of the advisors, a civic leader and a businesswoman who owned a multi-million dollar company, stopped to ask me a question.

The businesswoman asked me a computer question. I said that I didn't know the answer, but I knew who would know, and gave her the name and phone number of one of my computer consultants. The other asked me an investment question, and I said I didn't know the answer to that either, but I knew a great financial planner and gave him her number. Then I was asked a legal question, which I referred to an attorney I knew who specialized in that area.

In the pause as they wrote down all this information, I laughed deprecatorily and said, "I myself know nothing. I just know people who know."

I never forgot the businesswoman's response. She said, "Ah. A true leader."

One of the definitions of the word "lead" is "to show the way." You don't have to know the way yourself. You just have to know who knows.

Today, take time to ponder. Mumble if you must. Then delegate.

Today's Affirmation: "I am a leader and a way-shower. I help all around me find the right path."

275
Philosophical Conversation

"Look at every path closely and deliberately, then ask ourselves this crucial question: does this path have a heart? If it does, then the path is good. If it doesn't, then it is of no use."

—Carlos Castaneda

I had an interesting philosophical conversation one evening with a man I met in a restaurant. (*Okay*, a man I picked up in a bar.) I often get into conversations about the meaning of life and the nature of reality with people, since I think that's one of the most important things to figure out while we're here on the planet.

I remember telling him about my philosophy of choosing beliefs that make me happy. He seemed to get hung up on whether my beliefs were really true or not. Since beliefs about God, religion, metaphysics, and the purpose of life tend to be scientifically unprovable, I kept trying to explain that it didn't matter to me whether the beliefs I had chosen were true or not. They had to be taken on faith, and I had just decided to have faith in things that I thought worked with a universal theory of good and made me feel good to believe them.

After about an hour of this conversation, he finally understood my meaning.

"Oh," he said, realization dawning. "It doesn't matter to you if your beliefs are true. It makes you happy to believe them and that's enough for you. Is that right?"

"Yes!" I answered happily. "That's it exactly!"

"I see." We were quiet for a few moments as we digested our conversation.

Finally, I asked him, "What do you do for a living?"

"I'm a philosophy professor at U.C.L.A.," he replied.

I was sure he was joking. "You are not," I rebuked him.

"Oh, yes, I am," he said, smiling.

"Show me your I.D. then," I said, thinking I'd caught him. He pulled out his identification and sure enough, there it was written on his U.C.L.A. card: Associate Professor of Philosophy.

"That's really funny," I said. "I didn't realize I was talking to a pro. How'd I do?"

"Well," he said. "I'd give you an A!"

What do you believe? Does your path have a heart?

Today's Affirmation: "My beliefs make me happy and spiritually rich!"

276

It's All Just Stuff

"Thieves respect property. They merely wish the property to become their property that they may more perfectly respect it."

—Gilbert Keith Chesterton

I was robbed at gunpoint one evening after work.

It was dusk, about six o'clock, and I had pulled into my parking space in the underground garage at my condominium. I was about to open the trunk of the car to get some things, when I heard a deep voice behind me say, "Give me your money!" (This is not one of the affirmations I teach in my workshops.) My heart sank as I realized I was about to live out one of Los Angeles' less desirable statistics. Sure enough, I turned around and there was this big guy holding this big gun.

Well, I figured robbed was bad enough—I wasn't going to go for murdered—so I handed over my purse immediately. Next he said, "Give me your jewelry" and I gave him that, too. Then he ordered me to lie down on the ground. I didn't like that very much, but hey, he had the gun. As I laid down on the cold cement, heart pounding, a neighbor drove into the garage and scared the robber, who took off running. Whew!

I dusted myself off and went immediately to the building manager's office and reported the theft to the two gentlemen in the office. They were very upset, called the sheriff, and asked if they could get me anything. I said, "Yeah, honey, I need a cigarette! Mine were all in my stolen purse." They bought me some from the machine in the hall, and listened to my story with wide eyes while I smoked one. After a while, one of them looked at me closely and said, "You certainly are taking this well. You seem very calm." I said, "I am calm. All this guy wanted was my stuff. I can always get more stuff. In fact, I'll have *better* stuff next week!"

You see, several years before that, I was attacked at 3:00 A.M. in my bedroom. That guy wasn't just after stuff. That was a different experience entirely. I actually was very lucky in that encounter because I was able to fight him off. But it made me really appreciate life and safety. I'll fight to defend my life, but I'm not willing to die for my stuff.

I think this is one of the benefits of having had some bad experiences in life: You develop perspective. When minor bad things happen, I can usually look back and say, "Oh, well, I've lived through worse." It makes me good at recovery.

Today's Affirmation: "All my experiences teach me positive lessons and help me grow."

277
Help

"A man arriving in Heaven got to ask God one question. He asked, 'The world I left had so much poverty, disease, and evil. Why didn't you send someone to help?' And God answered, 'I did. I sent you.'"

—Unknown

My friend, Gary Tharler, sent me that story. One day, he picked up a brochure advertising the "AIDS Ride across Alaska." It changed his life.

Gary decided to participate in the ride. In order to do it, he had to devote most of his spare time to training himself to ride long distances on his bicycle. He trained for an entire year.

He said that Alaska was wild and majestic, and by the time he got there, he was well-trained for the miles and the hills. But no one was prepared for the weather. It was bitterly cold, and rained almost every day. The second day out was particularly harsh. They had to ride 75 miles and gain 3500 feet. After the first 20 miles, the temperature dropped, the rain turned to hail and then to sleet and finally, snow. He said that the advertised theme for the ride was *Impossible* broken into *I'm Possible*. After that brutal second day, someone suggested a more fitting theme: *I'm Popsicle*. But they all kept going, lifting each other's hearts and hands over the long miles, dedicated to completing the ride and raising money to stop a dreadful disease.

When Gary wrote all his supporters to tell us about his adventures on the ride, he said this: "It is so wonderful and fulfilling to challenge yourself to something over a year. Please, go ahead...proclaim something. Get out that screenplay, those tap shoes, those dried up oil paints. Go public with it. Devote sacred time to make it real. Be laser-focused and yet enjoy all that's around you, ride through or over obstacles, but remember your humanity. Be great. The truth is, you can't miss."

He wanted to raise $3,000. He raised $6,000. He was so inspired by this experience that he applied for and got a job working for the company that puts these rides together.

Thanks, Gary, for your willingness to put yourself on the line for others. Thanks for the call to others to do the same. Success is yours. Ride on.

Today's Affirmation: "I have the heart, soul, and ability to be of service to all mankind."

278

Reaffirm Your Affirmations

"If a ship has sunk, I can't bring it up. If it is going to be sunk, I can't stop it. I can use my time much better working on tomorrow's problem than fretting about yesterday's. Besides, if I let those things get me, I wouldn't last long."

—Ernest J. King

It is tempting, when things go wrong and break down, to focus on your limitations and problems. Since what you concentrate on is what you get more of, this just creates more limitations and problems. People around you can feel that you are tense and unhappy and tend to shy away from you during this down period, creating even more scarcity, both personal and professional. Then you're in a famine period.

At some point, you will decide you've had enough and take back control of your own fate, and do something creative to better your circumstances. On some conscious or unconscious level, you come to the conclusion that things aren't going to get better until you make them better, and then you take action. Take a class, read a book, listen to a motivational tape or lecture, *really listen* to some good advice given by a friend and then do something different, based on this new information.

Proceeding from the decision to change and the action that backs up the decision, your life will start to improve. When you want to experience more good in your life, do more positive affirmations and start thinking more positively. As you think more and more positively, you send out more ships, so more abundance flows in. And you will begin feasting.

So what makes you go back to famine again? Somewhere along the line, a fear creeps into your thoughts. A deal falls through, an associate or relative criticizes you in a vulnerable moment, the car breaks down, the stock market declines. A chill goes through your bones, and suddenly, you doubt yourself again. You stop thinking positive thoughts and start thinking negative ones. You start listening to the negative voice of the committee inside your head. Fear and doubt creep into your conversations, your plans, and your actions. Famine looms again.

Take control of your thoughts. Reaffirm your affirmations. The hardest time to do them is when you most need to do them: when you're at your lowest point—and when you're at your highest. At your lowest point, your negative voice is loud, you feel hopeless and depressed and it's really hard to think and feel positive. And at your highest point, you tend to be less diligent, thinking you don't need to do affirmations anymore because everything is going well. I rode this roller coaster myself until I saw that I needed to be positively focused and do my affirmations with spirit and energy every day no matter what.

Every day. No matter what.

Today's Affirmation: "I am loving my positive thinking every day!"

279

Mind Is the Builder

"The universe is full of magical things patiently waiting for our wits to grow sharper."

—Eden Phillpotts

People who become very successful have a single-minded devotion to purpose. They focus on the positive goal they desire, not the problems to be overcome. The roadblocks just mean there's a road on the other side. They focus on the road, not on the block. And they are very optimistic about the outcome. As Chesty Puller, an American Marine Officer, when surrounded by eight enemy divisions during World War II, said, "All right, they're on our left, they're on our right, they're in front of us, they're behind us...they can't get away this time!"

Years ago, a friend who lived in my apartment building was trying to lose weight without success. She came over to my apartment one day crying with frustration. She told me she was hardly eating anything and hadn't been able to lose a single pound. When I went back to her apartment with her, I immediately saw the source of the problem. All around the apartment she had posted signs that said "You're too fat!" "You're as big as a horse!" "You don't fit into your clothes!" Horrified, I told her to rip all of them down immediately. They were negative affirmations that kept her focused on the problem instead of the goal. I told her she needed to put up signs that said "You are slim and beautiful!" and "Your weight is ideal!"

She said, "But that's a lie."

I told her, "No, it's just telling the truth in advance."

She giggled, and I saw her attitude shift in that instant. She now looked happy and hopeful, with a positive expectation.

She lost five pounds that week.

Today's Affirmation: "I am slim, trim, and beautiful!"

280

Ease On Down the Road

"Too often we underestimate the power of a touch, a smile, a kind word, a listening ear, an honest compliment, or the smallest act of caring, all of which have the potential to turn a life around."

—Leo Buscaglia

The traffic on the roads in major cities can be a considerable cause of stress. Most people have heard of "road rage"—when tempers flare so badly that people do crazy things as anger overcomes normal sensibilities. When the flow of cars stops and it seems as if you're in a parking lot instead of on a freeway, it is frustrating and you are helpless. You can't get where you want to go. The anger you feel gets compounded when you see other people make stupid driving mistakes: They pull into your lane without looking, making you slam on the brakes to avoid hitting them, or they tail-gate and make you afraid they're going to run into you.

Years ago, my friend Stan Sudan, developed a new attitude for driving the busy streets of Los Angeles. He had gotten into the habit of fuming over the traffic and this put him in a negative frame of mind each time he got into his car. A self-aware thinker, he noticed that the problem was his own, and that he was the one suffering because of it. It was not healthy or productive for him to be constantly angry about a fact of life that he couldn't control. Accepting that he couldn't change the traffic situation in Los Angeles, he realized that what he could change was his reaction to it.

It was up to him to project a peaceful and loving attitude toward driving. Instead of being solely concerned with himself and what he wanted, he chose to approach the situation from a desire to help others. He decided that he was in charge of his section of the road. It was his job to see that everyone on his section got down the road safely. This put him in a positive, helpful frame of mind. When someone wanted to change lanes, he slowed down and waved them over with a smile. When someone tailgated him, he moved over so they could pass him. He did everything in his power to make sure that other drivers had a pleasant driving experience while around him. If somebody did something stupid, he would just shrug and say, "Oh, well. I've made that mistake, too."

This new focus of helping others on the road transformed his driving experience to one of happiness and helpfulness instead of anger and frustration. Imagine if everyone approached traffic with this attitude! Try this out for yourself today. You will find that when you get where you're going, you will arrive with a peaceful and loving frame of mind. You will feel better about others and better about yourself. Instead of "road rage," you'll have "street peace."

Today's Affirmation: "I help everyone around me to joyfully ease on down the road."

281

Pain-Full or Pain-Free

"It's the repetition of affirmations that leads to belief. And once that belief becomes a deep conviction, things begin to happen."

—Claude Bristol

In tears, Letty called me. A vibrant, happy mother and partner in her husband's computer consulting business, she wore braces to correct the alignment of her teeth. She had been to the orthodontist and got bad news. Several things were not going as planned, and the orthodontist needed to do some major work on her teeth today. Although she was supposed to come to class this evening, she called me to cancel, fear projecting her into the pain, swelling, and suffering she expected to undergo.

"Chellie," she said, "I need some positive affirmations for this process! I'm so depressed and scared that I can't get my mind on anything but the pain I expect. I know that if I expect pain, I'll get pain. Help me!"

"Good job, Letty!" I told her. "You have identified the problem and you know what will help alleviate it. But you don't need me to give you the affirmations—you can do them yourself.

"First, take a piece of paper and draw a line vertically down the middle. At the top of the left hand column, write 'Fear' and at the top of the right hand column write 'Affirmation.' Now start writing down every fear you have about today in the left hand column. Write until you've thought of everything. After you've completed the 'Fear' column, start countering each fear with a positive affirmation on the right hand side of the paper.

"When you have written an affirmation for every fearful thought, fold the paper so you can only see the affirmations, and start saying them out loud, with positive visions of health and good feelings. Use the mirror technique, and say them aloud while you look yourself in the eye. Say them in the car while you drive to the orthodontist. Focus on them and your vision for your beautiful face with perfect teeth throughout the procedures. Every procedure is bringing you closer to your perfect vision. You may feel sensations as the doctor works, but no pain. And it will be fast and easy!"

I have used this technique myself on many occasions and had pain-free medical procedures that I was told were going to be pain-full. I remember channeling my anger at having to have the procedure into a determination not to have the pain they told me I was going to have, so that I basically hypnotized myself into a comfort zone from which I refused to emerge. The energy of emotions can be channeled this way: feel the power of the fear, get mad at whatever made you fearful, feel the power of the anger build, control it, harness it and then channel its flow to the positive vision. You win!

Today's Affirmation: "I am healthy! I feel fine, and I feel wonderful!"

282

On a Blue Day

*"You must learn from the mistakes of others.
You can't possibly live long enough to make them all yourself."*

—Sam Levenson

I was feeling sad and vulnerable on Monday. But I had an appointment, so I went to the dentist to get my teeth cleaned.

"Oops," the dental hygienist said. "I don't like the look of these two teeth. I'm going to call the doctor." I never like it when dental professionals or airplane pilots say "Oops."

Dr. Neil McLeod, a wonderfully kind man and terrific dentist, peered into my mouth and said, "We need to take some x-rays of these teeth."

I smiled gently back at him. "Okay," I said. "But not today."

"Why?" he asked curiously. "It won't take but a minute, and if the cost is an issue, we can make payment arrangements."

"It's not that," I assured him. "I'm just feeling a bit blue today. If there's nothing wrong with my teeth, then the x-rays won't matter. If there is something wrong, I just can't handle it today. I'll come back another day, when I'm stronger."

On a blue day, keep all bad news at bay. You may not be able to choose the news, but often, you can choose the timing.

Today's Affirmation: "I overcome all challenges—when I'm good and ready!"

283

Cruise Ships or Speedboats?

"Every great oak tree was once a nut that stood its ground."

—Unknown

Big goals take longer to achieve than small ones. It's like the difference between the ponderous sailing of big cruise ships and the darting action of speedboats tearing through the waves. The speedboat will get to its destination quicker, but there will be more cargo to unload at the dock when the big ship comes in. When you have a big goal, the most important thing is to work on it regularly. Every day, do a little work on it, and one day it will be accomplished. It's the Ulysses S. Grant theory, per Michael Korda in *Another Life*: "Provided you're always moving forward, even if it's only a foot a day…eventually you will get to Richmond."

When I was president of the Los Angeles Chapter of the National Association of Women Business Owners, I learned an important lesson about sailing big ships. As the owner of a small business with four employees, I was used to getting things done quickly in my little speedboat. It was my show, so if I thought something was a good idea, we did it. But here, I had a twenty-member board of directors, who all had a say in whether or not something got done. Not only that, they were all business owners used to getting their own way, too. My skills of persuasion were going to get quite a workout here.

Not yet conscious of this situation, however, I tried to pass a motion at my very first board meeting to establish a new program. Pandemonium! I had had lots of time to think about what a great idea it was, but it was a complete surprise to everyone else. They needed time to consider it, discuss it, argue for and against it, identify problems, and come up with solutions. As every board member jumped in with their opinions, I called for a recess. I resumed the meeting sweetly saying, "There are no problems, only opportunities for growth"; there were hoots of laughter. We established a committee to study the feasibility of the new program. Everyone was happy with this idea, and I learned another lesson in patience.

A year later, the board approved the program. Then we had to go to the national board and get them to approve it. That took another year. But it was worth it. It was a great program and is still in place today. The important thing was, I learned to take the time to prepare before launching a big ship. The next time I had a program I wanted put into place, I sent a promotional package outlining the entire project and backing it up with reams of information. I called each board member individually to ask their opinion of the idea and garnered their support.

Work on your big ship today. Load some cargo, hire some sailors, check the rigging, store some provisions, set your course. Launch day will come.

Today's Affirmation: "I gather help and support from everyone I meet for my big projects!"

284

Income Possibilities

"By mistake, a man received his pay envelope without a check inside. He asked: 'What happened? Did my deductions finally catch up with my salary?'"

—Anonymous

It is critically important to do the math and count your money. This is particularly important in the planning stages of creating income either by opening a business or getting a new job. As important as enthusiasm and dreams are, they don't make you successful unless the numbers add up.

Michael, an energetic young man in the seminar business, sent me his goals for the year, and outlined how he was going to achieve them. His goal was to make $5,000 per month teaching seminars. He had three different seminars, and this was his enrollment plan:

15 people in Seminar #1 at **$30 per person**

10 people in Seminar #2 at **$50 per person**

15 people in Seminar #3 at **$50 per person**

As I looked at his plan, I noticed that he hadn't listed the total amounts he would earn from each seminar, so I did the math:

15 people x $30 = $ 450
10 people x $50 = $ 500
15 people x $50 = $ 750
Total Income: $1700

Try as I might, I couldn't make this enrollment plan add up to a $5,000 per month income. It is $3,300 short! Clearly, this man would be constantly disappointed in trying to meet his income goal of $5,000 per month. He needed to enroll more people or charge more for his seminars.

Remember that the first three steps to financial stress reduction are:

1. Think positive.
2. Send out ships.
3. Count your money.

The first two are important, but you can't forget about the third.

Today's Affirmation: "Money is piling up in all of my accounts."

285

To Get Your Goals You Have to Ask the Right Questions

"A good plan today is better than a perfect plan tomorrow."

—George Patton

Ted and his girlfriend, Tina, were two young chiropractors building their lives and their businesses together. Cheerful, upbeat, and fun, they enrolled in my workshop in order to get clarity and focus on their financial goals. They mentioned that they knew one of the best ways to expand their business would be to buy another existing medical practice. I congratulated them on their astute reasoning, as it is often much easier and faster to buy a business than to build one patient by patient on their own. They asked me to keep a lookout for a business they might buy.

As often happens when a goal is clearly stated, a plan mapped out, and then presented to people who might assist with its accomplishment, it wasn't long before a friend of mine, Ken, who owned a holistic medical center told me he wanted to sell his practice. He was delighted when I told him I might have a buyer! Excited at the prospect of helping three people achieve their goals by playing matchmaker, I couldn't wait to tell Ted and Tina when they came to see me that afternoon.

"How much money does he want for it?" was the first question Tina asked.

"$250,000," I replied.

"That's too much money!" she exclaimed. "Forget it."

"Wait a minute," I interrupted. "You have asked the wrong question, didn't like the answer and now you're about to reject this deal without investigating further!" (In AA circles, they call this "contempt prior to investigation.")

Tina paused. "Yeah, but we can't afford $250,000," she started to say, then caught herself as I shook my head and reached for a "No Yeah, but" button. "Okay," she laughed. "What's the right question?"

"The most important question is not how much it costs, but how much money does the business make," I replied. "If the business generated $35 million per year, you'd find a way to come up with $250,000 wouldn't you? Because that would be a fabulous profit for you." Tina and Ted laughed. "You're right about that!" Ted said. "And maybe we could make payments over time or get a loan to purchase the business outright. Give us Ken's number and we'll look into this further."

Although this particular deal did not materialize, Tina and Ted learned the importance of asking the right questions. How many times do we stop ourselves from going for our goals because we asked the wrong question or let an old belief or attitude convince us we couldn't have it? It is a habit of thought that begins "That won't work because..." Replace that thought with "How can I make this work?"

Today's Affirmation: "My mind is open to receiving my heart's desire!"

286

Bringing in the Gold

"My optimistic nature would have me going after Moby Dick in a rowboat and taking the tartar sauce with me!"

—Zig Ziglar

"I hate you!" the voice on the answering machine ended, laughing. I was laughing, too. Anne was one of my class participants, and had been resisting sending out ships. I was coaching her about it, and she had called me to report. This was what she said:

"I went home from class thinking about the golden phone. I know you keep saying that calling people on the phone is what brings in the business, but I didn't believe it. I decided to prove you wrong. So, the next morning, I pulled out my 'Dead File'—the file of prospects that I felt were never going to buy from me. One by one, I started calling them. I made about twenty calls. And wouldn't you know it, I made two sales! I couldn't believe it. Rats! Now I'm going to have to keep doing this. I hate you!"

Cracked me up.

Okay, so hate me all you want. But make those golden phone calls and bring in the gold.

Today's Affirmations: "I send out my golden ships and bring in the gold!"

287

The Rule of Three

"Yesterday is a canceled check; tomorrow is a promissory note; today is ready cash—use it."

—Kay Lyons

I had just received a large cash settlement from an auto accident I had been involved in. Gleefully, I held the $12,000 check in my hand. I thought about what I should do with all this money. At the time, I had debts, so I considered using it all to pay down my debt. That felt good, but not great—I wouldn't have anything fun to show for my good fortune. Then I thought, I could save all the money, but here again, I wouldn't have any enjoyment of the money right now. What I really wanted to do was spend all the money on fun and extravagance. But that didn't feel very responsible. I wrestled with the problem a while, then called a friend of mine, Gale Johnston, a certified financial planner.

When I confessed my dilemma, Gale laughed and told me about the "Rule of Three." This is what she told me to do:

1. Take a third of the money and put it towards the past—pay off debt.
2. Take another third of the money and put it towards the future—invest it.
3. Take the last third of the money and have a good time in the present—spend it.

I did as she suggested, and felt responsible, and had fun at the same time.

I'm praying you receive a large windfall soon, so you can try this out for yourself!

Today's Affirmation: "I am successful, generous, and happy!"

288

Are You Keeping Part of What You Earn?

"Dig a well before you're thirsty."

—Chinese proverb

Okay, here's another of those pages bugging you to save money. So, have you started yet?

Just think for a moment about all the money you have had pass through your fingers during your lifetime. From your first childhood allowance or your first job to your current salary or business gross income. How much is that? Or if that is too overwhelming to contemplate, just look at your gross income for the last ten years. How much is that?

What is left over after all that money has been in your hands? How much did you keep? What is the sum total of all the money you currently possess? At a seminar given by Consumer Credit Counselors, I learned that the life savings of the average fifty-year-old is $2,700. If you have more than that, congratulations! If less, you have some work to do.

During several months in 1999 and 2000, the American savings rate was a *negative* number. That means we borrowed more than we saved. And in the best economy mankind has ever known!

Start the savings habit *now*. Open a savings account for any amount of money and start. Then put 10 percent of all you earn into it—throughout the month with each bit of income you get. You will find that the money you need to pay the bills still comes in. It is part of the way you create abundance—by committing to it and then taking action to do it. Live on 90 percent of your income—you do it when things get tough, so why not do it now in order to save for your future?

If you can't do 10 percent, then do 5 percent or whatever it takes to get you started. Just get started. You'll like yourself—and your money—when you do.

Then if you get thirsty, you'll have a well.

Today's Affirmation: "I invest wisely and well and my money makes money!"

289
College Costs

"Too caustic? To hell with the cost, we'll make the picture anyway."

—Samuel Goldwyn

According to census figures, here are the average annual earnings of Americans, based on their level of education:

Education Level	Male	Female*
No high school diploma	$16,818	$8,861
High school diploma	$25,453	$13,407
College diploma	$47,126	$26,401

Think it might be a good idea to go to college? College graduates make nearly double the income of high school graduates who don't go to college.

If you want to attend college, but are afraid of the cost, read on:

College is more affordable than people think. A 1997 American Council on Education survey found that 71 percent of respondents said that a college education was "not affordable for most families." They also thought that the cost of getting a college degree was much more than it actually was. In another study, respondents guessed the cost of annual tuition at a four-year college was nearly $10,000 when in reality it was closer to $3,000.

So much is written about the high cost of a college education that many people never investigate the possibility. They know it's expensive so they don't bother to look into it any further. But there are many financial aid programs available to help at every stage of the process. Contact the financial aid office at the colleges you are interested in. They will assist you to get the help you need, direct you to scholarship possibilities, work-study programs, grants, and loans. Read Anna and Robert Leider's book, *Don't Miss Out: The Ambitious Student's Guide to Financial Aid*. Written from a consumer's point of view, they list hundreds of scholarship, grant, and loan sources.

Compare the cost of going with the cost of not going. If you or someone you love wants to go to college, get busy finding creative ways to get there. Don't let the thought "It's too expensive" stop you. Rather, think "It may be expensive, but I'll find out how to do it anyway!"

*There is still a wide discrepancy between what women earn and what men earn. The reasons for this are still widely debated, and beyond the scope of this book; for an overview of the problem and potential solutions, I suggest you read *Sex and Power* by Susan Estrich. For our purposes, if you are a woman reading this book, consider that these are aggregate figures for the entire population, and do not apply to *you*. Because you are practicing affirmations, sending out ships, counting your money....

Today's Affirmation: "I always generate plenty of money to do what I want to do!"

290
Tuna

"Never hope harder than you work."

—Rita Mae Brown

A bright young man of about thirty-five, Bob sat in my office and explained that he was looking for bookkeeping help for the new computer company he was trying to get off the ground. I asked him a lot of questions about his background and his prospects. He told me that he had received a $400,000 inheritance the year before. "Great!" I thought to myself, "a client who can afford to pay for my services!" I asked if he had a financial planner or stockbroker who was helping him to manage his assets. "No," he told me, "the money is all gone now."

I felt so sorry for him in that moment. What a gift he had wasted! Here he was, hopeful that he could make back his fortune with his start-up company, which now had no operating capital. He had several potential buyers for his product, a lot of hope, a lot of dreams—but no money. We tried to help him with some bookkeeping for a while, but his company never got off the ground, and he couldn't pay for our services, so we parted ways.

He sent me a prospectus on another new start-up company a couple of years later. He wanted me to send it out to possible investors I might know. At the end of the letter, he mentioned I could reach him at a certain phone number and then said if the phone was disconnected ("Oh, the life of an entrepreneur") I should try his roommate's number.

Would you invest your money with this man? Would you ask your friends to invest money with him? No matter what his dreams, his plan, his optimism, Bob had proven himself incapable of managing money. He's thinking positive which is good, and sending out ships, too. But he hasn't been counting his money. This makes him a tuna. He may become a dolphin one day, but until there's proof, only another tuna would give such a person more money.

Anyone like Bob in your life? As a friend of mine named Clancy said, "Teach him Spanish. I suggest you start with 'Adios!'"

Today's Affirmation: "I invest with success in people who are smart money managers like me!"

291

Allan Learns His Lesson

"If you lend someone twenty dollars and never see that person again, it was probably worth it."

—Anonymous

Allan is a sharp, young attorney in his own private practice. Like many sole practitioners, he leases office space from a larger law firm, and shares some of their equipment. He pays them for use of their copier and fax machines, for example. It is a co-operative, dolphin relationship that works in harmony for both parties. Most of the time.

Recently, Allan spoke to me of his growing irritation with the senior partner of the law firm.

It seems a shark fin or two was beginning to mar the surface of their relationship. On one occasion, Allan had a prospective client in his office, who he realized needed an attorney specializing in a kind of law that he didn't perform. The larger law firm did perform this kind of law, however, so Allan hailed one of their attorneys, David, and introduced him to the prospective client. David said he was sure he could help, and escorted the client off to his office.

A few days later, Allan saw David in the hall and asked, "Whatever happened with that client I introduced you to?" "Oh, it turned out great!" said David. "He hired us and I've spent the last two days just working on his case!" And David rushed off.

As Allan stood there, glad to have helped out but wishing he had gotten a thank you for his trouble, the head of the law firm approached him. "You're not paying enough money for using the fax machine in this office. We're going to have to start charging you more!"

Poor man. He had no idea just how terrible his timing was.

Well, Allan bought his own fax machine the next week. And his client referrals are going to another law firm—of dolphins who say, "Thank you!"

Take another look at the people around you. Are they saying "thank you" enough? Are you?

Today's Affirmation: "I thank God and all the people around me for my abundant blessings!"

292

Great Expectations

"The winds and the waves are always on the side of the ablest navigators."

—Edward Gibbon

Young and single, I had been focusing on my work life, to the detriment of my personal life. My friend and fellow business owner, Janice, was in the same boat. We decided it was time to make our reappearance on the dating scene. Never comfortable with making small talk in bars, we decided to go sign up with the "Great Expectations" video dating service.

When we arrived, the salespeople insisted on splitting us up for their presentations. Each of us was taken separately to a small room where we were pitched on the wonderful "shopping mall of men" (my expression, not theirs). Well, Janice and I were "pre-sold" buyers—we went there knowing we were going to sign up. We were happy to find out all the details of how it worked, but whether or not we were going to sign up was never an issue. We were signing up. The only issue was price.

Diligently, my salesman coaxed me to sign up at the going rate of $1,500. Luckily, I knew that prices on these kinds of services could be negotiable. I countered with a lower price. We haggled back and forth, and came to agreement at around $1,000. But now I played my trump card.

"I'm not signing or agreeing to anything until I talk to Janice," I said.

"Why?" asked the salesman.

"Because Janice is a better negotiator than I am!" I replied. "And I will be very unhappy if I walk out of here with her and find out she got a better deal than I did. So I want to know now, and I want the same price she's getting."

He hemmed and hawed and tried to tell me that was against their "rules" etc. I said fine, I am happy to leave without signing up. As I got up out of my chair, he quickly said, "Okay, you win," and went off to find Janice.

A few minutes later, he reappeared. "Well?" I asked.

He grinned sheepishly. "You were right," he said. "Your friend Janice is a better negotiator. She got another hundred dollars off the price. So I will give it to you for the same price that she got." Happily, I signed the deal, paid the money, and was a happy client of "GE" for years.

The moral of the story is that you don't always have to *be* the best negotiator. You just have to *know* the best negotiator.

Today's Affirmation: "I am always able to negotiate the best deal there is!"

293

Running Bad

"If you can't be a good example, then you'll just have to be a terrible warning."

—Catherine Aird

The bag lady I might become is never all that far from my mind. She lurks in hidden corners, waiting to catch me unaware. Just when I think I have the money thing licked, there she is, breathing her hot, stale breath on my neck. Sometimes I think I must play poker just to invite her back for tea when she's been away a little too long. Poker keeps me humble. I fancy myself a sharp card player and I love to play; the luck runs for me and against me at different times regardless. Maybe on my unlucky days I play more poorly. I am sure that on my unlucky days I am poorer.

With high hopes, I head for the poker club, expecting to make a few dollars and have a few laughs. And I get *pounded*. Nothing works. I can have the best shot at making a perfect hand, like three aces on my first three cards. Then every card after that is a brick, and against all odds, someone with a pair of deuces calls every bet I make and gets two more deuces on the last two cards. Four twos?! Then I get to experience anger and frustration and see how I am truly not kind to others after all. I am selfish, egotistical, and *unlucky*. It's not fair! I am "running bad." (This is a poker term used to describe an execrable flow of bad cards and bad luck.)

Eventually, I run out of money and temper. I drag myself back home and check in on my home office computer. Aha! A fax...from someone who has decided not to take my workshop after all and has written me a note to cancel. Perfect. The bag lady pats me on the shoulder. "There, there, dear," she commiserates. But she smiles her secret smile that warns me I mustn't feel too safe here in my nice office in my nice house. I howl at the moon. (Silently, so as not to wake the neighbors.)

The bag lady whispers to me all night long. In the morning, I write her this testimonial, giving her space and voice and time. She fades like a wraith in the morning sun, her mission accomplished. I have been reminded. There but for the grace of God go I. I pray and I meditate. I practice my affirmations. I revise my budget. Somewhere in the process, I recover my good humor and my love for my fellow man.

But not for the guy who got four deuces. Maybe tomorrow.

Today's Affirmation: "I love and accept myself and my fellow man."

294

Gulp and Go!

"The man who leaves nothing to chance will do few things badly, but he will do very few things."

—George Savile Halifax

I was a drama major about to graduate from college when a classmate called. An agent from Hollywood was coming to see him in a play, and he hoped I would sit next to the agent and say good things. I agreed; I was delighted to help my friend.

Frank Levy was a new agent at Creative Management Associates (now ICM), one of the top two agencies in the world. We hit it off right away, discussing plays, films, and performances—and my friend, Joe, naturally. It was an enjoyable evening, although it didn't pan out in a deal for my friend.

A week later, I got a call from Frank. His secretary had just quit and he offered me the job. I was so astonished, I almost "Yeah, butted" him out of it: "But I don't take shorthand." "That's okay," he said, "I don't dictate much." "And I don't type really well," I admitted, wanting to be honest. "That's okay, too," he answered, "What I really need is someone who can read scripts and write opinions on them. You can do that." I took a big gulp of air and plunged in. "All right. I'll do it!"

Reality set in my first day on the job, when I was faced with an electric typewriter. I looked all over it but could not locate the "on" switch. I went looking for help and found Sandy, another secretary. "How do you turn this on?" I asked, pointing to the typewriter. She flipped the switch underneath the keyboard. "Oh, Sandy, I never went to secretarial school and I don't know how I'm going to keep this job! Will you please help me?" I threw myself on her mercy, she laughed and said of course she would help, and we became fast friends from that moment on.

Soon, I was working for both Frank and Joe Funicello, Annette's brother. Stars came and went from the offices daily, and I met many of them. But I wanted to be one of them, not their agent's secretary. Eventually, Frank helped me get my first union acting job, and I left.

Years later, when I was looking for a literary agent, a friend put me in touch with Jim Jermanok, who had once been a top executive at ICM. When I called him, I said I used to work at ICM, too. "What did you do?" he asked. I told him and he laughed, saying, "I know Joe Funicello!" Synergy established, he referred me to Lisa Hagan, who became my agent. The ICM lessons are:

1. When someone offers you a job, don't try to talk them out of it.
2. When you don't know how to do the job, ask someone who does, and follow instructions.
3. Gulp and go!

Today's Affirmation: "All my relationships are valuable in expected and unexpected ways!"

295
Fear

"Whether you know it or not, fear has developed your likes and dislikes, picked your friends, and raised your children."

—Rhonda Britten

Fear is what stops us from living our passion, from developing our dreams, from rising to the heights of success we envision. We are afraid we won't be safe; we don't feel secure; we're in uncharted territory. Thoughts of the worst that can happen flood our minds and we're afraid to take the chances.

In the Hypmovation seminar I attended, we were told that it is normal and natural to have fears, but that we should "Face it; Examine it; Accept it, Reverse it." It is a helpful anagram to remember, as is this one: "False Evidence Appearing Real." But when I mentioned this in my class, everyone burst out laughing when one woman blurted, "Oh! I thought it stood for "F@%# Everything And Run!"

That's a funny comment, but we all know that running from your fear won't take you in the direction you want to go. My friend, Rhonda Britten, a deeply courageous author and speaker, has helped many break the bonds of fear. In her book, *Fearless Living: Live Without Excuses and Love Without Regret*, she shows how all of us are controlled in some ways by our "wheel of fear" which keeps us from our "wheel of freedom." When we understand the fears that limit our behavior, we can free ourselves of the limiting past and create new lives full of adventure, promise, and happiness.

Whatever your fear, you have to face it and move through it. Don't let it stop you. We risk failure, but failure is often just a step forward to success. We almost always fail at first. Your first time at bat—did you hit the ball? Chances are you didn't. (When I first started playing tennis, I needed three courts to play in because I couldn't hit the ball where I wanted it to go.) You accept that you will improve with time and practice. Hopefully, it doesn't keep you from ever picking up the ball in the first place. Have you ever watched a small child trying to learn to eat? They're terrible at it. Food goes everywhere. But they keep on trying. You don't see them give up and say, "Well, I hope Mom sticks around to feed me because I suck at it." So why expect perfection from yourself on the first try in the areas of business and money? Falling down and bumping your head a little is part of the deal.

Change the way you look at the feeling of fear. Instead of a nervous energy of anxiety, hold it as the energy of excitement. Great actors always say that they get butterflies in their stomach before every performance. If they don't get butterflies, they know they aren't going to be good. They need the energy of the excitement to transform their performance and make them soar. You need it, too. That's what it's there for. It's not nerves—it's energy.

Harness those butterflies. Use that energy. Gulp and go!

Today's Affirmation: "My energy and excitement help me reach my highest goals!"

296

Suit up, Show up, and Shut up

"Sometimes you have to make the right choices and let your feelings catch up with them."

—Dr. Phil McGraw

We pay too much attention to our feelings. We want to *feel* like making that cold call before we make it. We want to *feel* love for our fellow man before we donate to charity. We want to *feel* joy in our work before we work. When we don't feel these things, we don't make the call, love humanity, or do the work. But we've got it backwards. The feelings we want come after we take the action, not before.

We need to take the action that we know is the right action, regardless of how we feel about it. We can be terrified, angry, humiliated, sad, tired, or depressed, fighting our mental battles against doing what we know to be right, but the end result is that it doesn't matter how we feel about it, what matters is that we do the right thing.

In Alcoholics Anonymous, they have a wonderful saying about this: "Suit up and show up." This is the instruction given to newcomers who are struggling with the new practice of being sober. Alcoholics often struggle with emotions that feel overwhelming when they no longer have the alcohol to escape into. If you asked them to "feel like going to an AA meeting" before they went to one, the room would probably be empty. So the instruction is "Suit up and show up"—just get dressed and go. How you feel about it doesn't matter. What matters is that you do it.

When I made the decision that I was powerless over alcohol and became willing to turn my life around, they told me to go to ninety meetings in ninety days. I laughed. "Do you know what my schedule is like?" I asked incredulously. "I run my own business and I'm president of a trade organization. Impossible! Surely my case is different." They smiled at me beatifically. "This is what you have to do to remain sober," they told me. "How do you know?" I protested. "We're sober and you're not," they replied. "If you want what we have, you have to do what we do."

I wanted what they had. I wanted it bad. I went to their damn ninety meetings in ninety days. I didn't feel like it. But I got sober. I liked that. And I liked how I felt about it after I did it.

To "Suit up and show up" I have added "and shut up." When I was going to the midnight meeting on Sunset Boulevard, I whined about it. When I had to get up early and make the 7:00 A.M. meeting in Pacific Palisades, I whined about that, too. No one was interested.

Shine the cold, clear light of objective reason on the passage of your life. What's not in it that you want? Go get it. Forget how you feel now. The good feelings come after you do it. That is the secret of becoming happy, joyous, and free. And rich.

Today's Affirmation: "I am happy, joyous, and rich!"

297

Dig the Reservoir

*"After winter comes the summer. After night comes the dawn.
And after every storm, there comes clear, open skies."*

—Samuel Rutherford

When I think of all the time and energy I have spent trying to convince people to take my workshop when they really weren't that interested, I could cry. I finagle, I plead, I use all my fancy "closing techniques," trying to convince them to do what I want them to do instead of letting them off the hook I want to reel them in on. I'm sure at these times that Chellie "has a lean and hungry look." I am just as sure that it is not attractive.

Desperation appears when we fear not having enough. Enough participants in the workshop, enough money in the bank, enough salary, raises, promotion, accolades, jewelry, cars, clothes, children, space, time. We grab, we horde, we corral, we fight, we scream. Fear-based decisions rule our minds, hearts, actions. The more we grasp at abundance, the more it eludes us. Frantically, we try to push the river.

"Summertime, and the livin' is easy," reminds the song in *Porgy and Bess*, by George Gershwin. Life is slow and easy and rich in the summer. We are comfortable. We trust. We relax. We have dug the reservoir; the water flows in to fill it. Many people love me, love my class, can't wait to attend. These are the fish who can swim in the lake I have created. The other fish aren't bad, aren't wrong, aren't anything—except other fish who need a different lake.

When I remember this, I know my job is just to dig the reservoir. My fish will come.

Today's Affirmation: "It's summertime, and my livin' is easy!"

298
Navigating Stars

"Never let your head hang down. Never give up and sit down and grieve. Find another way. And don't pray when it rains if you don't pray when the sun shines."

—Satchel Paige

Zane, the movie director, was stuck. He had made a wonderfully funny short film and was having difficulty getting it seen. We met for a couple of hours to discuss his situation and figure out what new ships he needed to send out. At the end of the meeting, I told him that sometime you just have to ask God to give you a sign. He liked that idea and promised to try it.

A short time later, I received a note from him. He told me that he had been doing some serious talking with God for several days. Apparently, it was a fairly one-sided conversation and he wasn't getting an answer back. So he asked for a sign: that either one of his scripts would get sold or it would become abundantly clear that he should change the direction of his life.

Still, there was no sign. In exasperation, he told his wife, Julia, that since God wasn't cooperating, Zane was going to make a sign himself and hang it in his office. It was going to say: "Dear Zane, You are a successful writer, director and producer of feature films and television. Love, Your friend and confidante, God."

Before Zane had a chance to actually make the sign, his publicist called. She had spoken with an agent at Creative Artists Agency who was sending a messenger to pick up a tape of Zane's film. The agent said that he would get back to her in a week and that he would try to help out in any way he could. Zane was ecstatic.

He ended his note to me with this comment: "Admittedly, nothing has happened yet but it looks really bright. Seeing you last Saturday really helped me get my head on straight and chart my ship on a proper course. I look to the stars for aid in navigating my ship. And you are one of the brightest in the firmament. Thank you so much. Love, Zane."

Isn't that a lovely note? What every teacher/consultant/leader hopes for is having a student who actually follows your suggestion and then has success because of it. Getting notes like this is the icing on the cake: what we're all working for, hungry for, panting for. Be a bright star in someone's firmament. Be there. Help out. And remind everyone to ask God to play on the team.

Today's Affirmation: "I have many bright stars that help me navigate my ship!"

299

There's Always Enough Time to Do What You Really Want

"The trouble with many of us is that we just slide along in life. If we would only give, just once, the same amount of reflection to what we want out of life that we give to the question of what to do with a two-week vacation, we would be startled at our false standards and the aimless procession of our busy days."

—Dorothy Canfield Fisher

People fit amazing amounts of activity into their schedules. When you really are committed to your vision or your dream, somehow you find the time. It is almost like time literally expands and you accomplish incredible feats in nano-seconds instead of in hours. Days elongate as your focus and concentration put you in "The Zone," that space where everything flows naturally, easily, effortlessly. After spending time in "The Zone," you sometimes return to consciousness, amazed at what you've produced, half the time not even recognizing it as your own.

Mystery writer Sharyn McCrumb told of her experience with this in *Writer's Digest*. She said that in 1986, she sold a four-page book proposal, but with a catch: the editor needed the completed novel in six weeks. Gulp. She was working full-time, teaching a night class, and taking two graduate classes that both required research papers. She was also the mother of an eight-year-old daughter, with another child on the way. She had lots of "yeah, buts" to choose from.

Instead, she wrote the book in six weeks. Not only did she do it, but she did it so well that it won the Edgar Allan Poe Award for Best Paperback Novel in 1987!

This is a great example of a life "sprint." Sprints are wonderful, and you can do anything when a fantastic goal makes the sprint worthwhile. Just a small caution: don't make sprinting a full-time habit. And make sure to take a time-out when you've finished one.

Today's Affirmation: "I have abundant time to manifest my abundant riches!"

300

Nurturing Yourself

"It isn't the great big pleasures that count the most; it's making a great deal out of the little ones."

—Jean Webster

The class on accomplishing goals was intense. Each week for eight weeks, the participants met and outlined their strategies for achieving them. Most of the people in the class were high achievers, energetic personalities.

At the first class session, Korey listened quietly as each person listed their dreams and desires. She, too, was a successful businessperson, an entrepreneur who had started her own tutoring business and built it into a thriving business with ten employees.

But Korey was in crisis. In her determination to succeed, she had forgotten how to play. The goal-getting mode had become her constant setting, drive and determination her normal way of life. She was out of balance. She was unhappy.

One by one, each of the class participants outlined their goals. "My goal is to double my income," said one. "I want to expand my business internationally," said another. All of them had major, challenging, big business and big money goals. Each goal was met with applause and approval. As the last of the group, all eyes turned to Korey. "My goal is to nurture myself," she said. "I will bring in a list each week of all the things I did during the week to take care of myself, to pamper myself, to have fun, and to relax."

Pandemonium. Frowns. Quizzical looks. Anger and sarcasm. Everyone in the room protested her choice. "That's not an appropriate goal for this class!" they argued. "This class is about achieving success!" "What good is success if you're too tired to enjoy it?" she retorted. The instructor quieted everyone and allowed that Korey's goal was a legitimate one and she could proceed with the class.

Every week, the class participants shared their successes: "I just got my SBA loan for $100,000," "I made forty-five sales calls and closed three major deals," "I was just elected president of my national association." Korey brought in her nurturing list: "I walked on the beach in the middle of the afternoon; I painted pictures and listened to music; I took a bubble bath and lit the room with candles; I had a "Pajama Day" and read and watched movies in bed; I made a list of my best qualities and acknowledged myself for them." The other participants listened enviously.

By the end of the course, everyone was asking for copies of her list.

Why not start your own list today?

Today's Affirmation: "I relax, let go, and lovingly nurture myself."

301
Pet the Cat

"Life is a romantic business, but you have to make the romance."

—Oliver Wendell Holmes

I was rushing off to work one morning, when I reached down briefly to pat my cat on the head and say goodbye for the day. I caught myself suddenly as I stood up and thought, "Why am I rushing so that I can't take two minutes to really see, feel, and connect with my kitty that I love?" I put my briefcase, purse, and keys back down on the table, picked up Yoda, and just hugged and petted her for a while. At the office later, I tried to remember this experience and take the time to really see and hear and know and relate to the people behind the tasks at work.

I believe it must be possible for every thought and act to be performed in that state of grace called love. We occasionally see some people operating from this state and often they become famous as religious leaders. But I also see, as I really look around at the people I know and meet, many different levels of expertise at the practice of this concept. Look at the possibility if each individual had "spread love and peace" as his goal each day.

I can see the people who operate from love: they shine. Someone told me once that the definition of a friend was someone whose face lights up when they see you. You know what happens next—your face lights up, too! It looks to me that some people are lighting up a lot of other people. Wouldn't it be great to be among them, and light up faces everywhere you go?

In the business world, too, this is possible. Take time to understand the human being behind the transaction, the spiritual being behind the contract. The goal of business doesn't have to be just more profit. The possibilities are bigger than that. Business can spread light, love, and peace in the world.

Today's Affirmation: "Today I spread light, love, and peace in the world to all God's creatures."

302

There Are People Praying for You

"You, yourself, as much as anyone in the entire Universe, deserve your love and affection."

—Buddha

In the middle of the seminar, *How to Build Your Speaking and Writing Empire*, Mark Victor Hansen suddenly turned around on stage, looked out at the audience, and said emotionally, "There are people praying for you to publish your book!"

A chill ran down my spine—it was a goosebump moment. I thought of all three hundred plus of us writers in the room who had messages of hope and love and learning to share. Yes, for each of us, there is an audience, a group of people who need our message in order to live better, healthier, happier, or more fulfilled lives. People who would laugh or cry over our writings. People we could help. People who would, in turn, help us by reading and sharing our thoughts and dreams.

There are people praying for you, too.
There are people praying for you to open your restaurant.
There are people praying for you to produce your record.
There are people praying for you to paint your masterpiece.
There are people praying for you to give them a massage.
There are people praying for you to negotiate their contract.
There are people praying for you to teach them what they need to know.
There are people praying for you to sell them a car.
There are people praying for you to take their picture.
There are people praying for you to type their letters.
There are people praying for you to improve their health.
There are people praying for you to help them save their marriage.
There are people praying for you to help them be more beautiful.
There are people praying for you to give an exciting performance.
There are people praying for you to take care of their pets.
There are people praying for you to help them save money.
There are people praying for you to plan their vacation.
There are people praying for you to keep them safe.
There are people praying for you to write your computer program.
There are people praying for you to learn interior decorating.
There are people praying for you to get your degree.
There are people praying for you to invent your invention.
There are people praying for you to open your store.
There are people praying for you to ____________.
There are people praying for you.

Today's Affirmation: "There are people praying for me and I succeed in order to serve them."

303
A Love Letter to Yourself

"Life isn't about finding yourself. Life is about creating yourself."

—George Bernard Shaw

I attended a weekend women's retreat years ago, and seminar leader Suzy Prudden gave us the assignment to write a love letter to ourselves. We were to do this during our afternoon break. "It should begin, 'My darling, my dearest one,'" she said, "and praise all of your best qualities." Everyone tittered a bit; it was uncomfortable. I saw that no one had much experience with self-praise.

I went to my room to relax, meditate, and think about all I had experienced so far at this retreat. I had some resistance to writing the love letter to myself, but finally picked up pen and paper and started. "My darling, my dearest one," I wrote...and started to cry. I cried the entire time I wrote the letter. Finally, it was done and almost time to reconvene with the others. I washed my face with cool water and tried to repair the damage to my makeup.

As I walked into the conference room, I noticed a lot of women's eyes were red. We sat in a circle and Suzy said, "Now we're going to share our letters." Oh, dear, I thought, how embarrassing. The first woman who read her letter made it to about the middle of the second sentence before she started to cry. She was not alone, for we were all crying with her. We all cried for the entire time we shared our letters. Love swelled in the room and as we cried, we bonded. It was a tremendously moving experience. Not embarrassing at all.

Oh, how I cry for us all, we imperfect, perfectly beautiful beings who try so hard to be what's true, do what's best, and measure up to the impossible standards we set for ourselves. We constantly strive to fix what's broken, add what's missing, fill the unfulfilled longing. There's always room for improvement, never be satisfied, never give up. Have we tried hard enough, given enough, loved enough? How much is enough? At what level of attainment do we get to acknowledge and praise what we have accomplished instead of bemoan what yet remains to be done?

Write your love letter to yourself and keep it close by. Take time to praise yourself, acknowledge yourself for a good job well done this day, this life. Celebrate your wins, cheer for your own accomplishments, and nurture your creative soul. Be at peace, you did enough. You are enough.

Today's Affirmation: "I love and honor myself for all that I am and all that I do."

304
Believe in Magic

"I can live for two months on a good compliment."

—Mark Twain

Dwayne Garman is an upbeat, enthusiastic young magician. Everyone in class cheered the day he shared with us that he had accomplished a major lifetime goal: he auditioned for and was accepted as a member of Los Angeles' famed magician's club, the Magic Castle.

After accepting his accolades from the group, he shared with us how testimonials had helped him keep working when many other magicians were struggling. Several years before, he was working under contract with a local restaurant to provide close-up magic for their diners. He would move from table to table, performing various sleight-of-hand and card tricks to the amusement and delight of the restaurant's patrons.

The engagement was going well, but it was difficult for the restaurant owner to track the effectiveness of the entertainment on the bottom line. Was it really a draw to keep customers coming back? Did the act have a measurable impact on the dining experience? Dwayne could see that the restaurant managers were unsure.

So Dwayne created some "Feedback" cards to leave with the diners after he finished each performance, and asked them to fill them out. He would collect the cards from the tables later.

That's not what was so original about his idea—many people ask for feedback input on cards or forms. It's what he did next that made all the difference.

Dwayne made photocopies of the quotes from all the testimonial cards, by lining them up on the copier so that just quote after quote showed through. He then presented this list to restaurant management along with his bill at the end of each week.

Not only did he get paid promptly and happily, he worked for this restaurant chain until the parent company canceled the national program.

Send your testimonials along with your invoices—great idea! If you're on salary, you can still send updates on accomplishments and testimonials to your managers, along with "thank you" for your paychecks. Where else can testimonials work in your life?

Today's Affirmation: "I am wonderful—and I have proof!"

305

Send Ships into Someone Else's Harbor

"We are each of us angels with only one wing and we can fly only by embracing one another."

—Luciano de Crescenzo

Sometimes, no matter what I do, it seems that nothing is working. Every call I make to enroll someone in the workshop is a "no," people who I thought were enrolled for sure call to change their mind, a bill I wasn't expecting crops up unannounced. I find myself fighting fear of financial stress—again. All systems are not go. I do not pass go; I do not collect $200.

Breakdown. We all have these times. Who knows why? Something isn't centered within our own thoughts and beliefs, we have a new challenge or a new lesson to learn, it's a full moon, Mercury's in retrograde, or it's the economy, stupid.

I only know what works to get me past it—help someone else. As Zig Ziglar is fond of saying, "You can have everything in life you want, if you just help enough other people get what they want." I take this to heart on these days that trying to get my own needs fulfilled isn't working. I pull out my list of contacts and instead of focusing on who wants to buy my services, I concentrate on a magical question: "Who can I help today?"

On these helping days, I put aside all thoughts of myself and my business and dedicate the day to serving others. I enroll in someone else's course. I buy makeup from my beauty consultant. I peruse all my networking contacts to see who could benefit from each other. I call anyone I can think of who could use the services of someone else I know and tell them about each other. I invite people to come to networking meetings with me. I call people to tell them I'm thinking about them, and is there anything I can help them with today. I write testimonial letters to tell people I think they're wonderful. I make it my business to spread happiness and good cheer.

What happens when I do this seems almost magical. As I help others, I help myself. When I make someone else happy, I become happy. My day brightens as I brighten someone else's day. And then the dam breaks. Whatever was holding me back, disappears. Referrals start calling me "out of the blue." People call whom I've never met, referred by people I've never met! Money and good start flowing to me again.

Whenever you're not getting, give. Then watch the dam break, and the flood of good flow over you.

Today's Affirmation: "The abundance I sent to others returns ten-fold to me!"

306

What Looks Like Good News Isn't Always Good News

"There is no death—only a change of worlds."

—Native American proverb

I remember well, that horrifying day years ago, when the space shuttle *Challenger* exploded into space. My father had worked in the space program nearly all his life, and helped design the navigational system for the shuttle. On many mornings, my sisters and I had gotten up in the early dark before dawn to watch another space launch: the Mercury program, Gemini, Apollo, and all the shuttles. *Star Trek* fans, we cheered when the first space shuttle was named the *Enterprise*.

We girls had grown up and moved out, but we still watched Dad's space ships take off. He had been working on the *Challenger* launch for three days in a row, but was off duty on that fateful day when the weather froze and the O-rings failed. I called him immediately, crying on the phone. He was aghast, the worst fears of all having been realized. We shook our heads, and prayed for the adventurous souls who had been lost, and the families they left behind.

As I drove along the ocean on my way to my office, Barbra Streisand's version of *Somewhere* from *West Side Story* played on the radio. I thought about the teacher, Christa MacAuliffe, who had perished in the explosion. I had seen her on television and the competition for the title "First Teacher in Space." I saw the moment when she was announced the winner and saw her joy and happiness over having been selected. She was fun, she was funny, she was a dedicated teacher. None of us knew then that winning this prize meant her death.

I thought, too, about the woman who came in second in the running for this prize. How disappointed she must have been on that day when the winner was announced and it wasn't her. She had lost the prize—but it meant that she lived.

Think about this when you cry over your next loss: what looks like good news isn't always good news and what looks like bad news isn't always bad news. There are plans and purposes to life beyond our knowledge. As Richard Bach stated in his book, *Illusions*, everything in life boils down to two things: fun and learning. If you're not having fun, you're learning something. And when your mission has been accomplished, you leave the planet.

Mission accomplished, Christa, Dick, Michael, Ronald, Ellison, Gregory, and Judith. We remember and honor you.

Today's Affirmation: "I thank God for my time upon this rich Earth!"

307
Habits of Feeling

"You can't see the sun when you're crying."

—American proverb

Feelings run our lives. We go to movies, theater productions, watch television, and listen to music in order to feel the emotions they evince in us. Emotions are the game. We choose "three-hanky" movies, scary horror films, super-spy thrillers, fast-action adventures, romantic fairy tales, racy sex sagas, uplifting spiritual stories, dark, seamy, sordid stories of hopelessness and despair. We want to feel the sparkling joy of the lovers, the anxious fear of the threatened heroine, the shrieking mourning of the lost, the epiphanies of the saved. Sometimes we walk out of the theater wishing our lives were really like that. Sometimes we walk out and thank God our lives aren't like that. But in each case, we go there for the emotional fix, that adrenaline juice cocktail that spices up our lives.

The problem is that we think that it's the movie that produces our emotions and that it's our lives that make us feel the way we do. But the opposite is true. We choose the movie, and we choose the life in order to feel particular emotions we've gotten into the habit of feeling. That's why some people choose fulfilling marriages, while others choose emotional firing ranges. We look at the outside circumstances of our lives and then say the circumstances are responsible for the way we feel. But we choose the circumstances in order to feel this particular way, just like we choose a movie. Then habit takes over, and we reproduce the same circumstances and the same emotions over and over, forgetting that we set it up this way.

Want to feel richer? Happier? Calmer? More loved? Each day, sit quietly and think about a past incident in your life when you felt the positive emotion you want to feel again. Remember the exact circumstances, where you were, what the place you were in looked like, what season of the year it was, what smells, sounds, textures were present, who was there with you. Then concentrate on what happened and how you felt, moment by moment. Feel the feelings as if it were all happening again, right now in this moment. This is a technique, called "emotional recall," that actors use to reproduce emotional states.

Practice feeling the emotions you want in your life. And stop reveling in emotions you don't want. Don't tell the abuse story anymore, don't argue with your spouse over the same old thing, don't talk about your exhaustion, your resentment, your depression. Don't go to the horror movie today. Decide to live in the emotional space you desire and your outer circumstances will start to change to match.

Today's Affirmation: "I feel happier, richer, and more loved and loving every day!"

308

You're Wearing Your Thinking

"Most of the shadows of this life are caused by our standing in our own sunshine."

—Ralph Waldo Emerson

You're wearing your thinking.

It's on your face: your emotions show. If you're angry, I can see it. If you're happy, I can see that. I know if you're depressed, exuberant, alert, sleepy, cocky, defiant, joyful, excited. Your expression tells me if you love your life, love your fellow man, love me.

It's on your body: I can see the self-respect of the person who dresses carefully, neatly, cleanly. The flamboyance of loud colors states clearly you are unafraid of my opinion. The nose rings and multicolored Mohawks of the young people on Melrose Boulevard speak to me of teenage rebellion and worse (although I could be wrong about the worse). Rich fabrics and fine jewelry tell me you have manifested some wealth in your life. Rags tell me you haven't.

Studies have shown that some 75 percent of our opinions about other people are formed in the first thirty seconds we meet them through non-verbal clues.

You're talking your thinking.

After the visual, the verbal clues declare themselves. When you talk, you betray your culture, your upbringing, your education, your intelligence, and your beliefs. When you say "yeah, but" I see where you are stuck along the path to your dream. When you ask questions, I believe you are interested. When you never ask questions, I assume you are not. When you talk with energy, I catch your excitement. When you complain about things, I catch your resentment.

Some people are wearing Heaven. Some people are wearing Hell.

So. What are you wearing today?

Today's Affirmation: "I am proud to wear the abundant thoughts that I am thinking today!"

309
No Excuses

"The Lord will drench you with His showers but He will dry you with His sun."

—Czech proverb

So many people sit with their "yeah, buts" and their "I can't succeed becauses." They'd rather give you evidence for failure than ask how they might succeed in spite of their drawbacks. Everyone has drawbacks of some sort. But you can rise above them. Other people have. And if one person has done it, you can do it. Here are some people who have effectively canceled your excuses:

A poor black girl from Mississippi, from a broken home, abused as a child, had a dream and believed she could make it come true. She became an award-winning talk show host and one of the richest people in America: Oprah Winfrey, Talk Show Host.

A poor student, who continually failed in school, crippled with dyslexia when they didn't even know what dyslexia was, wanted to write. He earned riches and accolades as the creator of many long-running and popular television series: Stephen Cannell, Writer, Producer, Director

These are famous people and many know their inspirational stories. But dig deeper into the stories of people you know, and you will find many tales of triumph over disasters. I once met a woman who had been badly injured in an automobile accident. While lying in the hospital for the year it took her body to mend, she thought, "How am I going to work? I need to make money." She thought about all the limitations of her body and the things she couldn't do. Then she concentrated instead on what she *could* do: she could talk on the telephone. So she started an executive search firm from her hospital bed. She worked the phones every day, matching people who needed jobs with companies that needed employees. When finally she healed, she continued her work, and expanded her business into a very successful, moneymaking company.

If they can achieve their dreams in the face of these obstacles, so can you.

In a world where fad items like hula hoops, pet rocks, and virtual pets can make millions, anything is possible.

Today's Affirmation: "The world is filled with exciting opportunities for me to make money today!"

310
True Colors

"Colors are the smiles of nature."

—Leigh Hunt

The world is rich in color: the bright orange of a sunset deepening to purple at the edge of night, luscious yellow daffodils perched in forest green gardens, gold and russet leaves falling from dark brown trees. Who has not marveled at the iridescence of a peacock's plume, the pure white of a swan, the mottled magnificence of a leopard?

We humans have colors, too. If you want to look and feel rich, it is important that you develop your color style, and dress in the colors that are most suitable for you. When I met Jennifer Butler, a color stylist, she told me that if you wear your best colors, people will be unconsciously attracted to you without knowing why. I thought that would certainly be an asset in my profession, and I promptly hired her.

Jennifer's system subdivided the usual color categories of Spring, Summer, Autumn, and Winter and she determined that, with my red hair and green eyes, I was a "Metallic Autumn." She showed me samples that included a lot of shiny, sparkly material. But I love all colors so much, my wardrobe was filled with choices in other colors—colors that looked beautiful on the store mannequins but were a complete washout on me. Jennifer and her team came over to help me go through my closet for the weeding out process. Amid shrieks of "No, no, not that one!" about half my wardrobe ended up at the Goodwill. When I just couldn't bear to part with a particular outfit, Jennifer suggested I designate a special section of my closet for the color misfits. I was relieved, but she smiled and told me I might take them out and try them on, but I wouldn't wear them again.

She was right. I never wore the loud, navy-blue-and-white-striped dress again. Once I became accustomed to wearing the colors I looked best in, I couldn't bear to wear something that didn't suit me. I got more compliments on my appearance, but more important people paid me more attention, listened more closely to what I had to say. My income rose with my self-confidence. I saved money, too, since I no longer bought things on impulse that later hung in the closet because they really didn't look that good on me.

I recommend you get your colors done by a professional—the money you spend is an investment in yourself and will be worth it. In the meantime, you can get yourself started by ruthlessly going through your closet and giving away those clothes that don't make you look and feel fabulous. A good test for color appropriateness is to hold the fabric up to your face and see if it makes your skin glow and your eyes sparkle or if it washes you out and makes you look pale or tired. Get a friend who will tell you the truth to help you shop.

Because very few people really look good in chartreuse.

Today's Affirmation: "My true colors are shining through and I look and feel great!"

311
Need and Want

"It's possible to own too much. A man with one watch knows what time it is; a man with two watches is never quite sure."

—Lee Segall

"Let's go shopping—I need to buy some clothes!" I told my friend, Shelley.

"Need?" she asked.

She caught me. "Well, no," I admitted. "I already have clothes, so this isn't about need. It's really about having some fun at the mall!"

"That sounds good," she replied. "Let's go!"

We often overuse the word "need." It's been mentioned by various prosperity teachers that using the words "need" and "want" create a feeling of lack and limitation rather than abundance and wealth. If you're needy, you're poor; if you *want* things, it's because you don't *have* them. The dictionary definition of want includes: "1. A lack; shortage; 2. Poverty; 3. Craving; 4. Something needed." Need is partially defined as "1. Necessity; 2. Lack of something desired or required." These words are better avoided if we desire (almost said want!) prosperity.

Watch your usage of these words today. When you use them, how are you feeling? Are you feeling anxious from a sense of lack and limitation?

If you aren't having that kind of negative feeling, then don't worry overmuch about this. Don't get too involved with semantics. Many words we use out of habit and convention, and don't have negative feelings attached to them. This is merely another sign to pay attention to if you are in the habit of feeling *needy*.

Then you might have a richer experience of life if you focus on your desires from a recognition that you already possess great abundance and are merely adding to your stores of wealth. I practice this by saying "I desire" rather than "I want." The definition of desire is "1. To long for; crave; 2. To ask for." The definition of desirable is "worth having; pleasing." So desire desirable things for added pleasure and enjoyment in your life!

Then remember all desire is just entertainment.

Today's Affirmation: "I richly enjoy my rich life!"

312
The Benjamin Franklin Close

"Much ingenuity with a little money is vastly more profitable and amusing than much money without ingenuity."

—Arnold Bennett

When I can't decide whether or not to do something, I use a sales technique called "The Benjamin Franklin Close." (I don't know why it's called that.) I take a piece of paper, draw a line vertically down the middle of it, and label the left hand column "Pro" and the right hand column "Con." I write down all the reasons I can think of for taking the action in the left column, then all the reasons for not doing it in the right. By the time I am finished, it is clear to me which is a longer, stronger list.

Years ago, when I was trying to decide whether or not to keep my office or move my business into my home, I used this technique. Here's how it looked:

Pro	**Con**
Save money on rent	Cost of hiring mover
Convenient—no driving to the office	Cost of hiring professional organizer
Larger room for giving workshops	Cost of reprinting stationery
Only need one phone	

It was clear to me that I really wanted to move and that in the long run, it would not only be more convenient, but would save money. Since all of the "Cons" involved expenditures of money that weren't on my regular budget, I started thinking about how I might "find another way to get what I wanted." I wanted to hire a mover who was in my LeTip networking group, and I remembered that he had mentioned an interest in my workshop. I called him and asked if he'd like to do me a favor and move me and I would do him a favor and let him take my workshop for free. He said "Yes!" with alacrity.

Flushed with success, I thought the same offer might hold with the professional organizer in the group, and also the printer. They both happily agreed. So the net cost of my move was—zero!

Is there something in your life you are undecided about? Try the Benjamin Franklin Close. If that doesn't work flip a coin. By the time the coin lands, you'll know on which side you wanted it to land. You can tell because that's when you toss it again, telling yourself, "Well, two out of three…."

Today's Affirmation: "I give of my bounty to others and they bounce it back to me!"

313

Big Wedding, Small Price

"Creativity is inventing, experimenting, growing, taking risks, breaking rules, making mistakes, and having fun."

—Mary Lou Cook

An issue of *People* magazine ran a story about a young couple who wanted to have a beautiful dream wedding, but didn't have much money to invest in it:

"You may now kiss the bride...after a word from our sponsors."

Okay, the minister didn't quite say that at Tom Anderson and Sabrina Root's August 23 wedding—but he could have. To pull off their 250-guest dream nuptials, the cash-strapped but enterprising Philadelphia couple persuaded twenty-four local businesses to chip in some $32,000 worth of essentials—everything from the gold wedding bands ($500) to the exotic floral arrangements ($2,500). In exchange, the groom thanked each sponsor before the first toast and provided plugs on the invitations, on cards at the buffet, and on scrolls on the dinner tables.

"I always wanted a fairy-tale wedding," says Anderson, 24, a bartender who hit on the idea, he explains, after soliciting prize donations for a raffle. His bride, a 33-year-old hairstylist who met Anderson when she walked into his bar in June, 1998, the day she received the divorce papers ending her one-year first marriage—was skeptical at first. "I knew people were thinking, 'Will this be tacky?'" she says. But she eventually gave in. "Neither of us wanted to ask our parents for money," says Anderson, who labored for nearly a year to line up the sponsors.

Among the goodies: sushi, broiled salmon and Italian pastries from eight area eateries; a deejay to play Disney ballads; limos; a handmade tulle veil; even a weeklong Cancun honeymoon. The two laid out just $8,000 of their own money to rent a Glenside, PA. castle, hire food servers, buy liquor, and pay for Root's $1,600 dress. Weren't the guests scandalized by such blatant commercialism? If so, they weren't saying. "It was terrific," insists Root's mother, Elizabeth. "Tom was just a genius."

This is a perfect example of "find another way to have what you want." They were creative, determined, and clearly, good at sales! They got the wedding they wanted and the vendors got publicity, good will in the community, and great advertising at an event with a large captive audience. Everybody won.

What is it you want that you can't get through the usual channels? Get creative! Gather a team of friends to brainstorm ideas with you (dolphins only, please). What do you have to trade? What can you contribute to someone else in exchange for what you want? Make a plan then take action. Anything is possible.

Today's Affirmation: "With the help of friends and my creative ability, I make my dreams come true!"

314

What You Don't Do Will Cost You

"A pessimist is one who builds dungeons in the air."

—Walter Winchell

A group of friends who were all women business owners and I gathered together at a fine restaurant. We laughed and told stories while we ordered luscious meals from the menu. Charlene, a successful young chiropractor, quietly ordered a small dinner salad and hot water. My face expressed a look of shock as she pulled a tea bag from her purse. She looked at me sorrowfully and said that she just couldn't afford to buy dinner.

She had taken my workshop a couple of years before, and I knew her business had been doing well. After her responses to a few pertinent questions, like "Are you still doing your affirmations?" (to which the answer was "No"), I told her it might be a good idea for her to come back for a refresher course. She agreed.

One homework assignment was for everyone to fill out a personal balance sheet, listing all of their assets and liabilities. Charlene called: "I just can't do this homework, Chellie! Can I come to class early and have you help me with it?" I said, "Of course," and when she arrived, we got to work. First, we started listing all her assets. No problem there. She had business and personal checking accounts with healthy cash balances, and a money market account as well. She had savings, a retirement account, and owned a condominium. "Hmm," I wondered to myself, "Perhaps her problem is her debt load."

Sure enough, as we started to work on the liabilities, Charlene got nervous. I asked if she had any credit card debt. "Yes," she said weakly. I *thought* this was the problem. "Okay," I said calmly, "How much is it?" With a lump in her throat, she whispered, "Five thousand dollars."

"Is that *all*?!" I exclaimed. "You're this upset over only five thousand dollars?" She looked at me wide-eyed. "You don't think that's a lot?" she asked. "No!" I blurted out. "That's *nothing*! I often see people who owe fifty thousand, sixty thousand dollars. You could pay off this five thousand dollar debt tomorrow with the money you've got in your money market account."

Charlene changed in front of my eyes. She started to smile and then to laugh. She told me that she hadn't done the balance sheet exercise the first time she took the class because she was too embarrassed about her debt to write it down. She had continued to feel bad about herself because she didn't have a healthy perspective about her financial affairs. She spent two years with the Low Budget Blues unnecessarily. She asked me to tell her story to all my subsequent classes with the warning "What you don't do in this class will cost you!"

Today's Affirmation: "I count my money and watch the count go up every day!"

315

Read All the Fine Print

*"Education is when you read the fine print.
Experience is when you don't."*

—Unknown

After my bankruptcy, I needed to reestablish good credit, so I applied for a "secured credit card." This is a credit card that is issued when you put money in a savings account at the bank that issues you the card. The credit limit on the card is equal to the amount of money in your savings account. With time and a good credit history, they may periodically raise your limit without requiring that you deposit additional funds in savings. (Of course, they are dealing with people with problem credit, so they charge you a hefty interest rate for any money you borrow on the card.)

I was pleased to receive a letter from them after several years, stating that because of my "excellent record" with them that I qualified for a $1,000 upgrade reward certificate. (After problems with credit, hearing that you have an excellent record with anyone is music to your ears.) I thought the additional credit might come in handy some day. The letter requested that I sign a form and send it back to them. I started to do this immediately, but, habitually wary of small print, I continued reading the letter.

Am I glad I did. They wanted a fee of $75 for the upgrade, which basically meant I was paying cash for the privilege of giving them the opportunity to earn more money. I didn't like that very much, but thought perhaps the fee would be worth the increased limit on the card.

I kept reading. Then, on the back page, at the bottom, in small print, I found a statement that made my blood boil. If you accepted their offer, the annual percentage rate would be changed—from an already high 19.8 percent to 23.99 percent! As if 19.8 percent wasn't bad enough. Thank heavens I read the entire letter. But I know most people don't.

I wrote them a letter immediately, declined their offer, and strongly protested their campaign and business ethics. I never heard from them. But several months later, there was an article in the newspaper describing a class action lawsuit that had been filed against them for unfair business practices. What goes around, comes around.

Ignored any fine print lately? Mark Twain once said that the person who doesn't read good books has no advantage over the person who can't read them. That goes for reading the fine print, too.

Today's Affirmation: "I am an intelligent consumer—I know all and see all!"

316
Live within Your Means

"Annual income twenty pounds, annual expenditure nineteen nineteen six, result happiness. Annual income twenty pounds, annual expenditure twenty pounds ought and six, result misery."

—Charles Dickens

Notice that you can add any amount of money to this formula and the result is the same. If you make a million dollars a year but spend $1.2 million, you're in just as much misery as the person who makes $30,000 and spends $32,000.

The problem is over-spending. Human beings are basically just desire machines. It sometimes seems we can't get enough of anything. I know it's impossible for me to go shopping in the mall without seeing at least $10,000 worth of stuff I'd like to buy. It's amazing how fashion designers are always able to create more beautiful, fascinating clothes that I want. It doesn't matter how much I already have in my closet, there's always a new cashmere sweater or tweed skirt or cut-velvet scarf that attracts my eye. The sporty gold Lexus I'm driving is great, but, hey, did you see that new Jaguar over there? It's impossible for me to visit a bookstore without leaving with more books I just have to read....

One of the worst cases of spending bulimia I ever saw was illustrated in an article in the *Los Angeles Times* entitled *The Ultimate Material Girl.* It was the story of an accounts payable clerk who embezzled $1.5 million from the manufacturing company for which she worked. Distraught over the troubled relationship she had with her daughter, she stole in order to keep pace with her daughter's spending. Trying to buy her daughter's love, she bought her a Mercedes, a Porsche, a Saab, and a Jeep Cherokee. The daughter's closets were filled with designer fashions, $400 shoes, Louis Vuitton luggage, receipts for a $10,000 birthday party and $113,000 in home decorating services. She shopped every day. As long as the mother stole only $10,000 a month, her theft went undetected. But when the daughter tried to cash a check for $45,000, the bank manager got suspicious, and the jig was up.

The hole these people felt was not in their wallet but in their souls. It could never be filled with material goods. Surrounded by wealth, they were miserable. At some point, you have to decide that whatever you have is enough, and that what you will spend is only whatever is on your budget to spend, and no more. Then look for life's riches in friendships, helping others, being of service, and appreciating all the good things the world offers that are free to us all.

Live within your means. Love above your means. And both will increase.

Today's Affirmation: "My heart is filled with love and my bank account with money!"

317

The Emotional Bank Account

"You leave home to seek your fortune, and when you get it, you go home and share it with your family."

—Anita Baker

Sometimes when I speak to groups, I tell my story of having come to Hollywood to be a star. I pause, look around the audience and ask, "Anybody recognize me?" There is usually a good laugh at that, but once a hand shot up in the back of the room and a shout rang out, "I do! I do!"

I looked out into the audience, recognized the speaker and said, "Thanks, Mom!"

That was one of the endless deposits Mom and Dad made into my emotional bank account. Sometimes the "Bank of Mom and Dad" made deposits into my monetary bank account as well. They were always there for me, no matter what. I think they saw every play I ever performed in, whether driving to Santa Barbara or flying to Eugene, Oregon. The haven of home was the safety net that allowed me to leap out to catch the flying trapezes that filled my life.

In 1974, I was performing in Lubbock, Texas at the Hayloft Dinner Theater. The play was *Love and Kisses* and the star was Lyle Talbot, most recognizable as the neighbor on *Ozzie and Harriet*. Just before show time one Saturday night, I got a call from my Dad. He just had to tell me that at the office one day, he had mentioned that I was appearing with Lyle Talbot and his boss exclaimed that Lyle was his cousin! What a coincidence! We laughed and talked awhile and then Dad said, "Well, how do I get to the Hayloft?" "How do you get here?" I asked. "Where are you?" He said, "I'm at the airport in Lubbock."

I couldn't believe it. He had had a business trip to Houston, and thought he'd make a surprise side trip to Lubbock to surprise me. I was so excited! I told everyone backstage what had happened and that my Dad was coming to the show. Lyle Talbot spoke to the audience, told the story, and introduced my Dad, having him stand up and take a bow. Dad and I were both beaming. We made big deposits into each other's emotional bank accounts that night.

In the ebb and flow of life and relationships, sometimes we're making deposits, and at other times withdrawals from other people's emotional bank accounts. Relationships die when the withdrawals exceed deposits. Some bank accounts go untended for years until finally the accounts are closed and the proceeds distributed to the winds.

Who's minding your emotional bank account? Where are you making deposits? Where are you making withdrawals? Are you in the black, or are your accounts dripping red ink? Who are your depositors? Your lenders? Your borrowers? There is great emotional wealth in countless gold minds around you. Make some deposits today.

Today's Affirmation: "I give and receive endless blessings of love."

318
Dad

*"It doesn't matter who my father was;
it matters who I remember he was."*

—Anne Sexton

My dad is great. Growing up in the Great Depression, he lived on thin money much of the time. He met my mom when she was a secretary and he was a young cadet. They married in the midst of World War II. When he returned from active duty, he got his engineering degree—and me. Employment called him to Chicago, and my sister Jane made her appearance. When a man from California was heard bragging in February about mowing his lawn in his shirt-sleeves, Dad dusted the snow off his boots and moved us to Los Angeles. Third daughter, Carole, joined us there.

Dad worked in the space program at North American Rockwell. Dad loved us, encouraged us, helped us with our homework, disciplined us when we needed it, made the best jokes and the best hamburgers, and was our rock, our support, our stability. A quiet man, he dispensed wisdom in little nuggets when we needed advice and financial support in big checks when we needed money. I learned about positive thinking; he encouraged us to send out ships, although he didn't call it that; and he taught us to count our money and save. He was always there when the seas got rough, and cautioned us that not all the fish in the sea were dolphins. He taught us ethics, he taught us responsibility, he taught us humor.

Dad is in his eighties now and should be the poster child for enjoying retirement. He gets together with friends regularly, has weekend golfing getaways, takes piano lessons, and is learning to compose music on his computer. He's almost busier now that he's not working than when he was! But he always has time for the family, his daughters, sons-in-law, and grandkids, and his laughter and generous spirit brighten all our gatherings. He always has some new story to share, correspondence from an old friend, an article cut out of the paper, or a new book to read. His fascination and love of life inspire us all.

He showed me a letter he had written as a young man of twenty-two to my mother's parents. I read with tears his earnest promises of love, devotion, and support for Chellie LeNell, and for the family they would raise. I acknowledged him for having made such a beautiful mission statement for his life—and for having lived it completely.

Many times over the years, I have read in the *Dear Abby* and *Ann Landers* columns the recommendation that you write your parents a letter, thanking them for their gifts of light and life and love; that such a letter is treasured beyond gold. This is mine, Daddy. I love you!

When you've got dolphins in your life, appreciate them. Thank them. Give your parents of birth or your parents of choice this gift. Write them today. It feels so good to do it, you'll find it's a gift to yourself as well.

Today's Affirmation: "I bless and thank my parents, who taught me about life and love!"

319

Tic-Tac-Dough

"What do I think about when I strike out? I think about hitting home runs."

—Babe Ruth

Back in the seventies, my sister, Jane, went on the game show *Password*. She was their all-time champ, reigning for a total of nine days. In those days, big money was a few hundred dollars, and she made $5,000! The whole family celebrated and loved watching one of our own have her fifteen minutes of fame and fortune on television.

Well, I wanted to do it, too. I watched the show daily for several months, practiced with my sister, and then went down to the *Password* audition—and yes! I was selected to be on the show. I arrived at the television studio, heart thumping and dollar signs shining before my eyes...and then, I didn't win. Boo, hiss: the agony of defeat instead of the thrill of victory.

By now, you must have figured out that I am a proponent of the "If at first you don't succeed, keep on trucking until you do" school. So I made a few other non-noteworthy attempts at game show stardom, then in 1985, was selected to appear on *Tic-Tac-Dough*. This was my kind of show: play tic-tac-toe by answering fairly easy, general questions, and win money.

And I won! I was on the show a total of three days. They filmed five shows a day, so you had to bring changes of clothes so it looked like you were coming back on a different day. By the filming of the third show, my brain wouldn't work any more, and I was out of the show after missing the question, "What was the name of the TV show starring Michael Landon in which he played an angel?" Oooh, it's on the tip of my tongue, something-way, I think, I know *Stairway to the Stars*? Nope. *Highway to Heaven*. My short reign as champion was over.

For my three days' work, I took home a refrigerator, a stove, a typewriter, a trip to Hong Kong, $5,000 cash and an aromatherapy record player device—about $10,800 worth of cash and prizes. I was delighted. Another goal accomplished!

What's the lesson in this story and how can you apply it in your own life? There are always many layers in these stories. Here's a few to get you started:

1. Look for opportunities to make extra money and have fun.
2. Step outside your comfort zone and take a risk.
3. Study the winners and see how they do it.
4. Keep on truckin'.
5. Life is a game show.

Today's Affirmation: "I am a winner in the Game of Life!"

320
Hong Kong

"At the celebration of the Chinese New Year, one of the most honored observations is that of paying off all old debts. And we send missionaries to China!"

—Anonymous

After I won the trip for two to Hong Kong on a game show, my mom called to tell me that she was inviting herself to come along. Several friends of her's had been there, and she was itching to go. Then, as the two of us excitedly made our plans, Dad said he didn't want to be left behind, so we included him, too.

I wrote the Holiday Inn Harbor View to see if I could arrange for a rollaway bed in the room. I said I would pay whatever extra charge they might have for this service, but they wrote me back a lovely letter, saying that they were happy to have all of us at no extra charge.

I had the idea that since I had won this trip and the hotel wasn't making any money from our stay, that we would get a simple room in an undesirable location at the back of the hotel. Nothing could have been further from the truth! We were treated like royalty from the moment we arrived, from the limo service (yes, the Black Limo!) to the three managers who greeted us upon arrival. They showed us to our beautiful room overlooking Hong Kong harbor. There was a basket of fruit, a spray of orchids and a bowl of candy waiting for us next to three plush bathrobes, slippers, and the rollaway bed. It was delightful!

We spent the next seven days exploring all of Hong Kong—a fabulous city, teeming with life and energy. We shopped until we dropped, and every shop owner seemed to greet us with wide smiles and special offers (especially if we were the first customers of the day, as it was considered very lucky to sell something to your first customer).

The joy was contagious. I'm grinning to myself right now, just thinking about these people who radiated such positive expectation, I couldn't bear to disappoint them. I think I bought something in every shop I visited.

Take joy in your customers, your co-workers, your boss. Treat every customer as though they were the "lucky first customer" of the day. Like them a lot, and let them see that you do. Make them feel good about buying from you. You'll get rich if you do.

Today's Affirmation: "I radiate joy and positive expectation for my very rich life."

321

Family of Choice

"Everyone is a moon, and has a dark side which he never shows to anybody."

—Mark Twain

I have written of the wonderful blessings of my family. If you have not been one of the fortunate ones born to a supportive family, this page is for you.

I know people whose fathers were absent and others who wish their fathers had been absent. I am aware of people whose mothers abandoned them for drugs or drug dealers. I remembered my own father telling me that there were people who looked like human beings, talked like human beings—but they weren't human beings. So what do you do if you were tied to one at birth?

1. **Get out physically.** A friend of mine told me that his wife put herself in a foster home when she was a youth because of the terrible circumstances of her home life. What courage and determination that must have taken! In her action is part of the answer: remove yourself from the poison. Whenever you have the realization that where you are is not healthy, get out as soon as you are able to do so.
2. **Get out mentally.** If your family of origin is awful, create a family of choice that's beautiful. Get as much professional therapy as you need to understand and let go of your terrible past so that you can create a wonderful present. Find other successful escapees and ask them to mentor you and help you gather courage.
3. **Get out spiritually.** Find a religious philosophy that uplifts you and gives you peace. Find a spiritual practice that affirms that there is light, beauty, solace, and comfort for you. Find a God that loves you. Many years ago, I heard Elizabeth Kubler-Ross tell the story of a young girl who was dying of cancer but couldn't let go of life. When Dr. Kubler-Ross asked her why she couldn't go, the girl replied that she was afraid to die because she might not go to heaven. She was afraid that she must have been very bad to be punished so severely with cancer. Gently, Dr. Kubler-Ross asked the girl if she was a good student. "Oh, yes," the girl replied, "I loved school." "So then you must have gotten the easiest assignments," Dr. Kubler-Ross nodded. "No, not at all," the girl protested, "the teachers always gave the hardest assignments to the best students...." The girl's eyes widened and her mouth made a round "O." "I understand," she cried, and smiled, and let go.

Today's Affirmation: "I celebrate my family of choice!"

322

Shark Bait

"The wolf will hire himself out very cheaply as a shepherd."

—Russian proverb

One of my big disappointments in business was discovering that there are people who will hire you, take and use the gifts you deliver, and then won't pay you. Even worse, they never *intended* to pay you.

A local businessman rang up my bookkeeping service one Thursday afternoon with a rush job. He had a meeting with an accountant scheduled for the following Monday, but his books hadn't been reconciled. He was panicked—he needed a year's worth of bank reconciliations done by Friday. I said we could help him and he brought in all his bank statements.

Jim, one of my top staff bookkeepers, worked that evening and Friday morning to complete his work on time, and he thanked us profusely when he picked up his records. I gave him an invoice and he said that he had forgotten his checkbook, but he would drop off a check on Monday.

Well, you know the end of this story. Monday came and went—no check. A week went by, then two—no check. Finally, after several bills and a demand letter, he informed me that the work we did was no good and he wasn't going to pay us. (This is a favorite defense for these people—they complain about the quality of the work in order to have a justifiable reason for not paying.)

Now, Demon Chellie started howling at this point. Righteous indignation consumed me and I felt abused and betrayed. I sued him in small claims court and the judge split the difference and ordered him to pay us half the total bill. He didn't pay that either, and after a while, I wrote it off as a bad debt and vowed to learn my life lessons in this case: 1) Get a deposit before starting work, and 2) Don't let them have the work until you get paid. (After all, you don't leave Ralph's with groceries without paying for them first.)

Now I had to work on the inside job. I had to rid myself of anger, resentment, and the mental reprimands I was giving myself for being stupid. I remembered the Law of Karma, that what goes around comes around, and that "Judgment is mine sayeth the Lord." I moved on to better thoughts and better customers.

Well, the Lord's judgment works pretty well. The next winter, in a year where torrential rains and mudslides plagued the Los Angeles area, I opened up the local paper to discover that this man's house had slid off a cliff and was completely demolished. A moment of complete glee overwhelmed me as Demon Chellie rejoiced in the misfortune of her enemy. Saint Chellie had to do some major coaxing to get me back into a more compassionate state of mind.

Amazingly enough, two years later, this man called me again and asked me to do some bookkeeping work for him. I'm sure he was puzzled by my laughter as I exclaimed, "No thanks!"

Today's Affirmation: "All my clients are rich and wonderful and happy to pay me!"

323

Woe Is Me

"Things are going to get a lot worse before they get worse."

—Lily Tomlin

"Help me, Chellie, I'm in crisis!" cried Ellen. Having embarked on a new career in real estate eleven months before, she was having a difficult time and had not yet sold a piece of property. "I'm not doing my affirmations, I'm in denial about my finances, I can't do the budget homework, and I'm not sending out ships. I just can't do it!" As we talked, she laughed at herself and told me I should get some "Woe is Me" buttons to go with the "Yeah, but" buttons.

At times like these, life just seems so hard. We know what we should be doing, but the power to do it escapes us. We look at the wreckage we have created and want the *deus ex machina* of the Greek playwrights to come lift us up and carry us off to paradise. But there is no God machine and no Black Limo. The only paradise we find is the one we create for ourselves.

But how do we lift ourselves up out of the muck of our distress and move on? That's where pain comes in. Ellen reminded me of my friend Gracie, who had had similar problems.

Gracie was stuck in the muck. Her last relationship had ended badly, she was underpaid in her teaching job; depression and bills were piling up. I tried to make helpful suggestions, all of which were roundly rebuffed, especially the idea that she might want to see a psychotherapist. Finally, I gave up, realizing that I could do nothing to help but sympathize and listen.

Two years later, we sat huddled together in her living room while a storm raged outside. Some surprise bill had made a nasty appearance in her mailbox that afternoon and had sent Gracie into a crashing tailspin. Her life looked as black as the rainy night, and she stormed and cried in harmony with the thunder. Finally she sobbed, "I know you think I should go to a therapist, but I just can't!" "Well," I sighed, "I guess you don't hurt badly enough yet."

The next morning, Gracie asked me for the telephone number of a therapist. Amazed, I asked what had changed her mind. She said she didn't want to hurt any worse than she did then, and if I thought seeing a therapist might help, she would try it.

Within a year, Gracie had a new job, a better salary, and a husband. Paradise.

I told Ellen this story. She grumbled, giggled, then got back to work. Four weeks later, she sold her first house for $750,000—and two more the next month.

Pain is there to make us move. Our highest good is on the other side of the pain. When it hurts badly enough, we will go get it.

How bad are you hurting?

Today's Affirmation: "I live happily in the rich paradise I have created."

324

You Are a Winner!

"To dare is to lose one's footing momentarily.
Not to dare is to lose oneself."

—Soren Kierkegaard

Felicia Rose Adler was depressed. Reality was not living up to her dream.

She sunk gloomily in her chair and looked at her book. *Master Dating* is a fun, powerful book designed to help singles navigate the treacherous waters of the dating scene. A first-time author, she found a publisher, got an advance, suffered the torments of editing and rewriting, and worked hours on publicity, doing television, radio, and print interviews. She thrived on the hustle and bustle of book promotion, and her eyes lit up whenever she talked about her book.

A year later, she had sold one thousand books. Her vision had been to sell one million books. She dreamed of making a powerful impact on millions—and making millions.

Alone in the darkness, she realized she had made the success of this one book too important. She saw its lack of best-seller status as a reflection of her unworthiness. She identified so completely with the book that if someone rejected it, they were rejecting her. It was personal. It was devastating.

Suddenly, a thought struck her with complete clarity: "I am not my book." She got out of her chair and tied one end of a string around the book and the other end around her finger. She paced the room for a while, dragging the book behind her, looking at it from different angles, feeling the tug of the baby for its mama. Then she cut the umbilical cord and was free.

Many people never even try to get what they want. I believe it may be because they don't want to experience the death of the dream. If they never actually try to achieve the goal, they get to have the illusion that they could get it if they tried. Then the goal is always shining there as a possible future. But if they try and fail, the possibility of achievement no longer exists. Reality is cold. It is selling one thousand when you wanted to sell one million.

Cheer up, Felicia. Many people in the world will never write a book, never sell one copy, let alone a thousand. Revel in your accomplishment. Take joy in the learning and the doing and the being that you are that has changed with this experience. You have reached out to others with your story and a thousand people heard you. Maybe those thousand people achieved part of their dream because of knowledge you shared with them through your writing. Write on. You are not your book. You are not alone.

To all of you whose ships have been lost on the rocks, I say hold on. Take heart! Your life is not one ship. There is always another chance for you—another day and another ship. You are not alone. And you are not done.

Today's Affirmation: "I desire, I dream, and I revel in my accomplishments!"

325

Tomorrow Is Another Day

"What! No star, and you are going out to sea? Marching, and you have no music? Traveling, and you have no book? What! No love, and you are going out to live?"

—French proverb

Today I was cranky. Tried not to be anxious—failed. Played poker—lost. Was invited to dinner—canceled.

I am so upbeat most of the time, joy is practically my normal state. When I get moody and out-of-sorts, it is ugly. Mostly to myself. Feels like I took my brain, rinsed it in some muddy water, then put it back in my head. Ugh. The quality of my thoughts on days like this is distasteful. I dare not answer the phone. Getting into bed and turning the electric blanket up to "Nurture" is the only activity permitted.

I remember calling a woman one day who was clearly in the above state of wretchedness. The voice that croaked "Hello?" was trashed, beaten, debilitated, forlorn. Shocked, I blurted, "What's the matter with you?" She told me how tired and worn out she was from some 'round-the-clock project. I suggested she take the rest of the day off, go to bed, rest, and relax. She wasn't going to get any effective work done today from the state of being she was in; in fact, she could do herself harm by trying to talk to prospective customers from her depleted state of energy. I heard a huge sigh of relief on the other end of the line. She thanked me for giving her permission to opt out of the work she had planned for herself and thought she had to stay committed to do.

So I give myself the same permission to play hooky for a day. I pack myself off to my bed, my haven of dreams, my refuge of the night. Here I will not inflict myself and my misery on others. I read, I meditate, I pray. I shower my brain with as much white light and harmonious energy as I can muster, and gradually the dark dirt of desperation dissipates.

Like a cat with the cream, I purr my contentment.

Like Scarlett O'Hara—not everyday, but just this day—I say to all concerns, problems, and troubles: "I won't think about that today. I'll go crazy if I do. I'll think about that tomorrow. After all, tomorrow is another day!"

Today is for playing hooky.

Today's Affirmation: "All things are working together harmoniously for my greater good!"

326
Get off the Fence

"If American men are obsessed with money, American women are obsessed with weight. The men talk of gain, the women talk of loss, and I do not know which talk is the more boring."

—Marya Mannes

My friend, Kathy, was unhappy with her weight. She complained about it all the time and agonized about trying to lose weight. She didn't diet, mind you, she just *talked* about dieting and whether or not she should go on one. Every time we got together, it was, "Oh, I just know I'm too fat!" and, "Do you think I look too fat?" (Usually, we were eating rich, fattening foods at the same time she was complaining about her weight.) I began to get bored with this topic of conversation because there was never any action, never any movement, just endless repetitions of the dilemma. Kathy was all talk, no ships.

Finally, one day as she passed a mirror, she looked at herself sideways and then turned to me and said, "Do you think I look fat?" and I said, "Yes." The look of shock on her face told me I had her attention.

"Kathy, you're my friend and I love you," I said. "I don't care how much you weigh. My relationship and quality of friendship with you will be the same, whether you wear a size 6 or a size 16. Your weight has nothing to do with the wonderful times we have sharing our hopes and dreams, our philosophies and laughter. What matters is that you're happy. Happy people are generally more fun to be around. Now, you can be happy as a size 16 or happy as a size 6—it doesn't matter to me. But please just choose a size you want, go there, and be content. I will support you and love you, no matter what your choice."

She stared at me for a long moment. Then, thoughtfully, she said, "I think size 6 sounds good."

I said, "Great! Then let's go to the healthy salad bar place for lunch today."

During the next six months, Kathy dropped forty pounds. And she was happy every day doing it, because she got off the fence, chose a goal, and sent out a ship every day towards its achievement. Her dieting ships were: join a gym, exercise every day, eat healthier foods, eat fewer foods, think thin. Her rewards were compliments, new clothes in smaller sizes, and self-satisfaction.

If you want to lose weight, do what it takes to lose weight. If you don't want to do what it takes, choose to be happy with the weight you've chosen. Remember that Marilyn Monroe was a size twelve. Find role models at the weight you are—these days, they come in all sizes, shapes, and ages.

But in any case, don't talk about it.

Today's Affirmation: "I am a beautiful soul, wrapped up in a beautiful package!"

327

Thanks Givings

"If only the people who worry about their liabilities would think about the riches they do possess, they would stop worrying. Would you sell both your eyes for a million dollars...or your legs...or your hands...or your hearing? Add up what you do have, and you'll find that you won't sell them for all the gold in the world. The best things in life are yours, if you can appreciate yourself."

—Dale Carnegie

Having a sense of balance and perspective is this: knowing that there will always be someone who has more than you do—and someone who has less.

Think you don't have enough money? Donate a few hours working at the Union Rescue Mission, a homeless shelter, or a haven for runaway kids on the street. Then when you go home, take another look at all the riches you possess, remembering all those who do not have so much.

Think your health is poor? Maybe some people are worse off than you. Take flowers, songs, or poetry readings to a hospital or a nursing home. Make a donation to one of the many organizations that are searching for cures for what ails us.

Wish you were more intelligent? Notice the joy on the faces of the children in the Special Olympics and think again. Volunteer to teach a class; help an illiterate person learn to read.

Wish you were married, had a significant other, or even a date? You're only alone because you don't want the people who want you. Take another look and say yes to someone.

Wish you were single? Get single and give your mate a chance to find someone else who will really love them.

Wish you were more beautiful? Rent *The Elephant Man* then get to work on developing the inner beauty that he had.

Whatever it is you think you lack, there are those who have less than you. Whatever it is you think you have, there are those who have more than you. That is the state of this existence. You can be happy about it or you can be miserable. Your choice.

But the basic, glorious, joyous fact of life is this: you breathe, you think, you love, you hope, you cry, you laugh, and so does everyone else. Thank God, or whatever cosmic force brought you into being, for this spark of divine consciousness that gives you life.

Today's Affirmation: "Thank you, God, for filling my life with glorious riches!"

328

Happiness Is an Inside Job

"Gold, like the sun, which melts wax and hardens clay, expands great souls and contracts bad hearts."

—Antoine de Rivaroli

Studies have shown that, once above subsistence level, having more money and material success won't make you any happier. You already have to be happy. If you haven't learned how to be a happy person, how to take pleasure in the daily gifts the world offers to all of us, material goods will not satisfy you. Everyone can point to rich people who are lonely, bored, angry, or depressed. Having money just made them comfortable in their misery. The single-minded pursuit of money can distract them from their despair for awhile, but in the end, if they are curled up in their castle alone with no friends, all their millions will be cold comfort.

Some people are afraid to have a lot of money, because they think the money will make them selfish, uncaring, lonely, and miserable. But money doesn't do that. It's what is done with the money that is either good or evil. If you would do evil if you had money, then you are evil now—just without power. Money does provide power. The more money you have, the more you can manifest your material desires. The downside is that one can get distracted by all the material manifestations and neglect the spiritual ones. But of course, being poor can keep you focused on the *lack* of material success, and that can keep you from manifesting your spiritual desires.

So what is the answer? Learn to live rich, inside and out. There is joy in both internal wealth and external wealth. Focus on joy, happiness, your relationship with God, your relationships with other people, the meaning of life, and the mission of your life. Rich or poor, you can meditate and pray and make these your priorities. When you are joyful and grateful for what you have, you create the space for more. When you sense that there is a purpose to life and a mission within it for you to fulfill, then you act in harmony with God and the Universe. Open yourself to manifesting abundance in all areas of life, including financial success, knowing that you will use them honorably and with wisdom for the good of all around you.

Today's Affirmation: "I live richly and happily—inside and out!"

329
Worry

"Most people spend their lives running away from something that isn't after them."

—Unknown

Whenever we were upset about the possibility of something bad happening, before it actually happened, Mom would smile and say, "Don't borrow trouble. That hasn't happened yet. If it does, we'll figure out what to do then. Worrying about it today isn't going to help." This kind of conversation was usually preceded by the phrase "What if...": "What if I don't get accepted by the college I want to go to?" "What if I don't get a date for the school prom?" "What if I don't get the part I want in the play?"

Now, this is the same mother who was sick with worry if we were late getting home from our dates, but that was worry for a real event happening in the present. She didn't waste energy being concerned about our being late days before the actual event.

Worry is a negative affirmation. When you worry, you focus all your attention on the negative, scaring yourself with pictures of disaster and failure. Worry is different from contingency planning. Certainly, you want to have a backup plan in place in case your first effort fails. Mom had us apply to several colleges instead of just one, plan something fun to do if we didn't go to the prom, audition for other parts in other plays. Contingency planning enables you to await outcomes with equanimity. As a successful woman business owner once said, "Plan A is always the ideal picture. But it is usually a dream bearing no relation to reality. By the time I get to Plan F, I've got a plan that has some chance of actually succeeding."

I make my plans, put my dreams and goals onto paper and send out my ships. I hope they will come in. But I know I am never in charge of when they come in—or which ships come in. I am only in charge of sending them out. At that point, the winds of destiny and the hand of God take over. Worrying about those ships won't see them safely past the rocks and the waves. I trust that some of the ships will reach my harbor safely. God will choose which ones. And even if, at first glance, they look like leaky rowboats, they will turn out to be the right ships for me—golden galleons in disguise.

Today's Affirmation: "All my golden galleons are arriving safely in my harbor now."

330

Treasure Ships

"Men trip not on mountains. They trip on molehills."

—Chinese proverb

Sally called again today. "Help!" she cried. "My business has slowed down recently and I'm afraid I should cut my prices back in order to get more customers. But I like my new price and think I'm worth it. What should I do?"

A talented hair stylist, Sally had just finished my workshop several months before. She raised her prices and had great success in getting new customers during the course, but had apparently drifted back into some fear thinking since then. Her fear started manifesting in fewer clients and reduced income.

After checking with her that she was still doing her affirmations, I asked how many ships she was sending out. Well, it was the holidays, so not so many. Aha. I asked her how many clients she needed to have in order to make the income she wanted to make.

"One hundred," she answered immediately.

"So if you've been keeping track of how many ships you send out on your ships log, you know how many sales calls you have to make to get one customer," I said.

"Oh. I guess I haven't really exactly filled out a ships log...."

I smiled. "Okay, then, I suggest you start making calls and logging your results. But in any case, start making calls."

"How many calls do you think I should make?" she asked.

"As many as it takes until you have one hundred customers!" I replied. "There are nine million people in Los Angeles and you only need one hundred, so you aren't going to run out of opportunities."

She sighed and promised to get busy.

This is the road to success: being willing to do what it takes to get what you want. Send out your ships—your treasure awaits you. People are praying for you to show up, but they're just as afraid to pick up the phone as you are. Someone has to go first, and since you're the one reading this page, that someone is you.

Today's Affirmation: "I reach out to others because I am brave enough to be first."

331

The "Take it Away" Close

"I had a terrible thing happen to me yesterday. Opportunity knocked on my door and by the time I unhooked the chain, pushed back the bolt, turned the two locks, and shut off the burglar alarm—it was gone!"

—Robert Orben

My seminar series was going very well. For eight weeks, I taught the *Financial Stress Reduction® Workshop*, people were getting great results and now they often wanted to continue the process. So, I invented a course for graduates, called the *Money Mastery Network*.

I was delighted when I filled the class with just the first few phone calls. "Uh, oh," I thought, "I'd better call everyone else to let them know the class is sold out so they won't be disappointed if they can't come at the last minute."

What happened next was really funny. The typical telephone conversation went like this:

"Hi! This is Chellie. How have you been?"

"Great, Chellie! What's happening with you?"

"Classes are going wonderfully. Did you get my flyer on the new class I've started for graduates?"

Their tone of voice would change at this point: "Oh, yeah. Listen, I'm not sure about..."

"Oh, I'm really sorry," I would break in, "but I'm just calling to tell you that you can't come. The class is already sold out."

Immediately, now that they *can't* come, they *want* to come: "Oh, no! I was planning on rearranging my schedule so I could come. It sounds wonderful." "Well, I could put you on the waiting list," I would say. "Then if I have an opening, I could call you. Or I might start another group on a different night. What night would work for you?" I filled up another class that same week, solely because people didn't want to be left out. When I told them they couldn't have it, the people who had been unsure, suddenly became sure: they wanted it!

This is why you will see lots of advertising based on a limited time offer or discount that will expire. It is a classic sales principle—create a sense of urgency.

Where can you use this idea in your life? Instead of forcing spinach on the kids, or trying to wheedle them into it, why not make it special—and there's not enough to go around? If you need an audience for the charity show, instead of begging people to come, tell people there aren't enough seats for everyone, so they'd better make their reservations early. People don't want to be left out; they want to be in on things.

Today's Affirmation: "More and more people are happily buying my services today!"

332
Prizes

"Don't put people down, unless it's on your prayer list."

—Stan Michalski

Vince taught me about prizes you give to yourself. He was an executive search consultant for the recruiting firm where I first learned bookkeeping. A very cheerful, upbeat guy with a great smile, he always set goals for himself. And he told everyone in the office about them!

Every month, Vince would have a sales goal. "I'm going to make $20,000 in placement fees this month!" he would declare. "And when I do, I'm going to buy myself a brand new...." You can fill in the blank, he always had a new prize that he wanted, something *extra* to strive for beyond just getting enough money to pay the bills. Something *sexy* as they would say in Hollywood, something with sizzle, with pizzazz.

One month, in particular, I remember that his prize of choice was a Gucci wallet. He declared his goal and showed everyone in the office a picture of this beautiful leather article. He put a picture of it on the wall where he could see it as he made his sales calls.

The first month, he didn't meet his goal, but that just made him work harder, and he redoubled his efforts the next month. Finally, the day came when Vince let out a whoop and literally danced into the front office. "I did it!" he cried. "I made my goal and now I'm going out to buy my Gucci wallet!"

And he did. He left right then in the middle of the day, went down to the department store and bought that wallet. He was beaming as he brought it back to the office and showed it around to admiring oohs and aahs from all of us. "What a nut," some people thought. But I just thought he looked happy.

And, I noticed, he sure was making a lot of money. Picked out a prize for yourself lately?

Today's Affirmation: "Life has many treasures for me to enjoy and I deserve them!"

333

A Lesson in Negotiating

"Everything is worth what its purchaser will pay for it."

—Albert Einstein

Sarah Edwards, with her husband Paul, has written many books on creating the life you want to live, including *Working from Home*, *Secrets of the Self-Employed*, and *The Practical Dreamer's Handbook*. Years ago, she called me to say that a local department store was looking for speakers for a series of events and she had given them my name. I thanked her for alerting me to the opportunity, and when they contacted me, the department store representative asked what my fee was. When I said, "$1,500," she explained that it was a trial program and they didn't have a large budget. But it would be great publicity and exposure for me in my local area. Would I be willing to negotiate my fee? I agreed, and discounted my speaking fee to $1,000.

Sarah called me back a few hours later and said that they were asking her to speak as well, and wanted to know the amount of fee they were willing to pay. Speaking fees are very diverse, and it is often difficult for speakers to know what kind of budget the company has in mind. If you ask for too little, you don't look professional and if you ask for too much, you can price yourself out of the market. I was happy to share with her my negotiations with them, since she had gotten me the job.

She called me back two days later, laughing on the phone. She said she just had to tell me this story. Knowing that I had lowered my price for the department store event, and figuring they would try to negotiate with her as well, she decided to ask for more to begin with. So she told them her price was $2,000 and settled for $1,500. But that wasn't all. The next day, another friend who had also agreed to speak for them called Sarah to compare notes on pricing, too. That woman had said her price was $3,500 and settled for $2,500! It was a perfect lesson in negotiating.

Look again at your price. Who picked that number?

Today's Affirmation: "I am worthy of glorious abundance!"

334
Free Seminars

"The minute you settle for less than you deserve, you get even less than you settled for."

—Maureen Dowd

When I first started doing the *Financial Stress Reduction®* *Workshops*, I modeled my business on other seminar leaders and did what they did that seemed to work. Many of them put on free introductory seminars and asked everyone they met to come to them, and this was the first stage of the enrollment process. A percentage of the people at the free seminar would get excited and enroll on the spot for the fee seminar, and that's when they made money.

I followed this example for about six months. My experience was this:

1. Lots of people will say "Yes!" to a free seminar. Only about half of them will actually show up. (It's unfortunate, but many people don't consider it a commitment unless they've paid money for it.)
2. When you're listening, you're selling. When you're talking, you're not. And you're rarely listening at a free seminar because you're talking. You still have to follow up later.
3. It takes a lot of time and energy to plan, enroll, and teach a free seminar.
4. It takes no more time and energy to enroll someone for a paid workshop than it does to enroll them for an unpaid one.

After I figured this out, I decided to stop giving free seminars. It was too much work for too little reward. I looked for another way.

And found it: speak at the monthly meetings of local organizations. There are many of them, from Rotary and Kiwanis Clubs to Women in Management and National Association of Women Business Owners. They do all of the planning, enrolling, organizing, marketing, advertising, selling for you! Plus they give you a free meal. All you have to do is show up.

And "sing for your supper."

Today's Affirmation: "I love to speak and sing and people love to hear me!"

335

Smart Shopping

"The owner of a second-hand car knows how hard it is to drive a bargain."

—Unknown

There is a guiding principle to smart shopping that has nothing to do with searching out the lowest price. While looking for bargains is certainly a good idea—why pay a higher price if you can avoid it?—too many people will buy *anything* if it's a bargain. They end up with closets and houses full of mismatched objects they got a great deal on, but that they don't really like or look good in.

Debbie Leaper, president of StylePoints, maintains that a good wardrobe can actually help your bottom line by increasing your income. When someone meets you for the first time, 55 percent of what they think about you is determined before you even say a word. Their opinions begin the moment they first see you and are based on your appearance and your body language. In the first seven seconds of meeting you, your audience makes ten rapid-fire decisions about you, including what you do for a living, how trustworthy you are, how much money you make, and how successful you are.

Debbie lists these things to avoid when shopping for clothes:

1. Impulse purchases of fad clothing that will soon be out of style.
2. Unusual or trendy colors that coordinate with nothing else in your wardrobe.
3. Colors that look good on your friends—but not on you.
4. Fabric that is shiny, itchy, or cheap.
5. A "can't resist" markdown that will fit when you lose five pounds.

She then suggests that buying more expensive clothing may actually be cheaper for you in the long run. Debbie gives a formula for calculating the "cost per wearing": Take the cost of the item and divide that by the number of times you expect to wear it. For example, a pair of dark wool gabardine pants that costs $150 could be worn once a week for nine months, or thirty-six times annually. If they last three years, each of the 108 times it is worn costs $1.39. Not such a bad deal, when compared to $50 bargain trousers made from cheap synthetic fabric. This so-called "bargain" will be worn approximately six times before the fabric starts to lose its shape, develops a sheen, or starts to pull. The cost per wearing in this case is $8.33—not such a bargain, after all. Try buying fewer items, but more expensive, quality ones. The few pieces you have you will treasure, and you'll feel "like a million" wearing them.

Today's Affirmation: "I am gorgeous! I am beautiful! I am divine!"

336

Smart Spending During Holiday Season

"A man is a person who will pay two dollars for a one-dollar item he wants. A woman will pay one dollar for a two-dollar item she doesn't want."

—William Binger

People often moan about their budget-busting behavior during the holidays. They shop from their "See-it-want-it-get-it" mentality. As they bustle through the malls, shopping for the perfect gifts for their husband, children, boss, Aunt Sally, and Uncle Harry, they lose all control over spending. They forget their spending priorities, giving their credit cards a major workout. They remember—too late!—when the bills start arriving on January 2.

Who wants to spend the first three months of the New Year regretting—and paying for—their bad behavior at Christmas time?

Here is a plan for smart spending during the holidays:

1. Write special abundance affirmations, such as, "I find the perfect gifts at the perfect price for everyone on my list," and repeat them out loud each day. Make sure to say them on your way to the mall.
2. Do some of your shopping at crafts fairs, church, or neighborhood boutiques. You can often find beautiful handcrafted items that are very reasonably priced because people enjoy making them as their hobby, rather than as a profit-making venture.
3. Shop early—look for presents when a sale is on at your favorite store.
4. Remember that your closest friends and family might be on Low Budget—they might heave a huge sigh of relief and be very grateful to you if you suggest a spending limit for your gift exchange.
5. Give someone a gift certificate to their favorite store. On many occasions, I've given gift certificates to my nieces and nephews to toy stores, hobby stores, and bookstores. (Who can keep up with the clothing styles, musical tastes, and movie star crushes of teenagers anyway?) I've stayed on budget and the kids had fun shopping.
6. Give food. I've never seen anyone be disappointed by a gift of delicious homemade bread, or cake, or candy. Gloria Winter, down the street from my dad, made delicious candy every year, and I regarded it as one of my favorite things each Christmas.
7. Get involved in a charity. Spend a few hours serving food at the homeless shelter, collecting toys for needy children, singing Christmas carols at the hospital. A chiropractor I know has one day during the holiday season when the price of an office visit is canned food that will be donated to the needy. Nothing will do more for your sense of peace, joy, and goodwill.
8. Thank God for your abundance.

Today's Affirmation: "I give and receive all gifts with love and appreciation."

337

Endless Potential

"I am definitely going to take a course on time management... just as soon as I can work it into my schedule."

—Louis E. Boone

One of the benefits of our fast-moving, technology-enhanced lives today is the wide variety of choices we are offered. It's wonderful to have the freedom to choose where to live, our work , our friends. This is also a major cause of stress. Frantic to "live up to our potential," we run through our lives like we're trying to jump on a moving train. Then we're scared we've chosen the wrong train, so we keep jumping on and off, changing trains at every station.

In my hunger for experience and fear of missing out on something, I always seemed to take on too much. As a high school senior, I was Pep Chairman, Secretary of Girls League, Worthy Advisor of Rainbow Girls, and the lead in the school play all at the same time. During one period in college, I performed in a semi-professional dance company, choreographed and appeared in a campus main stage production, and rehearsed a reader's theater production from midnight until four A.M. because that was the only time I was available. Meanwhile I carried a full schedule of classes.

The over-commitment habit continued in my professional life as I juggled building a business with community service and holding board positions in organizations. It seemed I couldn't join an organization without being president or vice-president, often holding board positions in more than one organization at the same time.

But as I hurried through my life, with no time for reflection or thought, once in a while I would meet a business owner who was calm. They would smile serenely and say they used to be like me. But after building their businesses, working constant eighty-hour weeks, they finally sold their businesses and became consultants, working out of their homes. I didn't understand why on earth they would want to work at home.

Then one day my frantic life began to fall apart, like a plate-twirling circus performer who put too many plates in the air at once only to see them all crash in pieces on the ground. The crash seemed awful at the time, but in actuality what a gift it was! As I sorted through the wreckage, I picked back up only the valuable pieces. I cleared space in my life for reflection, meditation, friendships, a slower pace of work. I simplified my life to contain only those things I most cherished. I became a consultant working out of my home.

Now, I take time to be happy and to know that I am. And I have no intention of living up to my potential.

Today's Affirmation: "I now claim and celebrate the abundance of my life!"

338

Me or We?

"When one door closes another door opens; but we so often look so long and so regretfully upon the closed door, that we do not see the ones which open for us."

—Alexander Graham Bell

I have to solve the problem of me before I can solve the problem of we.

I learned this from trying it the other way around. In the whirlwind of my mad searching for the prince who would carry me off to happily ever after, I saw princes everywhere. I whirled and danced and obsessed and drank. When I got sober, my AA friends told me not to get into a relationship for a year. "Why not?" I cried. "That's an eternity!" They knew that the alcohol kept me hidden from myself, and that when I stopped drinking and started facing myself, I was going to change. In a year, I would be a different person, with different needs, different goals. I was an infant about to grow up, and I needed to wait until I was adult before I would have a chance at choosing a healthy relationship.

Well, that made sense to me. God knew, I hadn't chosen any healthy ones up until that point. I was willing to give it a rest and see what I would become....

I relaxed into myself and my work, and now I relish the freedom and power of being single. I am happy where I am. The whirlwind gave way to peace. Perhaps someone may join me on my path one day. But I know this truth: we must choose which road we want to travel before we can choose appropriate companions for the journey. Whatever road you choose, focus on its adventures, its benefits, the gifts it provides. Make the choice and be willing to pay the price. The difficulties are your teachers, designed to strengthen you in ways you have chosen to be strengthened.

If you are in a relationship, and especially if you have children, remember that not everyone is so fortunate. Bless the companions you travel with. Give thanks to God and then to them each and every day. Praise them, make deposits to their emotional bank accounts, acknowledge them, help them up when they stumble, nurse them when they are sick, and let them in to know you. Receive the sharing of their self with you with humility and grace. And love them. Whatever it takes to renew your love over and over, this you must do. Without the commitment to love, the dust of the road will clog your mouth and blind your eyes and boulders block your way. Notice that this road is, after all, paved with gold.

Life's treasures are more than numbers on a balance sheet, a bank statement, or a stock certificate. Your storehouse is also filled with the sweet drooly kiss of a one-year-old, laughter shared with a friend, and the warmth of a hand that sneaks into yours.

Today's Affirmation: "I give and receive love, joy, and laughter everywhere I am."

339
Dating

"Smooth seas do not make skillful sailors."

—African proverb

My friend, Shelley, and I were talking this morning about dating. She had just been out on a date, and was recapping for me what had transpired. Although she had no interest in pursuing this particular relationship, she said it had served its purpose.

"What purpose is that?" I asked.

"Well," she said, "I want to be more social, spontaneous, comfortable talking with men. Usually I'm uncomfortable."

"I know what you mean," I replied, "I get uncomfortable too."

She said, "Well, at least you go out—you joined that dating service."

"I certainly don't use it much now," I rejoined.

"Why?" asked Shelley.

"I don't like the energy when someone really likes me and I don't feel the same way." I pondered a moment, then said, "And I don't like the other energy either—where I like them and they don't feel the same way." I sighed. "I guess the only energy I like is when I love them and they love me back."

"But the price of getting that is you have to risk the other!" Shelley exclaimed.

"Yeah. It's frog kissing—and sometimes I'm the frog!"

We laughed ruefully over the age-old conundrum. It struck me then how this dilemma that keeps people from dating, also keeps people from making sales calls, looking for a new job, or asking for a raise. We feel tense and uncomfortable both when people don't respond well to us, and when we don't respond well to them. We like it when our energy is in sync: harmonious, receptive, loving, thoughtful, generous, and kind.

We need courage to confront the potential negative feelings. Without risking the down side, there can't be any up side. And I realize as I type this that I can't do anything about anyone else's energy—only my own. If I take care to center myself, to come from a loving place with my fellow beings, perhaps our interactions will be more comfortable.

The more I risk, the more love—and money—I allow into my life.

Take a risk. Go somewhere you can meet people. Smile at a stranger. Go on a date.

Today's Affirmation: "The world awaits in friendly fashion, happy to grant my desires today!"

340
Hidden Agendas

"Two monologues do not equal a dialogue."

—Nick Harrison

Tom and Linda are engaged to be married. Tom is nearly fifty, divorced with no children. He was married once before to a very wealthy woman, didn't have to work, and so has a rather sporadic work history.

Linda is from a wealthy family, very taken with Tom's charm and good looks. She has always resisted taking money from her family and works full time at a lucrative profession. Her goal when they get married is to quit her job, raise three children, and live on Tom's salary.

Tom's goal is to quit his job and live on his wife's money.

Neither of them has declared these intentions to the other. Their agendas are hidden. They don't know that their dreams are at cross-purposes.

Can this marriage be saved?

Can yours? Get all your agendas into the open where they can see the light of day and you can see the inside of your spouse's mind. Tell each other the truth and then make plans for each of you to get your needs met. Negotiate and compromise. It's possible if you are honest with each other. Impossible if you are not.

Today's Affirmation: "I speak the truth and declare my dreams so that others can help them come true!"

341
Boundaries

"If you don't concentrate on counting the money, people soon realize that money is not the focus of your consciousness, so they give you everything other than money: kudos, acclaim, praise, etc., etc. And sooner or later you'll be in trouble."

—Stuart Wilde

What are you working for, in lieu of the money? Perhaps you really need acknowledgment, so you take a job that pays less than you desire because the boss is friendly, compliments you, and makes lavish promises of future rewards. Perhaps you like to feel needed, so you give away your expertise for free to everyone who calls on the phone with a question. Or maybe you keep working with that difficult client because you're afraid to confront him with the fact that he complains too much, demands too much, and doesn't pay enough for your time.

That was my problem with George. He started up a business with several partners. He called me immediately, wanting to hire my bookkeeping service. But there was a hitch. They were a start-up company and didn't have a lot of money. Could I please, please give him rock-bottom rates, and they'd pay me handsomely later when they became successful. I was flattered. I was wanted. I said, "Sure!"

What followed was about seven months of excruciating financial and emotional disaster. The reports we gave him were never exactly what he wanted, he always needed additional work done—for no additional charge, of course—and he called every month to complain that our bills were too high. Compliments disappeared. But that was his fatal mistake. Had he kept on giving me wonderful praise, I probably would have done his bookkeeping forever.

One afternoon, he was in my office complaining about something and shook his finger in my face. That did it. Something in me snapped and I said, "Just a minute! You're talking to me like I *have* to work for you—and I don't. I have clients for two reasons: Number one: I make a lot of money; and Number two: I have a lot of fun. Now, I'm not making any money on you and you are not being fun. Something is going to have to change or we're not working together any more!"

I have never seen a more surprised expression on someone's face as I saw on George's that day. He had the grace to laugh, and he recovered his sense of fun. But he had not totally understood my declaration of my boundaries. Two days later, he called to complain about my latest bill. "That does it!" I declared into the phone. "Either get a check into my office for the full amount of the bill or come pick up your stuff!"

A check arrived a few hours later. I raised his rates the next month and he paid promptly without complaint. And he called regularly just to compliment us on the great job we were doing!

Do you want compliments or money? They are not mutually exclusive. Why not set it up so you get *both*?

Today's Affirmation: "I am extravagantly praised and paid for everything I do!"

342
The Color Purple

"Speak when you are angry and you will make the best speech you will ever regret."

—Ambrose Bierce

We rub up against each other the wrong ways sometimes. Like trying to force a jigsaw puzzle piece into the wrong slot, we try to make others fit into our picture. We listen but do not hear, because our understanding is blocked by the stone walls of our own perception.

Linda, my friend, fellow writer, and proposal coach, called today to offer help with my book proposal. I had gotten a very positive response from a publisher and was waiting to hear whether they were going to make an offer to buy it. Linda thought that we could spend additional time and energy polishing the proposal and the combination of our positive focus and work would help the project along. I thought she was telling me the proposal wasn't good enough yet.

"The proposal is fine just as it is!" I exclaimed. "It doesn't need to be redone a fourth time! One of these publishers is going to buy it soon and I don't have to polish it again!" Linda quickly backpedaled, tried to explain; I wasn't buying it. Here was Linda, trying to help, and I bit her nose off. Playing the waiting game while trying to keep my thoughts positive was stretching my fragile nerves tauter than I realized. St. Chellie would never have responded this way.

We hung up the phone quickly, but both of us sat with the negative energy and fought mental battles. She wrote me a letter, I wrote this page; I called her back. We explained our intentions, our feelings, our love, mutual admiration, and respect. Our friendship held, peace and equanimity restored.

Sometimes our words belie our intentions. "Do unto others as you would have them do unto you," doesn't always work. What they want done isn't always the same as what we want done. As an actress, I watched directors at work—some yelled at all the actors; some coddled all the actors. But the best directors yelled at the ones that needed yelling at, coddled the ones that needed more confidence, left alone the ones who needed to work things out alone. Linda is a fabulous writer, and in her meticulous attention to detail produces work much closer to perfection than I. I rush to completion, let the details fall where they may, and get done faster. They are different styles of work and behavior, and we each have much to gain from the other.

When her blue meets my red, a clash may occur, but if we keep talking, reaching for understanding with compassion and love, we create purple.

Today's Affirmation: "I enrich my life with wonderful friendships in rainbow colors."

343

Take Your Stand

"Honest criticism is hard to take, especially from a relative, a friend, an acquaintance, or a stranger."

—Franklin P. Jones

At lunch with a group of friends, we were dreaming about the big time. We wanted to fill more classrooms, write bestsellers, and help more people with our heartfelt work. We dreamed of appearing on *Oprah, Rosie, Sally, Montel, Charlie, Today, Good Morning America, Good Night Whatever.* Of sharing the lessons we had learned through difficult, personal traumas so that others might take a shorter road to success and happiness. And of course, we hoped to be listened to, acknowledged, photographed, loved. We smiled at the thought of how our lives would be perked up, new, improved, bigger, better, richer, more.

Then, because we are a thoughtful, balanced group, we talked about the down side of the big picture, of even fifteen minutes of fame. The long hours, the responsibilities, life on the road in a series of hotels, airports, endless smiling, and talking with countless strangers. And criticism—in print! I thought of all the terrible reviews I had read in the papers and how they must have hurt the people they criticized. As my friend Ann Hancock says, they're called critics, not praisers. I saw the sacrifice that is involved in going wide with your dream.

"Oh, I don't like that part at all," I gulped. "Can't I just have the good stuff?"

That's when Rhonda Britten, author of *Fearless Living: Live Without Excuses and Love Without Regret*, who had been listening to the discussion, nailed me. "You have to be willing to pay the price," she said, "or your fear of it will stop you from getting it. To take a stand in the world, you have to be willing to be loved that much—and hated that much."

So I take the risk; I make my stand. Maybe my message will reach thousands—or maybe only a few. Armed with the power to say no, if I remember to stay in the balance of what I have written in these pages, I will retain control over my life. I will march to the drummer I hear, with faith that there will be others who hear it, too.

Stand for what you believe. Do your work in the world, as wide as your purpose will allow. Your People will find you. There will be praisers who love you, and you may learn something from the critics. Faith, courage, and your mission will sustain you. Everything else will fall away.

Success is not a place you get to—it's a state you live in. If you enjoy the process, instead of being attached to the result, you will be a success every day of your life.

Today's Affirmation: "I enjoy my process and live in the state of success every day!"

344

Own a Nightclub

"I wanted so badly to study ballet. But it was really all about wearing the tutu."

—Elle MacPherson

"I want to own a nightclub!" crowed Laura. Middle-aged and with a sunny personality, Laura lit up every room she walked into with her positive energy. She had a million-watt smile and a can-do attitude, and I knew she could do anything she wanted to do.

"What interests you about owning a nightclub?" I asked. Laura was currently working as a massage therapist, and nightclub ownership looked like a very different career step.

"I just love to dance!" she replied. "I go dancing just about every night. I love the music and the people I meet and everything about it."

"Have you ever worked in a nightclub?" I pursued.

"No."

Immediately, I went in to "Goal Getting" mode: "I recommend that you get a job in a nightclub so you can learn what it takes to run one successfully. You need to learn about the financing, marketing, promotion, food and beverage, hiring acts or DJs, etc. You can take some classes at the local community college, too. Ask the owner of the nightclubs you go to if they will give you some advice...."

There were thunderclouds racing across Laura's face. I saw the "Yeah, but" before it issued from her mouth. Oh, resistance, you drag your feet across all our lives....

"I don't want to get a job in a nightclub," Laura protested. "I just want to own it, and go there and have fun!"

"Well, if you don't learn how to run it, you probably won't own it for long!" I exclaimed.

Laura stopped and looked at me pityingly. "Chellie," she said, "I don't really want to own a nightclub. I just want to have the *fantasy* of owning a nightclub."

We stared at each other for a moment...then we cracked up laughing. "Okay!" I said. "The *Fantasy Island* nightclub is yours!"

Fantasies add a lot of pleasure to our lives. They're dream diversions, escapes from everyday realities, and playgrounds for our minds. Enjoy them, and let others enjoy them, too. We don't have to take action on all of them. Let someone else do the ownership thing. Go dancing. In a tutu. Dream on.

Today's Affirmation: "I am dancing in the sunlight and moonlight of my life!"

345

Channel KGOD

"Two hundred seventy-eight channels and there's nothing on. Time to turn on the God channel."

—Lisa Morrice

It's hard for any one of those two hundred seventy-eight channels to hold my attention for long. I zip by them with my trusty remote, a kaleidoscope of whirling colors and images: Arctic explorers in a blinding snowstorm, "snow" on a channel that doesn't come through, thoroughfares in downtown London, a Dove soap commercial (I watch to see their current trend; maybe I could do another commercial for them), sitcom, sitcom, cartoon, no, no, zip, zip, zip.

I stop at James Lipton interviewing Neil Simon on *Inside the Actors Studio*. I've seen it but I watch it again, because Neil makes me laugh. Bravo, *Bravo*. Commercial, zip, a gorgeous hunk throws another gorgeous hunk to the wrestling mat—ouch!—zip, a panting girl suddenly screams, a knife, blood—ick—zip! Zen music: I relax. The men and women on the Korean channel are gorgeous in their ancient regalia, but I don't speak Korean and it's subtitled in another oriental language. Zip.

A couple of religious channels, but the big hair is pink and the mascara's running, and I don't think this is the God channel I'm looking for. Zip. Roy Dupuis, playing Michael on *La Femme Nikita*. Thud. Now there's a God. I tape this to drool over later.

VH1 has the "whatever happened to" stories and they're fun but I zip by after I find out David Cassidy is happy now. I'm glad. I met his mom once, Shirley Jones. Lisa Morrice and I had a singing gig at The Oaks spa in Ojai and I was singing my solo, *Desperado*, at dinner just as Shirley walked in with her husband, Marty Ingles. Perfect. The best soprano in the world walks in while I'm singing my toughest song...she was very gracious and complimented both of us. (I'm eternally grateful for that kindness, Shirley.)

Out of the depth of my reminiscent dream, a sudden thought freezes the remote in my hand.

I've had adventures. Why am I watching other people on television talk about their adventures? I need to go out and have more adventures of my own! And if I think I ever want to be on television myself, I'd better write about my adventures. Write. I can't watch one more person, real or fictional, talk about the life I want to be leading. I need to lead it.

Channel KGOD has broken through. "This is the day that the Lord hath made. Let us rejoice and be glad in it." I smile. I get up. I go. I write. Who knows? If I play my cards right, I may get to meet Roy Dupuis.

Today's Affirmation: "I rejoice and am glad in the adventures of my day today!"

346
Bon Jovi

"Age is something that doesn't matter. Unless you are a cheese."

—Billie Burke

Why does the music business target only teenagers and twentysomethings? As a middle-aged female, I'm a member of what seems to be the "despised demographic"—the one nobody cares about. Although youth and beauty are lovely qualities, they don't hold a candle to the ones developed later in life: self-esteem, wisdom, success, depth, and happiness. We still have passion and excitement, and money, too! The Screen Actors Guild reported that Americans over the age of fifty own 77 percent of all financial assets, account for 40 percent of total consumer demand, and control a net worth of nearly $7 trillion. Don't you think someone in the music business ought to sit up and take notice of that?

Because I became a Bon Jovi fan at age fifty-two. It took me by surprise. I happened across them on a segment of *Behind the Music* on VH1 and was struck by the band's passion and charisma. Joy of life and living throbbed through their music. I watched the entire show, and before long, I was hooked.

The next day, I bought their greatest hits album and sang along with it for the rest of the week. Then I bought all their other albums and a video and signed up for their fan club.

I admit I struggled with myself at first. We don't break out of boxes without interior battles. I'm a grown woman; I own my own business. I'm not a young chicky to be seduced by a heavy metal band. I didn't think I fit the hard-rock profile at all. I loved Country, Bach, Broadway, and the Beatles. But I broke out of my music box and found a passion for a hard rock band.

Am I having a mid-life crisis? Have I lost some part of my sanity? Well, maybe I have. But if so, then I recommend it. Lose your sanity; your self-descriptions that keep you locked in your current self, making each day a replay of the last. Life is a banquet; it's rich spread lies before you in glorious diversity. You may like fried chicken, but if you don't keep exploring, you may never discover the chicken curry, chicken cacciatore, or Chicken Kiev. White rice is wonderful, but if you stop there, you miss the shrimp fried rice, the rice pilaf, the curried rice, the basmati rice. There's a world of delightful tastes beyond what you know. Don't let anyone tell you you're too old to enjoy it.

Break out of your music box today. Join another party; feast at another banquet. Eat up life. Who cares if it's young, or new, or "just not you"? Your capacity for joyful experience is immense, but you have to take it out of the box and use it.

Today's Affirmation: "I'm glad to be alive and enjoying the rich music of life!"

347
Little Wins

"Celebrate what you want to see more of."

—Thomas J. Peters

My mother often got nervous if I got excited about something. I remember once having met a nice young man and hoping that he would call. He did. After I hung up the phone, I danced into the living room and crowed, "Steven asked me out—we have a date for tomorrow night! I'm so happy!" Mother visibly cringed and said, "Now, honey, don't get your hopes up."

Ouch! This really put a damper on my mood. She was afraid for me to expect or want anything for fear it might not turn out the way I wanted and then I'd be disappointed. But I was just happy over the little win—I wanted him to call and he did. I wanted him to ask me out and he did. I wanted to celebrate the wins I got—I didn't know what was going to happen on the date. Maybe it would be a win and maybe it wouldn't. That took away nothing from the win today.

Some people never want to get excited so that they won't get depressed if it doesn't work out. But the trap they set up for themselves is that they talk themselves out of feeling anything other than caution. When we talk ourselves out of emotion and circumvent our feelings, it becomes a habit that deadens us to the world and each other. I think that's why we revere actors so much—they show so much real emotion. Most people don't. They keep a "stiff upper lip" and die inside. Once I said enthusiastically to a man, "This is stupendous!" He looked at me quizzically and said, "I never use words like stupendous. Nothing seems to rate that much excitement to me." How sad! Someone in his past must have told him that it wasn't okay to get excited.

Pick some exciting words and use them! It's fabulous, terrific, stupendous, extraordinary, superior, amazing, astounding! Write in exclamation points! Celebrate your little wins and enjoy them. You earned it! And your happiness will infect everyone around you, too.

Today's Affirmation: "I celebrate all my stupendous wins every day!"

348

My Favorite Enrollment

"You have to take it as it happens, but you should try to make it happen the way you want to take it."

—German proverb

"My friend, Judy, told me I had to take your workshop. When is your next one?" said the female voice on the phone. I was so happy to get the call—a ship coming in to harbor that I didn't send out!—that I made a classic mistake: I answered her question.

"The next eight-week session begins on Wednesday from 3:00 to 5:00 in the afternoon." I replied.

"Oh, I can't come in the afternoon!" she exclaimed, "I work during the day. Where are you located?"

"I'm in Pacific Palisades."

"Oh, no. I'm in Pasadena, that's much too far away for me. How much does the seminar cost?"

"One thousand dollars," I answered.

"Oh, no! There's no way I can afford that!"

Do you see the problem? This woman called to enroll in my seminar and proceeded to ask questions about the features of the seminar (when is it, where is it, etc.) instead of the benefits of the seminar (how will it improve my life?). I then proceeded to answer her questions, instead of telling her what she really wanted to know. It is a classic mistake salespeople often make. I gave control to the prospect, I talked instead of listened, I addressed the wrong issue. Finally, having realized my error, I turned the conversation around:

"I understand," I said sympathetically. "But let me ask you a question. If the seminar was at a time you could come, a place that was convenient, and a price you could afford—what would you want to get out of it?"

"Well, I don't know exactly, but I have a lot of stress around money in my life...."

With one question, I had taken back control of the conversation. I asked more questions: What do you see as your biggest problem with money? How long have you had this problem? What would you most like to change about the money in your life? And so on. After she answered these questions, and told me her vision of success, I saw that she would benefit from taking my course. Then I shared with her the success stories of people just like herself who had benefited from the workshop in the specific ways she wanted to benefit.

By the end of the conversation, she got so excited about the possibilities, she exclaimed, "Okay, I'm in! Tell me how to get there." She voluntarily threw out all her objections and enrolled in the class, because she wanted the benefits.

What do people come to you for? How do they benefit? That's what you have to give—and what you have to sell.

Today's Affirmation: "People love to buy from me!"

349
For Your Children

"Always be nice to your children because they are the ones who will choose your rest home."

—Phyllis Diller

"I have no trouble selling someone else's products or services, I just have trouble selling my own!" Joan despaired. A chorus of agreement rumbled through the class.

"I used to be much more motivated when I had children," she went on. "I knew I had to make a living to support them. I was willing to do whatever it took to make that happen. But now the kids are grown, I have enough money to get by, but I want more. But I just can't seem to make the calls and do the work."

An idea came to me: "I want you to get four pictures of yourself," I said. "One picture of you as a baby, one from third grade, one from high school, and one from college. Put these pictures on the wall above your desk: These are the children you're working for now. They all still exist in you and deserve your best efforts. Nurture them, care for them, and love them. Work to buy them things to enjoy, work to make them happy. They deserve 'above and beyond money,' not just 'getting by money.' And you deserve it, too!"

I've met many women who work easily "on behalf of the children." It makes them feel less selfish. Usually these same people can promote and sell someone else's products or services much better than their own. To promote their own feels too much like bragging. It's the "good girl" syndrome: don't brag, don't be forward, be nurturing, be giving, be nice. If this was your upbringing, you're going to have to work to get over it. Or use it: it's not bragging if your service can really help the other person—it's your *duty to them* to convince them to buy the service that will make their life better. It's perfectly okay if you benefit, too, and make a profit! If you don't make a profit, you'll be out of business, and then you can't help anyone any more.

See how this works? It's called "re-framing" in psychology circles. Give yourself good, positive reasons to be successful, and help people at the same time. You don't have to choose. You can do both.

Today's Affirmation: "My wonderful contributions flow into the Universe and great wealth flows back to me."

350
Doubts

"We are each the parents of our dreams, so we must support them as best we can until they can support themselves."

—Paul and Sarah Edwards

Two of my favorite singers are Emmylou Harris and Linda Ronstadt, so I eagerly bought their *Western Wall: The Tucson Sessions* CD as soon as it was available, and enjoyed it immensely.

Robert Hilburn interviewed them for the *Los Angeles Times*. One of the things that most impressed him was how much they talked about other artists they admired. Generous in praise of each other, Emmylou spoke of having seen Linda for the first time in the late sixties. Harris was living in New York then and trying to get started in her music career. She said, "I thought I was pretty good. But when I heard Linda do this a cappella thing, I thought that no voice could be that beautiful."

Hilburn asked if that intimidated her, and I was struck by her reply: "Absolutely. I knew I could never sing like that. It really shook my confidence. So for a while, I thought I'd concentrate on writing songs. Then I went to the Philadelphia Folk Festival, and I heard Joni Mitchell and Bonnie Raitt. I thought, 'How can I compete as a songwriter?' because Joni was singing my heart and my soul. Then Bonnie got up there, playing slide guitar and singing great. At that point, I sort of gave up pursuing a career for a short period of time." I couldn't believe what I was reading. Emmylou Harris, with one of the most beautiful, angelic voices I've ever heard, felt intimidated by the competition?

Then Linda was asked the same question about the first time she heard Emmylou and she answered, "It was really a crisis for me. I felt she was doing (country rock) much better than I was. She was so much farther down the road. It was a time where I had to say I can either let this make me feel really terrible and I won't get to enjoy the music or I could accept it as really great and enjoy it. And that's the choice I made. And it was a great lesson, because music isn't a horse race and you can't have it be a competition....There's room for us all, and we all have our own stories."

This interview was amazing to me. Here they were, two wonderful, brilliantly talented, successful musicians—and they were talking about their feelings of inadequacy! I had forgotten that incredible people have doubts, too. Sometimes I think I'm the only one who thinks like that. Who do I think I am to be writing a book? I'm not as funny as Annie Lamott, I'm not a financial planner like Suze Orman, I'm not as good at sales as Zig Ziglar....Thanks, Linda, for reminding me: there's room for us all, and we all have our own stories. I'll be the best me I know how.

Today's Affirmation: "I am loved and acknowledged for my unique and wonderful talents!"

351
Ownership

"Few things are necessary to make the wise man happy while no amount of material wealth would satisfy a fool."

—Og Mandino

Ownership is a myth. As we travel through this brief life, we have temporary possession of some things, that's all. In a larger sense, we have joint ownership of many things: the air we breathe, sunshine and moon-glow, a meadowlark's song, the laughter of children playing in a park. Since we leave everything behind when we die, what's all the fuss about ownership?

What matters is usage and enjoyment. A Vincent Van Gogh painting was once auctioned for about ninety million dollars. I wonder how much time the person who owns it spends sitting in front of it and looking at it? I'll bet it's not that much. If a possession is just locked away and not looked at, admired, and enjoyed on a regular basis, ownership is just a number on a piece of paper. Some people have many numbers on many pieces of paper, but no enjoyment.

Years ago, I visited the Van Gogh museum in Amsterdam. It was fabulous. It is so clear, when you stand in front of one of these masterpieces, why it's a masterpiece. Energy and power radiate from the brushstrokes and the colors shock you with emotion. I enjoyed that experience immensely, and I carry the memory of it with me. I own the experience. That's as much ownership of a Van Gogh painting that I need.

We can make ourselves unnecessarily unhappy because we lack ownership of things we desire. We can lust after the new dress in the store window and cry and moan that we "can't afford" to buy it. Or we can treat shopping like a sightseeing trip where we can see, admire and enjoy the beauty of wonderful creations, without having to take them home and put them out of sight in our closets. The enjoyment of an experience is a pleasure we can treasure.

Erik Dreyer-Goldman, a computer whiz in Los Angeles, devised a creative solution to the ownership dilemma. He was driving along the Pacific Coast Highway one day with his wife, when she said, "I'd like you to buy me a Porsche convertible to drive along the beach." He had already looked into the expenses involved in Porsche ownership, and they totaled a larger percentage of his budget than he wanted to commit to an automobile. So he said, "Why don't we just rent a Porsche whenever you want to go driving on the beach? Then we are paying for what we want when we want it, and not paying for it when it's just sitting in the garage." She laughingly agreed that was a good plan. So you might see them breezing down the road, laughing and enjoying the sun in their favorite automobile in a very cost-effective outing!

What do you use and enjoy that you don't have to own?

Today's Affirmation: "I appreciate and enjoy all the beautiful treasures of my abundant life!"

352

Storage Lockers

"Teach thrift to all with whom you come in contact; you never know when you may need their savings to finance one of your ventures."

—Don Marquis

One Saturday, I went to a local bookstore for "The Largest Writing Workshop in the World," which hosted local authors to speak on the craft of writing. As I had just signed the contract for my first book, I had several agendas: 1) I wanted to participate and learn something new about the craft of writing; 2) I wanted to find out how events like this were done; and 3) I wanted to introduce myself to the store manager, let him know of my upcoming publication, and see if I could arrange to speak and do a book signing at his store (sending out ships early!).

The first speaker was author Billy Mernit, who has written *Writing the Romantic Comedy*. Charming and upbeat, he introduced himself, telling us that he was an expatriate New Yorker. "Once a New Yorker, always a New Yorker!" he exclaimed laughingly. His eyes twinkled as he confessed that he still had a storage locker in New York filled with couches, lamps, tables, chairs and other furniture, along with "forty to forty-five boxes." He shook his head as he considered the quirk of character that kept him paying $100 per month for this piece of home in New York.

My ears picked up at this news. "How many years have you had this locker?" I asked.

"Ten!" several members of the audience shouted, as Billy now tried to claim only "nine." Everyone laughed as Billy sheepishly acknowledged the total expense he had accrued in order to keep his toehold in New York: $12,000.

To a New Yorker in Los Angeles, this expense to remain a New Yorker is probably worth it. But the rest of you might take a look at where your past is dragging money away from your future and let go.

Billy led us through some thoughtful writing exercises, then told us how he had created his latest book, *That's How Much I Love You*, with his wife of two years, artist Claudia Nizza from Italy. They had met on a moonlight hike in Hollywood and love blossomed quickly. They dated for several weeks before her vacation was over and she had to fly back to Rome. He bought her a ticket back to Los Angeles, but she couldn't return for several months, so they talked on the phone often. He would ask, "Have I told you how much I love you?" Claudia would say, "No," and he would make up little stories to explain his deepening love for her. And one time he called and she said, "Okay, we do a book." They married on a hilltop in Malibu and their book is beautiful.

Everyone laughed when I asked if she had a storage locker in Italy. "No," he replied. "But she has a studio there!"

Today's Affirmation: "I am rich in life and love and all the world is my home!"

353

Storage Lockers—The Sequel

"Isn't it frightening how soon later comes, after you buy now?"

—Earl Wilson

After the "The World's Largest Writing Workshop" at the Barnes and Noble bookstore, I wrote to Billy Mernit, thanking him for his time, his expertise, and his relaxed and friendly teaching style. I enclosed a copy of the "Storage Lockers" page and asked if he would allow me to print it and use his name. I also mentioned that if he had any changes he would like to suggest, I would be happy to make them.

I was delighted to receive his charming response, in which he said he was flattered and happy to receive my story and letter. However, he let me know that "the storage space only cost $60.00 when I first rented it—and has gone up in price at $5.00 increments every year since—so the sum total of my 'toehold debt' is actually a bit less (you do the math) than $12,000." He went on to say, "If you can find a succinct way of stating that (i.e., in a sentence that doesn't distract from your narrative flow and brevity), I'll feel a little less silly—and your point will still be made. If you feel it messes up your story, on the other hand, you know what they say: print the legend."

I thoroughly enjoyed his letter, and his term "toehold debt," which will now become a part of my vocabulary.

As requested, I did the math, so the actual "toehold debt" Billy has on his storage locker is, as of this writing, only $9,900 instead of $12,000, so that correction is here noted. However, I noticed that since the price will escalate $5 per month next year and the year after that, etc., it will be $12,600 by 2002. By 2010, barring any increases, the total cumulative expense for the storage locker for twenty years will be $22,680. But what if a similar amount of money were saved instead of spent? To use round figures, if $100 per month were invested at 8 percent rate of return for twenty years, it would result in a total of $56,991.

The Billy Mernit lessons are:

1. Write thank you letters—they're fun to give and fun to receive.
2. Do your research—people care that you get your facts straight.
3. "Toehold debt" accumulates over time—keep track of how much you are willing to pay.

Today's Affirmation: "Whatever I pay for gives me a great payoff."

354

Joe To Go Coffee

"The only person who never makes a mistake is the one who never does anything."

—Theodore Roosevelt

My friend, Erik, gave me a pound of Joe To Go Coffee. It was a delicious blend called "Chocolate Hazelnut." I thoroughly enjoyed it, and when it was gone, I wanted more. So I called Erik to find out where to get some, and he offered to order a five-pound bag for me. Delighted, I said, "Great!" and waited for the delivery of my yummy coffee.

And waited.

And waited.

No coffee.

Finally, I called Erik and asked what had happened. He assured me that he had ordered the coffee and the company had said they shipped it. "I'll call them today and find out what happened," he said.

He called back a few minutes later and said that somehow my coffee got shipped to Boston. He apologized for the mistake and said I should get my coffee in a couple of days. Sure enough, two days later, I got my coffee and considered the matter settled.

Five days later, I received another package from Joe To Go Coffee—two five pound bags, one of Vanilla Nut and the other of Chocolate Amaretto. "Oops!" I thought. "Another mistake. I didn't order this. These people are going to have to get their act together."

I called Erik and reported this new error. Imagine my pleasure and surprise when he told me that the company had sent these ten pounds as a gift to apologize for their late shipment to me of my original order! They could have blamed the shipping company, they could have blamed a "clerical error" or "computer glitch," they could have said nothing and done nothing. Instead, they sent me a present.

I am loving my coffees. I serve it to all my clients and guests. And I tell them all this story. I am giving Joe To Go Coffee oodles of free publicity, great testimonials, new customers, and now they're in this book. They not only have a high quality product, but they have high quality care for their customers: they cared enough about me to send me a present to apologize for a mistake. I was delighted and impressed. For ten pounds of coffee, they got a customer for life. Send out a little ship, in comes a big ship.

So what do you do when you make a mistake?

Today's Affirmation: "I blaze trails of happiness everywhere I go!"

355

A Fire in Malibu

"All that is gold does not glitter; not all those who wander are lost."

—J.R.R. Tolkien

Be careful whom you judge. Sometimes the person who looks like a shark and swims like a shark isn't a shark.

I remember hearing Tom's story, right after a big firestorm had raced through Malibu canyon. He told me how scared he and his neighbors were the night that the fire approached their homes. They waited breathlessly by their radios and television sets, waiting for news, waiting to hear if the wind had changed direction, was coming their way, if they'd have to evacuate. They leaned on each other for help and support.

No one paid any attention to the old man at the end of the block. He was a gruff old codger, not very friendly, always complaining about too many cars being parked in front of his house. By general consensus, they left him alone.

Finally, the word came; they had to get out of the canyon. They had to leave their homes to the caprice of the winds and the fire. Frantically, they searched through the piles of their belongings, deciding which treasures to take with them as they made their escape. As the first flames leapt over the ridge above their homes, they knew that time had run out. Now they had to run. They hugged each other, said prayers and goodbyes, and fled.

The next morning, the fire had run its course; the firemen had once again performed their miracles and drowned the flames. Tom and his friends steeled themselves to drive to their homes. Would they find them still standing? Or would only ashes greet their eyes? Anxiously, breathlessly, they drove up the canyon. All around them were blackened tree stumps and brick chimneys—all that remained of the beautiful houses that once stood there. Their hearts beat heavily and their mood was somber as they reached their street and rounded the corner.

What a glorious sight met their eyes! Although every house around them had been destroyed, all of the five houses on Tom's street were still standing! And in front of them all stood the gruff old codger, with a garden hose. He had stayed behind and watered down all of their homes, all through the night. He had saved every one.

Is there anyone on your street you have written off as an "old gruff codger?" Take another look.

Today's Affirmation: "I appreciate the goodness, seen and unseen, in everyone around me."

356

Terry the Terror Temp

"There may be a hundred things you know about a person—all of them bad. But there may be just one thing you don't know, which if you did know, would completely change your opinion."

—A Nigerian Christian

When I was the bookkeeper at an employment agency, one of my duties was to prepare the weekly payroll for all the temporary employees the company had sent out on assignments. This was a simple task and for the most part enjoyable, as I got the pleasure of handing out paychecks to happy recipients each week. It was fun to give people money!

But one temp, Terry, was an absolute terror to work with. She always seemed rude and demanding to me. She would show up before the checks were written and say she was in a hurry and had to have her check right then. I felt used and abused and dreaded seeing her. Every time I saw her, my heart sank, and I got tense and irritable, expecting problems. Since I was expecting them, she made sure to deliver.

One Thursday, there she was again.

"Where's my check?" she demanded as she walked through the door.

"I haven't gotten to it yet," I replied huffily.

"I need it now because I have to get to work." Steely-eyed, Terry plopped herself down on the chair in my office.

"All right, all right!" I exclaimed angrily and flounced to my desk to write the check.

She took it without a thank you and left. I marched into Holly's office to complain and moan about what a nasty piece of work Terry was.

Holly put me straight in short order. She listened to me complain and then asked, "Do you know Terry's story?"

"No," I grumped, not caring very much either.

"Terry is working three jobs," Holly said. "Her father left her mother with five kids years ago. Last year, her mother died, and all of the kids were separated and packed off to foster homes. Terry is saving every penny she earns so that she can she can provide a home and get her brothers and sisters back together with her as a family once more."

"Oh." I felt very small and very ashamed. I thanked Holly for telling me and slunk back to my office, resolved to be a kinder, friendlier person—not only to Terry, but to all the people whose stories I didn't know, whose pain I didn't comprehend.

Be kind, for everyone you meet is fighting a battle.

Today's Affirmation: "I am gentle, kind, and loving to all I meet today."

357

Superman

"There is only one of you in the world, just one. And if that is not fulfilled, then something has been lost."

—Martha Graham

Last night in my class, we were playing "The Glad Game" and listing all of the things we are grateful for. We talked about maintaining an attitude of gratitude and I said that one of the things that always gets me back to center, being appreciative of what I have instead of what I don't have, is to think about Christopher Reeve. There was a pause as I contemplated his tragic accident, then I mentioned how awful I thought life would be if I was paralyzed. Jennifer, a young saleswoman, looked at me in surprise, then laughed. She said that wasn't what she thought I meant. She thought I liked to think about "cute boys!"

This morning I sit with a smile on my face, thinking how far Christopher Reeve had come in our consciousness past the terrible break of his body. In the agonizing days after his accident, he could have given in to death, but his loving wife, Dana, said, "You're still you!" That gave him the courage to fight for life. He didn't just fight for himself, but became a spokesman for all those with spinal injuries, and he continued to work, proving that he was still an artist with talents to share with the world. He succeeded wonderfully, achieving great notices as a director as well as an actor, to the point where a friend of his jokingly exclaimed that his paralysis was a "great career move." He chronicled his journey back from the brink of death in his book, *I'm Still Me*.

This body is a machine we inhabit, and sometimes machines break down. But while we live, we still have missions to perform and purposes to fulfill. Life can still be filled with love and wonder and opportunity. We can be "cute" even if we are in a wheelchair or a hospital bed.

Where there is breath, there is life. Where there is life, there is hope. Our future remains to be written. Anything can happen. Everything is possible. Whatever is happening in our lives, we can all write a book called *I'm Still Me*.

Today's Affirmation: "I am rich and wonderful just because I'm me!"

358

Karen

"The smallest effort is not lost. Each wavelet on the ocean tossed aids the ebb-tide or the flow; Each raindrop makes some flowerlet grow; Each struggle lessens human woe."

—Charles Mackay

My friend, Karen, was an artist with makeup. She believed every woman was beautiful, and helped many to discover their own unique beauty. I had been buying her products for four years.

I saw her at a networking luncheon: "Hi, Karen!" I said. "You look gorgeous, as always, you tiny thing!"

"Oh," she said self-deprecatingly, "my friends tell me I look anorexic."

"Hah," I scoffed. "You're naturally thin—they're just jealous."

She gave me a big hug, and suggested some new makeup I might try. I said sure and ordered a few items. She called me the next week to say that she had ordered my makeup and it would be delivered in a day or two. I thanked her. I didn't know that was to be our last conversation, mundane and ordinary.

Six days later, she took her life.

I know I couldn't have done anything to change her mind. Her inner pain was too great, and her focus on it too intense. Friends said that she had planned it for a long while, gotten her affairs in order, had her will notarized, written her goodbye letter.

But I *wish* I could have. I wish I could have made a difference, talked her into staying, given her a reason to go on. We shared poetry and dreams—of books we would write and places we would go. She left before she could see her dreams come true.

Goodnight, sweet Karen. May "flights of angels sing thee to thy rest."

To you I say, don't give up the ship! The way is often stormy, sometimes painful. Life may not have given you what you want so far, but tomorrow might be the day. You may not have gotten the best start in life, but you could have the best finish. Others have done it, through some of the worst childhoods, tragedies, and disasters imaginable.

Some people are fighting for money; others are throwing it away. Some people are fighting for their lives; others are throwing them away. Sometimes the biggest win is just to survive today in order to rise again another day. Find your mission. Help someone less fortunate than you—and there's always someone.

Stay alive.

Today's Affirmation: "I love and am loved. I have a unique and wonderful place in this world."

359

My Staff

"Many times a day I realize how much my own life is built on the labors of my fellow men, and how earnestly I must exert myself in order to give in return as much as I have received."

—Albert Einstein

Isn't it wonderful that there are people who do some things better than you? And have chosen careers in which they can perform these tasks so you don't have to do them? Aren't you *glad*?

I'm so happy that I have a car to drive—and I didn't have to design it, build it, paint it, or fix it when it breaks. I don't have to collect parts for the car either, or create/run an insurance company to cover myself for loss of the car. I didn't design the highway system, or city streets, or traffic signals.

I'm delighted that some people run restaurants, so I can get gourmet cooking whenever I want it, without having to struggle alone in my kitchen. I love beautiful jewelry, meticulously crafted by other hands, and wool sweaters. I don't want to dig out the raw ore from the mines or shear a sheep. I tried sewing a dress once, and trust me, it wasn't pretty. My thanks to everyone who helps design/sew/sell/ship beautiful russet clothing for the titian-haired.

I love coffee—but don't want to grow my own. I'm glad I can eat corn without shucking it myself, drink water without hauling it myself, and I don't want to know where the sewer pipes go but I'm glad they're there. I certainly couldn't build a computer or tell you how the Internet works, but I use them every day.

Mel Gibson works to entertain me. (Now there's a thought!) I'm glad that he and Kevin Costner, Antonio Bandaras, Harrison Ford, Russell Crowe, and Gene Hackman chose to be actors so that I can watch them—they get my $8.50 every time. So do the glorious women like Susan Sarandon, Julia Roberts, Meryl Streep, Sigourney Weaver, Whoopi Goldberg, Juliette Binoche…I wish I had more room on this page! They have faces and feelings that draw me in to celluloid lives. Many people make beautiful music for me: Bon Jovi, Phil Collins, Whitney Houston, Bernadette Peters, Emmylou Harris, and the Dixie Chicks. All the comedians work to make me laugh, and I do. I'm glad that Issac Asimov wrote science fiction, Richard Bach wrote *Illusions*, Herman Hesse wrote *Siddhartha*, and a group of sages wrote the Bible. Mitch Albom spent *Tuesdays with Morrie* and Shirley MacLaine went *Out on a Limb* for me. George Lucas and Stephen Spielberg take my imagination to thoughts, places, and worlds I have never been. All these people work for me. I grow, I learn, I am entertained.

Every day, so many people are serving me. In the business of my life, they're my staff. I take this day to remember to be grateful to every one of them for this rich life I lead, full of fun and learning. Thank you!

And if you're reading this, I'm on *your* staff.

Today's Affirmation: "I love and appreciate all the people of this rich world."

360
We Are Not Alone

"Anyone can cut an apple open and count the number of seeds. But who can look at a single seed and count the trees and the apples?"

—Dottie Walters

I smile to myself as I write the title of this page. "Hmm," I wonder, "will the reader think I am saying we are not alone in the universe, that flying saucers and little green Martians abound, that I am a UFOer?" I will tell you, I have not ruled it out.

I have a picture of "several hundred galaxies never before seen" as captured by the Hubble telescope. There are approximately one hundred billion stars in one galaxy—and then this new looking glass shows us several hundred of these collections of one hundred billion stars that no one knew was there. As I marveled over this picture, my father pointed out to me that the picture only showed one tiny keyhole portion of the night sky, and that the camera could be pointed in any other direction for three hundred sixty degrees and find stars and galaxies ad infinitum. "Billions and billions" of stars, as Carl Sagan said. Infinity.

Infinity: boundless, countless, endless, eternal, everlasting, incalculable, incomprehensible. I grasp at the fringes of the idea, a blind woman trying to imagine a painting. How vast is this void in which we hang suspended, tiny bits of flotsam in the cosmos sea. My mind creaks open to the possibilities of existence in other star systems, other dimensions, other times. Alternate realities. Imagination soars outward, yet balks finally at the enormity of the task. My thoughts fall back to Earth, the one teeming ball of life I know.

It doesn't matter if we are alone in the Universe or not. What is important is that we are not alone on the planet. Whatever you believe about the Universe and its inhabitants, the congregation of beings with which you exist collectively on this globe have primary importance for you. Each individual can do very little alone but exist, and sometimes not even that. Yet together we can build communities, cities, airplanes, space shuttles, telephones, computer networks, pyramids, and Eiffel Towers. We write books for others to read, produce food for others to eat, manufacture cars for others to drive.

I believe there is meaning and purpose to life, and the clues are hidden in other people. Search them out, it's a monster jigsaw puzzle—and it's fun. The answers are not for you to discover alone in a void; if it were so, we would all be on our own little individual planets—with instruction books, tapes, and videos. There are certainly enough planets to go around. We are here together for a reason. Your purpose in life is to figure out what that reason is. And every other person here is your teacher.

Today's Affirmation: "I celebrate the wonders of the Universe and my place in it!"

361

Close Encounters of the Third Kind

"Like buried treasures, the outposts of the Universe have beckoned to the adventurous from immemorial times."

—George Ellery Hale

I grew up reading science fiction. So much of what we take for granted in our everyday lives had its precursor in sci-fi: the radio, television, microwaves, space travel. What man can imagine, he usually later invents. For countless centuries, people were ruled by the suspicion that many things were impossible or unknowable. Now, we live in an age where nothing seems impossible—it's just a matter of inventing the right technology.

When John F. Kennedy said that we would put a man on the moon within ten years, the technology to do that didn't exist. He called for it to come into existence, and scientists jumped to make it so. And so it was.

I remember, "One small step for man, one giant leap for mankind." I stood in awe on the sidewalk outside my house, front door open so I could see the small figure walking in moon dust on the television set, and looked up at the moon in the night sky at the same time. Dad told me that the real miracle was not that a man was walking on the moon, but that we were all *watching* a man walking on the moon.

So I was excited to see *Close Encounters of the Third Kind*, Steven Spielberg's brilliant movie about the first human contact with an alien civilization. I went to a showing with my friend, Gaye, and my boyfriend, Stan. We were all riveted in our seats as the story unfolded in front of us. I was enthralled, I was *there*—it seemed so real and exciting to me. By the end of the movie, tears were rolling down my cheeks.

I had only known Stan for a short time. He didn't understand what I was crying about. He thought this a very strange reaction. He turned to Gaye and whispered, "What is she crying about?"

Friends for decades, Gaye knew me well. She softly answered back, gesturing at the great mother ship flying into space:

"She wanted to go."

I did. Still do.

Some people send out a ship. Some people send out a space ship. Humankind's spirit of adventure is the wind in the sails of them both. It's what gets anyone off the couch and out of the house.

Can you look at the stars and not wonder what marvels are out there? Can you look around at this world and not wonder what marvels are down here that you haven't experienced yet? What sparks your imagination? Expand your vision. Adventures await you. Reach out. Reach up.

Reach for the stars.

Today's Affirmation: "I reach for the stars, and find love, happiness, and fulfillment along the way."

362
Purpose

"We are not here merely to make a living. We are here to enrich the world, and we impoverish ourselves if we forget this errand."

—Woodrow Wilson

Food. Shelter. Clothing. These are the basics that we need to sustain life. Everything beyond that is entertainment. There is purpose and reason to our lives—beyond sustenance and beyond entertainment.

What is your purpose? What is your mission? What's it all about? My guess is that it isn't about just staying alive, and it isn't about who's got the most stuff.

When you answer this question, from your heart and your soul, you will know true financial peace. You have what it takes to survive, to stay alive—because, after all, here you are, alive after all these years. When you understand that the search for wealth, riches, beautiful things, etc. is just for your entertainment, you'll know you can be happy whether or not you have those things.

When I make High Budget money, I spend more. When I make Low Budget money, I spend less. Financial stress reduction is about being fluid and flexible with money—if you've got more, enjoy it; if you've got less, enjoy other things. Change your focus.

Beyond staying alive and entertaining yourself: what are you here for?

Today's Affirmation: "I am happily fulfilling my life's mission every day."

363
Roads

"The life of man is a journey, a journey that must be traveled, however bad the roads or the accommodations."

—Oliver Goldsmith

As a teacher, I try to act as a signpost to others, pointing the way down the road to success. But sometimes as I lecture, I know I'*m* the one I'm talking to. "Oh yeah, that's a good idea, Chellie; why aren't you doing that?!" says the voice in my head. I know that people point to leaders and teachers, whispering that they're "not walking their talk" and quail when I know I don't always walk mine. But I only learn to walk it after I talk it for a while and watch myself fail to connect, to measure up, to succeed at what I know I should do, what St. Chellie would do without blinking or thinking twice. Talking with my friend Korey, I agonized over the road I have taken and how many foibles and failures marked the way. I regretted the many times I strayed from the road I knew to be straight and true, the path to health and well-being, to financial success, loving relationships, spiritual peace.

"Why did I leave the road so many times?" I moaned.

"You were still on the road, Chellie," she told me. "You were just in the shitty part of it."

I still laugh over that description, but with that one sentence, she changed my picture of life. I had seen the map of life as a series of roads, with highways and byways and detours, but always one clear shining path that we were supposed to stay on. If you were on that bright path, the path was always straight and the sun always shone. It was only when you left the road that troubles loomed.

Now I see that roads are not so straightforward. You choose your road for the promised destination but the journey is never what you expect. Sometimes the way is steep, lined with sharp stones; sometimes it is a walk in the park. On some parts of the road the sun smiles; on others the wind howls. Sometimes other roads line up with ours and we trudge for a time side by side with another traveler. When we stumble, another can reach out a hand to steady us. Then the roads diverge again; our paths change; they keep north while we veer east. But always we are on our road. The one less traveled, the one we have chosen. The road beckons and we follow. We have chosen the destination and the road will take us where it wills. Its troubles train our endurance, strengthen our commitment until we are worn shiny smooth like rocks in a tumbler.

I stumble. I fall. I pick myself up. I repair the road. I learn. Success lies just over the next hill…or the one after that.

Today's Affirmation: "The road is clear and the way open to all the success I desire!"

364
The City at the Summit

"You cannot put the same shoe on every foot."

—Publilius Syrus

The whitewashed walls of the city of Santorini sparkle atop the steep cliffs that rise majestically from the cerulean blue waters of the Mediterranean Sea. Ships nestle in the harbor, surrounded by three islands that some say are the remains of the mythical city of Atlantis.

From the boat dock, you can climb the one thousand steps to the summit, or, if you prefer, you can ride a donkey—the local guides take groups up every half-hour. Tour buses can take you around the island before dropping you off at the top. The fastest way to the city is to take the cable car. Some people find their own precarious way up the mountain, slowly and laboriously climbing over the rocks.

A few visitors go directly to the city. Others take the detour around the island, looking at ancient ruins, and arrive at the summit later in the day. Some play all day on the beach, and still others stay on the ship and just gaze at the stars from below.

Among the visitors, there are sometimes arguments about which is the better way to get to the summit. "The cable car is faster!" some claim. "But it's more fun to ride the donkeys!" others retort. Those on the tour buses say, "Why go directly to the top? Enjoy the rest of the island first." "Climbing is good for your health!" say the rest. But no one says you won't get to the summit unless you take their route. The cable car riders don't go to battle with the donkey riders. The rock climbers don't throw rocks at the people on the stairs. No one ambushes the buses. It is clear there are many paths, and all lead to the city.

The citizens of Santorini are happy to greet the visitors, whoever they are and whenever they arrive. It makes no difference to them what mode of transportation the visitors choose or what time they appear. They may laugh gently at the slow climbers who choose the most difficult way. And they may wistfully regret that the sun-bathers at the beach or the star-gazers on the ship don't make it to the summit this trip. Oh, well, they shrug, maybe next year.

You may come when you wish, how you wish. All roads take you to the top. Whatever path you choose, when you reach the city, you are welcomed.

Today's Affirmation: "Whatever path I choose is the perfect path for me."

365
Accomplishments

A Prayer for us All

"I honor the place within you
Where the whole universe resides.
I honor the place within you
Of love, of light, of truth, of peace.
I honor the place within you,
Where, when you are in that place in you,
And I am in that place in me,
There is only one of us.
Namaste."

—Nepalese prayer (contributed by Lesleigh Tolin)

Thank you for walking this road with me; for sharing space on the planet Earth, and being who you are. (If you have gotten to the end of this book, I'll bet you're one of My People!)

At the beginning of this book, I asked you to write down your "Intended Results," to list your financial, emotional, and spiritual goals for the next year. What was your intention in reading this book? What did you want to have achieved by the end of it? Did it happen? Did you grow? Did your money grow with you? What did you get that surprised you?

Make a list of your accomplishments, and celebrate them. We need to take every possible occasion to praise and honor ourselves. You have succeeded! You are a success! Celebrate!

Whatever remains undone, transfer to a new list of "Intended Results" for next year. And begin again. This book is a tool that can help you along the way every year.

I leave you with a final affirmation of abundance for your life:

Today I declare that I am free.

I declare my financial freedom and demand that all the rivers of my good flow abundantly to me now. Gold and goodness heap upon me, and all that I take in I use in righteousness and truth. In return, I shower abundance on those before me. The world benefits from my presence. I live my life as fully as possible to shine the light of power and possibility over all who enter my circle of influence. I am free to be. I am free to be me. I am free to be me abundantly.

I pass this gift to all who hear it, see it, feel it. I am great, I am magnificent, I am radiant. I am perfect, whole, distilled, clear, farseeing, and farseeking. My place in the universe is assured and special. I matter. At peace with the earth and sky, rivers, fields, mountain, streams, and dreams, sparkling diamonds in the sunlight of life, I call to all in harmony with the ages. I am ageless, I am one, I am all. I am satisfied, I am content, I am filled. Thank you, God.

Peace be with you. May your life be rich—inside and out.

Today's Affirmation: "I am free. I am free to be me. I am free to be me abundantly."

About the Author

Chellie Campbell is the creator of the popular Financial Stress Reduction® Workshops now taught by certified Coaches throughout the country. Owner of a bookkeeping service with 13 employees for 12 years, she is the author of *The Wealthy Spirit* and *Zero to Zillionaire*, both published by Sourcebooks, Inc. She is one of Marci Shimoff's "Happy 100" in her *New York Times* bestseller *Happy for No Reason*, quoted as a "Financial Guru" in James Arthur Ray's *New York Times* best-seller *Harmonic Wealth*, and contributed stories to Jack Canfield's recent books *You've Got to Read This Book!* and *Life Lessons from Chicken Soup for the Soul*. She has been prominently quoted as a financial expert in *The Los Angeles Times*, *Pink*, *Good Housekeeping*, *Lifetime*, *Essence*, *Woman's World*, *Fitness*, and more than 45 popular books. Voted "Most Inspirational Speaker" by Women in Management, "Speaker of the Year" by the Association of Women Entrepreneurs and "Rotarian of the Year" by the Pacific Palisades Rotary Club, she is a past president of the Los Angeles Chapter of National Association of Women Business Owners. An avid poker player, she plays No-Limit Texas Hold'em tournaments in Los Angeles and Las Vegas, and enjoys birding, science fiction, and chocolate. For "30 Days to a Wealthy Spirit" daily inspirational emails and other information, visit her website www.Chellie.com or email her at Chellie@Chellie.com.